ROUTLEDGE LIBRARY EDITIONS:
ACCOUNTING HISTORY

Volume 45

VOLUNTARY ANNUAL REPORT DISCLOSURE BY LISTED DUTCH COMPANIES, 1945–1983

T0384427

VOLUNTARY ANNUAL REPORT DISCLOSURE BY LISTED DUTCH COMPANIES, 1945–1983

KEES CAMFFERMAN

Routledge
Taylor & Francis Group

LONDON AND NEW YORK

First published in 1997 by Garland Publishing, Inc.

This edition first published in 2021
by Routledge
2 Park Square, Milton Park, Abingdon, Oxon OX14 4RN

and by Routledge
52 Vanderbilt Avenue, New York, NY 10017

Routledge is an imprint of the Taylor & Francis Group, an informa business

British Library Cataloguing in Publication Data
A catalogue record for this book is available from the British Library

ISBN: 978-0-367-33564-9 (Set)
ISBN: 978-1-00-304636-3 (Set) (ebk)
ISBN: 978-0-367-49902-0 (Volume 45) (hbk)
ISBN: 978-0-367-49909-9 (Volume 45) (pbk)
ISBN: 978-1-00-304807-7 (Volume 45) (ebk)

Publisher's Note
The publisher has gone to great lengths to ensure the quality of this reprint but points out that some imperfections in the original copies may be apparent.

Disclaimer
The publisher has made every effort to trace copyright holders and would welcome correspondence from those they have been unable to trace.

VOLUNTARY ANNUAL REPORT DISCLOSURE BY LISTED DUTCH COMPANIES, 1945–1983

KEES CAMFFERMAN

GARLAND PUBLISHING, Inc.
NEW YORK & LONDON / 1997

Library of Congress Cataloging-in-Publication Data

Camfferman, Kees, 1966–
    Voluntary annual report disclosure by listed Dutch companies, 1945–
1983 / Kees Camfferman.
        p.   cm. — (New works in accounting history)
    Originally presented as thesis (Ph. D.)—Vrije Universiteit,
Amsterdam, 1996.
    Includes bibliographical references and index.
    ISBN 0-8153-3011-1 (alk. paper)
    1. Financial statements—Netherlands—History. 2. Corporations—
Netherlands—Accounting—History. I. Title. II. Series.
HF5681.B2C329 1997
338.7'09492—dc21   97-17768

Printed on acid-free, 250-year-life paper
Manufactured in the United States of America

Contents

Acknowledgments

This book was written as a PhD-thesis, completed at the Vrije Universiteit, Amsterdam, in 1996. The occasion of this edition by Garland Publishing not only provided the opportunity to make a number of minor changes in the text, but also allows me to repeat the following acknowledgements:

The Faculty of Economics, Business Administration and Econometrics at the Vrije Universiteit, in particular the Department of Financial and Management Accounting, generously provided the opportunity and the facilities to research and write this book.
I wish to thank most sincerely prof. dr J. Klaassen, my thesis supervisor, for his brisk guidance and confident support.
I thank the referees, prof.dr T.E. Cooke and prof.drs J.W. Schoonderbeek, for their interest in this project and their many helpful suggestions.
Prof. dr S.A. Zeff, though not associated with this project in any formal capacity, has been and still is, an invaluable teacher and guide. Throughout this book, I have tried to do justice to his example.
In addition, I would like to thank Maarten Gelderman, Tom Groot, Esther IJskes, Rudy Schattke and Peter Smidt for their most welcome assistance.

Amsterdam

April 1997

Main abbreviations used in the text

(Abbreviated company names are listed in Appendix B)

AICPA   American Institute of Certified Public Accountants
APB   Accounting Principles Board (UK)
ARB   Accounting Research Bulletin (USA)
ASC   Accounting Standards Committee (UK)
CAB   Commissie van Advies inzake Beroepsaangelegenheden (Advisory Committee on Professional Matters)
ED   Exposure Draft
EEC   European Economic Community
FASB   Financial Accounting Standards Board (USA)
GAAP   Generally Accepted Accounting Principles (USA)
IASC   International Accounting Standards Committee
ICAEW   Institute of Chartered Accountants in England and Wales
NIvA   Nederlands Instituut van Accountants (Dutch Institute of Accountants, 1895-1967)
NIvRA   Nederlands Instituut van Registeraccountants (Dutch Institute of Registered Accountants)
NV   Naamloze Vennootschap (Limited liability company)
OK   Ondernemingskamer (Enterprise Chamber)
RJ   Raad voor de Jaarverslaggeving (Council on Annual Reporting)
SEC   Securities and Exchange Commission (USA)
SER   Sociaal-Economische Raad (Socio-Economic Council)
SFAS   Statement of Financial Accounting Standards (USA)
SSAP   Statement of Standard Accounting Practice (UK)
TO   Tripartiet Overleg (Tripartite Study Group)
VAGA   Vereniging van Academisch Geschoolde Accountants (Society of Academically Trained Auditors, 1925-1967)
WJO   Wet op de Jaarrekening van Ondernemingen (1970 Act on Annual Financial Statements of Enterprises)

Voluntary Annual Report Disclosure by Listed Dutch Companies, 1945–1983

Chapter 1
Introduction

1.1 'The international disclosure bandwagon'

The three decades following the Second World War were a key period in the development of modern financial reporting by public or 'open' companies. Before this period, company financial reporting in many countries, including the Netherlands, consisted of little more than the publication of terse abstracts from the accounting records. But by the beginning of the 1980s, the annual reports of many companies had changed into rather attractive and often voluminous booklets in which an expanded set of accounting data was presented in a context of extensive non-financial information about the company in question. By that time, annual reporting had acquired a substantial part of its current outward appearance.

One explanation for this change is the introduction of more extensive regulation governing the contents of annual reports. Gerhard Mueller drew attention to the transformation of financial reporting during this period, and emphasized the importance of regulation. His analysis (Mueller, 1972) will be used to introduce the subject of the present study.
Commenting on the situation in Western Europe in the late 1950s, Mueller observed that 'financial reporting and disclosure were generally in a sad state of virtual non-existence' (p. 118). In many countries, legal requirements and established practice were generally in favour of highly secretive financial reporting. Differences among countries existed, to be sure, but even the relatively open British reporting standards 'tolerated [annual reports providing] almost no details concerning results of operations' (p. 119). At that time, only the United States could serve as a benchmark of openness in financial reporting because of the influence of the Securities Acts of the 1930s.

1

A process of change began in the early 1960s, and it increased in scope as the decade progressed. Throughout the developed world, legislatures undertook the task of revising company legislation, almost as if acting on an agreed programme[1]. Relevant legislation was introduced or changed in the United States (1964), Germany (1959, 1965), Japan (1963, 1967), France (1966), the United Kingdom (1967), Canada (1969), the Netherlands (1970), and somewhat later, in Spain (1973) and Italy (1974). During the 1960s, the Nordic countries were also at work at a common programme of company law reform. A common concern of most of these reforms was to increase annual report disclosure. For this reason, Mueller characterized the almost wave-like spread of new legislation as 'the international disclosure bandwagon'.

A direct impetus for a disclosure wave in the 1960s came from the United States in the form of a campaign by the SEC for greater voluntary disclosure (see also Hobgood, 1969). However, a more fundamental reason for the increased emphasis on disclosure, and one apparent in many countries, was a growing demand for reporting information, resulting from increased attention for companies on the part of investors and the general public.

Increased disclosure requirements were considered at the time as a relatively easy approach to meet this demand, given the difficulty of obtaining agreement on stricter rules on income determination and valuation. Changing demands for financial information, and changing patterns of financial statement usage were not confined to the United States but could be observed in a number of countries. Despite differences in institutional structure, this led to a basic similarity:

> [M]odes of achieving better and more financial disclosure differed from country to country. (...) despite the different routes utilized for arriving at higher disclosure plateaus, the outcome

---

[1] Details about the historical development of financial reporting legislation in various European countries can be found in Walton (1995).

2

(i.e., the disclosure rules and requirements instituted) brought about a fair degree of international similarity. (p. 122)

Mueller's analysis does not suggest that disclosure practices in the Netherlands were notably different from those in other continental countries. The conclusion regarding the Netherlands would therefore have to be that it shared in the general 'sad state' of affairs, and that, like other countries, it had to be lifted from this state by means of legislation (enacted in 1970) which was part of a common movement of legal reform affecting wide parts of the Western world.
However, one can also find expressions in the literature of an alternative view of the development of Dutch financial reporting. In contrast to Mueller's emphasis on regulation in bringing about improvements in disclosure, this other view stresses the role of voluntary improvements in Dutch financial reporting.

1.2   Perceived importance of non-mandatory improvements in Dutch financial reporting

A number of authors have emphasized that the development of Dutch financial reporting has been different from that in other countries. Such assertions can be found in the Dutch literature, and, from the 1960s onwards, in the international literature as well. They range from the simple characterization that '[t]he Netherlands is a sophisticated maverick in the international accounting community' (Da Costa *et al.*, 1978) to more elaborate attempts at international classifications of accounting practices. Among the latter, the well-known Nobes (1983) classification probably has done much to spread the view that Dutch financial reporting evolved along quite distinct lines. The most striking aspect of this difference has, of course, been the Dutch conceptual and theoretical framework for asset valuation and income determination on the basis of current values. It has been argued that this provided an effective alternative to regulation as a guide towards improved financial reporting. Bindenga (1995) has described the *Sonderweg* of Dutch financial reporting by distinguishing three 'orientations' or 'lines of development' in the history of financial reporting: an 'Anglo-Saxon (Commonwealth, USA), a 'Roman' (continental European) and a 'Dutch' line of development (See also Bindenga, 1993). The latter is characterized as follows:

> In the Netherlands, financial reporting has derived its character in particular from the development of business economics. As such, the Dutch situation is incomparable to that in other continental European countries, or to the Anglo-Saxon line of development. Until 1970, there was no legislation on or regulation of financial reporting. (...) The founding of a normative and objective school of business economics between 1920 and 1950 has had an important influence on financial reporting in the Netherlands. (...) Although the roots of financial reporting in the Netherlands can be found in business economics, this tradition has been broken. Confronted with processes of harmonization in Europe and with influences from American regulation, the legal element is now clearly present in the Netherlands as well. (p. 11)

Bindenga goes on to credit the Dutch auditing profession with playing an important role in the practical application of business economic theory. Although he refers primarily to issues of income determination and valuation, his strong assertion that before 1970 and before the impact of European harmonization, financial reporting developed under the influence of non-regulatory forces may have implications for disclosure as well. It would, after all, be somewhat curious to find that there were substantial voluntary improvements in accounting principles used while the issue of disclosure was neglected.

In fact, it has been observed that the Netherlands has been different in the area of disclosure as well, in the sense that in this respect Dutch practice is (and has been) more like that in the United States and the United Kingdom than like that in neighbouring continental countries (Choi and Mueller, 1992:421). Furthermore, it has been noted that openness in financial reporting practice in the Netherlands did not rest to any great extent on formal regulation, but on the same auditing profession to which Bindenga referred to explain the influence of business economics on valuation practices. A strong statement of this view can be found in Scott (1968), who presents the situation in the Netherlands as a goal to which developing countries trying to improve their accounting systems might want to aspire. After noting that the Dutch environment at the time was characterized by relatively light regulation, he remarks that:

> Dutch firms are widely regarded as the most progressive and innovative with respect to external financial reporting. The Dutch accounting profession appears to be very effective in showing Dutch companies the advantages which accrue from thorough and realistic disclosure of financial affairs to the public and has helped to create a strong and positive attitude toward accounting among all elements of the business community. (p. 61)

More recent observations on the role of voluntary action in Dutch financial reporting practice include the comment that '[u]ntil recently, [an] important feature [of Dutch accounting] has been the combination of almost extreme permissiveness with high professional standards' (Nobes and Parker, 1995:217).

Furthermore, in a review of current financial reporting practices by Traas in an address to the 1991 Rotterdam Financial and Management Accounting (FMA) Congress, it was concluded that Dutch financial reporting practice had, during the 1970s and 1980s, consisted largely of devising and complying with regulations. In contrast, it was argued that if financial reporting was to continue to improve, inspiration for the future should be drawn from an earlier period, in which voluntary action played a much larger role:

> (..) the necessary improvements [in financial reporting] may have to be brought about by voluntary action. (...) In fact, a development along these lines is nothing new. In the postwar period, during the 1950s and 1960s, this approach was used as well. And certainly not without success. (Traas, 1991:53)

5

Earlier in the same address, an appeal was made to 'revitalize the process that as early as the 1950s and 1960s led to a sustained improvement in reporting practice' (Traas, 1991:40).

In sum, the literature provides quite definite expressions of the point of view that postwar Dutch reporting displayed a distinctive tendency towards voluntary improvements. Although the literature is usually careful enough not to assume a past 'golden age' of voluntary improvements in reporting, the general image of the period is quite positive[2]. Although this point is generally stated with reference to valuation and income determination, one can find it applied to issues regarding extent of disclosure as well.

It will be noted that this view of developments in the Netherlands contrasts with Mueller's (1972) analysis of European financial reporting, discussed in the previous section. Mueller argued that European disclosure did not significantly improve before the wave of disclosure legislation in the late 1960s. Even though part of this apparent contrast may be explained by assuming that Mueller's observations of disclosure practices were confined mainly to the larger continental countries as France and Germany, this would still leave a presumed difference between these countries and the Netherlands which would merit further investigation. In short, the cursory review of the literature presented here gives rise to an empirical question about the actual extent of voluntary disclosure in the postwar Netherlands. It is this question which will be addressed in this book.

---

[2] See also Burgert, van Hoepen and Joosten (1995:21-22) for the view that substantial accounting regulation arrived relatively late in the Netherlands (in 1970), but that, nevertheless, many companies had reached fairly high standards of reporting practice on a voluntary basis.

1.3 Previous empirical research in the Netherlands

There has been little previous research into the long-term growth of annual report disclosure in the Netherlands. A factor of obvious importance in this respect is the traditional emphasis among Dutch accounting academics on the development of normative theory on valuation and income determination (see Klaassen and Schreuder, 1984). This has diverted some attention that might otherwise have been directed at empirical issues in general, and at disclosure issues in particular. Dijksma (1973:369) observed that before 1973, there had only been eight previous published surveys of (aspects of) Dutch financial reporting practices. Although the number of eight studies is a bit too low[3], the conclusion that empirical work before 1970 was remarkable primarily by its absence seems uncontestable. Following 1971, there have been regular but incompletely comparable surveys of reporting practices[4]. Dijksma and van Halem (1977) is a rare example of a cross-sectional empirical disclosure study modelled explicitly after foreign examples. Since 1986, a second regular series of empirical surveys has been published, containing much information on various disclosure issues[5]. Even more recently, other materials relevant to the development of Dutch financial reporting have been published, including a history of Dutch financial reporting regulation (Zeff *et al.*, 1992), an analysis of this regulation in terms of economic consequences (Maijoor, 1991) and a longitudinal study of the introduction of consolidated reporting in the Netherlands (Blommaert, 1995).
Altogether, the available survey data do allow a reasonable recon-

---

[3] Munnik (1931), Polak (1933) and Sternheim (1933) can, despite their rather casual approach, be considered as other examples of pre-war studies of actual practice.

[4] *Onderzoek Jaarverslagen,* published in the series *NIvRA Geschriften* (Amsterdam: Nederlands Instituut van Registeraccountants, 1973-1992).

[5] The series *Jaar in — Jaar uit*, initiated by the accounting faculty of Erasmus University, Rotterdam (Groningen: Wolters-Noordhoff, 1986-1995).

struction of post-1970 trends in disclosure. But an assessment of the differences or similarities between post- and pre-1970 reporting with respect to disclosure cannot be made on this basis. The Blommaert study is the only study to date that has expressly dealt with the issue of reporting development over the entire postwar period (over the 20th century as a whole, in fact).

1.4 Objectives and method of this study

1.4.1 General
The preceding sections have shown that within the literature, one can find support for the view that postwar Dutch financial reporting distinguished itself from its continental neighbours by a relatively large extent of voluntary improvements. In the absence of extensive previous empirical research, two possible interpretations offer themselves. It is possible that Dutch financial reporting was in fact somewhat different from that practised in other countries in terms of an unusually extensive reliance on voluntary improvements. To the extent that this is correct, this phenomenon would offer itself as a subject of further research in terms of its origins and nature. Another possibility is that there was not, in fact, a significant amount of voluntary disclosure in the Netherlands.

In the light of either possibility, the research objective of this study can be stated as: to describe and appraise the role played by voluntary disclosure extensions in the development of postwar Dutch financial reporting.

The next sections contain a further discussion of the research question, and the approach by which it will be addressed.

1.4.2 Definitions: voluntary annual report disclosure
In the context of financial reporting, *disclosure* refers to the transmission of information by enterprise management to recipients outside the enterprise. Disclosure is fundamental to financial reporting, which may be defined as 'communicating information that

relates, directly or indirectly, to the information provided by the accounting system'[6].

Despite this fundamental nature of disclosure, it is hardly ever formally defined. The word is generally used interchangeably with expressions as revelation, release, publication, making available or communication. In reporting practice, the absence of an accepted definition and the often casual use of the word 'disclosure' generally do not pose any problems. For this reason, this study will adhere to common usage and not attempt to define disclosure in a very strict way. The types of changes in annual reports discussed in this book include the following[7]:

- the breakdown of items included in financial statements that previously were added or netted;
- the inclusion or expansion of notes to financial statement items that provide information on their calculation or that provide additional information intended to facilitate their interpretation;
- the inclusion of figures in the notes showing the effect of alternative accounting treatments;
- the inclusion of completely new statements (as consolidated statements or funds statements).

This broad way of looking at disclosure helps to lessen the importance of the traditional distinction between disclosure on the one hand and recognition, valuation and income determination on the other hand. A change from historical cost accounting to current cost accounting in such a way that most of the historical cost information can still be retrieved from the financial statements or the notes might be considered as an extension of disclosure.

The subject of most studies in *voluntary* disclosure is disclosures that are not governed by legislation or accounting standards. A more

---

[6] FASB, Statement of Financial Accounting Concepts No. 1, ¶ 7.

[7] See Marth and Murphy (1994) for a considerably more elaborate classification of disclosure items.

precise name for these disclosures would therefore be 'non-mandatory disclosure'. Nevertheless, to keep in line with common usage, in this study the word 'voluntary' will generally be used to refer to non-mandatory disclosures. It should be kept in mind that disclosures may be induced by all sorts of non-regulatory pressures which may make the decision to disclose anything but spontaneous to those involved in that decision.

This study is limited to disclosure in *annual reports*[8], as opposed to disclosure through other channels. This limitation is inspired by practical considerations. The notion that annual reports are not produced and read in a vacuum, but are merely an element of the total set of financial and economic information disseminated by enterprises, was to some degree current in the Netherlands during the period studied here (*e.g.* Weisglas, 1955). Additional insights might be gained by comparing annual report disclosures with information published through other sources, to assess the 'openness' of enterprises in all its aspects. This will, however, not be attempted.

1.4.3 Approach to empirical work
An important part of this study consists of an empirical investigation of published annual reports. In brief, the study described in this book consists of a survey of the published annual reports of about 30% of the companies listed on the Amsterdam Stock Exchange over the 1945-1983 period. For these companies, a longitudinal study of disclosure changes in nine separate areas was conducted, covering a total of about 30 different disclosure positions. The details of the research design will be described and discussed in later sections of this book.
The main reason for the choice of period (1945-1983) is that it is the

---

[8] 'Annual report' will be used in this study to translate the traditional sense of the Dutch word *jaarverslag,* which refers to the entire document issued annually by enterprises and which includes the financial statements as its core.

widest interval within natural boundaries that can be drawn around the critical period at the end of the 1960s. As will be discussed below, the Second World War clearly demarcates this period from the previous period. In 1984, the adaptation of Dutch law to the Fourth Company Law Directive of the (then) European Communities took effect. This ended a period during which Dutch financial reporting regulation was free to develop purely under the influence of national factors. The almost 40 years covered provide sufficient room to observe disclosure changes in the long run, and to appreciate the changes effected around 1970 against their proper historical background.

The structure of the empirical study can be envisaged as follows. The question as to the nature and extent of voluntary disclosure in the Netherlands can, on a common-sense basis, be broken down into sub-questions at three different levels:

- The national level. Questions at this level are directly derived from the discussion in sections 1.1 and 1.2 on the perceived specific nature of the development of financial reporting in the Netherlands. But an assessment of the overall development of annual report disclosure during the postwar period also requires an investigation of the process of disclosure extension at two lower levels:
- The level of the disclosing company. Questions at this level are concerned with differences among companies in their participation in the assumed process of voluntary disclosure extension, and whether these differences can be associated with company characteristics.
- The level of the individual disclosure item. At this level, questions are considered relating to the characteristics of the process by which new disclosures were introduced and disseminated.

In order to arrive at answers to these questions by means of an empirical investigation, points of reference are necessary that assist in designing the data collection process and that assist in interpreting

11

and appreciating the findings. At each level, points of reference come mainly in two types (although the significance of the types differs from level to level):

A first set of points of reference consists of elements from the historical background. At a national level, one would have to know what kind of regulatory system was in place at various points in time, how it differed from or corresponded to comparable systems in other countries, and how, if at all, the balance between regulation and free development embodied in the particular requirements was rationalized. At a company level, one would have to know in outline the composition of the population of companies that is being studied and to be aware of major changes in, for instance, mergers and acquisitions activity and sources of company finance. At the level of disclosure items, one would have to know some particulars about specific changes in regulation, and about the degree to which knowledge of potential disclosures was available, for instance in the professional literature.

A second set of points of reference can be derived from the extant body of relevant theory and (international) empirical accounting research.

Theories about the development of accounting at the national level are relatively scarce, although one might consider the Nobes (1983) framework, mentioned above, as an instance of this type of theory development. At the company level, there is a fairly rich body of empirical research linking the extent of disclosure to selected company characteristics[9]. At the disclosure item level, theory development has proceeded mainly on the basis of insights derived from information economics[10]. These analytical theories are supplemented by some empirical work[11]. At both the company and the

---

[9] Typical examples include Whittred (1986), Chow and Wong-Boren (1987), Cooke (1989) and Wagenhofer (1990b, 1990c).

[10] See, for instance, Verrecchia (1983), Dye (1985), Dye and Sridhar (1995).

[11] See, for instance, Wong (1988), Forker (1988) and Craswell and Taylor (1992).

disclosure item level, there have been scattered attempts to establish links between specific theories of accounting development to the general framework of innovation diffusion studies.

The combination of a research question distinguishing three levels of analysis with points of reference drawn from a wide variety of sources gives this study a rather broad character. Each of the three research levels listed above would merit a more thorough study than is possible within the confines of this book. Moreover, an extensive research literature on the subject of annual report disclosure is available, suggesting a number of lines along which more narrowly focused studies might be conducted. Gibbins, Richardson and Waterhouse (1992) in their survey of disclosure research, identified a broad range of theoretical perspectives on disclosure, covering 'a large number of economic, institutional, managerial and other forces that lie behind disclosure' (p. 2). Each of these perspectives might be used as the framework for the analysis of annual report disclosure in the Netherlands.

Yet, given the present state of the literature on the development over time of financial reporting in the Netherlands, a rather broad exploratory approach was preferred over a more narrow approach. The focus of this study will therefore not be on a particular aspect of disclosure in general, but on the process of disclosure development in a given country and during a specific period. This study is directed at a better understanding of the development of disclosure in the Netherlands, rather than at the justification or elaboration of a particular theoretical perspective.

Given this objective, it is desirable to take into account a fairly broad array of different aspects of disclosure by means of an eclectic use of the approaches suggested in the literature, to arrive at a composite picture of disclosure development.

1.5 Chapter outline

To recapitulate, the objective of this study is to arrive at an understanding of the extent and nature of the process of expanding voluntary annual report disclosure attributed to the postwar Netherlands.
This phenomenon will be considered by an empirical study of
changes in disclosure of individual items and disclosure practices of
individual companies.

Chapters 2, 3 and 4 provide the background for the empirical study.
Chapter 2 provides a general introduction to the subject of annual
report disclosure by reviewing the analytical, economics-based
disclosure literature. It doing so, it lists the major points of reference to be derived from the analytical disclosure literature at the
company and disclosure item level.
Chapter 3 contains a reconstruction of the development of opinions
on financial reporting in the Netherlands, with an emphasis on the
importance attached to voluntary improvements in financial reporting. This chapter provides much of the historical background
material on the national level.
Chapter 4 reviews previous empirical research in disclosure, which
is concerned mainly with the company and disclosure item levels.
On this basis, and on the basis of materials provided in chapters 2
and 3, the design of the present empirical study is described.

Chapters 5 and 6 contain a discussion of the empirical findings.
Chapter 5 presents an analysis of differences in disclosure behaviour
among companies, and therefore coincides largely with the second
level of the research question as described in section 1.3. Various
measures of 'aggregate' disclosure over time are developed to test a
number of hypotheses concerning the relationship between disclosure
and company characteristics.
In chapter 6, differences in disclosure patterns among disclosure
items are studied. In this chapter, the most detailed level of the
research question, the level of the individual disclosure item, will be
discussed.   Attention will be paid to the role of various external

influences on disclosure such as the law and accounting standards. This chapter essentially consists of a series of more detailed case studies of disclosure change. Each case study is set against a reconstruction of its context based on primary and secondary historical sources. The studies of the several disclosure items will also include a comparison with changes in disclosure abroad, to the extent that relevant data are available.

Finally, chapter 7 contains a summary and discussion.

Chapter 2
Theoretical views on voluntary disclosure

2.1 Introduction

This chapter provides a general introduction to the issue of voluntary annual report disclosure by means of a survey of the theoretical literature on disclosure of accounting information. In terms of the outline of section 1.4.3, this chapter is concerned mainly with establishing the points of reference at the disclosure item level, and, to a lesser extent, at the company level.

The literature surveyed in this chapter is specific subsection of the wider body of literature usually referred to as accounting theory.
As to accounting theory, it is commonly observed that there is presently no single generally accepted accounting theory or approach to theory formulation. The 1978 *Statement on Accounting Theory and Theory Acceptance*[1] identified three basic 'theory approaches' to accounting theory formulation that could not easily be reconciled one to another. More recent surveys of accounting theory, as Belkaoui (1992), have identified four, or, by a different classification, six competing or complementary 'paradigms' in accounting research. What is true for accounting in general is also true for the more specific area of disclosure of accounting data. A recent overview of the disclosure literature (Gibbins, Richardson and Waterhouse, 1992) identified a substantial number of theoretical 'perspectives' in use. Nevertheless, despite apparent variety, a large part of the theoretical disclosure literature displays a fundamental unity. This unity is

---

[1] American Accounting Association, Committee on Concepts and Standards for External Financial Reports, *Statement on Accounting Theory and Theory Acceptance* ([Sarasota, Fl.:] American Accounting Association, 1978).

derived from an explicit or implicit underlying point of view, which may well be summarized by the following observation made by Chambers in 1951:

> The function of accounting is to convey facts. If any manager considers it necessary to detract from, to add to, to explain, or to belittle the importance of such facts, for financial or other purposes, that should be regarded as his affair. Disclosure is to be considered as a matter of managerial policy, not a matter of accounting doctrine. According to this view, disclosure is the outcome of the action or agitation of interested groups (including the managerial group) in the community; it is the response of management to the demands of other groups.[2]

This policy perspective on disclosure makes it clear that disclosure issues, if they are to be considered in the accounting literature at all, need to be studied in the context of the interaction of the interests of company management and other interested parties. The contemporary accounting literature tends to analyze and interpret this interaction in the language and with the methods of economics, notably those branches of economics known as information-economics and contracting cost theories.

This section of the accounting literature has flourished especially since the late 1970s[3], in response to the recognition of disclosure as a general economic issue and the development of information econ-

---

[2] 'Disclosure is a matter of managerial policy, not accounting doctrine', report of address by R.J. Chambers, *Journal of Accountancy*, August 1951, p. 223. See also Chambers (1955:22-27) for a fuller discussion of these issues. It is indicative of the development of the meaning attached to 'accounting theory' that more recently it could be stated that 'a manager's incentive to disclose or withhold information whose revelation is not required [is] arguably (...) the quintessential accounting problem' (Verrecchia, 1990a:245).

[3] That is, most of the theoretical literature discussed in this chapter appeared after the end of the period studied in this book.

omics. Since the economics-based literature has provided the largest and most coherent body of disclosure theory in the accounting literature, it will occupy the largest part of this chapter. Various other perspectives on or approaches to theory formulation have also been used in the literature on disclosure, but generally in more or less isolated studies. These will be discussed towards the end of the chapter, and contrasted with the more elementary information economics models. The result is that this chapter presents theories of disclosure in an order of decreasing abstraction, starting with the most elementary disclosure models in section 2.2. and adding complexities and additional considerations in subsequent sections. As will be seen, there is considerable scope for adding such complexities, especially when theoretical models are developed for highly specific disclosure situations. A purpose of this chapter is to illustrate the capacity of the disclosure literature to develop, on the basis of a relatively small number of basic themes, an almost limitless number of variations. In doing so, this chapter makes the point that, at least for the time being, the development of general-purpose economic theories of disclosure is not to be expected. However, a number of recurring themes can be identified accross the range of the available disclosure literature that, while not complete disclosure theories in themselves, can be used to interprete disclosure behaviour in specific situations. These basic themes, together with materials from the next chapter, which supplies the necessary situation-specific information concerning the development of financial reporting in the Netherlands, will form the frame of reference for the empirical research discussed in the latter part of this book.

2.2 A game-theoretical approach to information disclosure

A useful approach to voluntary disclosure at a high level of abstraction is by the type of economic modelling known as game theory. Game theory has been increasingly used during the 1970s and 1980s in disciplines such as finance and accounting. Its application to voluntary disclosure in a financial reporting context dates from the middle 1970s[4]. Although the literature discussed in this and subsequent sections is typically based on formal mathematical models, the discussion will be confined to the assumptions, intuition and conclusions underlying the different models.

2.2.1 Setting up a disclosure game

Game theory is a tool of economic analysis, comprising formal mathematical models that are examined deductively (Kreps, 1990:6). Because of the deductive reasoning employed, the insights gained from these models depend crucially on the nature of the assumptions made. In this section, a particular disclosure 'game' is constructed, with its own set of assumptions. As will be shown in subsequent sections, varying these assumptions will result in different outcomes.
The disclosure game outlined in this section should be seen as merely a convenient starting point for the discussion of some other, related game situations discussed in the literature. For that purposes, the game in this section has been constructed to reflect as much as possible the common denominator of the games discussed later on[5].

An elementary disclosure game requires some scope for the disclosure of information. This entails the assumption of a multi-person world, in which information is not freely available to all. Instead, it is assumed that information endowments are not equal among actors (a situation known as information asymmetry). It is assumed that firms exist, abstractly represented by streams of future cash flows. Some actors are assumed to be 'manager-owners'. These actors possess the right to future cash flows and information about these cash flows that other actors do not possess. Furthermore, it is assumed that these rights to future cash flows can be traded between

---

[4] See Ross (1979) for an early review.

[5] Formal representations of games resembling the one outlined here can be found, for instance, in Verrecchia (1983), Dye (1986), Wagenhofer (1990a) and Darrough and Stoughton (1990).

20

manager-owners and other actors ('investors').

One possible and simple game structure would therefore be as follows. Manager-owners are initially endowed with information on the value of their firm. This information is a particular, clearly circumscribed item of information concerning the future cash flows of the firm. In the most simple case, the manager-owners would know the amount of future cash flows with certainty, and would therefore know the value of the firm. Subsequent to receipt of the information, the manager-owners can decide to disclose or not to disclose that variable to investors. Following disclosure (or nondisclosure), claims to the firm's cash flows are sold to investors in a competitive market. Manager-owners seek to maximize the price of their ownership rights, investors seek to minimize the price to be paid. After trading, the cash flows are realized by the owners of the claims.

Before it can be deduced what strategies will be chosen by the players, the model needs further specification on a number of points:

(1)   Investors and manager-owners are assumed to act on rational expectations concerning the behaviour of other parties in the market. Participants try to make optimizing decisions them-selves, and they expect others to do so as well. Moreover, the expectation of rational behaviour is mutual. This allows the construction of so-called sequential equilibria[6]. In a game setting where players take action consecutively, a player will take action knowing that others will base their actions on inferences drawn from his observed action, and that these other players know that he knows that they know, and so on.

(2)   The number of participants in the market may influence the outcome. One could develop particular versions of this game

---

[6] See Kreps and Wilson (1982), Postlewaite (1989).

with one firm and one investor, with one firm and numerous investors, or with numerous firms and numerous investors. The precise market mechanism may also be of importance[7]. By assuming that investors are homogeneous in their expectations and utility functions, the differences between various possible market structures will be reduced. It is assumed here that investors (not firms, nor manager-owners) are homogeneous, and that both manager-owners and investors are price-takers.

(3)   Investors know that manager-owners possess information and can therefore observe whether the latter are withholding information. In other words, the 'information structure' (who holds what type of information) is common knowledge, even though the actual information is not. As will be seen, this assumption is of particular importance in determining the results of this type of model (see also Postlewaite, 1989).

(4)   Investors have pre-disclosure expectations concerning average returns. Without this assumption, there would be no basis to deduce investor behaviour in the case of nondisclosure.

(5)   Manager-owners cannot disclose false information.

(6)   Manager-owners can disclose information without cost. This assumption simplifies the analysis by restricting it to considerations of investor reactions to disclosure.

(7)   A one-period setting is assumed, in which all cash flows are realized after one round of trading. An equivalent assumption would be that the game could be repeated a number of times, but that the outcomes in one period do not affect the

---

[7] See Fishman and Hagerty (1989) for an example of an analysis of disclosure effects in an explicitly defined securities market.

expectations or outcomes in following periods.

2.2.2 Outcome

This game and its solution are a specific version of a more general type identified in Akerlof's (1970) exposition, which is the starting point for most of the economic disclosure literature[8]. Akerlof uses the example of the market for used cars to analyze what happens in a market in which sellers are aware of the quality of the goods offered, but in which buyers can only establish this quality after purchase. The result of this information asymmetry and the resulting quality uncertainty is that buyers will not offer more than average prices for goods that might, because of their individual quality, command higher prices. This removes the incentive to supply goods of more than average quality. When these are withdrawn from the market, both average quality and prices are further depressed. In some circumstances, prices may fall so low as to discourage any trading at all.

These somewhat pessimistic implications, usually referred to as 'adverse selection', would not immediately apply to the simplified market for claims on future cash flows sketched above. The reason for this is the assumption that investors know with certainty that manager-owners are able to make verifiable claims as to the true value of their firms without cost. Investors would know that manager-owners expecting above average returns would have an incentive to disclose their information on superior earnings expectations in order to differentiate their firms from firms with lower expected cashflows. In this way, these manager-owners could realize higher returns on sales of ownership rights. But the assumption of rational expectations on the part of investors would make investors adjust their expectations concerning the average returns of non-disclosing firms downward, which would in turn induce more manager-owners

---

[8] Jovanovic (1982) provides a more formal exposition of Akerlof's theorem; Milgrom (1981) applies these notions to the more specific case of trade in ownership rights in firms.

to disclose their now higher than average prospects. So instead of driving the market for ownership rights out of existence, the forces at work in the simple model would lead to an equilibrium of full disclosure. To put it differently, the scepticism of the buyers would lead to so negative an assessment of the nature of undisclosed data that it will ultimately be in the interest of all manager-owners to disclose rather than have their firms valued at an extremely negative value[9]. This mechanism leading to full disclosure is generally referred to as the 'revelation principle'. The body of theory on which it rests is frequently referred to as 'signalling theory'.

2.2.3 *Limitations*
The value of the simple model sketched above is not its ability to predict voluntary disclosure in annual reports. The prediction of full disclosure is at odds with common experience. The model can, however, through its explicit listing of assumptions, help to identify factors that may be relevant in explaining partial disclosure in practice. The effect of relaxing some of the assumptions will be discussed in subsequent sections, in which the following elements will be introduced[10]:

- disclosure costs (section 2.3),
- uncertainty about the information structure, and lower quality information (section 2.4),
- investor heterogeneity (section 2.5),

---

[9] The specific implications in a disclosure setting of the adverse selection phenomenon introduced by Akerlof have been discussed by Grossman (1981), Milgrom (1981) and Milgrom and Roberts (1986). More specifically, Grossman (1981) suggests that under strong assumptions competition among firms is not even necessary: even a single firm could be forced to disclose all the information it is known to possess.

[10] A relaxation of the assumption that information must be truthfully disclosed will not be discussed. See, however, Newman and Sansing (1993) who allow for the deliberate disclosure of noisy information. The general result is that this prevents completely informative equilibria.

- multi-period models (section 2.6),
- an agency-setting (section 2.7),
- disclosure of financial accounting data as opposed to hypothetical information on the true value of the firm (section 2.8).

The analytical literature on voluntary disclosure has not progressed to a similar degree in all these directions. Elaborate models have been developed to accommodate some of the complicating factors listed above, but other factors have been discussed only in general terms.

2.3 Disclosure costs

One of the most important assumptions to be relaxed is the assumption that there are no costs associated with disclosure. The notion that disclosure costs may limit the extent of disclosure has been recognized for a long time in the professional literature[11]. Recent research has served to clarify concepts, to make more explicit a number of assumptions underlying the general notion of a cost-benefit trade-off, and provides a framework showing that many apparently different 'costs' operate in a basically similar manner.

As indicated by Benston (1969, 1980), the determination of the parties that incur the costs and reap the benefits of disclosure, and of the extent to which these parties take into account the interests of others present particular difficulties in analyzing cost-benefit trade-offs in disclosure. One hypothesis might be that 'managers [act] in the best interests of stockholders (..) [and] provide information to them and to other investors according to their best estimates of how the marginal costs and benefits accrue' (Benston, 1969:516). It is

---

[11] See also chapter 3. See Elliott and Jacobson (1994) for a recent review of the disclosure cost issue from a professional vantage point.

difficult, however, to formulate decision rules for management that do take into account the interests of different parties, and there seems to be no compelling reason (in economic terms) as to why management would consistently be concerned with overall welfare.

The preferred approach in the economics-based literature is to assume that those making the disclosure decision do not attempt to optimize the balance of costs and benefits for all parties involved. Rather, they are considered to act on behalf of their profit-maximizing firms, and to assume that each of the other parties external to the firm will act in its own self-interest. The situation in which the interests of management and the firm may deviate is discussed in a later section.

The assumption of self-interested behaviour allows for relatively unambiguous decision rules, once the effects of disclosure on the economic position of the firm have been specified. These effects are generally discussed under the heading of 'proprietary costs'.

Dye (1985:123) distinguishes two types of information. Proprietary information is defined as information whose disclosure potentially alters a firm's future earnings gross of senior management's compensation. Disclosure of this type of information affects the value of the firm because it influences current or future cash flows. Examples of such effects on cash flow following the release of information include possible competitive damage, government intervention or a revision of a firm's credit rating. These costs, incurred because of the disclosure of proprietary information, are referred to as proprietary costs. All other, non-proprietary information would not, on disclosure, affect future cash flows, although such disclosures might lead investors to change their expectation about these cash flows, and therefore might also change the market value of the firm[12].

---

[12] Non-trivial real-world examples of strictly non-proprietary information are rarely provided in the literature. The distinction between the two types of information should therefore be seen as a simplification to capture what is in effect a continuum ranging from very low to very high proprietary costs.

It can now be argued, along the lines of section 2.2, that non-proprietary information will always be disclosed as a result of the cascade-
effect induced by adverse selection. For proprietary information, the
result is different.

Verrecchia (1983) is one of the earliest analyses of the effect of
proprietary costs on disclosure. His argument proceeds in the
following manner. The firm is endowed with the realization of an
informational variable, that can take on values on a continuum
ranging from 'bad news' to 'good news'. On disclosure of this
information, investors will adjust the valuation of the firm in accord-
ance with the auspiciousness of the information. In addition, it is
assumed that the information is 'proprietary' in the sense that its
disclosure will impose a given fixed cost on the firm. Incurring this
cost lowers the value of the firm with the same amount, regardless
of the actual value of the variable disclosed. Under the continued
assumption of rational expectations, and still in the simplified one-
period setting of the previous section, investors will now interpret
the nondisclosure of information more cautiously. In this case, the
reason for non-disclosure might either be that the information is
unfavourable, or not favourable enough to warrant incurring disclosure costs. That is, the costs of disclosure exceed the discount in the
share price applied by sceptical investors who infer from the fact of
nondisclosure that the information being withheld is possibly
unfavourable. This uncertainty about the nature of the information
that is being withheld creates leeway for a disclosure equilibrium in
which not all information is being disclosed as investors will not
draw the most negative conclusion from nondisclosure[13]. Subsequent papers on this basis have used more elaborate assumptions
regarding disclosure costs, which Verrecchia simply assumed to be
constant, independent of the value of the variable disclosed, and

---

[13] That is, instead of assuming that the value of the undisclosed variable
is the most negative possible, investors will now assume, given the rational
motive for nondisclosure now in existence, that the value of the undisclosed
variable is the expected value conditional on this value being below the
known disclosure threshold.

incurred only on actual disclosure.

Darrough and Stoughton (1990), Dontoh (1989) and Wagenhofer (1990a) have developed models in which proprietary costs are not simply caused by the mere fact of disclosure. This effect is obtained by assuming the existence of a third party, or third parties, beyond the firm and the investors.

In Darrough and Stoughton (1990), this third party consists of potential competitors[14]. The firm is assumed to receive an item of information which may be more or less favourable, and which it may disclose or not disclose. The entry of competitors into the market of the firm depends on the information being disclosed. The relation between entry and information is specified by a nominal variable 'barriers to entry': when barriers to entry are high, the competitor will not enter the market unless favourable information is disclosed. When barriers to entry are low, the competitor will always enter unless negative information is disclosed. Entry of the competitor will bring about costs to the firm considering disclosure.

Competitive considerations are also studied by Dontoh (1989), who assumes that, in an oligopolistic setting, some firms are endowed with information about the total future market for output. Under the proper assumptions, such firms face a trade-off between using the information for their own output decisions (which is assumed to result in a maximal long-term value) or making the information public (which is assumed to maximize the short-term value of the firm if the information is favourable). The uncertainty about which firms possess information, and about the kind of value-maximizing strategy they follow creates the opportunity for an equilibrium in which not all information is disclosed.

Finally, in Wagenhofer (1990a), the third party is unspecified and could be a competitor, a regulator, a credit rating agency and so on.

---

[14] Further extensions of the entry-game disclosure model are provided in Feltham and Xie (1992) and Newman and Sansing (1993).

This third party will simply impose a cost on the firm if (a) the firm discloses information favourable above a certain threshold, or (b) it believes the value of undisclosed information to be above this threshold.

In all three studies, the firm is shown as striking a balance between, on the one hand, the increase of firm value that will follow the disclosure of favourable information to investors, and on the other hand, the decrease in firm value resulting from adverse action that may or may not follow upon the disclosure of favourable information. In all three models, the result is that, under the rational expectations constraints, sequential equilibria exist in which firms do not necessarily disclose all the information they are known to possess[15].

The previous discussion can be summarized by stating that (i) nonproprietary information will always be disclosed and (ii) proprietary information will sometimes not be disclosed. This observation is useful to the extent that a distinction can in fact be made between proprietary and nonproprietary information. In a model in which a firm possesses only one item of information, it can simply be assumed to be either proprietary or not. The same can be done for each item individually when the firm possesses an array of information, thus breaking down the problem in a number of unrelated disclosure decisions. But when firms have more than one item of information, it is useful to consider possible interdependencies among these items. Dye (1986) has considered the situation of a firm endowed with two items of information, x and y. It is assumed that knowledge of the realization of x can be used to improve estimation of y, because of a known relationship between the two variables. Disclosure of y is assumed to entail proprietary costs. Disclosure of x by itself would not be costly, but for its known relation with y. Therefore, x is proprietary when y is not disclosed, and non-

---

[15] Similar conclusions are reached in Gal-Or (1985, 1986) and Darrough (1993).

29

proprietary otherwise. It is shown that equilibria in which x but not y is disclosed are probable, while equilibria of complete nondisclosure are not.

Summarizing, under a variety of assumptions the existence of disclosure related costs may explain why firms do not fully disclose information they are known to possess, and which sceptical investors might otherwise elicit through adverse selection. The limitations of this approach can be shown by the fact that slightly different assumptions may lead to different conclusions. In Teoh and Hwang (1991) it is demonstrated that firms may choose to withhold favourable information that might be disclosed without incurring proprietary costs. This contrary result is based on the intuitive premise that firms may use nondisclosure of information to signal other information that cannot be credibly disclosed (such as prospects). If firms with bad prospects have an occasional piece of good news, they might be so eager to disclose that it may be worthwhile for firms with good prospects to differentiate themselves from the bad firms with nondisclosure. Even though these conclusions seem to be valid under fairly constrained assumptions only, they do show the impact that these assumptions may have in this type of analysis.

2.4 Information structure

The nature of the information that the firm is endowed with and the knowledge of investors about this information, are other important elements in explaining disclosure.

In the most simple case (*e.g.* Wagenhofer, 1990a), the manager of the firm might receive the realization of an information variable that is with certainty equal to the value of the firm. That is, the manager receives a value y, investors know that the manager has this information, and the manager knows that, on release of the information, the investors will correctly value the firm at y. Important changes occur when there is uncertainty about quality of the information (its usefulness in assessing firm value), or even about its existence.

Stochastic properties can easily be introduced into models of disclosure games, as in Verrecchia (1990b)[16]. It can be assumed that the information the manager receives is the realization of a random variable of unknown distribution with as mean the 'true' value of the firm and a given variance. It can be shown that the disclosure threshold is raised as the information becomes less precise (that is, as its variance increases). When the firm is known to possess information that is completely unreliable, the market will not penalize the firm with discounted share prices for withholding it. On the other hand, perfect information will not necessarily lead to total disclosure, since this simply reverts to the cases described earlier in which partial disclosure is feasible. This assumption therefore, does not change the overall tendencies of the more simple models.

The reason that it does not do so is because it leaves intact a very strong assumption underlying those models, that is, the assumption that the information structure, as opposed to the information itself, is common knowledge (see Myerson, 1979). Without discarding this assumption altogether, which would greatly hinder further analysis, its effects can be gauged by the introduction of more uncertainty concerning the extent of the manager's knowledge. Instead of assuming that the manager always receives some information at the beginning of the period, it can be assumed that there is a known probability that information will be received. That is, the manager either receives no information at all, or does receive information of the kind used in previous models. When he does not disclose information, this may be due to his not receiving any at all, or to its unfavourable nature. A model along these lines is presented in Dye (1985), with the conclusion that these assumptions may explain why some nonproprietary information (that is, information whose disclosure does not entail costs to the firm) may not be disclosed, thus

---

[16] These properties were already included in the model in Verrecchia (1983), but their implications are only fully considered in Verrecchia (1990b).

adding to the result of the previous section. These results are obtained only when the manager can not, or only at great costs, be made to make a verifiable statement that he has not received information: to assume otherwise would reintroduce the possibility of adverse selection. According to Jung and Kwon (1988) who refined Dye's analysis, this effect is essentially the same as the effect of disclosure-related costs: in both cases, information can be withheld because investors are not sure of management's motives for doing so. A laboratory test of this so-called 'Informedness-dependent disclosure' (IDD) model is reported in King and Wallin (1991b). The general assertion that disclosure thresholds increase with the probability that management is not informed was supported by a simple disclosure game played in the course of an experiment. The specific thresholds predicted by the model were not observed in the experiment, however. In King and Wallin (1991a), it was found by means of a similar laboratory experiment that an increase in the number of disclosure options, or unawareness on the part of investors of the full range of disclosure options, also enabled the establishment of equilibria of less than full disclosure.

A final step in this direction is to consider how managers can influence their own information endowments. Whereas managers may be protected from the full force of investors' scepticism by the fact that their information endowments are of low quality (Verrecchia) or possibly non-existent (Dye, Jung and Kwon), this protective cover may be removed again if investors know that managers can exercise discretion in determining the amount and quality of information they receive. More concretely, investors might know that managers can build information systems with an almost infinite variety of output, or that they have access to the services of analysts and advisers.

In an extreme case, suggested by Verrecchia (1990b), managers would be expected to choose to receive no information at all. If disclosure of information would lead a firm to incur proprietary costs, firm value would be maximized if the manager would choose not to receive information that he might have to disclose on the basis of the revelation principle. This result can only be obtained under strong assumptions, though:

- Risk is not priced, that is, investors attach no positive value to the reduction in uncertainty as to the value of the firm caused by the disclosure of information.
- Information has no intrinsic value. The reverse of this assumption can be envisaged as meaning that having a management information system helps the manager to improve management of the firm, and thereby increases its value[17].

2.5 Heterogeneous investors and risk-sharing

In the previous sections, the group of 'investors' was considered to be homogeneous. A next step would be to consider the effect of more types of participants or of richer assumptions concerning their relationships.

One line of research considers the role of disclosures in risk-sharing among investors who are endowed with different portfolios and different resources with regard to information acquisition and interpretation[18]. One of the basic findings of this line of inquiry is the assertion that at least some investors may prefer less information to more. If investors are endowed with portfolios that will yield different, independent and a priori unknown returns, investors might reduce their risk by trading their investments before the true value of

---

[17] *Cf.* Lanen and Verrecchia (1987), where the relationship between operating decisions and disclosure is considered. If managers use their information to make, for instance, investment decisions, any observed actions can serve as rough alternatives to disclosure.

[18] Another approach is taken by Fishman and Hagerty (1989), who take into account that studying firms' disclosures is costly and that investors are therefore limited in the number of signals that they can study. This provides (some) firms with an incentive to disclose information with a higher precision which is less costly to study and therefore attracts more traders to the firm's shares. This in turn enhances price efficiency with regard to these shares.

the portfolios is revealed (for example: before a dividend is declared). The amount of actual trading will be influenced by the release of information. Investors holding what turn out to be investments with less favourable prospects will experience an immediate decrease in wealth, which might, before the release of the information, have been shared among all investors. In short, disclosure tends to increase consensus among investors, which reduces the possibility of risk-sharing. This line of reasoning has been developed by Verrecchia (1982) and Hakansson, Kunkel and Ohlson (1982). The latter find, as a result, that from a social welfare point of view, no disclosure is preferable to public disclosure. However, as might be expected, from an individual point of view, private information gathering may well yield increased private results. It can be shown that, without public information, there will be a demand for private information, but that, ex ante, all investors would benefit from an enforceable ban on private information gathering[19]. In the absence of an enforceable ban, investors will tend to favour disclosure over nondisclosure.

Although the general effect of increased disclosure is often assumed to be an increase in consensus, Indjejikian (1991) has shown that there can be more subtle effects if it is assumed that the interpretation of disclosed data requires effort and a certain level of sophistication on the part of investors. In that case, increased information content ('quality') of disclosures increases the incentives for investors to invest resources in private data interpretation. This increase in individual activity decreases consensus among investors, which increases the possibility of risk-sharing.
The results from attempts to explain disclosure on the basis of its risk-sharing effects are heavily dependent on the often strong assumptions required to keep the analysis tractable. Bushman (1991) and Indjejikian (1991) comment on the crucial nature of the assump-

---

[19] Hakansson (1981), Diamond (1985). See, however, McNichols and Trueman (1994) where a different setting (including pre-disclosure trading) results in different attitudes towards private information gathering.

tion that there is no pre-disclosure trading, and on the effect of one-period models.

2.6 More realistic time frames

The usual adverse selection models present the disclosure decision as a unique event in the sense that the decision to disclose has to be made without considering similar future decisions. It is commonly assumed that soon after the disclosure decision is made the firm will be liquidated or that, if future cycles of information endowment/ disclosure/ trading do occur, these are not in any way influenced by events in previous cycles. Correspondingly, the decision rule of management is assumed to be the maximization of the current market value of the firm.

All of these characteristics are naturally at variance with the reality of annual report disclosure, but to say this does not imply that it is easy to trace the effects of more realistic assumptions. Nevertheless, attempts have been made in the analytical literature to make a beginning in addressing these concerns.

The initial models presented in earlier sections have been extended to account for the passage of time in two ways.

A first extension considers the possibility that disclosure decisions are not simply made on a 'whether or not' basis. The timing of the disclosure is included as a part of the disclosure decision. If firms are not confined to one particular moment in time at which they either may or may not disclose a part of their information endowment, they can influence the informational content, or relevance, of their disclosures by exercising discretion in selecting the moment of disclosure. In his 1983 study, Verrecchia has indicated a possible way of incorporating this element in his adverse selection model. The model specified a fixed, exogenous proprietary cost, which might be assumed to decrease with time. The consequence would be that 'good news' would be disclosed earlier than 'bad news' and that, if proprietary costs eventually tend towards zero, investors will

35

in the end force the firm to disclose all information it is known to possess[20]. This aspect is of some importance in bridging the gap between theoretical modelling and the practice of financial reporting. The latter tends to be dominated by accounting information with an essentially historical character, losing much of its relevance with the passage of time.

A second temporal extension consists in adding more periods to the essentially one-period models described above. Dye and Sridhar (1995) have analyzed the effect of a two-period model on what was described earlier as knowledge of the information structure. It was argued in section 2.4 that uncertainty on the part of investors as to the information endowments of firms could lead to lower levels of disclosure. This uncertainty, however, can be reduced by observing firms' disclosure behaviour in successive periods. Dye and Sridhar assume a two-period world in which firms receive information with a certain probability at the beginning of the first period. The receipt (not the content) of the information by the various firms is imperfectly correlated. According to the general logic explained earlier, some firms will decide to disclose their information in the first period. The number of disclosing firms will lead investors to revise their estimates of the likelihood that nondisclosing firms have received information, which in turn may lead to a second round of disclosures by previously nondisclosing firms. This model of 'herding behaviour' provides a first step towards the analysis of dynamic disclosure behaviour within a group of companies.

An essential feature of both the Dontoh and Dye and Sridhar approach is, however, that they still deal with a single cycle in which all disclosure and trading decisions revolve around one item of information. Following trading, there is a new generation of owner-

---

[20] However, Skinner (1994) found that there is a tendency for companies to disclose extreme bad news early. This effect was attributed to attempts to prevent negative reputation effects and the possibility of legal action in the US setting.

managers which may be faced with a similar disclosure decision, but this sequencing of single-cycle models does not amount to an explanation of long-term disclosures.

Suggestions for developing a truly long-term theory have been advanced by Wagenhofer (1990a), who raises the possibility that firms do not base their decision to disclose on the value of a particular item of information but instead commit themselves in advance to disclosure policies for future realizations of this variable. This notion of precommitment is not further developed. The results of adding this complication seem to depend to a very large extent on highly specific assumptions. On the whole, precommitments would seem to take away the uncertainty underlying the partial disclosure results: whereas in the basic case nondisclosure was tolerated because of ambiguity concerning management's motivation, this would now be reduced to uncertainty about management's reasons for choosing a strategy of full nondisclosure.

2.7 Agency relationships

Whereas a game-theoretical approach has not yet resulted in a model of long-term aspects of voluntary disclosure, a slightly different approach based on the notion of agency relationships has to some extent filled this gap. As indicated above, the simpler disclosure games rested on the assumption that residual interests in the firm (ownership rights) would be sold. This provided the mechanism by which owner-managers sought to maximize the price of these ownership rights whereas investors sought to minimize the price to be paid. The models ended with the transfer of ownership rights, and modelling successive periods amounted to modelling the behaviour of successive generations of owner-managers.

Alternatively, it might be supposed that the original owner-managers remain in charge as managers after all or some of the ownership rights have been sold to investors. This assumption provides a truly long-term setting for an analysis of disclosure in which subsequent periods are not repetitions of the first period. The framework of analysis based on agency relations has received widespread attention since the study of Jensen and Meckling (1976). Leftwich, Watts and Zimmerman (1981) contained a first application to disclosure issues[21].

A situation can be assumed in which owner-managers sell their ownership rights to investors, but remain in charge as managers. The original sale of ownership rights is governed by the revelation principle outlined earlier: the investors will discount the share price for all information they know or suspect the manager-owners to have but do not disclose. Hence, there is an incentive for full disclosure. But the assumption that the original owners will be retained as 'agents' provides a complicating factor. This introduces an unknown variable in the future cash flows of the firms: the extent to which agents will in future engage in self-interested behaviour[22] to the detriment of the investors (the 'principals'). Because this variable is indeterminate, and hence cannot be truthfully disclosed[23], investors will react similarly as in other situations of nondisclosure. That is, they will make a pessimistic assessment of the extent of future self-interested behaviour and apply a large discount to the share price offered.

Analogous to the full disclosure of the earlier models, the manager-

---

[21] It will be noted that the Jensen and Meckling (1976) and Leftwich, Watts and Zimmerman (1981) papers appeared before the development of an extensive game-theoretical disclosure literature. Therefore, the exposition of the agency approach provided here contains some anachronisms. Other studies on the relationship between signalling and derived demand approaches include Morris (1987) and Craswell and Taylor (1992). Ronen and Yaari (1993) provide a signalling model based on an agency setting.

[22] 'Self-interested behaviour' captures a wide variety of phenomena. In terms of the initial model of the firm as a series of future cash flows, one can think of these cash flows as given and interpret self-interested behaviour as attempts by managers to appropriate some of these cash flows for private consumption. One can also assume that cash flows are dependent on management performance in which case managers might have an incentive to choose lower levels of exertion.

[23] See assumption (5) in section 2.2.1.

owners will attempt to prevent discounts by introducing monitoring and bonding arrangements. These fulfil a similar role as a truthful disclosure that the value of the variable 'self-interested behaviour' will remain within certain limits. The monitoring arrangements may take several forms, but one frequently suggested mechanism is the regular supply of information. In this way, the assumption of an agency setting provides a rationale for disclosure in a multi-period setting, but it should be noted that there is no guarantee that an agency setting will result in the actual adoption of regular public disclosure as a monitoring device. This depends on the availability of alternative monitoring devices, and their cost relative to the cost of disclosure.

Costs of disclosure can be interpreted in the same way as in the earlier models, and proprietary costs are again an important component of the costs of disclosure. That is, if certain items of information that are useful for monitoring purposes entail the likelihood of adverse action by competitors, the government or other parties, it is likely that choosing alternative monitoring devices will lead to a higher firm value. The contribution of the agency approach is to point out that the choice of a committed disclosure strategy is a part of a comprehensive endogenous solution to the problem of optimizing the contracting network among the various interested parties in the firm. It can, in general, be hypothesized that in firms with a higher potential for conflicts of interest between agents and principals, there is a rationale for incurring higher monitoring costs, and hence the likelihood of a greater extent of regular disclosure.

Once it is assumed that firms exist indefinitely, the model can be extended to include the disclosure of incidental information (of the 'good news/bad news' type) to which the earlier models were largely confined. Several assumptions are possible. One set of assumptions would be that there is a continuous secondary market in ownership rights, and that the managers (agents) are allowed to participate in this trading. These two assumptions together provide an incentive for insider trading on the part of management. Rather than disclosing either good news or bad news, managers will use this information to trade on their own account. These assumptions on their own will therefore lead to a nondisclosure equilibrium (with regard to incidental information). However, to the extent that insider trading transfers wealth from current to prospective shareholders, contractual arrangements will be set up as part of the general bonding arrangements that prevent managers to engage in insider trading (see Ross, 1979). It is conceivable that the bonding arrangements will take a form in which management rewards are positively tied to share prices without the possibility of direct trading by managers (either through stock options or bonus arrangements). The model will then revert to the earlier case in which management has an interest in maximizing share price, and in which the management's disclosure decision will be based on a trade-off between the effect of a disclosure on investors and the possibility of adverse action.

It can be concluded that an agency or derived demand approach is especially useful to extend the more elementary signalling approach to cover long-term disclosure practices.

2.8 Relevance to annual financial reporting and implications for the present study

The previous sections have outlined the current state of theory development in the area of economics-based models of disclosure behaviour. This section contains an evaluation of this body of theory, looking at its applicability to annual report disclosure, its consistency with the professional literature, its comprehensiveness and its implications for the present study.

As indicated above, applications of signalling theory in the accounting literature have tended to be restricted to disclosure decisions in which the decision to disclose is based on the particular value of the variable to be disclosed. That is, the routine disclosure of a variable regardless of its particular value is not treated explicitly by this literature. In that respect, the applicability to annual financial report disclosures appears to be limited. It is possible to envisage an extension of the applicability of signalling models by reasoning that firms for which a particular variable is *on average* higher than the average across all firms would have an incentive to disclose this variable on a routine basis, thus triggering a familiar cascade-effect. This extension, although not implausible in the form of a casual argument, has not yet been attempted in the research literature.

As has been shown, the introduction of an agency setting, interpreted in terms of its adverse selection implications, does to some extent provide a formal explanation of routine disclosure. It provided a rationale for routine disclosures, even though it was concluded that such disclosures were a likely but not a necessary consequence of the assumptions inherent in such a setting. Any routine disclosures derived from an agency perspective are restricted to monitoring information. The framework does not provide an explicit explanation for the routine provision of information that may not serve any monitoring purposes but is aimed, instead, at facilitating investment decisions.

But even though a number of steps are still lacking in the formal analysis before the models discussed in this chapter can be applied to annual report disclosure, their general conclusions are quite compatible with those to be found in the more general, or professional literature on disclosure. The findings of this chapter can be compared with some of the observations in a review of practical disclosure issues in the mid-1950s by Horngren (1957). In his review, one can find the following elements:

- the relationship between a company and its investors as the primary force driving disclosure extension;
- the importance of tying management interest to share price (either through stock options or the threat of proxy contests) as an explanatory factor of increased disclosure;
- the need to consider the costs of disclosure in terms of competitive damage or government intervention;
- the impossibility of withholding information that the public knows is probably available to the company and the disclos-

ure of which is unlikely to cause substantial competitive damage;

- the importance of disclosure by other companies in assisting the investing public to revise its estimates of the probability that a nondisclosing holds that type of information as well.

This conformity of theoretical models with observations in the practice-oriented literature is not surprising. After all, such models set out to explain facts that are already familiar by demonstrating that there is a logical economic explanation for these familiar phenomena. The fact remains, however, that this correspondence between theoretical results and professional opinions is achieved despite the fact that the theoretical approaches outlined here ignore or do not address explicitly a number of factors that play a role in shaping the contents of financial reporting.

One of these factors is that disclosure decisions are not necessarily taken by single individuals. Rather, disclosure is the result of a group process within firms in which economic and non-economic factors may form a complex mixture. The introduction of bounded rationality in particular may seriously affect of the results of the rational expectations models described above.

The idea that the internal workings of firms with respect to the production of annual reports may be fairly complex is not new, although studies along these lines are scarce. Sorter *et al.* (1966) have formulated this idea in terms of 'corporate personality', and suggested that accounting practice may reflect aspects of personality as 'conservatism'. Their empirical study focused on measurement, not disclosure, and does not seem to have established a more permanent line of research. Gibbins, Richardson and Waterhouse (1990, 1992) is indicative of the current state of the literature on this point in that it still professes to be no more than an exploratory study, providing a tentative framework and vocabulary for analyzing the disclosure process within firms. On the basis of a relatively small number of detailed case studies, they conclude that firms have distinct 'disclosure positions', or stable preferences for the way

42

disclosure is managed. These positions can usually be clearly identified by participants in the disclosure process and can be described by the dimensions of 'ritualism' (uncritical or routine adherence to norms believed to apply to particular classes of disclosures) and 'opportunism' (active consideration of specific advantages in the disclosure of information). Disclosure positions are formed under the influence of a variety of influences in which less tangibles factors like company history and personal preferences as expressed in internal political processes are mingled with more objective factors as direct disclosure regulation, norms used by the financial press and the desire to maintain access to the capital markets. The handling of specific disclosure issues is influenced not only by the general disclosure position, but also by the way the issue is brought to the attention of and perceived by the firm, and by organizational structures for handling disclosure issues.

If the internal disclosure process within a firm contains a number of elements that are not immediately accessible to formal economic analysis, the same is true for the external environment of the firm. When one considers the process in which new norms for annual financial reporting are developed, questions are raised as to how new disclosures originate. At least to some extent, new disclosures are the product of a process of 'technological innovation' of which the earlier stages such as the inception of new ideas and their propagation by means of persuasion, education and imitation, are highly qualitative by nature[24]. In chapter 4, it will be discussed to what extent general theories of innovation-diffusion can be used to supplement the approach to disclosure outlined in this chapter.

---

[24] Examples of financial reporting research that explicitly take into account factors as group behaviour, knowledge generation and propagation and the influence of persuasion include Tritschler (1970), Comiskey and Groves (1972) and Edwards (1991). Chandra and Greenball (1977) is an attempt to chart the consequences of differences in perceptions between management and investors of potential disclosures and their costs and benefits.

Casting the net even wider, one may see disclosure and reporting issues in the light of the texture of the entire social system. Illustrations of this approach are the analysis of the introduction of the value added statement in Britain in the context of the contemporary socio-political situation by Burchell *et al.* (1985) and the interpretation of the annual reports of General Motors in the light of a changing pattern of gender relations (Tinker and Neimark, 1987). In the latter paper, the analysis is again explicitly based on an economic framework, but one radically different from micro-economic rational expectations approach described previously in this chapter[25]. Chapter 3 will document the historical context of financial reporting in the Netherlands, in order to identify factors of this kind.

On the basis of this chapter, it can be concluded that the economic approach to disclosure theory formulation discussed in this chapter is as yet incomplete. The formal steps leading from incidental disclosure to routine annual report disclosure have only begun to be addressed. Given the almost limitless scope for citing factors and variables that may have an influence on the highly complex disclosure process, it is not to be expected that comprehensive disclosure theories will soon appear. Rather, the literature appears to develop in the direction of ever more specialized models, dealing with highly specific situations and assumptions.
Yet, it appears equally justified to assert that a fairly limited number of key features of the disclosure process has been identified in the theoretical disclosure literature. Even though some or all of these features have been known in the professional literature for some time, they have been shown to be amenable to rigorous theoretical

---

[25] 'The political economy approach [to accounting] is concerned with explaining and assessing the ways various social protagonists use accounting information and corporate reporting to mediate, suppress, mystify and transform social conflict. The approach places class relations at the forefront of the analysis and is, accordingly, concerned with the effects of accounting information and corporate reporting on the distribution of income, wealth and power' (Tinker and Neimark, 1987:71-72).

justification. They include:

- The importance of the determination of the contents of the 'disclosure array'. Even though the existence of potential disclosures is often simply assumed, attention has been drawn to the importance of the process by which new disclosure options become available.

- The importance of knowledge of the 'information structure'. New disclosures do not only have to be available as options to management. Awareness of these options among outsiders to the firm has been shown to be a vital part of the mechanism of disclosure expansion.

- The vital importance of disclosure costs in preventing situations of complete disclosure. Moreover, the literature has begun to address the issue of the endogenous nature of disclosure costs, by considering the effects on disclosure costs of interaction between firms and between firms and third parties.

These elementary principles (and their underlying reasoning as outlined in this chapter) will play an important role as points of reference in the development of the empirical section of this book and the interpretation of its results. However, as indicated by the discussion in this section, they cannot be judged sufficient by themselves to explain and interpret the development of disclosure practice over time. For that reason, the next chapter adds to the frame of reference in this study by considering in more detail the historical background of annual report disclosure in the Netherlands.

Chapter 3
Views on voluntary financial reporting in the Netherlands

3.1 The notion of a 'Dutch system' of financial reporting

In this chapter, attention shifts from the generalized, abstract discussion of disclosure in the previous chapter towards the more specific topic of annual report disclosure in the postwar Netherlands. Whereas the previous chapter identified a number of general factors influencing disclosure, this chapter outlines the context in which such factors operated in the concrete historical period studied here. In this way, this chapter adds to the frame of reference required for the empirical investigation of Dutch reporting practices in subsequent chapters.

This chapter could be rather short, if its sole purpose were to demonstrate that there was in fact ample scope for voluntary annual report disclosure in the postwar Netherlands. Such a demonstration would merely consist of an enumeration of the rather modest legal disclosure provisions in force during this period. Such a short description of legal provisions would not, however, do full justice to the subject of voluntary disclosure in the postwar Netherlands. The reason for this is that the absence of major regulation did not occur by default. Rather, it came about in a climate of intensive reflection on what could and could not be achieved by means of company law in the area of financial reporting.

There is a definite relationship between the light regulatory regime in the Netherlands and the perception, sketched in chapter 1, that financial reporting in the Netherlands evolved along different lines from that in other countries. As indicated there, an important element in the perceived 'otherness' of Dutch financial reporting was a favourable development of reporting practice in an environment that was relatively free from regulation.

This chapter attempts to capture this intellectual background of Dutch financial reporting by describing the history of Dutch accounting regulation in the light of the development of thought and opinion on the respective roles of regulation and voluntary action.

The intellectual climate that this chapter aims to describe was made up of many different, changing and frequently conflicting visions. Yet one particular point of view seems to stand out. Many participants in or observers of Dutch financial reporting during the middle years of this century shared a similar perception of a mechanism by which Dutch financial reporting could hope to do without the degree of disclosure regulation considered necessary elsewhere. This notion that there was or might be a distinct 'Dutch system' or 'Dutch model' of reporting and reporting regulation represented the optimistic end of the spectrum of opinion on financial reporting. At the other end of this spectrum, one could find the opinion that Dutch financial reporting was of a low quality, and would not substantially improve without regulation. This view was less common, however, than its counterpart. For that reason, the notion of a 'Dutch system' has been adopted as the organizing theme of this chapter. By tracing its development, it can be used as a yardstick with which alternative, more pessimistic views that existed as well in the Netherlands can be compared.

A second note on the nature of this chapter relates to the definition of disclosure. Even though disclosure issues can generally be distinguished from issues of valuation and income determination, at the general level of 'national reporting systems' and 'reporting regulation', this distinction cannot always be maintained. In issues like secret reserve accounting, disclosure and valuation become inextricably mixed. Although the emphasis in this chapter is clearly on disclosure issues, the discussion will inevitably touch upon reporting issues of a broader kind.

This chapter is mainly based on the Dutch professional auditing literature. As indicated in chapter 1, auditors played a key role in the perceived mechanism of disclosure improvement. A second important source on which this chapter draws is the (professional) legal literature, mainly in the area of company law.

This chapter precedes the empirical chapters later in this book, and it was presented in chapter 1 as part of the framework required for understanding the development of reporting practice. In a way, this ordering of chapters is artificial as it is just as true that one needs knowledge of the development of reporting practice in order to understand the development of regulation of and opinion on financial reporting. One might, in fact, think in terms of a triangular relationship between reporting practice, reporting regulation and opinion on reporting in which developments in each area influenced the other two areas. In particular, as will be seen, the perception that there were substantial voluntary improvements in reporting practice played an important role in justifying the continued reliance on a light regulatory system. This chapter deals primarily with the interaction between regulation and opinion, while a discussion of reporting practice is deferred until chapters 5 and 6. Yet, for a better understanding of the present chapter, it is useful to point out that these later chapters do provide empirical support for the view that there were substantial voluntary disclosure extensions throughout the postwar period.

A final note on the nature of this chapter deals with demarcation in time. In order to appreciate fully the origins and development of the notion of a Dutch approach to financial reporting, it is necessary to go back before the beginning of the postwar period covered by the empirical study in later chapters. This chapter will take as its starting point the similarity in much of 19th century European company law, and sketch how, from this common basis, the Netherlands moved towards a distinctive position characterized by a comparatively light set of accounting regulations.

The chapter consists of three chronological parts, covering the period up to 1940, the 1945-1970 period and the period from 1970 to the middle 1980s. This breakdown roughly corresponds to the rise, the attainment of maturity and the start of the gradual disappearance of the notion of a 'Dutch system' of reporting and reporting regulation.

3.2 Developments prior to 1940

3.2.1 The company law reform movement in Europe (1800-1930)
It has frequently been observed that the development of company law, of the limited liability company and, more particular, of financial reporting has followed broadly similar paths in the various countries of nineteenth century Europe (see Walton, 1995:chapter 1). The national histories of financial reporting regulation for that period can be seen as variations on a few common themes: the widespread influence of French codified law, the consequences of the industrial revolution which made the first generation of company legislation obsolete, and the attempts at remedial legislation in which mandatory financial statement publication and disclosure regulation played an important role.

The French *Code de Commerce* of 1807 had an important influence on company law throughout western Europe. The regulation of the limited liability company in the *Code* had two important characteristics. On the one hand, the limited liability company as seen by the *Code* was an instrument of private economic initiative. The structure of a particular company was to be determined primarily by the contract entered into by the participants in its capital. On the other hand, the *Code* specified that the articles of incorporation of a new company had to obtain state approval before a new company could be created. This system of preventive supervision was aimed at preventing private agreements to the detriment of creditors or the general interest through the abuse of limited liability.
The growing number and size of limited liability companies in the second half of the nineteenth century ushered in a period of reflection on the nature of the firm, and especially about means of

controlling the economic power that began to be concentrated within limited liability companies. Thinking on the nature and use of financial reporting developed as part of this wider reflection. This background explains why financial reporting was initially seen as primarily a legal issue.

Throughout Western Europe, company laws were repeatedly changed during the period 1850-1914 to reflect the changing nature of businesses carried out in limited liability companies. A common feature of these revisions was the growing emphasis on the mandatory provision of information, financial and otherwise, to those with a financial interest in the doings of company managements (Van Slooten, 1900: 39). This was seen as a more effective control mechanism than preventive state supervision, and one that happened to be more suited to an age in which the notion of *laissez-faire* still played an important role.

This 'publicity principle' spread like a wave throughout Europe. Changes in French, British and German company laws[1] mutually influenced each other and provided the inspiration for a variety of regulations in minor European countries and overseas dependencies[2]. As a result, the various European companies acts all shifted the focus of regulation from preventive state supervision to publicity, but the particulars of these new regulations differed considerably among countries. European company law began to display a wide spectrum of regulations concerning the type of information to be disclosed, the audience to which the information was to be disclosed, the medium of disclosure and enforcement mechanisms and sanctions.

Developments in the Netherlands can be fitted into this general outline. The *Code de Commerce* was imposed on the country in

---

[1] The key points of reference were the French Act of 1867; the General (North) German Commercial Code of 1861, modified in 1870 and 1884, and its 1897 successor; and the British Joint Stock Companies Act of 1856 and Companies Acts 1862 and 1900.

[2] See, for instance, Walton (1986).

1811 and remained in force until 1838, when it was replaced by a domestic Commercial Code *(Wetboek van Koophandel)*. This Dutch Commercial Code closely followed its French predecessor. Even though the system of preventive state supervision did attract some criticism at the time, it was retained in the 1838 Code as the principal safeguard of the public interest. The possible alternative of using audited financial statement information for such purposes was only dimly perceived *(e.g.* Van Hall, 1834: 73).

A next stage in the development of Dutch company law began when neighbouring countries started to introduce reforms in the 1860s and 1870s. Stimulated by this foreign example, company law reform, including the possible application of the publicity principle, began to be debated in the Netherlands from the 1870s onwards. However, the Netherlands distinguished itself from almost every other European country by the fact that despite intensive debate, no new company law was enacted between 1838 and 1928. Rather than quickly adapting its legislation in line with the international trend, the Netherlands 'let the psychological moment slip' (Van der Heijden, 1925(a):34). Instead, a long process of attempted company law reform was set in motion in 1871 with the submission to Parliament of the first of a series of draft laws to revise the sections of the Commercial Code dealing with the limited liability company *(naamloze vennootschap* or *NV)*. Difficulties in formulating reporting requirements were a major cause of the fact that a reform law to modify the Commercial Code was passed only as late as 1928/1929[3]. This reform made publication of financial statements mandatory for large and/or listed limited liability companies and included some elementary disclosure requirements.

The Netherlands was not the last European country to require

---

[3] The date 1928/1929 refers to the fact that the main part of the law was passed in 1928, and that an amendment dealing specifically with financial reporting was inserted in 1929. An outline of the reform process can be found in Zeff *et al.* (1992: chapter 2). See also Walton (1995: chapter 10).

publication of financial statements[4], but it took longer than neighbouring countries to make up its mind about the type of regulation it wanted. In many other countries, company law reform was achieved in stages. A typical sequence of events would be for a first act to prescribe the publication of details of incorporation, and the presentation of an annual balance sheet to shareholders. Subsequent legislation would expand these provisions by requiring general publication of the balance sheet, for example through a commercial register or a national newspaper, and by imposing certain minimum disclosure rules on the balance sheet. In a similar way, publication requirements might in later stages be extended to cover the profit and loss account[5]. In the Netherlands, no such intermediary stages occurred. A complete basic companies act (publication of balance sheet and profit- and loss account and some minimum disclosure requirements) was introduced in 1928/29, replacing the relevant sections of the Commercial Code (1838) that were, at that time, the most ancient set of regulations in force in Western Europe.

A reason that is occasionally advanced (see Zeff *et al.*, 1992:33) for this relative tardiness is that the economic development of the Netherlands was relatively slow. This factor might help to explain why Belgium, one of earliest European countries to industrialize, introduced important modernizations in its company law as early as 1873, including mandatory publication of financial statements.
But although it is true that the transition to a modern economy started rather late in the Netherlands, a period of rapid change at the

---

[4] Austrian companies were not required to publish financial statements until 1938. Finland introduced mandatory publication in the same year as the Netherlands, in 1928.

[5] In Denmark, for instance, a business act was introduced in 1862 (and revised in 1899), requiring disclosure of details of incorporation. A book-keeping act was introduced in 1912, and a limited companies act, requiring publication of a balance sheet, in 1917. Minimum disclosure requirements and the requirement to publish a profit- and loss account were introduced in 1930 (Walton, 1995: chapter 5).

close of the nineteenth century resulted in an economic structure that could compare with that of the larger European countries in all respects except scale (Van Zanden and Griffiths, 1989:5-9). Even though there had been only 137 NVs in the Netherlands in 1850, their number had grown to almost 7000 in 1910 (Valkhoff, 1938:152). In addition, a growing number of NVs acquired a stock-market listing. In the 20 years up to 1900, the number of listed NVs grew at the remarkable average rate of 13 to 14 new listings a year[6]. In all, the economic structure of the Netherlands around 1900 seems to offer no compelling reason why the Netherlands should not modernize its company law, as countries like Spain (1869, 1885) and Switzerland (1881) had already done before.

A second possibility would be that the Netherlands was not affected by the sort of financial scandals that triggered company law reform in other countries[7]. This, however, was not true. A number of major financial scandals erupted between 1880 and 1910 that had wide repercussions. In 1905, the government was explicitly asked by parliament to speed up the process of company law reform for this reason[8]. In the end, though, scandals as these were apparently not a sufficient stimulus to complete the reform process.

Part of the slowness can be ascribed to factors not directly relating to company law, as in the disparaging comment, made near the end of the fifty-year reform process, that 'the legislative machinery works

---

[6] See Valkhoff, *loc. cit.*, and De Vries (1983:127). The number of listings is reported in Koert (1934:53-55), and De Vries (1976:33, 87). The latter counts securities rather than companies. Numbers refer to the total of Dutch and Dutch East-Indian companies.

[7] Such as the massive company failures in Germany during the period 1870-1873 (Schröer, 1993), the collapse of the City of Glasgow Bank in 1878 (Edwards, 1989:144) and the Danish Alberti-affair of 1908 (Walton, 1995:57).

[8] For the relation between scandals and reform, see Visser (1926). De Vries (1983:9-11) contains a short discussion of some of the more celebrated scandals.

hardly anywhere as slowly as in the Netherlands' [9]. However, it is more likely that the reasons for the long delay in making effective changes in the law should be sought primarily at a more conceptual level, in the existence of a strong and articulate opposition against the involvement of the law in publications by limited companies. The next section contains a closer analysis of the debate on company law reform in the Netherlands during the 1870-1930 period. Such an analysis is important, because during this period the ground was prepared on which a voluntary system of reporting was to be constructed. During this period, the role of the law in financial reporting was a question faced in all countries in Europe, including the Netherlands. In the Netherlands, it was eventually determined that the law should *not* play an important role in determining the contents of financial reports. This negative decision, which moved the issue of financial reporting largely outside the legal sphere in which it had originated, cleared the way for the emergence of an alternative view in which financial reporting was based on voluntary action.

3.2.2 The emergence of liberal reporting regulation[10]

Throughout the period 1871-1928/1929, the debate on company law reform, in particular on legal regulation of financial reporting, was carried on with varying intensity among lawyers, businessmen, the government and parliament, and, beginning in the late 1890s, the emerging auditing profession. As elsewhere in Europe, a key issue in was whether government supervision could be replaced by

---

[9] *Advies over het gewijzigd ontwerp van wet op de naamlooze vennootschappen* ('s-Gravenhage: Verbond van Nederlandsche Werkgevers, 1926), p. 4. See also Zeff *et al.*(1992:44-45).

[10] General sources used for this section include Cosman (1872), Mees (1872), Van Slooten (1900), Beerenborg (1907), Van Slooten (1912-13), Volmer (1914), Van Hasselt (1919), Van der Heijden (1925a and 1925b), Lampe (1925), Huussen-de Groot (1976), De Vries (1983 and 1985) and Zeff *et al.* (1992:chapter 2).

mandatory publicity, and if so, how the latter should be regulated.

The traditional argument in favour of government supervision had been that limited liability represented an economic privilege. In that light, it would be improper to allow the creation of such privileges by private agreement, and government had not merely the right but also the duty to impose some form of supervision in order to prevent abuse (*e.g.* Van Tricht, 1880). That premiss accepted, it might be argued that government supervision, especially if it was limited to preventive supervision exercised at the inception of an NV, was not the most effective approach to supervision. Mandatory publicity might be a more effective alternative. But the justification for imposing publicity would be the same: public availability of financial statement information was a price to be paid for limited liability. In this view, a case for mandatory publication of financial statements (or of at least a balance sheet) could be made on the basis of the nature of the legal form of the limited company *per se*[11]. The view of financial reporting as a corrective or a price formed the basis of the first two draft laws to be produced on the subject of company law reform in 1871 and 1890.

Given this view of financial reporting as an alternative safeguard against abuse of the limited liability company, it is natural that early interest in financial reporting deals to a large extent with its effectiveness as such, that is, with the possibility that this safeguard itself is abused. Some[12] believed that it would not be sufficient merely to prescribe the publication of financial statements, but that it would be necessary as well to regulate their contents in order to prevent the publication of meaningless or even misleading financial statements. This negative approach implied that the possibility of

---

[11] For this view especially Déking Dura (1886:149n), but also Van Slooten (1900, 1912-13), Beerenborg (1907), and Van der Heijden (1929:15).

[12] The main exponent of this view was G. Van Slooten, whose 1900 dissertation remained the point of reference in discussions on reporting regulation until well in the 1920s.

'voluntary disclosure' was seen as rather remote, or at least not as a reliable assumption for regulatory activity. The 1890 draft law did, for this reason, indeed contain a list of minimum balance sheet disclosures, allegedly based on the example of the Swiss 1881 *Obligationenrecht*.

Gradually, however, an opinion gained strength that placed less emphasis on the need for the public to be protected against abuse by the limited liability company, and more on the right of the limited liability company to be free from the imposition of the costs of publicity. This view seems to be part of a broader trend towards liberalism and deregulation that persisted throughout the period 1870-1930. Government intervention in the affairs of the limited company could be seen as a phenomenon from an earlier age, or even as 'reactionary'[13].

The most extreme position in this direction had been taken as early as the 1830s by Van Hall (1834) who had argued that a limited liability company ought to be free from any state interference since it arose from private agreement between free men, and since no one was obliged to engage in transactions with such a company. This view continued to be promulgated, especially in business circles, right until the 1928 Commercial Code revision[14].

Usually, however, a more balanced approach was adopted, aimed at reconciling the lawful interests of both the company and third parties. It was recognized that publishing financial statements might be detrimental to the welfare of the company, as it might provide actual and potential competitors with vital information (this corresponds to the notion of proprietary costs developed in the previous chapter). If it was assumed that the interests involved were substantial, and might actually involve the life or death of the

---

[13] Zeff *et al.* (1992:47). See also Zeylemaker ([1946]: 15) for the view that the period before 1870 was characterized by a greater inclination to interfere with the limited liability company.

[14] As in *Advies over het gewijzigd ontwerp van wet op de naamlooze vennootschappen* ('s-Gravenhage: Verbond van Nederlandsche Werkgevers, 1926), notably p. 23-24.

publishing company[15], it would not be correct for the state to attach conditions to its gift of limited liability without proper grounds. Such grounds might be found in specific activities or types of company finance. A common proposal was that companies should be required to publish financial statements only if they publicly floated securities, took savings deposits or sold insurance policies[16]. Although this more balanced point of view provided a middle ground on which most Dutch theorists were able to accept the usefulness of mandatory public financial reporting as an alternative to state supervision[17], implementing this idea in concrete legal provisions proved to be a difficult problem.

In the early 1870s, it was apparently often assumed that matters of valuation and presentation of information in balance sheets were so self-evident as not to require further regulation[18], or that they might be regulated satisfactorily by a few relatively simple rules. However, the development of accounting thought, notably the development of the idea of depreciation and the elaboration of accrual concepts eroded faith in unambiguous and 'true' balance sheets based on exit values[19]. In addition, disclosure became a practical issue. During the later part of the nineteenth century, a growing number of listed companies voluntarily started to publish summary balance sheets in the newspapers or as separate

---

[15] So J. Heemskerk Azn, cited in debates following Cosman (1872) and Mees (1872), p. 102.

[16] See, for instance, Volmer (1897). A similar view was expressed by Th.Limperg jr. See transcript of debate recorded in Van Slooten (1912-13:6).

[17] Van Slooten (1900: 85) hardly raised the issue of Royal Consent 'faute de combatants'. Some, however, did not want to dispense with Royal Consent altogether (See Volmer, 1914:110-111). In a modified form, it has survived up to the present.

[18] See Cosman (1872:108).

[19] Volmer (1914:32-33); Schmalenbach (1933:64-68).

brochures[20].   This prompted the question to what extent the balance sheet to be required by law might be such an abbreviated balance sheet (one, for instance, in which all the receivables were grouped under one heading instead of listing each individual debtor)[21].   And if so, what should be included in an abbreviated balance sheet and what might be omitted?

Gradually, it became an established fact that proper financial reporting was so complex and required such care in taking into account the circumstances of the individual company that it was impossible to give meaningful rules by law[22].   This point was duly reflected in the third attempt at company law reform.   A 1910 draft law, though building in general on the attempts of 1871 and 1890, dispensed for this reason with the regulation of the contents of balance sheets included in the 1890 draft[23].

In this way the position that regulation of the contents of financial statements was 'necessary and possible' developed into the view that it was 'necessary but impossible'.   But the latter view began almost immediately to give way to the position that regulation, was 'neither possible nor necessary'.

The basis for this development was the discovery of two additional safeguards against misleading financial statements that could replace detailed regulation[24].   One was the nascent auditing profession that since the late 1890s offered the possibility of independent audits. The earliest Dutch association of auditors, the NIvA *(Nederlands Instituut van Accountants),* had been founded in 1895.   By 1920, it

---

[20]   Van Tricht (1880:39), de Vries (1983:128).   Data concerning the extent of this phenomenon seem to be lacking.

[21]   See Cosman (1872), Mees (1872).

[22]   Van Slooten, who had in 1900 argued for publication by all NVs according to a generally prescribed balance sheet format, later modified his position by conceding that regulation, if necessary, should proceed by industry (Van Slooten, 1912).

[23]   (Bijlagen) Handelingen Tweede Kamer, zitting 1909-1910, 217.3 p. 32.

[24]   Both to be found in 1910 draft, for the first time.

had consolidated its position as the leading professional organization[25]. As might be expected, the auditing profession appeared to be especially inclined to espouse the argument of industrial diversity against detailed regulation, as it could be used to argue for legal recognition of the audit profession and mandatory audits in which the auditor would determine wether or not financial statements were 'true' *(juist)*, in relation to the circumstances of the company, both in valuation and disclosure[26].

The other safeguard was the force of public opinion. It began to be assumed that the investing public would on the whole at least be able to distinguish informative from uninformative financial statements so that it might be expected to take care of its own interests by abstaining from investment in unduly secretive companies.

These two safeguards together formed a quite convincing framework, that fitted the mood of the times, the more permanent aversion of companies against interference and the aspirations to professionalism of the auditing profession. It was also the conception of financial reporting that was finally enacted in the 1928/1929 legal reform.

According to the revised law of 1928/29, large companies and companies with listed or bearer securities would have to publish both a balance sheet and an income statement by depositing these documents at a commercial register. Shareholders had the right to appoint an auditor. Furthermore, the law required a note on the valuation principles used, but companies were free in their choice of such principles. As to financial statement disclosure, the law as amended in 1929 listed 12 items that had to be disclosed, subject to applicability, on the debit side of the balance sheet. There were no mandatory disclosures regarding the credit side of the balance sheet or the income statement.

---

[25] References to the auditing profession in this chapter can therefore be understood as referring primarily to the NIvA, and, occasionally, to the associations with which it merged during the 1960s into the NIvRA *(Nederlands Instituut van Registeraccountants)*.

[26] See, for instance, Reiman and Nijst (1906:68-70).

The commission charged with preparing the draft amendment in which these disclosure requirements were contained, motivated its recommendation by an argument that summarized the traditional, nineteenth century view on the nature of reporting regulation. It was stated that there was a risk that mandatory publication of financial statements without regulation of contents might lead to uninformative statements. However, it would be difficult to extend any such regulation beyond 'a few generalities' without confining companies in too narrow a strait-jacket. The committee was able to resolve this problem by stating that the purpose of regulation was not to make financial statements give a more or less complete insight into the position of the firm, but 'the protection of the public' which could, apparently, be achieved with a minimum of information[27].

From this point of view, it is not surprising that balance sheet disclosure requirements were added almost as an afterthought at the end of a 50-year reform process. Nor is it surprising that their effectiveness was doubted by critics[28].

The course of developments in thought on reporting regulation outlined above differentiated the Netherlands from its continental neighbours. As indicated, the Netherlands shared a common heritage of the Napoleonic legal codes with other continental countries. The attempt to regulate financial reporting within the context of an overall revision of the Dutch commercial code is therefore reminiscent of, for instance, the approach to regulation in Germany. But here the similarity ended. Germany and Belgium, another close neighbour, introduced rather more strict regulation at an earlier stage. In Belgium, mandatory publication was introduced as early as 1873, and minimum disclosure requirements were added in 1913. By the end of the 1910s, the differences between the

---

[27] *Verslag van de Commissie benoemd bij Ministerieel besluit van 26 juli 1928*, reproduced in *De Naamlooze Vennootschap*, vol. 7 no 11, February 1929, p. 346-347.

[28] Sternheim (1929), repeated in Munnik (1931:37); Volmer (1929) and, at a somewhat later date, Jacobs (1932).

Netherlands and other continental countries had become quite apparent. Van Hasselt (1919:8) cites a number of critical Belgian and German comments on Dutch company law, indicating that regulation of limited companies in the Netherlands was perceived as virtually nonexistent, on a level with that in countries like Greece and Turkey and providing no serious protection for investors.

But a more favourable interpretation would be that the Netherlands, in its attitude towards the regulation of financial reporting, began, despite its continental legal tradition, to resemble the United Kingdom rather than its continental neighbours. The United Kingdom had not been influenced by the French movement towards codification. Nevertheless it started the 19th century with a strong tradition of state involvement in the creation of limited liability companies, which, on the basis of the 1720 'Bubble Act', could only be created by Royal Charter or Act of Parliament. In the mid-19th century, economic development prompted a reconsideration of company law, in which the basic tendency was to lessen or abolish the influence of the state in the creation of limited liability companies. Published accounting information was seen as an important alternative, and the view that 'the price of limited liability is the publication of accounts' was put forward (Napier, 1995:265). The Joint Stock Companies Act of 1856 (consolidated in the Companies Act 1862, which remained in force until 1900) introduced a model set of articles of association, containing extensive and rather modern accounting and reporting clauses that were available for voluntary adoption. Mandatory publication of balance sheets was imposed on public companies in 1907, but the contents of the balance sheet were not specified. Some elementary disclosure requirements were introduced in 1928, and at the same time the presentation of an (unspecified) income statement to shareholders was made mandatory (though not its publication).

In all, the arguments for and against extension of mandatory disclosure used in England during the run-up to the 1928 Companies Act revision were quite similar to those used in the Netherlands at the same time[29]. The result, in terms of the extent of mandatory disclosure and the types of company to which publication requirements applied, were also quite comparable. The main difference was that in the United Kingdom there was apparently a greater willingness to issue incremental legislation. In the Netherlands, attempts were made from 1870 onwards to regulate all aspects of the limited liability company with one comprehensive revision of the Commercial Code, which greatly increased the difficulty of arriving speedily at a satisfactory outcome. In the United Kingdom greater use was made of partial regulations for specific groups of companies. The accounting and reporting of companies with a definite public responsibility, such as railways, utilities and insurance companies were regulated by a series of Acts from the 1860s onwards. The 1907 Act introduced a distinction between 'public' and 'private' limited companies, which greatly facilitated the introduction of publication requirements for the former. Otherwise, differences between the Netherlands and the United Kingdom were slight indeed, and the more or less simultaneous company law reforms of 1928/29 brought the two countries in a virtually identical position.

By 1928/29, the decision had been made in the Netherlands that company law did *not* play an important role in ordering the contents of financial statements, even though it might play a role in their publication. This question originated and was solved as a *legal* question. The arguments used were primarily of a legal nature and were concerned with questions of what the law ought to do or could hope to achieve. The basis of what would later be seen as a 'Dutch system' of reporting regulation must therefore be sought in the area of company law development rather than the auditing profession or business economics.

---

[29] Compare Edwards (1976), on UK opinions on financial reporting regulation, with those documented in Van Hasselt (1919:118-132), Zeff *et al.* (1992: chapter 2).

The position reflected in the 1928/29 law was not exclusively Dutch. Despite contemporary perceptions of the 'national character' of Dutch company law (Van der Heijden, 1929:13-14), it differed in degree rather than kind from approaches to company law formulation elsewhere. Compared to the United Kingdom, where a similar abstinence of the law could be observed, the degree of difference was rather small.

Regardless of its origins or uniqueness, however, the abstention of the law in influencing the contents of financial statements left scope for other forces to play a role in the development of financial reporting. In the next section it will be shown that during the 1930s a clearer perception began to grow of the sort of forces that might or would play a role in this area.

3.2.3 The 1930s
In a stylized way, it might be said that around 1930, the first round of company law reform in Europe was drawing to a close. This first round, starting in the mid-19th century, had resulted in the insertion of a publication requirement and some rudimentary disclosure requirements into most European systems of company law. By 1928/29, the Netherlands had also completed, as one of the last European countries, a process of company law reform that belonged to this first age of reform. As indicated above, this brought the Netherlands to a position roughly comparable to that of the United Kingdom. The position was characterized by the recognition that the law could require publication, but did not have an active role to play in directing the contents of published financial statements.

It can be argued that the 1930s saw the initial stages of a new, second round of financial reporting regulation, or, more general, financial reporting change, that extended disclosure practices and disclosure regulations considerably beyond the limits of what was considered possible in the 19th century. This gave rise to the question of whether the Dutch decision to minimize the role of the law in financial reporting could be maintained in the light of these changing circumstances.

In 1931, the publication requirements of German company law were modified, partly in response to a number of financial collapses connected with the worldwide economic crisis. This resulted in a considerable expansion of required financial statement disclosure. Standardized schedules for the profit and loss account and the balance sheet were introduced which contained rigid and rather detailed requirements concerning the separate disclosure of various financial statement items. For instance, the 1931 schedules required separate disclosure in the profit- and loss account of both employment costs and social security contributions. As will be seen in chapter 6, this disclosure issue remained controversial in the Netherlands until the end of the 1960s.

In 1934, the US Securities and Exchange Commission (SEC) was created with a mandate to determine the standards of financial disclosure in financial statements issued for listing purposes. Subsequent legislation extended these powers to annual financial reporting to stockholders. The result was the introduction of extensive and, by contemporary standards, quite controversial disclosure regulation in the United States. As will be documented more fully in chapter 6, the introduction of mandatory sales disclosure in the US preceded a similar development in the Netherlands by more than 35 years[30].

In the United Kingdom, no changes occurred in reporting legislation during the 1930s. The company law amendments introduced in 1928/9 did not impose a strict regime of disclosure regulation, and hence did little to counter a tendency towards less disclosure that had become evident during the 1920s. However, even in the absence of legal spurs to increased disclosure, stagnation in the development of financial reporting was prevented by the impact of the Royal Mail case. According to Edwards (1989:127) the commotion caused by

---

[30] Strictly speaking, the difference was almost 50 years. It was not until 1983 that the sales disclosure requirement was made strictly binding, rather than strongly suggestive as it had been since 1970.

the revelation of the dubious reporting practices of the Royal Mail Steam Packet Company in a notorious 1931 criminal case 'probably had a greater impact on the quality of published data than all the Companies Acts passed up to that date'[31].

The Royal Mail case strongly reinforced an embryonic tendency among a small minority of British companies to follow voluntarily the trend towards fuller disclosure that could be discerned in the United States (see de Paula, 1948:265).

These developments abroad did not go unnoticed in the Netherlands. The remainder of this section will explore how thought on reporting, disclosure and disclosure regulation evolved in the Netherlands during this period.

In the Netherlands, the completion of the 1928/9 company law reform after a more than half a century of preparations ruled out any major revisions of the law during the foreseeable future. The law brought little that was new for companies that did already publish their financial statements before 1928, since the scanty disclosure requirements could be reconciled with most previous reporting practices (Jacobs, 1932). In the absence of the kind of major scandals that occurred in the United Kingdom or Germany, financial reporting practice was therefore left to develop in a context of relative calm[32]. At this stage, attention to financial reporting issues tended to shift from the legal to the auditing literature.

As seen above, the Dutch auditing profession had been assigned an important role in the revised Commercial Code. The absence of detailed regulation had in part been justified by granting shareholders

---

[31] The most important defect of the Royal Mail financial statements was that, during the 1920s, undisclosed reserves were released into income without clear disclosure of this fact. In this way, operating losses were transformed in apparent profits. Discussions of the Royal Mail case in the Dutch literature include Hageman (1932) and Spinosa Cattela (1948b:113-118).

[32] See Van der Grinten (1953:67) for the contrast between the extensive debate on publication by limited companies prior to the 1928/29 reform and the relative quiet afterwards.

the right to appoint an auditor. The auditing profession was faced with the task of determining the exact scope of its responsibility under the new law. Three points of view on this issue can, with some simplification, be distinguished in the professional literature of the 1930s: a traditionalist view, a view aimed at quite radical renewal of financial reporting, and a moderate view aiming to balance the two extremes.

The traditional view adhered closely to the letter of the law, which was based on the view that the role of financial statements was limited to safeguarding the interests of outsiders with a financial interest in the company. For this purpose, the financial statements did not need to contain more than a minimum of information. The role of the auditor was to establish that the financial statements did not present an unduly favourable picture of the financial position of the company. Whether the extent of disclosure was sufficient was to be settled between management and its shareholders, and therefore not a primary concern of the auditor. Some auditors expressly defended the rather secretive reporting practices of the time. For example, J.G.Ch. Volmer, a senior figure in the Dutch auditing profession, repeatedly voiced his opinion that publication of a profit and loss account ought not to be imposed on companies, that secrecy as reflected in contemporary practice was quite beneficial for business life, and that if shareholders did want more information, they could and should change the articles of incorporation of their company to impose such a requirement on management[33].

In contrast, other auditors displayed an awareness of changes in thought on financial reporting abroad, and advocated a more active stance of the auditor in improving levels of disclosure. One of the best publicized expressions of this point of view came from future NIvA-president H. Munnik at an annual NIvA study meeting in

---

[33] For instance, Volmer (1925, 1926, 1927). A similarly restricted view of financial reporting is displayed in the *Leerboek der Accountancy*, a textbook on auditing published during the 1920s and 1930s (see Nijst, 1929, chapters 2 and 3).

1931. In a paper on 'the rendering of a public account by the limited liability company by means of the financial statements', Munnik presented a vision of financial reporting in which financial statements were 'to give such information, that the state of the business and the course of affairs, as recently as possible, can be appreciated, even by outsiders' (p. 34). Munnik called this 'full publicity' *(volledige openbaarheid)*. On the basis of an extensive survey, he concluded that many financial statements failed to meet this standard. Munnik did not believe in detailed regulation of the contents of financial statements, and thought that the auditor had a task in ensuring fuller disclosure by refusing to approve financial statements deficient in this respect[34]. In addition, the literature of the 1930s contained other pleas for an active role of the auditor in modernizing financial reporting. A point of view that began to be aired during this period was the notion of comparability of financial statements. This notion assumed that financial statement information ought to serve more purposes than the simple guarantee of a minimum position. Janssens (1927) and especially Van Doorne (1935) argued that financial statements should contain the information necessary for a variety of decision-making purposes. There were other individuals arguing for a broader view of financial reporting, such as Knap (1931) advocating 'openness' and 'honesty' through the provision of more extensive data, and Koppenberg (1935) who pleaded for 'honest and complete', and preferably uniform reporting, a subject to which auditors payed 'too little attention'. To end this series of examples, J.E. Spinosa Cattela (1931) argued for an extension of financial reporting information (notably through interim financial statements) on the basis of the

---

[34] Munniks views were opposed by other senior members of the profession present at the meeting. E. Van Dien and A. Sternheim restated the position that the most that could be demanded from financial statements was that they were not misleadingly optimistic. 'Full publicity' as demanded by Munnik was said to be impractical, and would soon become detrimental to the interests of the company. Moreover, it was not part of the elementary task of the auditor (Munnik, 1931:37, 38-39).

American example.

Between the more extreme positions, there was scope for moderation. During the 1930s, one can observe the development of a view of financial reporting that was to play a significant role in the postwar period. This view acknowledged the possibility of improvement in financial statements, while maintaining that the primary stimulus for changes in reporting had to arise from the interplay between company managements and the readers of financial statements, rather than from the auditor. There was nevertheless a role for the auditor, however, since in this view the 'readers of financial statements' were considered in the aggregate, as the public at large, for whom the auditors played the role of representative, interpreter and educator.

A basis for this view was laid in the course of the 1928 Commercial Code revision. Even though the law enshrined a rather traditional view of reporting regulation, it also contained the seeds of a new departure[35]. The 1925 draft law that formed the basis for the law enacted in 1928 did not contain any specific disclosure requirements and was in this respect simply the successor to the 1910 draft law. When, in the course of the parliamentary debates on the 1925 draft, members of parliament produced the traditional argument that mandatory publication without specified disclosure would lead to misleading or uninformative financial statements, an amendment calling for the disclosure of a number of balance sheet items was submitted. The minister in charge of the commercial code reform replied, however, that it would not be necessary to specify by law what a balance sheet ought to look like. He argued that this was well enough known in the 'economic and social climate'

---

[35] According to current opinion, the 1928/29 Act is certainly not regarded as a milestone in the development of thought on accounting regulation. Burgert, Van Hoepen and Joosten (1995:21), dismiss the law as 'insignificant' ('stelde niet veel voor'); Klaassen and Bak (1993:16) ignore the law altogether and start their description of legislative history in 1970.

(maatschappelijk verkeer) in which the company in question operated[36]. The reference to this concept, already familiar as a general norm in civil law, implied that the proposed law did not need to contain explicit mandatory disclosures, but could rely on easily observable norms that did not draw their existence from and were not defined by the law.

The point to note is that this argument raised, in a careful way, the possibility that these unwritten norms would become part of the *legal* obligation imposed on companies. That is, the possibility was suggested that in a conflict between shareholders and company management over financial reporting a court of law might have recourse to general norms of accounting and disclosure in order to decide the issue in question. The words used by the minister on this occasion evoke a similar departure in civil law about a decade earlier. In a landmark case of 1919, it had been established that obligations in civil law could arise not only from damage caused by transgressing the literal clauses of the law, but also from damage caused by violations of unwritten norms of justice prevailing in the *maatschappelijk verkeer*[37].

It would take some time before this notion began to develop and to gain wider acceptance. During the enactment process of the 1928 law, it was mentioned only in the margin of the debates, and to begin with, the minister's use of the argument appeared to be unsuccessful since the 1929 amendment did result in some explicit disclosure requirements[38]. However, the fact that the disclosure

---

[36] Bijlagen Handelingen Tweede Kamer, 1924-1925, no. 69; Handelingen Tweede Kamer, 1928-1929, p. 1828-1829, p. 1832-1833. Both the phrase *maatschappelijk verkeer* and the more simple *verkeer* were used.

[37] See IJsselmuiden (1972:73) for the reference to the 1919 Lindenbaum/Cohen case implied in the *maatschappelijk verkeer* clause as used in financial reporting.

[38] Although the amendment which provoked the ministerial statement about the *maatschappelijk verkeer* was not carried when the reform act was passed in 1928, its contents were contained, more or less unchanged, in an amending law passed in 1929, which brought the 12 disclosure items referred to earlier into the law. The confused history of the amendment

requirements were presented as a minimum left the idea of unwritten norms governing the contents of financial statements ample scope. Shortly after its initial expression in parliament, the idea began to be echoed in the literature. In handbooks on company law, the unwritten norms to which financial statements had to adhere were referred to in interpreting the scant explicit disclosure requirements[39]. The explicit requirements could be and were presented as minimum requirements that might, on the basis of the law rather than at the requests of the current shareholders of the company, *have* to be exceeded according to the circumstances of the firm in question.

The notion of general, uncodified reporting norms also began to spread among auditors (Nijst, 1929; Knol, 1936; Van Gruisen, 1937), for whom it potentially had significant implications. From this point of view, the auditor could now no longer judge the adequacy of a set of financial statements with reference to a real or implicit agreement between the company and its actual shareholders, but he had to consider what would be expected of such a balance sheet by the public in general. This notion developed in close relationship with contemporary views on auditing. In that area, it began to be accepted under the influence of the views of Th. Limperg that it was not possible to limit the responsibility of the auditor by specific agreements between the auditor and his client, but that, instead, the auditor was bound by the expectations of the 'economic and social climate' with regard to the nature and scope of

---

provides ample illustration of the variety of opinions held on reporting regulation at the time. The original amendment was based on a petition to parliament by the NIvA. Given that before and after the event the general position of Dutch auditors was against formal disclosure regulations, it is not surprising that this action by the NIvA evoked some controversy among its own members (See also Sternheim, 1929 and Zeff *et al.*, 1992:54).

[39] Visser (1929:139), Van der Heijden (1929:354-356), *cf.* Van der Heijden/Van der Grinten (1955:551-552). In Van der Heijden (1929), the 'eischen van het verkeer' are connected directly to the penal sanctions governing publication of financial statements.

audits (see Camfferman and Zeff, 1994). As argued more fully in Camfferman (1994a), it became customary among auditors during the 1930s to refer to these general, uncodified norms for financial reporting by the name of 'sound business practice' *(goed koopmansgebruik)*. 'Goed koopmansgebruik', initially used interchangeably with the notion of the 'maatschappelijk verkeer' later was used as the name for the specific application to financial reporting of the more general concept of 'norms of the economic and social climate'[40].

The immediate practical effect of the introduction of these views on the nature of financial reporting was slight. As long as it was accepted that the 'economic and social climate' was content with the minimum information required to let financial statements play a role as safeguard against fraud, the practical effect would be that financial reporting could continue to use balance sheet and income statement formats dating back to the turn of the century. Criticism of secretive reporting practices therefore continued unabated until the end of the decade (*e.g.* Schoepp, 1939:212).

Nevertheless, two important consequences were to flow from the introduction of these concepts.

First, they blurred the dividing line between voluntary and mandatory disclosure. It could be and was argued that the small list of mandatory disclosures contained in the 1928/9 Commercial Code were only the most visible part of the total set of legal disclosure requirements. On the basis of this concept, therefore, those engaged in financial reporting practice were taught not to equate 'mandatory'

---

[40] See Hartog (1933:468) and Van Gruisen (1937) for the synonymous use of 'sound business practice' and norms of the economic and social climate with reference to accounting. See Keuzenkamp (1938:180) for the relation between the theory of inspired confidence and 'sound business practice'. In 1947 this usage was formalized when the phrase 'according to sound business practice' was introduced into the NIvA's rules of professional conduct to describe the meaning of an auditor's certificate (see Camfferman, 1994a).

disclosure with explicitly listed requirements.

Second, the notion of 'norms of the economic and social climate' had a distinctly dynamic potential. The unspecified demands of this 'climate' as represented by the combination of best practice, the theoretical and professional literature and the views of informed financial statement users, could presumably change over time, opening the possibility of progress and of ever higher demands placed on financial statements. As will be seen in the next section, exactly such a development occurred after the war: the differential between what 'ought' to be reported and the explicit minimum requirements of the law started to widen, giving rise to fairly extensive non-mandatory improvements in the information contents of financial statements.

3.2.4 Review of position around 1940

By 1940, a number of elements that might serve to justify the assumption of the existence of a particular 'Dutch' approach towards financial reporting and reporting regulation had begun to emerge. Most importantly, the question of whether or not the law ought to govern the contents of financial statements through formal disclosure clauses had been answered negatively. When legislation was finally introduced in 1928/9, the Netherlands positioned itself alongside the United Kingdom rather than next to its continental neighbours where a greater role had been accorded to the law. The opening thus created by the withdrawal of the law began to be filled in a rudimentary way by the doctrine that reporting in general and disclosure in particular need and can be governed not by specific legal requirements, but by reference to generally accepted, uncodified norms. For this reason, an important feature of Dutch financial reporting, at least in the eyes of Dutch auditors, was that the rather liberal legal requirements presupposed the existence of a strong and competent auditing profession.

At this stage, a growing consciousness can be discerned in the Dutch auditing literature of the differences between the Netherlands and other countries, even though the latter were for practical purposes mainly restricted to Germany, the United States and the United Kingdom[41].

With regard to Germany, it was not too difficult to stress the differences. Not only did German legislation precede its Dutch counterparts by several decades, the 1931 reporting regulations introduced an extent of mandatory disclosure that went well beyond anything contemplated in the Netherlands. The German requirements found few defenders in the Netherlands, and complaints in the German literature could be cited in the Netherlands during the 1930s to illustrate that such discontentment was only what might have been expected from excessive strictness in disclosure regulation (Van Rietschoten, 1934).

The United States began to figure more prominently in the Dutch auditing literature during the 1930s, but the emphasis was mainly on auditing technique. When US reporting was discussed, as in Munnik (1931), there is a tendency to mix admiration of certain outstanding qualities (such as the early date of publication) with the amused rejection of other aspects considered typical for US society (such as the extent of advertising in US annual reports). It should be noted that prior to the enactment of federal securities legislation in the 1930s, the approach to reporting regulation in the United States differed considerably from that in Europe. As seen above, European legislation had accepted the publicity principle as its main element. Until the 1930s, however, the relevant US regulations consisted mainly of state legislation in which a 'paternalistic' form of

---

[41] As a general indication of the geographical spread of attention to foreign developments in the Netherlands, one might look at the items discussed in the 'From Abroad' *(Uit het buitenland)* section in the journal *Maandblad voor Accountancy en Bedrijfshuishoudkunde*. This section contained extracts from foreign journals, news items and short comments. From 1930 to 1939, the section included a total of 154 items: 66 on the United Kingdom, 41 on the United States, 34 on Germany and 13 on other countries.

preventive supervision played an important role[42]. In most European countries, this type of regulation played at best a secondary role since the late 19th century. The heavy emphasis on disclosure in the Securities Acts, however, made US reporting regulation potentially more relevant to the European situation.

Among other countries, the United Kingdom played the most important role in the perception of Dutch auditors. British reporting was considered by Munnik (1931) as the standard to which Dutch reporting might aspire. The Royal Mail case, however, which was quite extensively covered in the Dutch literature, gave rise to comments that at least in the area of proper disclosure of releases from secret reserves, Dutch auditors adhered to stricter standards than their British colleagues (Hageman, 1932). During the 1930s the conviction grew in the Netherlands that Dutch accounting and auditing were at least on a level with their British counterparts and were developing in the same direction. In the United Kingdom, an evolution comparable to that discernible in the Netherlands occurred from a strictly legal interpretation of the responsibility of the auditor with regard to financial reporting, to an interpretation in which less formal criteria, notably the 'true and fair'[43] criterion, began to play an important role[44]. Moreover, the British literature of the 1940s paid increasing attention to the role of voluntary action as opposed to regulation in bringing about improvements in financial reporting. F.R.M. de Paula, a senior British accountant, commented on the UK Companies Act 1947 in the following manner:

---

[42] See Hawkins (1986:chapter 4) on these so-called 'blue sky laws', and in particular for the notion that they 'were based on a paternalistic regulation philosophy rather than the (...) disclosure philosophy embodied in the 1900 British Companies Act' (p. 128).

[43] Or 'true and correct', as it was used until 1947 (Parker and Nobes, 1994:1-4; Napier and Noke, 1992:40-41).

[44] See Nijst (1929:117-120) and Edwards (1976:297).

The development on the movement towards the improvement in the form of presentation of accounts and the establishment of an agreed code of basic accounting principles can be traced back some twenty years or more. In those far-off days, there was a small minority that was not satisfied with the general and accepted practices of the time. (...) It was the [Royal Mail case], in the writer's judgment, that gave this whole movement its first great impulse. Directors and auditors of companies immediately commenced to reconsider their methods and practices in the light of the lessons to be learned from that grim case. (...) The fundamental change [in financial reporting] has come about, it is submitted, in the most desirable way. It has not been imposed from above by law upon an unwilling public, but the law has followed the existing best practice. Practical men of affairs had read the lessons of the [Royal Mail] case and voluntarily and immediately commenced to evolve accounting principles and practices to comply with them. (de Paula, 1948:265)

This statement would presumably have met with the wholehearted approval of many Dutch auditors. Rather than speaking of a 'Dutch' approach to financial reporting at this stage, it would be more appropriate to refer to a common British/Dutch attitude. As will be seen in the next section, however, a certain divergence between the situation in the Netherlands and the United Kingdom began to appear with the passage of the Companies Act 1947 in the latter country.

Of course, the Netherlands and the United Kingdom could also be compared from a different point of view. Rather than interpreting the light touch of legal regulation of disclosure as the result of an enlightened form of liberalism, it might as well be argued that in both countries the Legislator had been unduly tentative if not simply negligent by continuing to condone reporting practices that were evidently inadequate[45]. This negative interpretation shows that at this time only the first, tentative steps had been set in the development of a convincing alternative to formal regulation. Whereas in the United Kingdom some proof of the effectiveness of such an approach had been forthcoming in the improved financial reporting in the wake of the Royal Mail case, in the Netherlands such proofs would not be seen until after the Second World War.

3.3 1945-1970

3.3.1 Overview
During the quarter century following the Second World War, significant changes occurred in the practice of financial reporting in many developed countries. As indicated in chapter 1, a striking aspect of financial reporting change during this period was the extension of financial statement disclosure. This tendency was discernible in many countries, even though the pace, extent and mechanism of change differed considerably among countries.

In the United States, the securities legislation of 1933 and 1934 was strongly concerned with the extension of disclosure, as is apparent from the subtitle of the 1933 Securities Act: 'An act to provide full and fair disclosure...' (Bevis, 1965:17). The acts marked the beginning of a significant increase in both mandatory and voluntary disclosure by US companies, and were followed by a distinct change in views on the nature and purpose of published financial statements[46]. From 1936 onwards, this process of disclosure

---

[45] See, for instance, Schoepp (1939:212), Knol (1948), Edwards (1989:141-142), Napier (1995:272-273).

[46] 'In recent years the annual reports of large corporations have changed from formal, technical documents to attractive and interesting reading matter. Instead of being directed merely to stockholders, the modern reports are also prepared to interest employees and the general public. In fact, they constitute part of the company's public relations program.' (Myer,

expansion involved the participation of the US auditing profession through the AICPA's Committee on Accounting Procedure (CAP), to which the SEC had granted a derived authority in this area. The intensity of the standard-setting effort continuously increased during the 1950s and 1960s as the CAP gave way to the Accounting Principles Board (APB). Ultimately, growing concern over financial reporting and the standard setting process during the 1960s would prepare the way for the creation of the Financial Accounting Standards Board (FASB) in 1973. As a result, at the beginning of the 1970s, the extent of disclosure in US annual reports was far ahead of that in annual reports in the United Kingdom, its closest rival in this respect (Benston, 1976a, 1976b; *cf.* Barret, 1977).

In Europe, however, tendencies towards greater disclosure were apparent as well. An area of difference was that in Europe the notion of accounting standards did not develop to any great extent before 1970[47]. Hence, company law reform continued to be the main focus of efforts to expand disclosure. In this respect, Germany and the United Kingdom were the two most important European points of reference for Dutch financial reporting[48].

In the United Kingdom,

> [t]he Companies Act 1947 (consolidated into the Companies Act 1948) marked the beginning of the 'modern era'. In contrast with most previous Companies Acts, its provisions were

---

1952:64)

[47] Even though the *Recommendations on Accounting Principles* issued on behalf of the Institute of Chartered Accountants in England and Wales (ICAEW) between 1942 and 1969 did constitute a form of standard setting, they differed fundamentally from the *Statements of Standard Accounting Practice* issued since 1970, as the latter were, for practical purposes, mandatory (Zeff, 1972:76).

[48] Although among auditors, attention for the United States and the United Kingdom was far more intense than for Germany (Van Viegen, 1956:257).

concerned more with the needs and rights of stockholders and investors with respect to a management over which they were presumed to have little control than with protection of creditors or a reaction to a specific scandal. The Cohen report, on which the Act was based, stressed the desirability of disclosure for stockholders and society in general, and rejected the earlier (predominantly nineteenth century) philosophy that a company's affairs were primarily a matter of contract among shareholders. (Benston, 1976:16).

Among the significant changes brought by the Companies Act 1947 was the introduction of disclosure requirements concerning the income statement, and the requirement to produce a consolidated balance sheet. For the first time, the 'true and fair view' requirement received substantial support from a set of mandatory disclosures (De Paula, 1957:148-150). The Companies Act 1947 therefore marked the end of the long period during which a direct influence of the law on the contents of financial statements had been largely ruled out. In contrast to the Netherlands, company law began to be recognized as a 'major progressive factor in the development of British financial reporting' (Napier, 1995:275). Company law continued to be a focal point in UK financial reporting change, as in the 1962 Jenkins report and the Companies Act 1967. As in 1947, considerations concerning accountability of the enterprise to society at large played an important part in the 1967 Act[49].

In Germany, the Companies Act was changed in stages. In 1959, a preliminary stage was completed in which the requirements concerning the published profit and loss account were modernized. In 1965, the main body of company law was revised. As in the (UK) Companies Act 1947, perceptions of a changing social role of the enterprise played a role in prompting German company law

---

[49] Hendriksen (1969:22,31-32). See also Sewart (1991) for a discussion of the tendency towards greater public accountability in the United Kingdom.

reform (Schoenfeld, 1970). In both countries, increased social accountability was cited to justify an extension of disclosure. The resulting expansion of mandatory disclosure further widened the gap between Germany and the Netherlands. Whereas, in 1959, the Dutch Commercial Code still included no disclosure requirements at all with regard to the profit and loss account, the new German law specified an impressive 32 line items to be disclosed (subject to applicability) in the income statement, including the controversial disclosure of gross sales.

In the Netherlands, there was considerable awareness of occurrences abroad, and these played an important role both in reporting practice and in debate on reporting regulation. Although there was some advocacy of a US-style approach to reporting regulation during the 1950s, the main focus of attempts to reform financial reporting was, in line with developments elsewhere in Europe, on changes in company law. The debate on the role of the law in financial reporting, considered closed in 1928/29, was therefore opened once again.

An important feature of the attempts to introduce new financial reporting regulation was that they were part of a wider legal reform movement. At first, changes in reporting legislation were considered in the context of the revision of the entire Civil Code. Later, such changes were treated as part of an integral revision of the provisions on corporate governance in the Commercial Code. As a result of this apparent desire for comprehensive reform, the enactment of any new reporting legislation had to await the settlement of a range of controversial issues ranging from worker participation to the structure of the board of supervisory directors. It was not until 1970 that a new reporting law came into effect. Apparently, no partial or interim legislation on financial reporting (as used, for instance, in Germany in both 1931 and 1959) was ever seriously considered in the Netherlands.

A key feature of postwar Dutch reporting is therefore that the relatively slow pace with which accounting law was enacted provided a 'grace period' during which a system of voluntary reporting improvements, as dimly envisaged at the end of the 1930s, obtained a rather unique chance to prove itself. Those who advocated that financial reporting could develop best in freedom were given the opportunity to prove that Dutch practice could develop in line with practices in the United States and the United Kingdom, but without the imposition of the relatively strict requirements in both countries.

The next two sections will analyze in greater detail how (a) developments in reporting practice provided the necessary support for the notion that there was in fact a viable 'Dutch' approach to financial reporting in which heavy regulation could be avoided, and (b) how the advocates of voluntariness attempted to carry as much of this 'Dutch system' forward into law when, after 1960, company law reform was finally under way.

3.3.2 1945-1960: Further development of a voluntary system

As seen in section 3.2, the prewar Dutch auditing profession had, on the basis of notions advanced during the period of Commercial Code reform in the first decades of the century, gradually developed a relatively simple theoretical framework that acknowledged, in principle, the possibility of progress in financial reporting. It was admitted in theory that reporting practices were likely to vary over time, and that once acceptable standards of reporting and disclosure might become unacceptable. In practice, however, the principle of adhering to norms of the 'economic and social climate' *(maatschappelijk verkeer)* or 'sound business practice' *(goed koopmansgebruik)* was applied in a way that equated such norms rather strictly with actual practice, precluding significant change (Burgert, 1953). Following the war, however, the dynamic potential of the notion of norms of the 'economic and social climate' began, to some extent, to be realized. An important underlying factor for this change was the influence of foreign example that began to make itself felt through various channels.

As argued in Zeff *et al.* (1992), the fact that a number of large Dutch companies acquired foreign (US) listings in the early 1950s was an important mechanism to confront Dutch companies and auditors with US reporting practices. The growing presence of US companies in Europe had a similar effect. According to Brands (1954), the growing volume of international capital flows implied that Dutch auditors would do well to take note of foreign practices. Van Viegen (1956) made a similar case and noted approvingly that the NIvA had, in fact, recently installed a committee on documenting foreign practices.

Awareness of foreign examples was not enough, however. A crucial issue was whether or not Dutch company managements would be willing to copy the more open financial reporting practices of the United States and, to a lesser extent, the United Kingdom.
Measured by the volume of criticism from the financial press, the amount of change in company financial reporting during the first postwar decade was not extensive[50]. However, such criticism was now strengthened by the fact that small numbers of companies did in fact begin to improve their financial statements, especially in terms of increasing disclosure. These companies could be held up as an example to others, and as proof of the proposition that fear of competitive damage was used too easily as an argument against fuller disclosure. The creation, in 1953, of the Henri Sijthoff award for the best annual financial report is symptomatic for the attempts in the financial press to foster a spirit of competitive improvement in financial reporting practice. A notion that received growing attention was the belief that financial statements, rather than present a minimum of information for the benefit of creditors, ought to give 'insight' into the financial position and the results of the company.

The most significant contribution to the cause of voluntary reporting

---

[50] See Knol (1948:97), who 'recently observed rather frequent remarks concerning financial statements in the press', and, rather late in the postwar period, a remark by Vecht (1954:97), that 'one can hardly read a discourse [on the NV] without encountering the complaint that the reporting by NVs is seriously deficient.'

was made by a report on recommended financial reporting practices issued in 1955 by the joint Dutch employers' organizations[51], and usually referred to, after the chairman of the drafting committee, as the Rijkens report. Up to the publication of the report, no unambiguous sign had been forthcoming to show that the concern for improvements was shared by company managements on any large scale. The 1955 report could be seen as such a signal, and its publication could well support an optimistic view regarding the future of financial reporting.

To contemporaries, one of the most arresting features of the Rijkens report was its quite outspoken disapproval of secret reserve accounting[52]. But the report also contained numerous recommendations on disclosure issues, which were presented as a consequence of the primary demand that financial statements ought to give 'insight'. Among the more conspicuous were recommendations to publish sales and cost of sales, comparative figures and multi-year summaries, information on pension and deferred tax liabilities, off-balance sheet liabilities, information on market developments, research and development activities, employment, and general expectations for the current financial year. The gap between these recommendations and general practice was stressed in a number of comments[53]. The contrast between the recommendations and current practice was so great that some commentators believed that without some form of compulsion, the majority of companies would never reach the minimum standard of

---

[51] *Het Jaarverslag,* Rapport van de Commissie Jaarverslaggeving van het Verbond van Nederlandsche Werkgevers, het Centraal Sociaal Werkgevers-Verbond, het Katholiek Verbond van Werkgeversvakverenigingen en het Verbond van Protestants-Christelijke Werkgevers in Nederland (Den Haag, 1955). See Zeff *et al.* (1992: chapter 3) for a discussion of the background and contents of the report.

[52] See, for instance, 'Hoe kan men de jaarverslaggeving verbeteren? — Commissie der Werkgeversverbonden brengt een rapport uit', *Algemeen Handelsblad*, 1 April 1955.

[53] See Slot (1955:81), and 'Maatstaf voor jaarverslag', *Elseviers Weekblad*, 9 April 1955, p. 21.

reporting described in the report[54].

The Rijkens report appeared at a critical moment in the post-war development of thinking on accounting regulation. The initially somewhat unfocused concern about the quality of financial statements as apparent from the financial press and parts of the professional literature had in the early 1950s begun to crystallize around the notion of a companies' commission. Sanders (1952), a publication that received much attention at the time, contained a plea for a *vennootschapskamer* or companies' commission, modelled on the US Securities and Exchange Commission[55]. At least to some members of the sponsoring employers' bodies, the Rijkens report was primarily an attempt to forestall government interference in financial reporting. From this point of view, the Rijkens report would serve as evidence that organized business was capable of taking care of financial reporting itself[56]. If this was in fact attempted, the attempt was highly successful. The publication of the Rijkens report turned out to be a strong argument in favour of the opinion that legal interference in financial reporting was not only undesirable but also unnecessary. It could be argued that experience had proven that companies could voluntarily improve their reporting, aided by non-binding guidance as provided by the employers' associations.

Neither the Rijkens report itself nor the accompanying statements of committee members to the press contained a hint that the report was the beginning of a more or less regular system of guidance on

---

[54] See v.Zw., 'Het Jaarverslag', *Handels & Transport Courant*, 4 April 1955, p. 1; J(ustus) M(eyer), 'Het goede jaarverslag', *Haagse Post*, 16 april 1955, p. 11.

[55] Less well-known than Sanders' plea is the observation by Brands (1952:232) that '[from improved US financial reporting] it is clear that there has to be a directing body — over there the Securities and Exchange Commission — to achieve really effective improvements'. He also speculated that in the Netherlands 'an institute' would probably have to be set up to give guidance to company financial reporting.

[56] For a contemporary view, see Brands (1955:24). See Zeff *et al.* (1992: chapter 3) for materials on the employers' perspective.

financial reporting. Nevertheless, the view that a kind of semi-regulatory system along these lines could be established began to be aired shortly after its publication. A clear statement of the belief that the Rijkens report was not an incident but the foundation of a 'system' of accounting regulation can be found in a discussion of the report for a German audience (Geertman, 1955). The author contrasted the English and German systems of accounting regulation, both of which were characterized by extensive regulation, with the Dutch environment, virtually free of legal interference. This regulatory vacuum was not to be seen as a weakness, but as a strength, as it allowed a more informal and flexible system:

> Recent developments appear to go in the direction that the statements of the employers' association are interpreted as a sort of law. Since the publication of the report of the employers' association, several newspapers have criticized departures from the recommendations.
>
> The Dutch system has produced the result that managements of all holding companies have taken care that consolidated balance sheets are prepared and published (...). In our view, the advantage of the Dutch system is that on the basis of a few legal requirements and the recommendations of the employers' associations a much greater degree of flexibility can be achieved than in other systems based on case-specific prescriptions. (...) Furthermore, it should be pointed out that this arrangement always allows the easy adaptation to new scientific insights, practical concerns and considerations from a Commercial Law point of view. (Geertman, 1955:368)

Geertman may have presented things in a more favourable light than he would have done if he had written for Dutch readers, but his feelings are only slightly stronger than those of others writing at the same time, when empirical evidence of the Report's effects could not have been extensive[57].

The Dutch auditing profession was not left unaffected by the developments outlined in the previous paragraphs, even though disclosure issues remained for some time in the shadow of the more traditional concerns of income determination and valuation[58]. In 1953, G.L. Groeneveld addressed an audience of auditors with a speech on 'new tendencies in published financial statements'. In his speech, Groeneveld discussed two recent developments in financial reporting: the increasing use of current cost accounting and a shift towards earlier publication of financial statements. On the whole, the impression conveyed by his speech was positive: due to a combination of developments in domestic thinking (elaboration and acceptance of Limpergian current cost theory) and of the increased importance of the American example, Dutch financial reporting was moving in the right direction. Groeneveld concluded that Munnik's (1931) demand for 'full publicity' would be fulfilled by the adoption of current cost accounting in financial statements. However, in a published reaction J.C. Brezet commented on this latter statement that it was not so much changes in income determination that were

---

[57] 'It seems to us that the road to be taken from here goes into this direction that the employers' unions proceed forcefully on the road chosen [in the Rijkens report], in cooperation with the Stock Exchange Association, which, as one of the most appropriate organizations in this areas, should do much more than it is doing now. This cooperation should lead to a series of perfected recommendations regarding financial reporting, which no right-thinking management board can ignore. Moreover, we see a pedagogical task for the two organizations that we mentioned. For many limited companies would like to choose the proper road, but do not now how. When they are presented with a properly elaborated schedule, prepared by such honourable organizations as the employers' unions and the [Stock Exchange] Association, the lesson will not lightly be put aside.' (De Tijd, 1 April 1955).

[58] See, however, Spinosa Cattela (1948a), one of a number of publications on foreign developments in accounting. See Foppe (1951) and Vecht (1954) for indications that disclosure issues began to receive serious attention among auditors.

required, but rather a more complete disclosure, especially of income statement items. Since tendencies in that direction were still very weak, as witnessed by a recent crop of deficient financial statements, Brezet urged auditors to remember the spirit of Munnik's 1931 paper (Brezet, 1953).

Following the Rijkens report, the notion that concepts such as the 'economic and social climate' and 'sound business practice' also had implications for financial statement disclosure became more apparent among auditors. In the opening paragraphs of a 1956 report on disclosure of information on commitments *(obligo's)* the NIvA, by way of its Advisory Committee on Professional Matters[59], gave what amounted to its first statement on the development of financial reporting over time:

> In forming an opinion on the specific question laid before the Committee, it is important to draw attention to the historical development of the demands that the economic and social climate places on information to be provided by means of the annual report. Data, disclosure of which in the annual report was initially just considered useful, but that might just as well be omitted, were later considered of such significance that their disclosure became necessary. (...)
> With the progression of the demands of the economic and social climate the borderline between what is considered as useful and what is classified as necessary in forming a picture of the enterprise has shifted. This has gradually resulted in an ongoing clarification of the picture given by financial statements. (p. 399)[60]

---

[59] *CAB*, at the time chaired by H. Munnik.

[60] 'Rapport van de Commissie van Advies inzake Beroepsaangelegenheden over het vraagstuk van het al dan niet verwerken van obligo's in de verslaglegging', *De Accountant*, vol. 62 no. 6, April 1956, p. 395-409. See also the section 'De verslaglegging van naamloze vennootschappen' in the committee's (CAB) annual report over 1956/57 in

The Rijkens report was cited as one of the most important among contemporary documents that could be used to determine the extent of the shift from 'useful' towards 'necessary' disclosure.

The position taken by the NIvA confirmed that the line dividing 'mandatory' from 'voluntary' disclosure was in fact blurred. Auditors were encouraged not to expect a clear set of prescribed disclosures with which to check financial statements. Rather, they were to exercise their professional judgement to determine what the circumstances of the case in question required. This was confirmed in a series of cases brought before the NIvA's disciplinary board (Raad van Tucht) in the latter half of the 1950s[61].

Around 1960, the feeling was well-established among Dutch auditors that the approach to financial reporting in the Netherlands was different, but sound.

'Freedom is good for the strong' was the way in which F. Van Amerongen (1963:497) described the hallmark of Dutch accounting for the benefit of English readers. And on the whole, the Dutch auditing profession did indeed feel itself to be strong enough to produce, in cooperation with company managements, reports of anglo-american quality without anglo-american regulation.

---

which the committee in effect stated that it was aware of the developing demand for 'insight' and of the 'deplorable' fact that many Dutch companies failed to meet this requirement. The issue was said to have its 'ongoing attention'. (De Accountant, vol. 46 no 2, November 1957, p. 116).

[61] Notably 1958-8, 1958-15 and 1961-11. Other cases in which the Disciplinary Board dealt with financial accounting issues included 1956-7, 1958-11 and 1959-6. In these cases the concept of goed koopmansgebruik was further interpreted, and explicitly applied to disclosure and presentation. In short, the Board confirmed that the circumstances of the case (among which potential competitive damage figured prominently), determined the application of goed koopmansgebruik to specific financial statements. Although the Board suggested that the threat of competition might be used too freely in practice, it refused to specify a definite minimum of disclosure. According to one of its rulings (1958-8), an income statement showing net income as a single item might in some circumstances justifiably be considered as 'prepared according to goed koopmansgebruik'.

Around 1960, therefore, it was possible to formulate a coherent view of why and how Dutch financial reporting was different through its reliance on voluntary behaviour. At the core of such a view was the idea that largely uncodified but nevertheless recognizable norms for financial reporting could be applied by competent auditors. These norms were formally indicated by the notions of '(norms of the) economic and social climate' and 'sound business practice', and materially by the requirement of 'insight'. Attached to these notions was an idea of dynamism and progress, of continually increasing demands that would be met by the basic willingness of company managements to comply with them. And most importantly, there was empirical vindication in the obvious improvements witnessed in the financial statements of a number of well-known companies[62] and in the expressed commitment of the employers' organizations to creditable reporting[63].

This view, of course, was an ideal. It was often pointed out that the rather roseate assumptions underlying it did not always correspond with reality. For instance, in discussing the Rijkens report, a cornerstone of any such 'Dutch system', one could either stress the impressive disclosure recommendations, or the numerous escape clauses, offering companies all kinds of reasons for not complying with the demands (Knol, 1955). One could argue that even the 'best' annual report (at least according to the panel of judges of the Henri Sijthoff award) showed serious deficiencies (Slot, 1958). In a similar vein, one could either see the distinctness of the Dutch approach to financial reporting as a source of pride, or one could warn that 'we [the Dutch auditing profession] have to be careful when we judge what is done abroad, and we must not be blinded by the conviction of our own superiority' (Van Viegen, 1956:257).

---

[62] See the statement by Kenneth S. Most: 'Today, the most modern and sophisticated accounting system in use by a public corporation is undoubtedly that operated by the big electrical and electronics company, Philips, in Holland' (Most, 1964:9).

[63] See Kraayenhof (1955:390) for an expression of the mutual confidence in goodwill and competence between auditors and management.

Even Van Amerongen (1963), quoted above on the strength of the Dutch auditing profession, conceded that there were 'weak brethren' among his colleagues and among company managements for whom a tightening of regulation might prove beneficial. Sobering thoughts like these played an important role in initiating a new round of company law reform at the beginning of the 1960s.

3.3.3 Renewed associated with company law reform
Following the completion of the Commercial Code reform in 1928, company law, at least as far as it affected financial reporting, entered a period of relative calm which lasted until the 1950s. As indicated above, during this period the field was left to practitioners of financial reporting, that is, to company managers and their auditors, to show that satisfactory levels of reporting quality could be achieved without strong legal backing.

From the late 1950s onward, however, forces external to the domain of financial reporting instigated a period of renewed attention for company law reform. As in the period 1870-1930, financial reporting was again caught up in a wider current moving towards legal reform. As in Germany and the United Kingdom, a concern for what might be called social issues was a central feature in demands for company law reform. Concerns like these could introduce a note of urgency in what might otherwise be a detached discussion among accounting and legal experts:

> Publication of fuller accounts is no narrow matter of company law, but a pressing social issue. In the long run, the question is not 'Shall we tell or conceal?', but 'Shall we tell the shareholders or the planners?' Tell we must. (Baxter, 1956:41)

In a similar way, financial reporting began to be linked in the Netherlands with the broader question of 'the socialization of enterprise' *(vermaatschappelijking van de onderneming)*. This question largely corresponded with the issues arising out of the separation of ownership and control analyzed in the US context by

Berle and Means (1932).

The idea that a degree of 'socialization' was imminent did not agree well with the traditional assumption that a firm was an item of property, to be disposed of according to the wishes of the owners. Although this view might still be valid for small firms, it was considered obsolete for large, open NVs of which the shares were widely distributed. Such companies had gained immense social and economic influence, while at the same time the disappearance of recognizable owners had created a power vacuum to be filled by more or less unaccountable managers.

Under the catchword of 'vermaatschappelijking', a variety of solutions to this apparent problem were offered from various parts of the political spectrum. In general, these solutions entailed setting up mechanisms to ensure that company managements would take into account the social ramifications of their decisions. From the late 1940s onward, political discussions on representation of labour on supervisory boards or the institution of works' councils were carried on with varied intensity. In this context, more informative financial reporting appeared as a possible instrument to make managements more susceptible to social control, or, conversely, as a concession made in order to prevent more consequential intrusions into managerial autonomy.

The debate on 'vermaatschappelijking', including the issue of financial reporting, received a strong stimulus by a 1959 report on 'The reform of enterprise' by the Dr Wiardi Beckman Foundation, the scientific bureau of the labour party[64]. This report emphasized the relationship between corporate publicity and the broader social responsibility of the enterprise that had played an important role in

---

[64] *De hervorming van de onderneming*, Herziening van het vennootschapsrecht in verband met medezeggenschap in en toezicht op de onderneming (Amsterdam: De Arbeiderspers, 1959). A more extensive discussion of contents, background and consequences of the report can be found in Zeff *et al.*, (1992:chapter 4).

the reform of British company law about a decade earlier[65].

In the wider context of a discussion of company law reform, the committee responsible for the report stated that, because of the very limited nature of the 1929 regulation 'most financial statements of our large N.Vs, banning some favourable exceptions, excel in vagueness.' (p. 46) According to the report, neither the complaints of the financial press nor the commendable initiative of the Rijkens report had materially altered this situation. The committee repeated the call for a companies commission *(vennootschapskamer)* to supervise financial reporting.

The report stirred up debate in the legal literature and the press, and it played a role in the installation, in 1960, of a governmental commission to draft proposals for reform of company law. The charge of this commission, referred to after the name of its chairman as the Verdam Commission, included an investigation of the effectiveness of a system that left much if not all responsibility for the improvement of the quality of financial reporting to the initiative of the business sector:

> In connection with the important role that the larger enterprises in particular play in the economic life of our country, it is of great importance that the annual financial documents — especially the balance sheet and the profit and loss account — give a clear picture of the state of affairs in the N.V. A committee established by the four employers' unions has made some suggestions in that regard a few years ago. It is, however, open to question whether it is possible to rely entirely on the views of business in this matter, and whether there is no task for

---

[65] See, for instance, the approving review of the Cohen Commission report, and in particular its espousal of the publicity principle, by J. Valkhoff (1946). Valkhoff subsequently was to chair the committee responsible for the 1959 Labour party report.

the legislature.[66]

That, indeed, was the question, and there was no lack of published opinion on the subject. The installation of the Commission gave rise to a new outpouring of views.

The Wiardi Beckman report had chosen to describe reporting quality in sombre colours, and others subscribed to this view with varying degrees of approval[67]. However, the Wiardi Beckman report also prompted publications of more cheerful views of financial reporting quality.

The installation of the Verdam Commission, and especially rumours of its quick progress in drafting a proposed law on financial reporting, made the question of whether or not there should be a new law on the subject somewhat academic[68]. Attention therefore focused on the nature of a new financial reporting law: should it merely give actual practice a legal footing, or should the law be an attempt to force changes in reporting practice?

The joint employers' associations stated their opinion in a revision of the Rijkens report, drafted by a committee chaired by J.A. Hamburger and published in October 1962[69]. The actual recommendations of the report differed little from those of the 1955 report, but they were now embedded in an extensive treatise on the position of the firm, on communication between the firm and interested parties and on the possible role of legislation. The

---

[66] *Herziening van het ondernemingsrecht*, Rapport van de Commissie ingesteld bij beschikking van de Minister van Justitie van 8 april 1960 (Den Haag: Staatsuitgeverij, 1965), p. 2.

[67] See, for instance, Kruize (1961) and Vecht (1960).

[68] As a matter of fact, the revision of the Civil Code had led, in 1958, to an acceptance in principle of more extensive accounting regulation even though the contents of future regulated remained to be specified (Zeff *et al.*, 1992:146n).

[69] *Verslaggeving verantwoording en voorlichting* door de besturen van naamloze vennootschappen ('s-Gravenhage: Raad van Nederlandse Werkgeversverbonden, 1962).

committee clearly expressed its views on the relative roles of reporting regulation and private initiative:

> In practice the contents of financial statements have grown in a pleasing way beyond the minimum requirements [of the law]. It can be said that in general the working of social forces — new insights on the part of company managements themselves, but also more in particular the public discussion and especially that in the financial press — is an important stimulus for the level of reporting.
> The development of this new spirit concerning the accountability process will certainly progress even further. (...) It is of the utmost importance that this development can take place in freedom. (p. 24)

The report acknowledged that codification might be useful at some stage, but maintained that regulation of the kind of information to be disclosed in financial statements should always be of a global nature. The committee evoked the picture of a formalized reporting process in which companies would not disclose more than required and in which reporting practice would be forced in a strait-jacket of inflexible rules reflecting old and possibly obsolete views on financial accounting. The word it used to describe such degeneration was *verstarring* (stiffening, with the overtones of 'ossification'). For the next decade, it was to become an often-used argument that any law had to be so flexible that the ill-defined but grim prospect of *verstarring* was avoided[70]. Not unnaturally, the word also began to

---

[70] Use of the word in this context was not an innovation of the committee, even though its report appears to have given it widespread currency. Van Doorne (1935: 69) and Koppenberg (1935: 130) had already raised the spectre of 'verstarring' in the context of reporting regulation. During the 1960s, the word occurred over and over again, as in Kleerekoper (1962), Berckel (1965), Laterveer (1967), Louwers (1970). It was also picked up in the Verdam report (p. 25) and the accompanying memorandum to the 1968 draft law.

play a role in stressing the dutchness of the 'Dutch system': *verstarring* was often presented as the result of deficiencies in foreign systems of reporting regulation[71].

A similar voice was heard from the Liberal party's scientific bureau in a report[72] intended to provide a counterweight to the Wiardi Beckman report. On the subject of financial reporting, this report saw some merit in adapting the law 'to what has become established practice' (p. 319). The law should not, however, attempt to effect significant changes in reporting practice. The report alleged that proponents of increased legal requirements 'project, without any ground, certain abuses in other Western countries on the situation in the Netherlands'. In fact, owing to the stimulus of social forces

> [t]he voluntary publication of data that exceed the legally prescribed minima, often presented in an attractive and easily accessible format, has, especially since the Second World War, been strongly developed by many N.V.s. If one compares the average content of the annual reports and prospectuses that are published today, one sees a remarkable improvement, both regarding contents and format. It is our impression that this development still continues, and with increasing swiftness. (p. 316)

In short, even though numerous opinions were offered on the quality of financial reporting, few authors referred to the necessity of evaluating the actual state of financial reporting[73]. An exception to

---

[71] As the official notes to the 1968 draft law (Memorie van Toelichting, p. 8); in Louwers (1970:407). In this sense, the word is already used by Vermeer (1955:159).

[72] *Open ondernemerschap*, De Groei van de Onderneming en het Vennootschapsrecht. Geschriften van de Prof. Mr. B.M. Telderstichting nr 9. ('s-Gravenhage: Martinus Nijhoff, 1962).

[73] Critical views, albeit in varying intensity, on the current state of reporting in Sanders (1963), Haccoû (1962), Brouwer (1962). In defense of current reporting practice, and/or optimistic about possibilities for voluntary improvements: 'Verantwoording en voorlichting', in: *De Onderneming*, vol.

this general trend was J.M. Vecht's suggestion that a committee be appointed to investigate on a sound empirical basis what had been the actual effects of the Rijkens report, and to what extent financial reporting was still deficient (Vecht, 1963:121).

As to auditors, the NIvA leadership understood quite early that legislation of some sort was unavoidable, but the refrained from taking a public position on the subject of company law reform[74].

3.3.4 The 1970 Act on Annual Financial Statements of Enterprises

The Verdam Commission installed in 1960 produced a report in 1965, which included a proposed draft law on the annual financial statements of enterprises. A modified draft law based on this report was submitted to parliament in 1968, and in 1970 an Act on Annual Financial Statements of Enterprises was passed. Given that previous legislation dated back to 1929 and represented in effect the conclusion of a late 19th-century debate, the introduction of a new and modern system of regulation could rightly be described as a 'breakthrough' (Nathans, 1969:76).

---

12 no. 19, 15 September 1962, p. 624-625; Philips (1961), Smulders (1965), Bloembergen (1961), 'Voor betere verslaggeving en voorlichting — Nieuwe aanbevelingen van commissie der werkgeversverbonden', *Handels & Transport Courant*, 13 September 1962, p. 3

[74] In 1958 the NIvA installed a committee to study the possible contents of new regulation in the framework of the Civil Code revision. The committee, chaired by A.Th.E. Kastein, spent considerable time studying various reporting issues on the basis of Dutch and international literature. Among other things, it supplied the NIvA management board with a draft response to the 1965 Verdam proposals. The attitude of the NIvA in taking public positions on reporting issues is stated clearly in the committee's files: 'In the past, the management board of the Institute has always adopted the position that the Institute should not seek publicity for any views it may have on financial reporting, but should stay in the background. It preferred to observe in a critical manner the work of other organizations. The knowledge of Institute members could, of course, be brought to bear through other organizations.' (Minutes of Kastein committee, 5 January 1966, CoKas 184; kindly supplied by J.W. Schoonderbeek).

The developments surrounding the enactment of the 1970 Act are well documented[75]. Here, attention will be focused on some aspects of the law that relate to the issue of voluntary disclosure. Essentially, it will be argued that the new law included and clarified many of the elements that in the previous sections were said to be coalescing into a perceived 'Dutch system' of reporting regulation. Without denying the character of a 'breakthrough' to the 1970 Act, this section therefore primarily stresses its historical continuity.

The proposed law on annual financial statements contained a considerable number of disclosure clauses. Most were taken over into the 1970 Act. The requirements in the final law consisted of an array of about 80 items to be disclosed in the balance sheet and income statement. This represented a substantial extension of disclosure regulation in comparison with the scanty regulation of the 1928/29 Commercial Code (which included on the same count some 12 items). By international standards, however, the extent of required disclosure was modest. The 1970 Act resembled the UK Companies Act 1948 rather than the German 1965 Company Law[76].

The status of the new disclosure requirements within the framework of the law cannot, however, be assessed entirely by their number. The law was clearly aimed at greater openness on the part of companies, but its approach was not based on the enumeration of required disclosures. 'Openness' was broadly interpreted, and included the use of more acceptable principles for valuation and

---

[75] English-language sources include Zeff *et al.* (1992: chapter 4) and Maijoor (1991: *passim*).

[76] In the Verdam report, the German and US systems of regulations are cited as extremes to be avoided (p. 35). British legislation is not mentioned, even though, for instance, the proposed arrangement of the income statement in the Verdam report quite closely resembled that in Schedule 8 of the 1948 Companies Act.

income determination[77]. Specifically, the law was aimed at ending the practice of using secret and hidden reserves[78]. But even to the extent that the law was intended to bring about improved disclosure, its specific disclosure requirements definitely occupied a secondary place in the law. This was already envisaged in the Verdam Commission's report (p. 35), and taken over in the new law. Much stress was placed on the requirement that the financial statements provide 'insight', a phrase equivalent in its effect to the British 'true and fair override' and referring back to views on reporting developed in the 1950s. Those articles of the new law (articles 2 and 3) that contained the 'insight' requirement were placed at a level different from the other articles, containing mainly the disclosure requirements. This latter part of the law contained merely an elaboration of the general principle of 'insight'. In order to convey such insight, financial statements would probably have to contain the information listed in the sections on disclosure, but it was not improbable that providing 'insight' might require more, different or perhaps less information[79].

This feature helps to understand why the disclosure requirements, especially as listed in the Verdam Commission's report, could make a rather haphazard impression at the time[80]. These listed disclosures were to be seen as suggestions rather than strict rules, 'giving guidance' in the application of the general principles[81].

---

[77] The somewhat dismissive opinion expressed by Beekhuizen and Frishkoff (1975:14, 21) that the law dealt mainly with disclosure seems to rest on a too superficial analysis.

[78] See J. Kraayenhof's remark in Handelingen Tweede Kamer, Zitting 1969-1970, p. 2913.

[79] Memorie van Toelichting, Bijlagen Handelingen Tweede Kamer, Zitting 1967-1968, 9595 no. 3, p. 8. The possibility of providing less information was added by amendment in parliament. See also Boukema (1975:80).

[80] See Coelingh (1965:5) and Van der Schroeff (1965:229).

[81] Memorie van Antwoord, Bijlagen Handelingen Tweede Kamer Zitting 1989-1969, 9595 nr 6, p. 2.

Although in the final law the lists of disclosure requirements were given a more systematic look, they retained the appearance of being suggestions rather than requirements. The interpretation of the disclosure requirements as 'recommendations' or 'examples' was taken over by commentators on the law[82]. In this way, the blurring of the distinction between mandatory and non-mandatory disclosure that had already become a standard notion in circles of auditors, and that was at least embryonically part of the 1928/29 law, was now firmly enshrined in the legal provisions on financial reporting.

Another familiar element introduced into the law was the notion that financial reporting norms, rather than being detailed in the law, might instead be derived from the 'economic and social climate'. The law contained few explicit prescriptions on valuation and income determination, but instead contained a general clause (article 5) that the 'principles on which the valuation of assets and liabilities, and the determination of income are based [shall] adhere to norms that are considered acceptable in the economic and social climate'. Subsequently, it has been understood that this clause, even though in its literal sense it referred to balance sheet valuation and income determination only, was understood to subject disclosure issues to the 'norms of the economic and social climate' as well (See IJsselmuiden, 1972:75).
An important aspect of this clause was that it provided a link with another important development from the past, as it provided the framework for a continued involvement of business in the development of reporting norms[83]. While the draft law was debated in parliament, the minister in charge publicly invited the accountancy profession and 'organized business' to prepare an inventory of reporting practices and to pronounce on their acceptability. This invitation resulted in the creation of the so-called 'Tripartite Study Group' *(Tripartiete Overleg)*, a private sector body

---

[82] On the Verdam proposals: Tempelaar (1965:39); on the final law: Sanders, Groeneveld and Burgert (1975:131).
[83] See Schoonderbeek (1981:4).

issuing recommendations on financial reporting[84]. In this way, of course, a mechanism rather closely resembling the system of regular guidance on reporting envisaged at the time of the publication of the Rijkens report was brought into existence. A modification introduced at this time was the participation of representatives from the labour unions, who now formed a third delegation next to the representatives of business and the auditing profession.

In all, the 1970 Act could be seen as the embodiment of continuity rather than change. Even though extensive legislation in the area of financial reporting was in itself a novelty, the new law was in agreement with many earlier ideas on the nature of reporting and reporting regulation. The process of legal change may even have helped to strengthen these ideas. It seems likely that for those who thought in terms of an actual or ideal 'Dutch system', the entire process of preparing and discussing the new law did result in a much clearer perception of what such a system did or ought to stand for. This appears from the number of publications appearing at the time that list or discuss in a rather consistent manner the perceived features of Dutch financial reporting. On the basis of such publications[85], it becomes possible to construct the following ideal notion of the Dutch reporting environment. Its key elements, of which the antecedents have been sketched in the previous sections, can be listed as:

- *A national, Dutch character:* there was awareness of other

---

[84] The organization of the group and the arrangement of its pronouncements were changed in 1981 without materially affecting the status of its pronouncements. The group is currently known as 'Council on Annual Reporting' *(Raad voor de Jaarverslaggeving)*, and its pronouncements as 'Guidelines on annual reporting'. See Zeff *et al.* (1992: chapter 5) on the origins and development of the Tripartite Study Group.

[85] See Tempelaar (1966, 1968), Laterveer (1967), Scott (1968), Nathans (1969), Louwers (1970), Los (quoted in Zeff *et al.*, 1992:189), Tyra (1970), Frederiks (1974).

approaches to reporting and regulation abroad, but it was nevertheless believed that the own approach was superior or at least the most suitable for the national circumstances.

- *The absence of a clear boundary between mandatory and voluntary behaviour:* beyond the explicit requirements of the law that were deliberately kept to a minimum, there existed an outer area within the circumference of the required 'insight'.
- *Progress:* the circumference of 'insight' was not fixed, but expanded in the course of time, as indicated by the reference to the presumably dynamic 'norms of the economic and social climate'.
- *Auditor competence:* to infer in each situation how the insight requirement resulted in concrete demands for the financial statements.
- *Voluntary participation:* entrepreneurs would willingly accept the requirements determined in this way with a view to their own interests. This willingness would extend to experimentation with new forms of reporting, providing the basis for Progress.
- *Proven by use:* the viability of the approach was considered proven by the quality of Dutch reporting, which was assumed to be comparable to that in other major developed countries.

The sense of continuity conveyed by the law presumably was one of the reasons why the law was accepted in parliament without great controversy. There was, to be sure, extensive argument over particular arrangements (especially the compliance mechanism), but debate was on the whole pragmatic and devoid of sharp conflict. It was with apparent justification that the justice minister expressed his satisfaction that 'there is such wide-spread agreement about the fundamentals of [this draft law].'[86]

---

[86] Memorie van Antwoord, Bijlagen Handelingen Tweede Kamer, Zitting 1968-1969, 9595/9596 nr. 6, p. 1. For an expression of similar feeling: Handelingen Tweede Kamer, Zitting 1969-1970, p. 2901.

3.4 1970 to the present.

In the years following 1970, the ideal of a 'Dutch system' of reporting and reporting regulation gradually began to lose some of its hold over the imagination of those who had shared in this vision. However, to trace this gradual waning of the ideal of a 'Dutch system' after 1970 is not a straightforward task. Since it was never universally shared, let alone formally adopted, it never was formally abjured or repealed either. It is undeniable, though, that views on financial reporting current during the first half of the 1990s differ considerably from the picture outlined in the previous paragraphs. Between 1970 and the present, a variety of circumstances and developments have affected and continue to affect the constituent key elements of the 'Dutch system' enumerated in the previous section. None of these elements was ever completely renounced or invalidated, but each of them has suffered in relevance, clarity or acceptability. The overall result has been that the composite ideal of the 'Dutch system' was left to fade away more or less unconsciously in the dissolution of its components.

In the following sections, the effects of some of the more important events and circumstances will be briefly discussed.

3.4.1 Developments among auditors

Enthusiasm for a particular Dutch approach to financial reporting had been strongest among auditors. It is therefore useful to start with a review of some of the general trends in the auditing profession.

At the end of the 1960s, the professional auditor literature was characterized by self-confidence. The auditing profession had achieved its lifelong goal of legal recognition in 1967. From that year onwards, all certifying auditors were united in one officially recognized body known as NIvRA *(Nederlands Instituut van Registeraccountants)*. The united profession could look forward to the introduction of an obligatory audit for a significant number of companies. It took pride in the knowledge that the high standards of professional life carried forward into the legal settlement were nothing more than what it had achieved already for itself in the days without legal protection. The sentiment was optimistic, and there was an eagerness to scale new heights[87].

Unfortunately, determining what new directions were to be taken in the course of further progress turned out to be a rather intractable problem. From the early 1970s onwards and lasting roughly throughout the decade, the auditing profession experienced growing uncertainty about its identity and about the proper response to new challenges. Two related developments disturbed the profession in particular. The most clearly felt, though perhaps not the most lasting, was the fact that the trend towards *vermaatschappelijking* that had resulted, among other things, in the 1970 Act on Annual Financial Statements, began to be felt within the auditing profession. It was believed that a growing participation of employees and the general public in corporate affairs required a

fundamental reconsideration of the role and responsibility of the auditor. Issues such as involvement of the auditor in management audits or the possibility of auditors serving as semi-officials on behalf of the public interest began to appear in the literature[88]. On a more practical level, it resulted in much attention being paid to the

---

[87] One of the clearest expressions of this sentiment is the speech of A.F. Tempelaar, NIvRA chairman, at the inaugural meeting of the reconstituted profession (Tempelaar, 1967).

[88] This development is marked by three study reports commissioned by the NIvRA (*De accountant, morgen?* rapport van de commissie toekomstverkenning aan het bestuur van de orde nederlands instituut van registeraccountants (Amsterdam: Nederlands Instituut van Registeraccountants, 1971); E. Zahn, *De organisatie van het accountantsberoep onder de loep* (Amsterdam: Nederlands Instituut van Registeraccountants, 1975) and *Neutraal, maar niet passief*, Discussierapport van de Werkgroep Dynamische Functieanalyse (Amsterdam: Nederlands Instituut van Registeraccountants, 1980). Two *accountantsdagen* were devoted to issues of change facing the profession (*Het beroep onder de loep* (1975) and *Stormen rond normen* (1976). A guide to this literature is Coret (1977).

auditor's involvement with interim financial statements and prospective information[89].

At the same time, the profession and its clients were confronted with rapidly expanding regulation in many areas, and of financial reporting in particular. This trend towards regulation resulted from the same general trend towards 'vermaatschappelijking', and it is not surprising that some members of the profession embraced regulation as a necessary or desirable way of coping with a perceived proliferation of new demands[90].

3.4.2 Empirical indications of reporting quality

The 1970 Act inspired curiosity about the extent of compliance with the new regulations, which in turn encouraged empirical research in financial reporting. During the 1970s, systematically gathered data on the actual state of financial reporting in the Netherlands became available for the first time. The NIvRA started to publish the results of biennial surveys of financial reporting from 1973 onwards. The aspects of financial statements surveyed corresponded, at least in the earlier years of the series, largely with the clauses of the 1970 Act. The image of Dutch reporting as revealed in this series of empirical studies did not quite match the ideal of continuous voluntary progress in financial reporting. On the whole, compliance was satisfactory. But the reporting practices expanded only slowly beyond the legal minimum. An academic study by R. Slot reached even more negative conclusions[91]. The overall result of the greater availability of empirical data on the actual quality of financial reporting was a

---

[89] A critical review of the trend towards a more widely defined audit function can be found in Groeneveld (1976:139-159).

[90] On the development and impact of regulation: Berendsen (1990:95-99). A contemporary analysis of developing regulation that betrays some of the bewilderment it inspired is a speech by NIvRA vice-chairman Van Emmerik (1977).

[91] *Vijftig jaarverslagen — Gewogen en te licht bevonden*, Economisch Instituut der Rijksuniversiteit Utrecht (Leiden: H.E. Stenfert Kroese B.V., 1975).

rather more subdued tone, replacing some of the optimism from the late 1960s, and removing some of the assumed empirical foundations of the 'Dutch system'.

3.4.3 Internationalization

As noted in previous sections, attention to other countries has never been absent from the Dutch accounting literature. Nevertheless, until the 1960s, Dutch auditors had been rather eclectic in their reception of foreign ideas and practices[92]. It has been argued, in fact, that the postwar Dutch auditing profession maintained a conscious distance towards foreign organizations of auditors. This was based on the perception that professional standards in the Netherlands were distinctly superior to those abroad, with the possible exception of the United States and the United Kingdom (De Hen, Berendsen and Schoonderbeek, 1995:18-21). By the latter half of the 1960s, elements of a different attitude towards foreign practices began to emerge. In the professional literature, there were increasing signs of a realization that foreign approaches to accountancy and auditing might, after all, be relevant. In the Netherlands, the changing appreciation of the value of foreign example coincided, and became inextricably mixed, with the internationally observable shift of attention from accounting 'principles' to accounting 'standards'.

The term 'standards' emerged in Britain, where the Accounting Standards Steering Committee was launched at the beginning of 1970. The first Statement of Standard Accounting Practice was issued in 1971. In the United States, the Financial Accounting Standards Board succeeded the Accounting Principles Board in 1973.

---

[92] An illustration of the mixture of approval and amusement with which the United States were viewed from a Dutch perspective is the extensive review by R. Burgert of the *Papers presented at the 67th Annual Meeting of the American Institute of Accountants* (Burgert, 1955/56). According to Burgert, this book 'brings us as Alice in Wonderland in the middle of our American colleagues' (p. 365).

Even though the word 'standards' did not originate in the United States, the Wheat Committee, which proposed the creation of the FASB, argued that in retrospect the work of the APB could be described more aptly in terms of 'standards' than of 'principles' (Solomons, 1986:41-42). In all, the advent of accounting standards represented a 'profound change' affecting financial reporting practices worldwide (Baxter, 1981:282).

During the second half of the 1960s, the Dutch professional literature displayed a clear awareness of trends in US accounting regulation, and of the possible implications for Dutch financial reporting[93]. Especially the work by Paul Grady, *Inventory of Generally Accepted Accounting Principles for Business Enterprises* (APB Accounting Research Study #7), drew much attention as it was seen to epitomize a new approach to financial reporting. Two issues of the professional journal, *Maandblad voor Accountancy en Bedrijfshuishoudkunde* were devoted to this study in 1966, and it was an important influence on the Tripartite Study Group.

During the 1970s, international influences made themselves more strongly felt in the Netherlands. These included the International Accounting Standards issued by the IASC, the rudimentary attempts at regulation by the OECD and the UN and attempts at harmonization on the part of the EEC. In all, by the later half of that decade it could be remarked that foreign example had not only gained in importance due to the 'torrent' of international developments, but that the Dutch accounting profession had without noticeable reflection embraced the principle of codification underlying the work of the IASC that was in marked contrast with traditional attitudes[94].

This increased attention for foreign developments reduced the necessity or even desirability of a 'Dutch' approach. At the same

---

[93] See especially Smulders (1965), Kruisbrink (1965) and Karelse (1965).

[94] Bindenga (1976); 'torrent': Steenmeijer (1976:17).

time, it provided a climate in which acceptance of more elaborate 'accounting standards' was quite natural. These trends continue to make themselves felt up to the present (Van der Wel, 1992).

3.4.4 Impact of the Enterprise Chamber

An important source of disparity in expectations regarding the 1970 Act was the uncertainty about the effects of the new compliance mechanism introduced by the Act. This took the form of an Enterprise Chamber *(Ondernemingskamer)*, a court created to investigate complaints by interested parties relating to the Act on financial statements, and empowered to give directions to companies regarding the drafting of financial statements. If the court were to be activated by frequent complaints, the accumulation of jurisprudence might result in a system characterized by a much higher degree of formal reporting regulation than would appear from the text of the underlying law. Consequently, liberal representatives in parliament professed to believe that the law would not result in major changes for many companies, since previous voluntary developments had already resulted in a general level of reporting as envisaged by the law[95]. On the other hand, a labour representative expressed the view that the law would be a 'first step', to be continued by an active role on the part of the Enterprise Chamber in the process of improving financial reporting[96]. The uncertainty was characterized by Groeneveld (1968:143) in the following way:

the development of a major body of jurisprudence cannot be

---

[95] Handelingen Tweede Kamer, zitting 1969-1970, p. 2863.

[96] Handelingen Tweede Kamer, zitting 1969-1970, p. 2860, 2861. Further instances of different expectations include the following. On the one hand, the investors' association 'Vereniging Effectenbescherming' expressed the view that lack of clarity in the law might well result in the Enterprise Chamber being 'flooded' with cases (Bijlagen Handelingen Tweede Kamer 1968-1969, 9595 no. 4, p. 2). On the other hand, Van Rietschoten (1965, p. 224) expected that the Enterprise Chamber would only be activated in exceptional cases.

ruled out, given that (...) the requirements [of the law] are to be considered as minimum requirements. The Enterprise Chamber is charged with the difficult task of determining exactly, in a particular situation, what the requirements, formulated in general terms and as minimum requirements, amount to.

According to Burgert (1982), the direct impact of the Enterprise Chamber on financial reporting has been quite marginal. He attributed this to the already 'reasonable' level of disclosure by the larger companies, and to the cumbersome procedures of the Enterprise Chamber which deter interested parties from filing complaints in all but the most flagrant cases of noncompliance with the law. Similar conclusions have been reached by Berendsen (1990: 56-59), and by Klaassen (1991).

Hence, the Enterprise Chamber has not done much to alter the balance between voluntary and mandatory disclosure in favour of the latter by producing clear and generally applicable pronouncements. However, the Enterprise Chamber has had a more general and presumably unforeseen effect on views on the desirability of explicit regulation of accounting. Its mere existence as an avenue to legal action has produced a rationale for reporting regulation that was unknown before. Whereas previously, from the point of view of companies, reporting regulation had few if any positive benefits, the existence of the Enterprise chamber made certainty concerning the actual contents of the legal requirements a positive good. That is, for the first time it was no longer necessarily in the interest of the companies to maintain a wide, blurred border area between voluntary and mandatory disclosure.

A similar development occurred among auditors. Whereas before 1970 the expressed fear had been that a detailed spelling out of accounting and reporting principles might lead to *verstarring*, now the problem emerged that without such an explicit regulation companies (and by implication, their auditors) might be subjected to judgements that were perceived as unpredictable if not arbitrary. Auditors, hitherto largely unaccustomed to courtroom practice in the context of financial reporting, experienced this new development as disagreeable or even threatening[97], especially when the new activity of the Enterprise Chamber resulted in serious negative publicity about the auditing profession in the national press[98].

3.4.5 The Tripartite Study Group and disclosure issues

As discussed above, a private-sector Tripartite Study Group *(Tripartiet Overleg)* was set up in 1970 to make an inventory of the 'norms of the economic and social climate' referred to in the 1970 Act. By common consent, these norms were understood to refer to disclosure issues as well. The publications of the study group, issued since 1971, therefore contained (and still contain) numerous discussions of disclosure issues.

The significance of the study group for the further development of the views on voluntary disclosure underlying the 1970 Act is quite complex, as it represents a mixture of continuity and change.

Continuity was most evident when the study group was seen as a continuation of the voluntary system based on recommendations by the employer's organizations. The study group was seen as a natural consequence of the involvement of the employers' unions with improving financial reporting in 1955 and 1962. In this sense it was a belated realization of what Geertman (1956) had already dubbed the 'Dutch system' (see also Smulders, 1965).

However, the study group could also be interpreted as a first step towards the introduction of a system of accounting standard-setting similar to that evolving at that time in the US or the UK. Such an interpretation could easily develop on the basis of the interest displayed in the Netherlands of around 1970 in US approaches to the codification of accounting principles. Moreover, the reference to norms considered 'acceptable' in the economic and social climate

---

[97] Meijer and Van Tilburg (1979:398).

[98] See J. Burggraaff, 'Voorwoord van de voorzitter', in *Verslag van de werkzaamheden 1 september 1977 - 31 augustus 1978* (Amsterdam: Nederlands Instituut van Registeraccountants, 1979), p. 6.

invited comparison with the notion of Generally Accepted Accounting Principles as used in the US (see IJsselmuiden, 1972:73).

The difference between these two ways of looking at the study group emerged during the 1970s and 1980s in recurrent discussions on the 'status' of the publications of the study group. It had to be determined whether or not these publications (known since 1980 as 'Guidelines on Annual Financial Reporting') contained binding accounting standards. Ultimately, the literature on this subject achieved a consensus, according to which the Guidelines are not binding, but derive their authority from their 'intrinsic worth'. What this means, in effect, is that they contain the norms that an individual company, with the help of its auditor, could and ought to have derived itself from its knowledge of the 'economic and social climate'. A company and its auditor could, at least in theory, apply the same process of reasoning, referring to the literature and reliance on experience as the study group would use in its drafting of Guidelines. Compliance is therefore at least theoretically ensured because the Guidelines are seen to represent norms that, even if unwritten, would have been equally binding on the company and its auditor. In this way the Guidelines represented a continuation of the blurred distinction between mandatory and voluntary elements in financial reporting that was indicated above as a key element in a 'Dutch system' of reporting. The fact, however, that this view could only be established (or re-established) after extensive discussion within the study group, in the literature and in the NIvRA indicates that, around 1980, support for a system of more authoritative guidance was rather widespread.

Such support came from organized business and was also manifest within the auditing profession that had for a long time contained the more outspoken supporters of a voluntary system. Some of the more general reasons for a change in attitude have already been indicated: it is likely that changing general attitudes towards regulation and an ever growing awareness of foreign practices in the area of standard setting may have accustomed auditors and business to expect more strict guidance from the study group. A more specific reason can be found in the role of the Enterprise Chamber. Calls for more authoritative Guidelines coincided roughly with uncertainty about Enterprise Chamber activity. Before the enactment of the 1970 law, when it was as yet unclear what role the Enterprise Chamber would play, there were calls for the audit profession to exert itself in the codification of accounting principles in order to prevent this area from being occupied by the new court (Kraayenhof, 1967:18). Comparable voices were heard in the later part of the 1970s when the court had actually become active: by then one could hear that the status of the Tripartite Study Group with regard to standard setting should be upgraded at the expense of the Enterprise Chamber (Meijer and Van Tilburg, 1979:400), or to provide the auditor with more viable defences in court (Klaassen, 1980:338). From a business point of view it was remarked that many company managements had 'become increasingly disquieted by the fact that agreement with the auditor does not offer a guarantee of the correct interpretations within the fairly wide margin allowed in many legal regulations and in areas not regulated by law' (Van Putten, 1980:11).

In addition, there was the need to come to terms with the International Accounting Standards being issued since 1974 and the desire to present the Tripartite Study Group as a viable alternative to a strict implementation of the Fourth Directive.

Even though, therefore, the work of the study group represented on balance continuity rather than change, it was nevertheless a focus for thought on change. In this way, the mere existence of the guidelines, coupled with the uncertainty introduced by the debate concerning their status, has tended to obscure some of the notions forming the 'Dutch system', or to change their perceived significance. One of these effects is that the study group has shifted the emphasis in thinking on voluntary behaviour. Instead of looking for beneficial effects of the harmonious cooperation of management and auditor in preparing the financial statements of the individual companies, attention shifted to cooperation in determining accounting standards. Whereas in the late 1960s the uniqueness of the Dutch system was sought in the fact that voluntary behaviour at the level of the individual firm had resulted in informative reporting, in the 1970s such uniqueness was found in the fact that accounting standards were being set in a system of voluntary cooperation (Frijns, 1979:659).

Although this shift of emphasis left the importance of voluntary action intact, it did have some consequences. For the individual firm and the individual auditor engaged in drafting a specific set of financial statements, the existence of a set of standards, whether voluntarily issued by their representatives or not, served to make the idea of voluntary reporting more remote. If such standards were to some extent binding, it meant that compliance with such standards, rather than professional determination of proper reporting, became a more characteristic part of the accounting process.

The study group has also served to bring to light some of the limits of a voluntary system. The assumption of willing cooperation has occasionally been put severely to the test by the inability of the delegations to reach consensus on important accounting issues. In one of the few disclosure areas where the study group has attempted to go significantly beyond legal requirements, segment reporting, issuance of clear guidance was prevented by strong disagreement (Zeff et al., 1992:327-328).

In short, the study group has been set up in harmony with the notions of the 'Dutch system'. Seen in this light, it is natural that its structure and status began to be questioned and perhaps even misunderstood as the ideal of the 'Dutch system' itself began to recede from the minds of those involved. But the study group itself has been a factor as well in bringing about this dissolution of the composite 'Dutch system', by leading to changes of attitude towards some of its important elements, notably the idea of a blurred distinction between voluntary and mandatory reporting practices.

3.4.6 The Fourth Directive

A further reduction of the 'Dutchness' of Dutch financial reporting was caused by the adaptation of Dutch law to the Fourth EEC Directive on Company Law, which was made effective in 1983.

Given that the 1970 Act had deliberately avoided a strict framework of disclosure requirements, one would expect some resentment in the Netherlands because of the significant changes in disclosure regulation required by the Fourth Directive. The Fourth Directive, especially in its earlier drafts, was based on principles that were quite different from those of the Dutch 1970 Act. The Fourth Directive assumed strict compliance with its disclosure requirements. The Dutch 1970 Act, on the other hand, was drafted in a way that consistently played down the importance of the formal disclosure requirements. The disclosure aspects of the Directive were contained in a set of mandatory balance sheet and income statement schedules, as used in German company law since the 1930s. In the Netherlands, the last time that such rigid schedules had been seriously considered as a legislative option was in the literature responding to Van Slooten's (1900) thesis. The Fourth Directive therefore represented a return of Dutch accounting legislation to a continental European mould. As indicated above, the Netherlands had since the days in which the 1928/29 Commercial Code revision was prepared, been orientated towards UK accounting legislation.

Some resentment because of this change was voiced in auditing circles[99], but not nearly to the extent that might be expected given the pleas for vigilance against *verstarring* that had accompanied the passage of the 1970 Act. Apart from the inevitability of the process of European harmonization, a major explanation for this seems to be the changing attitude towards regulation in general noted in section 3.4.1. Besides, it could be argued that the introduction of the Fourth Directive was not a change in principle. In the

---

[99] An item by item criticism from a NIvRA point of view appeared as '(Gewijzigd) voorstel voor vierde EEG-richtlijn - Rapport van de Commissie Ondernemingsrecht', *De Accountant*, vol. 81 no. 5, January 1975, p. 313-323. See also Pruijt (1971:40-41), Sanders (1972:15).

accompanying memorandum to the implementation act, it was claimed that the Fourth Directive was implemented 'while attempting to conserve what has already been achieved in the Netherlands'. Since 'the Directive implies that the draft law has a much more detailed character than the [1970 Act]', a guiding principle was that '[w]herever the Directive presents the member-states with an option, this has generally been used on behalf of the flexibility that practice requires in applying [legal] prescriptions'[100].

As a practical consequence of conserving previous Dutch achievements, both the 'insight'-override and the reference to the 'norms of the economic and social climate' were retained. Nevertheless, the reduced scope for discretion in using the 'insight' criterion represents another instance of an element of the 'Dutch system' that was not formally renounced, but that was allowed to diminish in importance.

An important effect of the Fourth Directive was that it weakened, to a certain extent, the assumption of auditor competence in determining proper disclosure. The introduction of extensive formal norms carried the risk that the judgmental aspects of the auditor's work would be replaced by mere checking of compliance (Bindenga, 1976). But there was a further effect. Much more than the 1970 Act, the Fourth Directive expanded the influence of Law in the area of financial reporting. Whereas the Dutch auditing profession could justifiably claim expertise in auditing and business economics, the structure of its education and the nature of past experience could not justify serious claims to expertise in legal affairs. This had already come to light in connection with the first cases before the Enterprise Chamber, but the Fourth Directive prompted even more activity in the nature of conferences, study meetings and articles aimed at preparing the auditor for this hitherto unknown dimension of his profession (Degenkamp, 1983:10).

---

[100] Bijlagen Handelingen Tweede Kamer, Zitting 1979-1980, 16236 no. 3, p.3.

3.4.7 Gradual change in views on voluntary reporting

The previous sections have indicated how various elements of the 'Dutch system' gradually came under pressure, were questioned or lost some of their validity in the course of the 1970-1985 period. To review some of these developments:

- The notion that there was or ought to be a particular 'Dutch' approach to reporting and reporting regulation came under pressure through the increasing importance attached to developments abroad. Especially in recent years, the desirability of having a purely national approach to reporting regulation has been questioned. The Fourth (and later Seventh) Directive constituted an immediate imposition of foreign reporting principles on Dutch law, which could therefore to a far lesser extent be seen as 'Dutch'.

- The practical significance of the idea of a wide border area between mandatory and purely voluntary disclosure has decreased because of the significant extension of legal requirements.

- The idea of specific auditor competence in determining reporting requirements specific to the circumstances has decreased somewhat in prominence by increased reliance on formalized rules and the increased importance of legal skills.

- The assumption of willingness among managements to provide information or to work for consensus with auditors has lost some of its validity in the light of occasional difficulties in reaching agreement in the Tripartite Study Group.

- The empirical validity of the 'Dutch system' could be questioned by its mixed results in providing good financial reporting as indicated by both domestic and international surveys.

The net effect of these developments on the role of an abstraction as the 'Dutch system' cannot be determined exactly. Participants in the financial reporting process would tend to perceive such an ideal with varying degrees of clarity, and would differ in their interpretation of such a view.

Nevertheless, it seems appropriate to conclude that the overall effect of the trends and factors enumerated in the previous sections has been that, at present, there would be considerably less support for the view that there is or ought to be a distinctly 'Dutch' approach to financial reporting relying to a large extent on unregulated action.

3.5 Conclusions

This chapter has provided a description of the rise and gradual disappearance of the practice of interpreting Dutch financial reporting in terms of a 'Dutch system' of financial reporting and reporting regulation. On the basis of the materials provided in this chapter, it is now possible to arrive at an appreciation of the view of a 'Dutch system' as applied to voluntary disclosure extension. The period during which a 'Dutch system' was seen to exist was a period (1) during which the exogenous development of company law in the Netherlands left the area of the contents of financial statements temporarily untouched, and (2) during which other factors, such as the auditing profession and company managements, were given a relatively free rein.

Taking a long-term perspective, it may be said that Dutch company law has changed in response to the same forces or influences that were active in Germany and the United Kingdom. In the late 19th century, financial reporting legislation was changed to replace preventive state supervision. In the period following the Second World War, change resulted from calls for wider corporate accountability. In both cases, the direction of change was identical across countries. Nevertheless, an important difference separated the Netherlands from both the United Kingdom and Germany in that the slower pace of legislation in the Netherlands resulted in a longer period during which financial reporting could develop autonomously. This provided an environment in a which the notion of a 'Dutch system' could develop.

That a 'Dutch system' could exist in this way by the grace of the law can be seen both at its beginning and at its ending. During the preparation of the 1928/29 Commercial Code revision, the decision to leave the contents of financial statements largely unregulated, despite foreign precedent, was arrived at on the basis of arguments on the proper role of the law. Such arguments could and were also used to determine the contents of company law outside the area of financial reporting. At end of the period studied here, the scope for a specific 'Dutch system' was considerably narrowed by the introduction of the Fourth Directive, which represented above all a change in the approach to legislation, rather than a change in views on financial reporting. It was this changing approach to legislation that reverted financial reporting regulation to a pattern of legislation renounced in the context of the 1928 Commercial Code revision.

Given that the law temporarily maintained an attitude of abstinence in the area of financial reporting, other forces were allowed to determine the shape of financial statements. As seen, the most important of these forces was the interplay between auditor competence and the willingness of company managements to innovate. To rely on these forces to bring about improvements in financial reporting, or to advocate reliance on them, was not unique to the Netherlands, however. As indicated, prior to the passage of the Companies Act 1947 in the United Kingdom, similar views were expressed concerning the importance of voluntary action in the development of financial reporting. Outside the Netherlands, men were definitely aware of the attractions of a voluntary system. However, in most countries the working of voluntary forces was inhibited or obscured by systems of regulations that were or became more elaborate and binding than in the Netherlands. Even in the United Kingdom, the country that for the longest time remained close to the Netherlands in the area of accounting legislation, the

Companies Acts 1947 and 1967 introduced restrictions not felt in the Netherlands until 1970 or even 1983.

Rather than concluding, therefore, that a specifically 'Dutch' line of development in financial reporting can be distinguished, it is more useful, at least with regard to the development of financial statement disclosure, to position the Netherlands at one of the more extreme ends of a continuum of approaches. On this continuum, the situation in the Netherlands most closely resembled, and was in fact for some time substantially identical to, the United Kingdom.

The discussion in this chapter established that there was a widespread perception in the Netherlands of the importance of voluntary improvements in disclosure. In addition, this chapter has offered an interpretation of how such a point of view could develop in the context of the history of financial reporting regulation in the Netherlands and in other countries. The main task of the empirical section of this book is now to demonstrate that important voluntary disclosure extensions did in fact take place, and to determine in more detail how these were brought about.

Chapter 4
Approaches to empirical disclosure research

4.1 Introduction

This chapter introduces the empirical section of this study. Section 4.2 reviews the existing empirical literature. Section 4.3 discusses the main choices underlying the research approach adopted here. Sections 4.4 and 4.5 discuss the selection of disclosure items to be studied and the sample of company financial statements in more detail.

4.2 Survey of previous empirical research

Interest in extent and form of disclosure in financial reporting practice is a long-standing feature of the accounting literature. Reports on studies of reporting and disclosure practices appeared well before the Second World War. Munnik's (1931) report on Dutch reporting practices, discussed in chapter 3, can be cited as an example. It is, however, not until after the war that the literature on this subject acquires a more systematic character, with sequences of studies starting to form a coherent body of research. At present, the empirical disclosure literature is rather well developed, even though not all potential avenues of research have been explored with the same degree of thoroughness. Table 4.1 shows an overview of recent publications with their main characteristics.

For the purposes of this chapter, the variety of approaches within the total body of published empirical research on financial statement disclosure can be ordered by means of two elementary dimensions. These are the level of aggregation with which disclosure is measured (single-item versus multi-item studies) and the number of periods studied (single-period versus multi-period studies). Section 4.2.1 discusses issues regarding the level of aggregation. Sections 4.2.2 and 4.2.3 review the empirical approaches used in single-period studies and multi-period studies, respectively.

4.2.1 Aggregation levels in disclosure studies

As indicated in chapter 1, the word 'disclosure' has a number of meanings, ranging from the act of making a marginal addition to the contents of a set of financial statements, to the total extent of information included in an annual report. Similarly, disclosure studies can take as their subject the disclosure of specific items of information, or the total extent of disclosure.

Hence, three basic types of disclosure study can be distinguished:
- Single item studies.
- Multi-item studies, not including a measure of aggregate disclosure.
- Aggregated multi-item studies.

Single-item studies do not pose specific issues with regard to the measurement of disclosure. Such measurement either involves a binary scoring (*e.g.* Wong, 1988, on the disclosure of current cost data, and Bazley, Brown and Izan, 1985, on lease disclosures) or the use of an ordinal scale with which various disclosure alternatives can be ranked (*e.g.* Bradbury, 1992, distinguishing four levels of segment reporting). A number of these studies are shown in the upper half (panel A) of table 4.1.

The group of multi-item studies without aggregation includes regular surveys of public reporting practices, such as *Accounting Trends & Techniques*. In addition, there are unaggregated multi-item studies that include more substantial analyses, such as Murphy (1988) on the development of Canadian financial reporting. Unaggregated studies tend to rely on qualitative interpretations of observed data.

Aggregated multi-item studies are characterized by the use of 'disclosure indexes' to measure total extent of disclosure. The origin of index-type studies is by common consent traced to the work of Cerf (1961). Typically, a disclosure index is used to capture in a single number the 'disclosure' aspect of a set of financial statements. This involves compiling a list of topics about which a company might provide information, assigning scores to a particular set of financial statements for each topic or item about which information is disclosed, summing individual scores to a single number and dividing this by the maximum total score that might have been obtained.

Marston and Shrives (1991), reviewing the disclosure index literature, report that disclosure indexes are used in a wide variety of studies. Apart from studies (*e.g.* Tonkin, 1984), disclosure indexes are used in cross-sectional analytical studies and comparative static studies. Table 4.1 (panel B) contains a list of studies using disclosure indexes. As the table shows, the use of disclosure indexes in the literature has, if anything, increased during the early 1990s, despite the fact that the index method suffers from a number of weaknesses. As indicated by Marston and Shrives, these consist mainly of the inevitability of subjective judgements, both in selecting items for inclusion in the index and in assigning scores to companies[1].

From table 4.1 (panel B), it appears that the number of items used in disclosure indexes varies from 14 to more than 200 elements. The typical number, however, is between 30 and 50 elements, with a tendency for larger numbers of elements in more recent studies. Various approaches have been used to select items for an index (apart from replicating earlier studies). Choi (1973) based his research on an explicit model of decision-making for investments from which he derived a list of required information. Interviews with investment analysts have been used to refine or calibrate such lists (Firth, 1980)[2].

---

[1] See also Dhaliwal (1980) for a critical commentary on cross-sectional disclosure research by means of the index method.

[2] A meta-analysis by Courtis (1992) has shown that a non-trivial degree of consensus can be established across temporal and national divides with regard to the perceived importance of disclosure items.

Table 4.1
Cross-sectional empirical disclosure studies

Study:	Country/year:	Object:	Covariates of disclosure:
Panel A: selected single-item studies:			
Salamon & Dhaliwal (1981)	US, 1967-1970	segmental information	**asset size** **new issues**
Leftwich, Watts & Zimmerman (1981)	US, 1937,1948	interim reporting	assets in place firm value debt/firm value outside directors **listing status** **inertia** industry dividend frequency **auditor**
Bazley, Brown & Izan (1985)	Australia, 1979	lease commitments	net assets auditor **industry** fin.rep. competition **foreign affiliation** leverage bonus schemes
Whittred (1986)	Australia, 1930s, 1950s.	consolidated reports	**cross-guarantees** **management share in parent equity** **# of subsidiaries**
Wong (1988)	New Zealand 1980-81	current cost data	effective tax rate **leverage** **market dominance** historical cost ROA **capital intensity** size (net income)

122

Table 4.1 (continued)

Bradbury (1992a)	New Zealand, 1983	segmental information	**firm value** **leverage** assets in place earnings volatility foreign affiliation
Bradbury (1992b)	New Zealand 1973-76	semiannual reporting	earnings volatility unexpected earnings size
Craswell & Taylor (1992)	Australia, 1984	oil & gas reserves	**auditor** **log assets** leverage cash-flow variance ownership dispersion
Roberts (1992)	US, mid-1980s	corporate social responsibility disclosure	**high profile industry** **PAC contributions** **age of corporation** public affairs staff **return on equity** average revenue ownership dispersion market beta **donations** debt/equity ratio
Forker (1992)	UK, 1988	directors' share options	size directors' equity **directors' options** auditor audit committee **dominant personality**
Lang & Lundholm (1993)	USA, 1985-89	analysts' ratings of disclosure	**size** **returns** variability of returns abnormal returns unexpected earnings **earnings/returns correlation** **issues of securities**

Table 4.1 (continued)

Wallace *et al.* (1994)	Spain, 1991	extent of dicslosure on 16 items	**size** gearing return on equity profit margin **current ratio** manufact/nonmanufact **listing status** big-6 auditor

Panel B: Studies using disclosure indexes

Singhvi (1968)	India, 1963-65	weighted index of 34 items	**asset size** **rate of return** **earnings margin** auditor **foreign affiliation** # shareholders
Singhvi & Desai (1971)	USA, 1965/66	weighted index of 34 items	asset size # shareholders **listing status** auditor rate of return earnings margin
Choi (1973)	Entrants Eurobond market 1954-1970	(un)weighted index of 47 items	**entry in Eurobond market**
Buzby (1974, 1975)	US, 1971/72	weighted index of 39 items	**asset size** listing status
Barrett (1977)	seven countries, 1963-1972	(un)weighted index of 17 items	**country** **year**
Dijksma & Van Halem (1977)	Netherlands, 1970-74	index derived Singhvi & Desai (1971)	**size** share price volatility
Firth (1979)	UK, 1976	(un)weighted index of 48 items	**listing status** **size** big-8 auditor

124

Table 4.1 (continued)

Firth (1980)	UK, 1973	(un)weighted index of 48 items	**market capitalization rights-/new issues**
Kahl & Belkaoui (1981)	Banks from 18 countries, 1975	weighted index of 30 items	**size**
McNally, Eng & Hasseldine (1982)	New Zealand, 1979	weighted index of 41 items	**total assets** net income/total assets growth total assets industry auditor
Cowen *et al.* (1987)	US, mid-1970s	unweighted index of social responsibility disclosures, 27 items	**size** industry return on equity existence of social responsibility committee
Chow & Wong-Boren (1987)	Mexico, 1982	(un)weighted index of 24 items	**firm value** leverage assets in place
Wallace (1988)	Nigeria, 1982-86	weighted indexes comprising 185 items on six disclosure areas	**perceived importance of areas according to survey**
Cooke (1989)	Sweden, 1985	unweighted index of 224 items	**listing status** size affiliation
Wagenhofer (1990b, 1990c)	Austria, 1990	unweighted index of 14 items	**log capital** industry return on investment leverage
Cooke (1991, 1992)	Japan, 1987	unweighted index of 106 items	**size** listing status industry

Table 4.1 (continued)

Raffournier (1994)	Switzerland, 1991	unweighted indexes of 24 and 30 items	**size** profitability ownership of shares leverage assets in place **export to sales ratio**
Hossain *et al.* (1994)	Malaysia, 1991	unweighted index of 78 items	**size** **ownership dispersal** **foreign listing** leverage assets in place big-6 auditor
Hossain *et al.* (1995)	New Zealand, 1991	unweighted index of 95 items	**size** **leverage** assets in place ratio big-6 auditor **listing status**
Hossain & Adams (1995)	Australia, 1991	unweighted index of 80 items	**size** leverage assets in place **big-6 auditor** **foreign listing**
Gray, Meek & Roberts (1995)	US/UK, 1989	unweighted indexes of 108 and 112 items	**country** **listing status**

Note: covariates are classified as **significant** or not significant according to the conclusions reached in the various studies rather than on the basis of a uniform criterion.

On the other hand, Cooke (1989) is an attempt to construct as wide-ranging a list as possible, not limited to a single group of users of financial statements.

A criterion used in a number of studies (Buzby, 1975; Barrett, 1977; Firth, 1980; Wallace *et al.*, 1994) is to select only those items that are applicable to all companies. This solves the problem that, when a company does not disclose a particular item, it is not always possible to tell if that follows from a reluctance to disclose or whether the particular item simply is not relevant for the company in question. Where appropriateness is not guaranteed by the selection of items, scoring involves judgement (as in Cooke, 1989) or the problem is simply ignored (as in McNally, Eng and Hasseldine, 1982).

4.2.2 Issues in cross-sectional analysis

In both single-item studies and in studies of aggregate disclosure, the extent of disclosure can be related to selected company characteristics or other circumstances. A typical approach is to use a form of multivariate analysis such as linear regression (in the case of disclosure indexes) or logit regression (in the case of single-item studies). Table 4.1 lists the covariates of disclosure investigated in the multi-item studies discussed in the previous section (panel B) and in a number of single-item studies (panel A).

Ideally, the selection of relevant company characteristics should proceed in the context of a theoretical framework, for instance as developed in the literature discussed in chapter 2. The studies listed in table 4.1 differ considerably, however, in their reliance on the existing theoretical literature on voluntary disclosure. Evidently, this in part merely reflects the relatively late development of such a theoretical literature over time. For this reason, earlier studies like Singhvi (1968) tend to base their research design to a considerable extent on common sense. Reliance on practical reasoning continues to play an important role in many later studies.

Another way of arriving at a set of explanatory variables is by following earlier empirical studies. In McNally, Eng and Hasseldine (1982), explanatory factors are selected simply because previous empirical studies have shown them to have a certain explanatory power. Regarding the selection of items to be included in disclosure indices, a similar perpetuating effect is visible. The studies by Cerf (1961) and Cooke (1989) have played an important role as examples for other studies.

In contrast, Wagenhofer (1990c) contains an elaborate attempt to derive a set of explanatory variables from an information-economics model. Interestingly, his selection of explanatory variables (size, rate of return, listing status, leverage, industry, degree of state ownership) is to a large extent identical to the selection used in the earlier 'common sense' models.

Finally, in the case of single-item studies, explanatory variables can be selected that are expected to be relevant for that particular disclosure decision. For instance, the factor 'cross-guarantees' was used by Whittred (1987) to analyze the incidence of consolidated reporting.

Despite the various approaches to selecting explanatory variables, the general tendency in the literature is to adhere to a relatively small number of variables that recur across studies. The general pattern of results obtained with these variables will be briefly discussed below.

Explanatory variables: Size
Size appears to be the single most important variable in explaining disclosure. A large majority of studies that have included measures of size have found a degree of statistical significance in the association between size and disclosure. It appears that this result is more or less impervious to variations in the size measure used. Total assets, assets in place, sales, number of shareholders, market value of equity, market value of equity and loan capital and logarithmic transformations of some of these variables have been used, singly or in combination, in many studies, and usually with consistent results. In general, a high degree of correlation between such measures as total assets, sales and market-based measures of firm value may be assumed, which accounts for the identical results obtained with different size measures (see Newbould and Wilson, 1977).

Explanatory variables: Listing status and capital market activity
Active involvement with the capital market has been found to be an important indicator of the extent of disclosure in a number of studies. Some authors (Singhvi and Desai, 1971; Cooke, 1989; and Gray, Meek and Roberts, 1991) have found that listing on more than

one stock exchange, or on an official market as opposed to an over-the-counter market, coincides with more extensive disclosure. New demands on the capital markets, for instance new issues, can be the occasion for increases in disclosure (Firth, 1980). Despite the contrary findings in Buzby (1975), capital market activity appears to be, with size, one of the strongest explanatory variables.

Explanatory variables: Industry
Somewhat surprisingly, industry has not received much attention in the empirical literature surveyed. Given that possible competitive damage is one of the most important determinants of disclosure mentioned in both the research and the professional literature, one would expect more attention to be directed to this factor, as industry may be a proxy for competitive pressure or possible competitive damage.

However, McNally, Eng and Hasseldine (1982) included industry among their explanatory factors without discussion. Bazley, Brown and Izan (1985) did so merely because empirical research had shown an association between industry and accounting method choice. Wagenhofer (1990b) includes industry as a proxy measure for proprietary costs.

Empirical results of the few studies that did include industry as an explanatory factor have been mixed. Drawing conclusions from these limited results is hindered by the fact that industry is not easily defined and that classifying companies according to industries is to a large extent a matter of judgement.

Explanatory variables derived from an agency perspective
Leftwich, Watts and Zimmerman (1981) is the most elaborate attempt published to date to test the usefulness of agency theory as an explanatory framework for voluntary disclosure. Specifically, they have tested for such variables as assets in place (fixed assets/firm value), leverage and existence of outside directors. These factors are assumed to be proxies for a higher incidence of agency costs (and hence positively related to extent of disclosure), or indicators that alternative monitoring systems are used. None of

these factors was strongly related to disclosure, at least not in ways predicted by the underlying theory[3]. Inconclusive results on assets in place and leverage have resulted from other studies as well (Bazley, Brown and Izan, 1985; Chow and Wong-Boren, 1987; Wagenhofer, 1990c; Craswell and Taylor, 1992 and Bradbury, 1992, although the last does have a positive result on leverage).

A primary reason for this lack of results might be that the effects predicted by the agency framework are concerned with such a level of detail that their occurrence cannot be established because of noise (Burton, 1981). However, it is not certain that more detailed studies will yield better results. Forker (1992) is a detailed study of the relation between corporate governance and disclosure on share options held by directors. Although the agency framework might be expected to be useful in this case, very few of the predicted associations were observed.

Explanatory variables: Auditor
The impact of audit firm is typically investigated by a binary variable: big-six/eight firms versus other audit firms. The rationale is that larger audit firms are more likely to have the technical competence required to identify possible disclosure extensions.

Most studies aiming to associate different disclosure practices with external audit firms have not found significant effects (Singhvi, 1968; Singhvi and Desai, 1971; McNally *et al.*, 1982; Bazley *et al.*, 1985; Forker, 1992). Studies that did find some association are Leftwich *et al.* (1981) and Craswell and Taylor (1992). On the whole, the evidence for a relationship between auditor and disclosure is weak.

---

[3] It should be noted that most empirical studies of financial reporting from an agency perspective have dealt with accounting method choice rather than with disclosure issues. As argued in Watts and Zimmerman (1990), empirical work in these areas has generally yielded results in support of the hypotheses suggested by the agency framework.

Explanatory variables: Nationality

A few studies have analyzed differences in disclosure among companies from different countries (Barrett, 1976 and 1977; Tyra, 1977; Gray, Meek and Roberts, 1991).

'Nationality' can make an impact in two ways. The most straightforward is the effect that companies in one country tend, in general, to be more open than companies in another. Barrett (1977) specifically addressed this kind of differences. In studies dealing with one country, such an effect may also occur when companies with foreign affiliations show differences in disclosure (*i.e.* Singhvi (1968) and Bazley, Brown and Izan (1985) on foreign-affiliated companies in India and Australia, respectively).

Another possible effect is that disclosure may be associated with different explanatory factors among different countries. For instance, in the English-language literature, size is very often reported to be strongly associated with fuller disclosure. However, Coenenberg, Möller and Schmidt (1984) report on the basis of a survey of German empirical literature that in Germany it is industry rather than size that is most consistently associated with differences in disclosure. A similar difference was found by Gray, Meek and Roberts (1991) who indicate that for US multinationals, disclosure is associated with multiple listings while such an association cannot be established for UK multinationals.

4.2.3 Issues in multi-period analysis

In the literature, three approaches can be distinguished to extend the time-frame of the analysis beyond a single period:

- Pooling of observations from different periods in event studies.
- Comparative static studies.
- Studies of change processes in absolute time.

Pooled-observation studies

Studies of this type focus on disclosure change rather than extent of disclosure, and therefore tend to be single-item studies. Whittred

(1987) and Blommaert (1995) contain examples of this approach. Both studies deal with the inclusion of consolidated financial statements in the annual report. In this approach, data are collected on first consolidations occurring within a given period for a number of companies. The decision to consolidate is related to financial or other characteristics of the company in the year of its first consolidation. In this way, the calendar year in which first consolidation occurs plays no role in the analysis, and observations across a number of years are pooled in a single analysis.

Comparative static studies
These studies compare disclosure practices at two distinct points in time, without observing the year-on-year changes by which disclosure changed during the intervening period. This approach can be used for single-item studies (Bircher 1988), multi-item but unaggregated studies (Murphy, 1988) and for index-type studies (Barrett, 1977). In all three examples, the analysis is qualitatively orientated, and relies largely on a discussion of changes in the environment in which financial reporting takes place. Leftwich, Watts and Zimmerman (1981), however, includes a statistical analysis of changes in disclosure practice described in terms of comparative statics.

Change process studies
Studies in this category would take into account the absolute time at which disclosure change occurs, or at any rate the timing of disclosure change by one company relative to that of other companies. As a framework for such studies, Gibbins, Richardson and Waterhouse (1992:51-52) suggest the body of literature known as 'innovation diffusion' studies. This framework has been used in a number of studies in financial reporting change[4], but most of these studies,

---

[4] See Rogers (1983). The earliest suggestion of the usefulness of this framework in financial accounting is Tritschler (1970). Empirical studies on this basis include Copeland and Shank (1971, on LIFO accounting), Comiskey and Groves (1972, on accounting for installment sales), Parker (1977,

including the examples cited by Gibbins *et al.* (1992), deal with valuation and income determination (*e.g.* the dissemination of LIFO) rather than disclosure.

4.3 Outline of present empirical study

This section outlines the approach to be used in the present study. This approach should be seen as a pragmatic continuation of the lines discernible in previous studies. In this section, the general framework of the analysis is discussed first, followed by a discussion of the main choices made in data collection.

4.3.1 Framework of analysis

The body of research on 'diffusion of innovations' has been chosen as a general framework for this study. As indicated in the review of previous empirical work, the use of a 'diffusion of innovation' perspective has characterized some previous research in the area of financial reporting. The present study, which was introduced in chapter 1 as an exploration of the characteristics of the process of disclosure change in the Netherlands, can be structured along the lines suggested by the more general model of innovation diffusion.

As described in Rogers (1983), 'diffusion' or 'innovation diffusion' processes can be observed in areas studied by a variety of scientific disciplines. These processes share some fundamental properties across discipline boundaries. Hence, recognizing a process in any area of research as a diffusion process gives access to a body of terminology, questions and hypotheses that help to structure an analysis of that process.

---

on consolidated financial reporting), Bao and Bao (1989, on LIFO accounting).

Diffusion can be described as the process by which (1) an innovation (2) is communicated through certain channels (3) over time (4) among the members of a social system (Rogers, 1983). Closely related to the notion of 'diffusion' is the concept of 'adoption'. Adoption relates to the demand side of innovation, to the question of whether individuals will accept or reject an innovation when it is brought to their attention. A diffusion process can therefore be envisaged as the result of numerous individual adoption decisions. On the basis of this definition, the change of financial statement disclosure in the Netherlands during the post-war period can be interpreted as an innovation diffusion process.

In general terms, an innovation is defined by Rogers (1983:11) as 'an idea, practice or object that is perceived as new by an individual or other unit of adoption'. In the context of financial statement disclosure, this implies that, as is frequently the case in diffusion studies, the boundaries of the innovation are not necessarily clear-cut. One might interpret every extension of financial statement disclosure as an innovation in its own right, or, conversely, one might consider the notion of 'openness in financial reporting' as a single innovation that was diffused in the Netherlands during the entire post-war period. For the present it suffices to recognize that the change in financial reporting during the post-war period represents at least one innovation in the sense of the word used here.
That this innovation occurred in the context of a definite social system was shown in chapter 3. By documenting the importance attached in the Netherlands to the notion referred to in that chapter as the 'Dutch system' of financial reporting and reporting regulation, it was made clear that financial reporting was not an activity undertaken by a collection of isolated reporting entities. Rather, it was observed that the population of companies formed a group that was clearly demarcated (by nationality and company law), where norms and values concerning financial reporting were communicated and to some extent shared, and which contained potential role models (large companies) and potential change agents (the financial press, the auditing profession).

To complete the discussion of the definition of 'diffusion', attention is drawn to the obvious facts that disclosure change, seen as a diffusion process, was characterized by a definite time dimension and relied largely (though not necessarily exclusively) on the use of communication channels rather than on repeated and independent invention by each individual adopter.

Once a change process is recognized as a diffusion process, the following aspects suggest themselves for analysis (Rogers, 1983: chapter 2):

1. The source of the innovation and the timing of its first and subsequent adoptions.
2. The rate of adoption of different innovations in a single social system and the characteristics of innovations that are related to the rate of adoption. Such characteristics can include the relative advantages, complexity and observability of innovations.
3. Correlates of innovativeness, that is, characteristics of adopters that are associated with their propensity to adopt.
4. Tracing interadopter communication channels or communication networks and identifying change agents.
5. Use of communication channels at different stages of the individual adoption process.
6. The rate of adoption of similar innovations in different systems.
7. Consequences of innovation.

In this study, these questions will be addressed under two main headings (which correspond to chapters 5 and 6).
Chapter 5 will discuss issues related to adopter characteristics. This corresponds mainly to question 3 listed above, although elements of question 4 will be dealt with as well. Relevant adopter characteristics can be derived from three sources. First, the general diffusion literature has identified a number of adopter characteristics that tend to be associated with propensity to adopt across research disciplines. Second, the cross-sectional disclosure literature discussed in this chapter has produced a degree of consensus on company characteris-

tics associated with propensity to disclose. Third, the historical background of developments in the Netherlands, outlined in chapter 3, suggests a number of relevant characteristics.

Chapter 6 can be characterized in terms of innovation characteristics. The discussion in that chapter revolves primarily around questions 1 and 2 listed above. Question 6 will be addressed in terms of a comparison with disclosure development abroad. Elements of questions 4 and 5 will be discussed as well. Question 7 is beyond the scope of this study.

4.3.2 *Outline of data collection*
The general framework outlined above, combined with the inevitable resource constraints, implies a trade-off in the collection of the required data. This trade-off involves the number of disclosure items, the number of years within the 1945-1983 period and the number of companies to be studied.

In this study, this trade-off has been resolved by the selection of a relatively small number of disclosure areas, to be studied on a year-by-year basis for a substantial fraction of the population of listed companies. In other words, quantity in terms of disclosure items has to some extent been sacrificed in exchange for quantity in terms of the number of years and the number of companies. While emphasizing that the choice as outlined here cannot rigorously be shown to be the most appropriate in the circumstances, some arguments can be cited to justify this approach. This takes up the remainder of this section. Sections 4.4 and 4.5 discuss the details of the company and the disclosure item sample.

The objectives of this study might be attained by either a comparative static study or a study of year-on-year changes in disclosure. A year-by-year study was chosen because of the scarcity of this type of study in the literature. As a result, data had to be collected for a relatively large number of years, which was compensated for by a reduction in the number of disclosure items. A positive rationale for limiting the number of items to be studied is the need for detailed studies by item. To understand the process of disclosure change, the circumstances in which each disclosure item was introduced and adopted in the Netherlands should be known in some detail. It was found in chapter 2 that, next to proprietary costs, the information structure was a vital determinant of disclosure. In order for a company to consider a disclosure, this disclosure must be part of the array of available disclosures. Moreover, one would not expect substantial disclosures if parties outside the firm were not aware of the fact that the item in question was part of the disclosure array. In other words, a disclosure must be 'discovered' and accepted as a potential disclosure, either by domestic invention or by observation of foreign practices. To understand the adoption of a particular disclosure requires that one knows the extent to which that disclosure was or became part of the common body of knowledge in financial reporting.

4.4 Sample of disclosure items

The quality of financial statements often referred to as 'extent of disclosure' defies attempts at exact measurement. Disclosure, as a characteristic of an entire annual report, can be thought of as the sum of a collection of parts, but neither the identification of these parts nor the determination of their weights in the total extent of disclosure are easily resolved issues.

Breaking down total disclosure into individual disclosures is hindered by the fact that there is no obvious downward limit of disaggregation in financial statement data. Obviously, financial reporting practice has coped with this difficulty by developing some commonly accepted data groupings that can be considered as basic disclosure units, such as 'cost of sales' or 'provision for pension liabilities'. This study will basically adhere to common usage, but it should be realized that such usage can cover considerable variation in meaning.

Even if disclosure elements can be identified and compared among different sets of financial statements, the contributions of such individual elements to 'total disclosure' are not easily assessed.

Again, in financial reporting practice the different importance of various disclosure items is readily accepted. This is true even though empirical research into the perceived importance of various disclosure elements has rarely proceeded beyond the precision of five-point ordinal scales and has fairly consistently shown considerable differences among various groups of parties involved in financial reporting[5].

This background indicates the margin of uncertainty involved in both the demarcation of disclosure items and the assessment of their importance. The following listing of disclosure items to be studied here is therefore the product of a selection process that relies to a substantial degree on a subjective assessment of developments in postwar Dutch disclosure. The considerations, criteria and constraints that played a role in this selection are discussed following the list of items. In this study, a total of 13 disclosure items were selected[6]. These items can be grouped into the following 9 areas:

1. disclosure of sales (or turnover);
2. inclusion of comparative figures;
3. disclosure of tax costs and tax liabilities (2 items);
4. employment-related disclosures (2 items);
5. inclusion of consolidated financial statements;
6. inclusion of a funds statement;
7. disclosure of current cost data (2 items);
8. disclosure of earnings per share.
9. disclosure of segmented sales and operating income (2 items);

---

[5] A number of studies on differing perceptions of disclosure are available from the period studied here, such as Chandra (1974), Benjamin and Stanga (1977) and Firth (1978). Lang and Lundholm (1993) contains more recent indications of varying perceptions of disclosure quality among financial analysts. See, however, Courtis (1992) for opposite results.

[6] Appendix A contains a full listing of these items and a description of the disclosure data gathered with regard to these items.

A number of criteria have been applied to arrive at this selection. Materials regarding the substantial correctness of the application of these criteria to the nine selected items will be found in chapter 6, where all of the items are discussed in detail. The criteria used are:

a. The disclosure should be an 'innovation' of the 1945-1983 period. There should be no or only limited disclosure in 1945, and a substantial degree of disclosure in the subsequent period. Universal disclosure need not be achieved during this period.
b. There should be sufficient scope for voluntary disclosure of the selected items. Since major regulation was not introduced until 1970, this requirement says in fact that a large proportion of the selected disclosures should remain non-mandatory following the 1970 Act.
c. The disclosures must be applicable to all or most companies. Otherwise (in the case of consolidated and segment reporting), it should be possible to decide on (in)applicability by means of relatively objective decision rules.
d. The disclosures should represent balanced diversity in the temporal patterns of their diffusion (*i.e.* some disclosures should be selected that are already being disclosed early in the period, and the selected disclosures should not all have reached universal adoption well before 1983).
e. Given the importance attached to costs of disclosure in the theoretical disclosure literature, an analysis of the relationship between the characteristics of a disclosure and the rapidity of its diffusion will have to take at least this factor into account. The disclosures included in the sample should therefore differ to some extent in their associated costs. A crude approximation of this characteristic can be found in the degree to which the mandatory disclosure of an item is opposed in the literature.
f. Some empirical material on the disclosure over time in other countries should be available.

On the basis of these criteria, a set of disclosures can be selected to serve as the basis for meaningful item-by-item comparisons among companies and for comparisons with developments in other countries. The operationalization of criterium e. is of course a major determinant in the confidence with which results from these individual item studies can be generalized to disclosure in general. As indicated above, assessing the importance of items, especially during the course of a 40-year period, is necessarily a subjective process. This criterion has been operationalized largely on the basis of a survey of the Dutch professional literature as used in chapter 3. The items selected are among those that played an important role in the 1955 and 1962 employers' reports discussed in that chapter, as well as in a number of other reports and studies on financial reporting practice during the postwar period[7]. In all, the selection of items would appear to capture a sizeable portion of improvements in disclosure during the 1945-1983 period. The number of items chosen for this study still places this study within the band-width of multi-item disclosure studies listed in table 4.1[8].

4.5 Company sample

Chapter 3 has provided no compelling reason why a study of voluntary disclosure in the post-war Netherlands should be restricted to listed companies. In fact, the voluntary publication of financial statements by some large non-listed companies was occasionally cited as yet more evidence of the suitability of a voluntary approach to

---

[7] Notably Otten (1954), the published norms of the Henri Sijthoff award; *Open Boek*, Een nota over de behoefte van werknemers aan informatie over hun onderneming (Amsterdam: Federatie Nederlandse Vakvereniging, 1976), the *Beschouwingen naar aanleiding van de Wet op de Jaarrekening van Ondernemingen* (Considered Views) published by the Tripartite Study Group from 1971 onwards.

[8] In fact, the number of disclosure items is approximately equal to that used in Wagenhofer (1990) when the effect of combining disclosure 'items' into disclosure 'areas' is taken into account.

financial reporting in the Netherlands[9]. Yet the relative scarcity of accessible collections of financial statements of non-listed companies has resulted in a restriction of this study to listed companies.

The population to be sampled was initially defined as all companies with shares listed at the Amsterdam stock exchange at any moment between january 1945 and december 1983. Companies meeting this requirement were identified by means of *Van Oss' Effectenboek*[10], supplemented by data from the financial daily *Het Financieele Dagblad* and the annual Stock Exchange guide commonly referred to as *De Effectengids*[11]. Figure 4.1 shows the development of the population of listed companies over time. As will be evident, the population has changed considerably during the post-war period. Whereas the 1950s saw an increase in the number of listed companies, the total number was reduced rather dramatically by a wave of mergers and acquisitions starting in the late 1960s. As a result of mergers and acquisitions, the identification of individual companies is not always straightforward. As a general rule, the continued existence of the legal entity, that is, the limited liability company of which the shares are listed, is assumed to imply the continued existence of the company. Changes in name or in the nature of the enterprise carried out within the limited liability company are, in general, assumed not to affect the continued existence of the company in question.

Exceptions to this rule have been made in cases of amalgamations of companies. For this purpose, a distinction is made between mergers and take-overs. This distinction is usually supported by indications

---

[9] *E.g.* 'Waarom publiceerde Honig N.V. haar jaarverslag?' (Honig, 1963), and 'Openheid bij de naamloze vennootschap: Het jaarverslag 1968 van de Steenkolen-Handelsvereeniging N.V. te Utrecht' (Brands, 1969).

[10] *Van Oss' Effectenboek* (Groningen: Noordhoff, 1903-1955; Den Haag: Leopold, 1956-1978).

[11] *Gids bij de Prijscourant van de Vereniging voor de Effectenhandel te Amsterdam* (Amsterdam: de Bussy, annually since 1888).

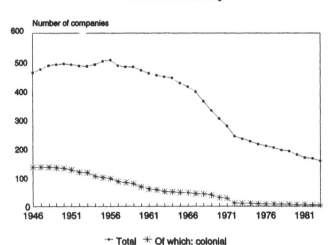

Figure 4.1 Listed companies
Amsterdam Stock Exchange

— Total ＊ Of which: colonial

such as the relative size of the companies involved, the type of process used in amalgamation and the name of the new combination.

In the case of a merger, rather than a take-over, the listing of both companies is assumed to have ended, and a third company is assumed to be newly listed. In the year of the merger, the population decreases by two and increases by one. When one company is acquired by another, the acquired company is removed from the population. The status of the acquiring company is unaffected.
These rules apply, with some modifications, to the situation in which only one of the companies involved is listed. The possible outcomes of these amalgamations are:

-   The listed company is considered the acquiring company; its status within the population is unaffected by the acquisition.
-   The listed company is considered the acquired company and therefore removed from the population.
-   The company resulting from a merger obtains a listing, in which case it is considered as a new listing replacing the merged

142

companies to the extent that they were listed.
- The company resulting from a merger is not listed, in which case any merging companies that were listed are removed from the population.

The population of companies defined in this way was been narrowed down by excluding companies whose financial reporting, with regard to extent of disclosure, was expected to be imperfectly comparable with that of the main body of listed companies. Eliminations on the basis of this criterion included investment companies, companies whose activities were largely confined to the Netherlands East Indies and companies active in the financial sector.

Investment companies
Companies whose activities are limited to holding securities of other companies were excluded since their most relevant disclosures are incomparable to those of operating companies. This group excludes recognized investment funds, but also ordinary limited liability companies that are dedicated to holding securities of specified listed companies (*e.g.* 'Calvé-Delft', 'Moeara Enim' and 'Dordtsche Petroleum').
Evidently, companies may change categories. A number of investment companies started life as operating companies (*e.g.* 'Moluksche Handelsvennootschap'). Their exclusion from the sample space required an element of judgement.

East-Indian/Indonesian companies
Companies with activities and assets exclusively or almost exclusively in the Netherlands East Indies/Indonesia have been removed from this population. The rationale for excluding this rather substantial number of companies is that, for the majority of these companies, normal operations were impossible during all but a few years of the period under study. Hence, their reporting practices were affected by overriding concerns that did not apply to the European companies.
From early 1942 until late in 1945, no operations were possible at

143

all, due to the removal of European personnel during the Japanese occupation. From 1945 until 1950, operations of most companies were made impossible or seriously hindered by the hostilities preceding Indonesia's independence. After independence, a brief period of tranquillity allowed some companies to recuperate. In 1957, however, Dutch investments in Indonesia were nationalized. What was left was a group of approximately 150 listed Dutch companies whose assets consisted almost exclusively of claims on the Indonesian government. Most of these companies continued a slumbering existence until 1970, when a final settlement was reached.

For these reasons, a considerable proportion of companies listed at the Amsterdam stock exchange from 1945 until 1970 are disregarded in this study. Evidently, there is no clear-cut distinction between colonial and non-colonial companies. A number of these companies have been retained in the population, as they managed by diversification to survive the nationalizations of 1957. On this basis, companies like 'Deli Maatschappij' and 'Rubbercultuurmaatschappij "Amsterdam"' have been retained in the population.

Banks and insurance companies
Empirical disclosure studies tend to leave out banks and insurance companies for the reason that at least part of their disclosures are incomparable with those of other industries. In this study, in which disclosure of individual items figures as prominently as the study of aggregate disclosure, banks and insurance companies could have been included in investigations of those companies that apply to all types of industries (number of employees, tax costs). However, these companies have been subject to a different regulatory regime than ordinary listed companies. Their disclosure choices may therefore have been affected by different forces. This study does not address this issue.

From the population as defined by the three exclusions listed above, a sample of companies has been drawn, according to the following procedure:

1. As indicated above, the sample should reflect the size of the population in the sense that for each year, the proportion of sample to population size should be constant. This proportion has been set at 30%. With this percentage, the absolute sample size varies between 45 and 101 companies, which corresponds to sample sizes in earlier studies[12].
2. From the population of companies that were listed on December 31st, 1945, a random sample is drawn of 30%.
3. Similar samples of 30% are drawn from the four subgroups of companies newly listed during the periods 1946-1955, 1956-1965, 1966-1975, 1976-1983. 'Newly listed' companies that are in effect the product of a merger including at least one previously listed company are not included in these subsamples.
4. The five chronological subsamples (or cohorts) are combined to form one sample. Each company sampled in any of the five cohorts remains part of the sample for each year from 1945 or its first listing until its delisting.

This sample is then modified in the following manner:

5. The listing of some sampled companies may end because of a merger. In that case, the company resulting from the merger, if listed, is included in the sample for the years following the merger.
6. The multinational companies Philips, Royal Dutch Petroleum/Shell, Unilever and AKU/Akzo have been selected regardless of the outcome of the procedure sketched above. These companies were selected because their foreign listings have traditionally led to the perception that they played an role in transmitting overseas reporting practices to the Netherlands (see also section 3.3.2).
7. Companies whose financial statements were not available in the collections of the Vrije Universiteit, Amsterdam; the Katholieke

---

[12] *E.g.* Chow and Wong-Boren (1987): n = 52; Cooke (1989): n = 90.

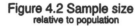

Figure 4.2 Sample size
relative to population

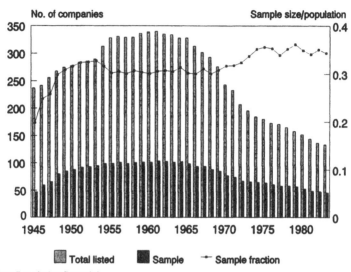

'total listed' excludes financial
and colonial companies (see section 4.5)

Universiteit Brabant, Tilburg and Erasmus Universiteit, Rotterdam were replaced by random draws from their respective cohorts (that is, a company listed in 1956-1965 is replaced by a company from the same age-group)[13]. The companies sampled according to this procedure are listed in Appendix B. The

---

[13] In all, the financial statements of 24 companies could not be retrieved, at least not for all the years during which they were listed. All three university libraries have attempted in the past to maintain complete collections of financial statements of listed companies. Gaps in the collections should therefore in principle reflect random causes. However, it is conceivable that library staff will go to greater lengths to obtain financial reports of large and well-known companies. Since size is bound to be related to disclosure, this may cause the sample to be biased. Whenever possible, results of the present sample will be related to results of such previous Dutch disclosure studies as are available in order to asses the extent of any possible bias.

relation between the size of the sample as actually drawn and the sample space is shown in figure 4.2. It appears that the ratio of sample to population size fluctuates for most years between 30% and 35%. Two remarks are in order:

First, for 1945-1948, the sample fraction appears to fall below 30%. This is due to the fact that for a considerable number of sample companies the resumption of normal reporting practices after the war was slowed down by such hindrances as destroyed records or inaccessibility of assets. Figure 4.2 shows the sample of annual reports rather than the sample of companies.

Second, from the late 1960s onward, there is a distinctly upward trend in relative sample size to 35% or more. This increase in relative sample size indicates that the companies included in the sample are, on average, slightly longer-lived than the population as a whole. However, such deviations from population characteristics can probably be classified as acceptable sampling error. Given the precipitous decline in the size of the population (falling at a compound annual rate of 5.7% between 1965 and 1975), it seems that sample size has followed population size in an acceptable manner.

147

Chapter 5
Company characteristics and disclosure

5.1 Introduction

In chapters 5 and 6 the data, gathered according to the procedures defined in chapter 4, will be analyzed. This chapter discusses the extent to which differences in disclosure behaviour within the sample of companies can be associated with company characteristics. As opposed to the next chapter, which investigates differences in disclosure among items, this chapter is therefore concerned with differences in 'total' disclosure among companies.

Although 'total disclosure' is an elusive concept, it can be captured in a practical and simple way by a disclosure index as discussed in chapter 4. The 'total disclosure' by a particular company in a particular year can be approximated by the number of items disclosed by that company out of the total list of thirteen disclosure items (see Appendix A). Figure 5.1 shows the yearly average levels of disclosure (expressed as a fraction of the total number of applicable items) for the entire sample of companies.

The image conveyed by this figure is that of a steady increase in disclosure. The increase slightly accelerates in 1969 and 1970, but otherwise progresses at a fairly constant rate throughout the postwar period. Figure 5.1 appears to be a good summary of the contemporary mental image of the development of Dutch financial reporting discussed in chapter 3. In particular, it appears to support the more positive views on the effectiveness of the voluntary system in use in the Netherlands: an overall tendency to increased disclosure that is only marginally affected by the introduction of the 1970 Act. Contemporaries were aware of differences in the extent to which companies participated in this process of overall improvement. Tempelaar (1966:272) observed:

Figure 5.1 Total disclosure by year
(average across all companies)

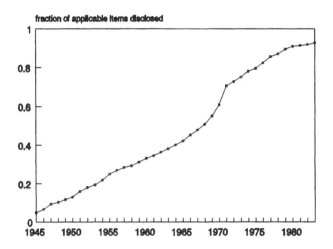

fraction of applicable items disclosed

(...) the results [of an informal survey of 1964 financial reports] will not be surprising to many, and, as confirmed in the comments of the financial press, display a tendency that can presumably be seen with listed companies in general: an interesting group of front runners, including the "internationals" that aim to provide shareholders and other interested parties with very good information; a tail-end of companies of which the boards apparently subscribe to Talleyrand's dictum that man has been given speech to hide his thoughts. And between these extremes one can see a large middle group aiming for improvements that are gradually being realized.

This chapter attempts to enlarge upon Tempelaar's observation by addressing questions as: how wide was the gap between the front runners and the companies making up the rear ? Is there more to be said about company characteristics[1] in relation to disclosure than that the multinational companies tend to lead the way ?

In order to answer these questions, this chapter takes the following steps:

Section 5.2 explores the extent of variance in disclosure among companies; that is, it characterizes the differences in disclosure among companies that subsequently have to be explained.

Section 5.3 demonstrates that there is in fact a certain consistency in the disclosure behaviour of individual companies: without consistency, there would be no point in trying to investigate systematic differences among companies by relating essentially fixed company characteristics to disclosure. On this basis, section 5.4 introduces various measures that can be used to summarize disclosure practices over longer periods of time.

Analyses of the relationships between these measures and various company characteristics are reported in section 5.5, which is the core of the chapter. Section 5.6 contains concluding remarks.

5.2 Variance in disclosure among companies

This section discusses in general terms the nature and extent of the differences in disclosures among companies and over time. Its main purpose is to assist in conceptualizing and envisaging the complexities involved in describing and analyzing the process of disclosure expansion witnessed in the sample of companies.

A first indication of differences in disclosure behaviour among companies can be obtained by adding more detail to the graphical representation of average annual disclosure, as in figure 5.2. Apart from the upward sloping curve of average disclosure for the entire sample (already shown in figure 5.1), some indications of the disper-

---

[1] Even though in the literature 'firm characteristics' is a more common indicator of the qualities referred to, the word 'company characteristics' will be used here because in this chapter the word 'firm' will be reserved for 'audit firms'.

151

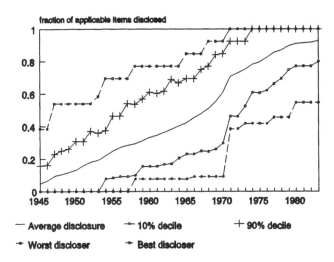

Figure 5.2 Dispersion of disclosure
(Total disclosure, all companies)

fraction of applicable items disclosed

— Average disclosure ●- 10% decile + 90% decile
●- Worst discloser ●- Best discloser

sion around this average have been added.

The two 'decile' lines shown in figure 5.2. represent the levels of disclosure not exceeded by 10% and 90%, respectively, of sample companies. Therefore, the area included between these two lines shows the variation in disclosure displayed by 80% of companies in the sample. As shown in this figure, this area or corridor gradually widens from about 15 percentage points in 1945 to a maximum of around 60 percentage points (equivalent to 6 to 8 disclosure items) in the late 1960s. After 1970, the differential declines again to about 20 percentage points.

Beyond the two decile lines, the best and worst disclosure scores for each year have been added to indicate the maximum disclosure difference between any two companies at a given point in time. This difference rarely falls below 50 percentage points and reaches a maximum of more than 80% in the late 1960s. At that time, some companies disclose almost all of the 13 disclosure elements considered here, whereas other companies disclose only one of the relevant items.

152

Figure 5.3 Disclosure trajectories
(illustrative companies)

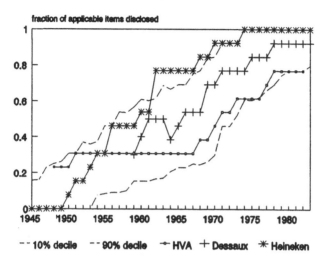

fraction of applicable items disclosed

--- 10% decile   --- 90% decile   —•— HVA   + Dessaux   * Heineken

Figure 5.4. Disclosure deciles
(illustrative companies)

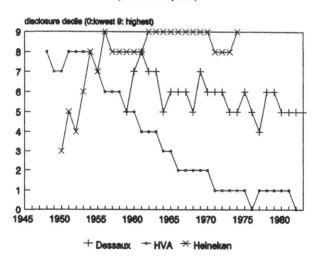

disclosure decile (0:lowest 9: highest)

+ Dessaux   —•— HVA   * Heineken

153

From figure 5.2, the influence of the 1970 Act is clearly from the strong increases in disclosure in or immediately before 1970. It may be noted that improvements in disclosure vary with the previous disclosure level: improvements are large for the worst disclosing company, and imperceptible for the best disclosing companies.

An important point to note is that this pattern of widening and then narrowing disclosure differentials is largely due to the choice of disclosure items. For all of the items, a substantial part of the introduction cycle from first to universal adoption falls within the 1945-1983 period. Hence, it is only to be expected that in the early years, disclosure differences are small since only few of the companies disclose any of the items at all. In the same way, at the end of the period when many companies disclose most or all of the items, there is little scope left for diversity. In other words, merely owing to the selection of disclosure items, the frequency distribution of total disclosure scores changes from sharply positively skewed in 1945 to a more or less symmetrical distribution in the mid-1960s, and finally to one that is negatively skewed in 1983. Nevertheless, it can be concluded that, with respect to the items studied here, there have, in fact, been large differences in disclosure among companies throughout most of the postwar period.

Within the total range of variation, one can envisage the disclosure histories of individual companies as in figure 5.3. In this figure, the 'disclosure trajectories' of three companies, HEINEKEN, DESSEAUX and HVA[2] are shown relative to the 10-90% interval described earlier. These companies were chosen to illustrate that companies need not maintain a constant position relative to each other.

DESSEAUX managed to maintain a position roughly around the average level of disclosure. HVA, on the other hand, did not increase its disclosure at all from 1950 to 1967 and hence, despite a

---

[2] Companies included in the sample will be referred to in the text by labels in SMALL CAPITALS. These labels are used to avoid ambiguities caused by name changes and mergers. Appendix B relates these labels to full company names.

promising start, was overtaken by most other companies. HEINEKEN started at a low level but sharply increased its disclosure over the period 1949-1956 and, from that time onwards, managed to maintain its position within the top 10% of disclosers.

An alternative way to represent the histories of these individual companies is by means of 'disclosure deciles'. These can be obtained by ordering, for each year, all companies according to their disclosure scores and dividing them in groups that each contain 10% of the total number of companies.

For the three companies shown in fig. 5.3, the decile profiles over time have been charted in figure 5.4. This way of envisaging the data clearly illustrates that 'good disclosure' is very much a relative concept. The failure of HVA to improve its initially good disclosure resulted in a gradual relative decline.

The fact that companies do not necessarily maintain their relative disclosure position implies that there may not be a group of individual companies that can unambiguously be classified as 'best' or 'worst' disclosers. Instead, companies may change status a number of times and may, in different periods, belong to different disclosure categories. For the group of best disclosing companies, this fact is illustrated by figure 5.5 which shows the disclosure experience of all companies that at one time or another during the 1945-1975[3] period belonged to the top disclosure decile.

As expected, the large multinationals (AKU (AKZO), PHILIPS, KONINKLIJKE PETROLEUM (Royal Dutch/Shell) and UNILEVER) belonged to the group of best disclosing companies for all or most of the period. More interesting, because less well attested in the Dutch literature, is the apparent fact that among the other companies that

---

[3] For the preparation of figure 5.5, companies with identical scores have been assigned to the same decile with the result that deciles do not always contain exactly 10% of the observations. From 1975 onward, the number of companies with identical scores of 100% disclosure becomes too large to be grouped into one decile. Therefore, figure 5.5 does not extend beyond 1975.

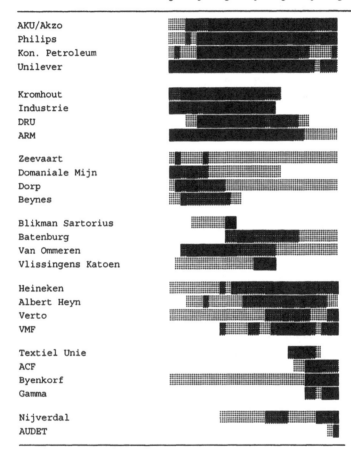

Figure 5.5
Partial disclosure histories of best disclosing companies

```
          1   1   1   1   1   1   1
          9   9   9   9   9   9   9
          4   5   5   6   6   7   7
          5   0   5   0   5   0   5
```

AKU/Akzo
Philips
Kon. Petroleum
Unilever

Kromhout
Industrie
DRU
ARM

Zeevaart
Domaniale Mijn
Dorp
Beynes

Blikman Sartorius
Batenburg
Van Ommeren
Vlissingens Katoen

Heineken
Albert Heyn
Verto
VMF

Textiel Unie
ACF
Byenkorf
Gamma

Nijverdal
AUDET

Period of listing
Company belongs to highest disclosure decile
Company belongs to second highest disclosure decile
Company belongs to any of eight lower disclosure deciles

156

appeared in the decile of best disclosing companies, there is a clear 'generational' pattern. These other companies succeed each other to occupy for relatively short periods positions among the best disclosing companies. During the late 1940s, one can see some ephemeral top disclosers (ZEEVAART, DOMANIALE MIJN). These companies presumably profited from the fact that during these years most companies disclosed no items from the list at all, which means that one or two chance disclosures could bring a company to a position in the top decile. These companies are soon eclipsed by more consistent disclosers, such as the multinational companies. More remarkable is a group of four or five smaller companies that consistently appear as top disclosers during the period to about 1960 (KROMHOUT, LOHUIZEN, DRU, ARM and perhaps VAN OMMEREN). In later sections, these companies will receive further attention. For the time being, it can be observed that some of these companies disappeared from among the top disclosers through delisting, while others were gradually replaced by companies that were already listed for some time, as HEINEKEN, ALBERT HEYN and VMF, or by new listings, as ACF and AUDET. The HVA and HEINEKEN examples mentioned above indicate that an absolute decrease in disclosure is not required for a company to disappear from among the top disclosers. Rather, companies that do not expand their disclosure will be overtaken by companies that do.

The point that companies may change their relative disclosure status over time has been made with some emphasis in this section, in order to provide a cautionary note regarding the results presented in the next sections. The remainder of this chapter relies to a large extent on measures of disclosure that try to capture companies' overall disclosure performance throughout the period in a single number. Given the sometimes large changes in relative disclosure, this will inevitably result in data loss. Against this background, the next section considers in more detail to what extent companies can be considered as consistently strong or weak disclosers, despite the fact that the relative disclosure status of individual companies can and does vary over time.

5.3 Consistent disclosure

Consistent disclosure occurs when companies that are among the early disclosers of one item are among the early disclosers with regard to other items as well. This section demonstrates the existence of at least a minimum degree of overall consistency, which is important in an investigation of the relation between fixed company characteristics and disclosure as measured by an all-period statistic.

To describe whether a company is an early or a late discloser, the most obvious measure is simply the year in which an item is first disclosed by the company in question. This measure will be used in principle to assess the degree of consistency among various disclosures, but with two modifications to take into account two complications in the set of observed disclosure data.

First, there is the problem that the data are censored. Companies enter the sample in 1945 or at the time of their listing and leave the sample in 1983 or at the time of their delisting. This implies that their disclosure history (if any) previous or subsequent to the sample period is not observed. Companies for which the critical event of first disclosure falls outside the observation period must be considered as left-censored (right-censored) cases. These companies have to be excluded from this analysis.

A second complicating factor is that companies may disclose some items incidentally. A particular item might be disclosed in one year because of special circumstances, but not in subsequent years. During the 1940s and 1950s, round-number anniversaries frequently prompted historical reviews including current data that were not regularly published[4]. To control for this effect, items are not considered as effective 'first disclosures' unless they were disclosed for a minimum of two consecutive years.

With these two modifications, 'observed first disclosure' (OFD) can

---

[4] Examples of this 'jubilee-effect' are documented in the next chapter. See also Munnik (1931:30) for a pre-war reference to this phenomenon.

for present and subsequent purposes be defined simply as the financial year in which a company first discloses a particular item[5].

Table 5.1 shows the correlation coefficients for the OFD's of all pairs of disclosure items. Inspection of this table shows that only four of the 78 correlation coefficients are negative, and none of these negative coefficients differ significantly from zero. On the other hand, the overall degree of consistency is not extremely high since, in total, 34 correlation coefficients do not (taken individually) differ significantly from zero.

To test the hypothesis that all correlation coefficients are zero, a test proposed in Steiger (1980) is used. This hypothesis can be rejected at the .001 confidence level[6]. Repetitions of this test for subsets of disclosure items showed that for all subsets with seven or more items, the hypothesis had to be rejected at the .001 confidence level.

It can be concluded that consistent disclosure involves (albeit to varying degrees) a substantial subsection of disclosure items.

---

[5] More formally, OFD is defined by the following operations:
- For each company and each disclosure item, the years are identified in which companies switch from nondisclosure to disclosure.
- 'Disclosure' is defined dichotomously, following the definition in Appendix A.
- Firms are to continue the disclosure for at least two consecutive years before a first disclosure is recognized.
- Firms already disclosing in 1945 are assumed to show an observed first disclosure in 1945. Similarly, firms not disclosing in 1983 are assumed to start disclosing in 1984. The requirement of two consecutive disclosures does not apply here.
- 'Observed first disclosure' is not defined when a company is right- or left censored with respect to a particular item in years other than 1945 and 1983.

[6] This involves the statistic $\Sigma (n - 3) * (z')^2$, in which z' is the Fisher transformation of the correlation coefficient and n is the number of observations on which that particular correlation coefficient is based. The summation is taken over all k possible pairs of correlations, and the statistic is Chi^2 distributed with df = k. The value found is 455 with df = 78, which is highly significant. Owing to censored data, the several correlation coefficients are based on different subsamples of the total sample of 140 firms.

Table 5.1 Correlation Matrix of years of observed first disclosure

	SALES	WAGES	EMPLOY	CONSOL	TAXINC	TAXBLNC	CCINC	CCBLNC	COMPF	FUNDS	SEGIND	SEGGEO
EPS	.37** (51)	.20* (52)	.32* (51)	.52** (40)	.15 (34)	.12 (42)	.23 (42)	.05 (48)	.41* (35)	.65*** (51)	.31* (42)	.34 (31)
SEGGEO	.51** (35)	.35* (38)	.42* (36)	-.07 (24)	.08 (30)	.19 (27)	.53** (38)	.50** (41)	.53** (28)	.41* (34)	.27 (33)	
SEGIND	.51** (37)	.16 (38)	.16 (36)	.50** (31)	.21 (27)	.20 (32)	.42* (37)	.09 (39)	.24 (27)	.35* (43)		
FUNDS	.40** (47)	.21 (50)	.45** (50)	.33* (36)	.38* (31)	.34* (38)	.38** (47)	.08 (46)	.44* (32)			
COMPF	.36** (60)	.41*** (50)	.33* (57)	.34* (55)	.29* (76)	.12 (72)	.13 (45)	.12 (67)				
CCBLNC	.15 (65)	.28* (63)	.24 (68)	-.01 (54)	-.01 (64)	.05 (65)	.55*** (60)					
CCINC	.29 (46)	.24 (50)	.27 (53)	-.03 (38)	.28 (40)	.51*** (46)						
TAXBLN	.34* (59)	.27* (57)	.36** (62)	.04 (57)	.49*** (69)							
TAXINC	.34* (56)	.32* (50)	.26 (54)	.27 (53)								
CONSOL	.41** (54)	.54*** (48)	.35* (51)									
EMPLOY	.44*** (64)	.48*** (69)										
WAGES	.45*** (62)											

two-tailed significance levels:
*** p < .001, ** p < .01, * p < .05
(): number of pairwise comparisons

disclosure items:

SALES — sales
WAGES — wage costs
EMPLOY — number of employees
CONSOL — consolidated statements
TAXINC — tax costs
TAXBLNC — tax liabilities
CCINC — current cost income statement
CCBLNC — current cost asset values
COMPF — comparative figures
FUNDS — funds statement
SEGIND — industry segment data
SEGGEO — geographical segment data
EPS — earnings per share

5.4 Measurement of multi-year total disclosure

This section introduces a number descriptive techniques for characterizing overall disclosure performance over longer periods of time. 'Overall multi-year disclosure' will be approached from a number of perspectives in order to compare the results of these various approaches and, as a result, to establish a degree of confidence in their validity on the basis of their correspondence. The measures of disclosure developed in this section will provide the basis for the analysis of differences in disclosure among companies in section 5.5.

5.4.1 Describing disclosure in terms of adopter categories

Innovation-diffusion terminology (see chapter 4) can be used to convert Observed First Disclosure scores to an overall measure of propensity to disclose. It has been found that innovation diffusion processes typically follow an 'S' shaped curve. If, in a graphical representation, time is plotted at the horizontal axis and the cumulative number of adopters of an innovation within a population is plotted at the vertical axis, it is generally found that the number of adopters rises slowly at first, then increases rapidly and finally levels of again. If the number of new (rather than cumulative) adoptions is plotted, the result will be a bell-shaped curve resembling that of the normal distribution.

This pattern can be used to define a number of 'adopter categories'. Normal distributions are symmetrical and characterized by their mean and standard deviation. This suggests a classification based on average moment of adoption (μ) and standard deviation of the moment of adoption (σ). A commonly used ordering of adopter categories distinguishes five categories:

1. 'Innovators': those adopting before $t = \mu - 2\sigma$
2. 'Early adopters': adopting before $t = \mu - \sigma$
3. 'Early majority': adopting before $t = \mu$
4. 'Late majority': adopting before $t = \mu + \sigma$
5. 'Laggards': adopting after $t = \mu + 2\sigma$

161

To the extent that disclosure changes do follow the S-curve pattern typical for innovation diffusion, it makes sense to classify companies according to their relative innovativeness following Rogers's classification scheme.

The adoption curves as observed in this study are not quite symmetrical (see also chapter 6). Hence, a classification scheme is used that is based somewhat loosely on Rogers' classification. The starting point is the cumulative frequency of adoptions implicit in Rogers classification. In normal distributions, the categories 1 to 5 correspond to the following cumulative frequencies:

1. the first 2.3% to adopt
2. those among the 2.4 - 18.2% to adopt
3. those among the 18.3 - 50% to adopt
4. those among the 50.1 - 84.1% to adopt
5. those among the 84.2 - 100% to adopt.

These percentages can be applied to asymmetrical distributions as well. When applied to the thirteen disclosure items, the results are as indicated in figure 5.6[7]. This figure shows how each company with

---

[7] Figure 5.6 is based on the following procedure:
- All instances of observed first disclosure (OFD) are ranked, by disclosure item, in order of occurrence. OFD is defined as in footnote 5 to this chapter.
- The ordered OFD's are divided into the five percentage segments listed above. This in turn establishes the cut-off years for the five groups. All companies first disclosing in a particular year are assigned to the same category, while the number of wrongly classified companies is minimized. When two consecutive first disclosures crossing a percentage boundary are separated by more than one year, the boundary year is assumed to lie in the middle.
- Finally, a correction is applied. On the basis of the cut-off years determined in the previous step, certain companies are added to the (1), (2) and (5) groups. Left-censored disclosing companies whose year of entry falls within the (1) and (2) groups are assigned to those groups; right-censored nondisclosing companies whose year of exit falls in the (5) group are assigned to that group. The total number of corrections

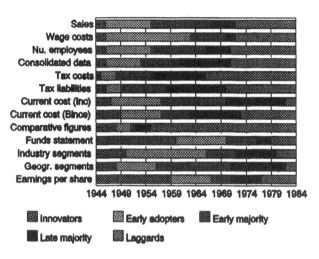

Figure 5.6 Adopter categories by item
(company characterization according to
year of first disclosure)

Sales
Wage costs
Nu. employees
Consolidated data
Tax costs
Tax liabilities
Current cost (Inc)
Current cost (Blnce)
Comparative figures
Funds statement
Industry segments
Geogr. segments
Earnings per share

1944 1949 1954 1959 1964 1969 1974 1979 1984

▨ Innovators   ▨ Early adopters   ▨ Early majority

■ Late majority   ▨ Laggards

an OFD for a particular item can be classified with regard to that
item. For instance, a company starting to disclose wage costs in
1965 would be regarded as an 'early majority' discloser.

To obtain a simple overall classification of companies, the numbers
'1' to '5' of the various adopter classes are taken at at their numerical value, and an average score is calculated across all disclosures.
The resulting averages should be treated with some caution, not only
because of the rather crude nature of the procedure in general, but
also because the averages of some companies may be based on only
one or on a small number of OFD's. An arbitrary threshold can be
introduced requiring that for an individual company at least 7 OFD's
must be available before a score for overall 'innovativeness' is
calculated following this procedure.   The 72 companies that meet

arising out of this procedure is less than 5% of the total number of
observed switches.

this requirement are listed with their average scores in table 5.2.

A general assessment of the validity of the ordering shown in table 5.2 can be obtained by comparing the top of that table with figure 5.5. As might be expected, the highest-ranking companies in table 5.2 are also the companies that occupy the top disclosure decile for longer periods of time. The large multinational companies appear near the top of the list, as well as a number of smaller companies like KROMHOUT, DRU and LOHUIZEN that, as shown in figure 5.5, were among the best disclosers during the 1950s.

The three companies discussed in section 5.2, HEINEKEN, DESSEAUX and HVA also appear at appropriate locations in table 5.2. HEINEKEN appears on a (shared) tenth place, slightly below the top because of its low disclosures in the late 1940s which cannot quite make up for its excellent disclosures after 1953. HEINEKEN's score is almost equal to that of ARM, a smaller company with a reverse disclosure experience (see figure 5.5): ARM disclosed very well in the 1950s but fell towards the rear in the late 1960s.

DESSEAUX and HVA provide other examples of similar scores hiding different disclosure developments. Both companies score close to average (3.8 and 3.7 respectively). DESSEAUX did in fact maintain its disclosure at a truly average level (see figure 5.3 and 5.4), but the average score of HVA is the result of good initial disclosures and a long subsequent decline.

In order to establish more formally whether the ranking of table 5.2 represents significantly consistent behaviour, a randomization test was carried out. For each disclosure item, the company classification scores (1 to 5) were randomly redistributed among companies. New average scores were calculated for each company. These data were reduced to a frequency distribution with eight categories. This procedure was repeated a number of times, and average frequencies calculated until these average frequencies were fairly stable.

These randomized frequencies were then compared to the data of table 5.2. The hypothesis that the actual data might have been obtained by means of a random sample from the averaged

Table 5.2

Companies ranked according to first disclosure across all items

Based on observed switches from nondisclosure to disclosure (OFD)

Observations/ Name	Average score based on 5-group classification	2-Group clustering
8 KROMHOUT	1.8	1
9 DRU	2.2	1
9 LOHUIZEN	2.2	1
13 UNILEVER	2.2	1
12 AKU	2.3	1
12 PHILIPS	2.3	1
7 IJSFABRIEKEN	2.3	1
13 KONINKLIJKE PETROLEUM	2.6	1
8 BLIKMAN SARTORIUS	2.6	1
9 THOMASSEN DRIJVER	2.7	1
13 HEINEKEN	2.7	1
10 NKF	2.8	1
10 VLISSINGENS KATOEN	2.8	1
12 ARM	2.8	1
10 MÜLLER	2.9	1
11 ALBERT HEYN	2.9	1
8 ASW	3.0	1
7 APELDOORN ZEPPELIN	3.0	1
13 VAN OMMEREN	3.1	1
12 OGEM	3.1	1
10 VMF	3.1	1
10 HV ROTTERDAM	3.2	1
--------------------------------- two group cut-off -------------------------------		
13 VERTO	3.2	2
12 NIJVERDAL	3.3	2
7 TWENTSCHE HANDEL	3.3	1
10 GROFSMEDERIJ	3.3	2
13 DORP	3.3	2
13 KNP	3.3	2
8 BALLAST-NEDAM	3.8	2
12 BIJENKORF	3.4	2
7 BLAAUWHOED	3.4	2
7 NIEAF	3.4	2
9 NETAM	3.4	2
8 HBM	3.5	2
7 VULCAANSOORD	3.6	1
13 FURNESS	3.6	2

Table 5.2 (continued)

8 GIESSEN	3.6	2
11 SCHOKBETON	3.6	2
9 BATENBURG	3.7	2
10 DESSEAUX	3.7	2
10 REINEVELD	3.7	2
7 ENOT	3.7	1
11 KEY	3.7	2
12 NIERSTRASZ	3.8	2
13 ROMMENHÖLLER	3.8	2
10 HVA	3.8	2
11 LINDETEVES	3.8	2
8 ZEEVAART	3.9	2
9 AIR	3.9	2
9 BEGEMANN	3.9	2
9 REISS	3.9	2
10 REESINK	3.9	2
10 STOOMVAART ZEELAND	3.9	2
13 CETECO	3.9	2
13 PONT	3.9	2
9 BERGOSS	4.0	2
7 DUIKER	4.0	2
13 HOEK	4.0	2
7 JONGENEEL	4.0	2
11 WERNINK	4.1	2
9 KOUDIJS	4.1	2
8 SCHUITEMA	4.1	2
11 TWENTSCHE KABEL	4.2	2
8 BEERS	4.3	2
8 HOUTVAART	4.3	2
8 OOSTZEE	4.3	2
10 REEUWIJK	4.3	2
9 WIJK & HERINGA	4.3	2
7 MARIJNEN	4.4	2
9 HOLDOH	4.4	2
7 ASSELBERG	4.6	2
11 KLENE	4.6	2

Note: 'Average score based on 5-group classification' is the average of scores across the 13 disclosure items. Companies are assigned scores ranging from 1 (early disclosure) to 5 (late disclosure) based on the timing of their disclosure relative to the average year of disclosure.

'2-Group clustering' is a nonhierarchial clustering of companies based on the years of observed disclosure for all items with pairwise deletion of missing data.

distribution was tested by means of a Chi^2 test, and was rejected at confidence levels of $p <$ .001 (Chi^2 = 27.6, df = 5). Hence, it can be concluded that the companies listed at the upper (lower) end of table 5.2 did, with some degree of consistency, disclose earlier (later) than those at the lower (upper) end of the table.

A clustering approach was used to determine a boundary between the 'upper' and 'lower' end of table 5.2. The 72 companies were clustered on the basis of the actual years of observed first disclosures. In a two-group clustering, the companies are divided in a group of 'early disclosers' consisting of 25 companies, and a group of 47 'late disclosers'. Cluster membership is shown in the second column of table 5.2. The clustering approach and the ranking on the basis of the 1-5 scores in the previous section produce almost exactly identical results. If the boundary between early and late disclosers is drawn at 3.21 (in terms of the average 5-point score), the clustering approach results in a minimum of three deviant classifications.
As a final indication of the validity of the ranking depicted in table 5.2, it can be shown that companies belonging to the upper half of the table were significantly more likely to win the annual Henri Sijthoff prize, awarded since 1953 for excellent financial reporting by listed companies (see chapter 3)[8].

5.4.2. Average Normalized Disclosure/Average Excess Disclosure
Using Observed First Disclosure has two advantages. The procedure relies on common-sense notions of disclosure timing, and can be interpreted in terms of innovation-diffusion. As discussed in the previous section, it produces results that appear to be quite plausible. An inherent disadvantage is that the method requires the actual observation of a first disclosure. Since observations on many

---

[8] Among the 72 companies in table 5.2 were 19 award winners, 16 with an average OFD score $<$ 3.5. Of the 53 non-winning companies, 17 had an OFD score $<$ 3.5. Chi^2 = 15.2 (13.3 with continuity correction); $p <$ .001

167

companies are right- or left censored, OFD-measures utilise a subset of the available disclosure data only. This section therefore proposes a pair of alternative measures based on all disclosure data for all companies. These alternatives are based on the total annual disclosure scores as depicted in figures 5.1-5.3.

In order to reduce the series of yearly disclosure scores of a given company to a single 'life-time' disclosure score, two approaches suggest themselves:

- The average over the life of the company of the differences between the annual disclosure scores and annual average disclosures can be calculated, resulting in a measure called Average Excess Disclosure (AED).
- Alternatively, the annual disclosure scores can be normalized before they are averaged, resulting in a measure called Average Normalized Disclosure (AND).

More formally:

$$AED_i = \frac{1}{(YrOut_i - YrIn_i)} \sum_{YrIn_i}^{YrOut_i} (d_{i,t} - \overline{d_t})$$

$$AND_i = \frac{1}{(YrOut_i - YrIn_i)} \sum_{YrIn_i}^{YrOut_i} \frac{d_{i,t} - \overline{d_t}}{\sigma_t}$$

Where $YrIn_i$ and $YrOut_i$ are the first and last years during which company i is listed; d is the disclosure score (as in section 5.1), either subscripted for company i or averaged across all companies for year t; and σ_t is the standard deviation of company disclosure scores in year t.

The *a priori* rationale of using AND rather than the more simple AED is that AND takes into account that the margin of variation of disclosure scores (compare the 10%-90% interval in figure 5.2) is not constant over time. In practice, however, the two scores differ

168

Table 5.3
Correlation of measures of overall disclosure

number of required observations of first disclosure :	> 0	> 6	> 9	13
number of companies:	139	72	38	12
correlation coefficients:				
AND/AED	.99	.99	.99	.99
AND/OFD	-.64	-.87	-.92	-.98
AED/OFD	-.63	-.87	-.93	-.98

All coefficients significant at p < .01.
'Number of required observations' sets a threshold for the number of uncensored observations of disclosure by a company. 'Number of companies' is the number meeting each threshold level.

little and are highly correlated. In the remainder of this study, the two measures will be used interchangeably. It should be noted that AND/AED is always calculated over a particular time period. Without further indication, this will be the 1945-1983 period. When AED/AND are calculated for subperiods, abbreviations will be used like AED5564 to indicate AED for the 1955-1964 period.

AED and AND can be compared with the scores based on observed first disclosure (OFD). Table 5.3 shows that the three disclosure measures are highly correlated, which provides a reasonable confidence that a classification of companies according to any of these measures will have sufficient validity to enable a meaningful analysis of the relationship between company characteristics and disclosure. As already indicated, however, OFD (and hence AED and AND) cannot distinguish between companies with identical average disclosure scores but with different trends in disclosure. Whether a company's disclosures improve or decline relative to other companies is not indicated by these measures. The next section discusses an additional measure to capture these differences in relative disclosure patterns.

5.4.3 AED/AND and changes in relative disclosure

For reasons indicated in the earlier discussions of the HVA and DESSEAUX examples, it is useful to combine the AED/AND measure with a second measure reflecting changes in the relative disclosure position over time. Referring to figure 5.4, one can image that trend lines are fitted for each company through the graph of disclosure deciles. The gradient of this trend line provides a simple indication of whether a company's relative disclosure position improves or deteriorates. This measure of the direction and speed of disclosure change can be plotted against the average level of disclosure in a scatterplot.

Figure 5.7 shows in general terms how such a diagram would have to be interpreted, while figure 5.8 shows the actual data for a selection[9] of companies. Figure 5.8 shows that there is considerable diversity among companies with similar AED scores. Naturally, companies with very high or very low AED scores tend to have gradients close to zero (if a company is already in the top decile, it is impossible to improve any further, and *vice versa)*. Companies with AED's close to zero display a wide range of gradients, indicating that their disclosure can be strongly improving, or deteriorating rapidly.

With this final extension, the descriptive apparatus required for the analysis of the relationship between company characteristics and disclosure is sufficiently developed. The actual analysis is the subject matter of the next section.

---

[9] Figure 5.8. includes companies which were part of the sample for 17 or more years. This restriction was imposed to exclude companies for which a disclosure trend line would be based on a small number of observations.

Fig 5.7. Types of disclosure histories

Change in relative
disclosure > 0

disclosure
lower than average
but improving

disclosure
better than average
and improving

AED > 0

consistently
worst disclosure

0

consistently
best disclosure

AED < 0

disclosure
lower than average
and declining further

disclosure
better than average
but falling behind

Change in relative
disclosure < 0

AED: Average excess disclosure (section 5.3.2)

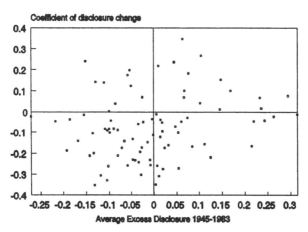

Figure 5.8 Average disclosure
and disclosure change

Coefficient of disclosure change

Average Excess Disclosure 1945-1963

All companies with 17 or more years'
annual reports available

5.5 Company characteristics and disclosure

5.5.1 Selection of relevant characteristics

This section briefly discusses the selection of company characteristics to be investigated in the remainder of this chapter. The factors selected here do not exhaust the possibilities in this respect. They do, however, represent a fairly wide range of company characteristics related to more than a single theoretical perspective. The selection of items should be appreciated, therefore, in the light of the exploratory nature of this study as outlined in chapter 1.

There are three sources suggesting company characteristics that may be associated with disclosure. First, there is the disclosure research literature discussed in chapters 2 and 4. Second, there is the literature on disclosure developments in the Netherlands discussed in chapter 3. Finally, the general diffusion literature has produced a number of frequently recurring characteristics of early (late) adopters.

On the basis of the previous disclosure research literature, company size and capital market activity are obvious avenues of investigation. Company size has been found to be significantly related to disclosure in nearly all previous empirical studies, an effect that can be explained in a number of ways. In terms of chapter 2, it might be argued that for larger companies the proprietary costs associated with certain disclosures are less because their data tend to be aggregated at a higher level. This lack of precision in the data may prevent or hinder some forms of adverse action. From an agency perspective, it has been argued that larger companies are faced with higher agency costs, which may justify incurring higher disclosure costs.
From an innovation diffusion perspective, it may be pointed out that, in general, size has been found to be an important covariate of innovative behaviour among companies (Brown, 1981: 156). Again, there may be more than one reason for these findings. One of these is that large companies have some advantages over smaller ones in adopting new innovations, such as greater command over specialist

172

knowledge. The relationship between size and disclosure will be examined in section 5.5.2.

A second important factor suggested by previous empirical disclosure research is capital market activity. It may be argued that financial reporting information can play a role in facilitating capital market transactions. As seen in chapter 2, the sale of ownership rights was one of the fundamental conditions necessary to create a simple disclosure game. More elaborate theoretical relationships between capital market activity and disclosure can be developed on the basis of agency considerations. Section 5.5.3 will address these issues in the context of the present study.

In previous empirical work, the relationship between industry and disclosure has not been shown to be as strong as that with size and capital market activity. Nevertheless, it does merit investigation. From a disclosure research perspective, industry can well be argued to be a potentially important factor in explaining differences in proprietary costs among firms. From an innovation diffusion perspective, industry can divide, to some extent, the total population in social subsystems with different patterns of communication and imitative behaviour. Industry effects are examined in section 5.5.4.

Size, capital market activity and industry have all been considered in previous cross-sectional disclosure studies. The present, longitudinal study offers the possibility of adding an additional dimension to these factors. It now becomes possible to see how these factors operate in the long run. As regards size, section 5.5.2 considers how company growth rates, that is, changes in size over time, are related to disclosure. Section 5.5.5 extends the analysis of capital market activity by considering the disclosure characteristics of newly listed and delisting companies. In section 5.5.4, dynamic aspects of the relationship between disclosure and industry investigated by considering the disclosure characteristics of growing and declining industries.

The innovation diffusion framework suggests that communication processes play an important role in innovation diffusion. Communication may take place through mass-media type channels, or through interaction among adopters and potential adopters. Both types of communication may play a role in disclosure improvements. A typical example of a potential 'mass medium' influence is the 1955 Employers report on financial reporting practices (see chapter 3). This type of influence will be considered in more detail in chapter 6. Communication between individual companies will be considered in this chapter. Section 5.5.6 discusses intercompany links through multiple board memberships. Section 5.5.5 considers the possible role of auditing firms in communicating new disclosures among companies. Even though 'audit firm' was not found to be an important explanatory factor in previous studies, the important role ascribed to the Dutch auditing profession (see chapter 3) would appear to warrant its inclusion.

5.5.2 Disclosure and size

Measurement of size
Several possibilities have been suggested in the research literature regarding the choice of a company characteristic to represent 'size'. Gross sales, total book value of assets, combined market value of debt and equity and other measures have been proposed (see Newbould and Wilson (1977) for a review). From the studies listed in table 4.1, it follows that sales or measures related to sales are the most frequently used size measures, but that other measures tend to be correlated with sales (see also Cooke, 1989; Watts and Zimmerman, 1978).

Lack of data prevents the use of sales as a size measure in this study for a large part of the period. It was not until 1969 that over one-half of the companies in the sample disclosed their sales. For this reason, total assets rather than sales are chosen to represent size, even though there are some problems associated with this measure. A potential problem is that it is not always possible to compare companies in industries of differing capital intensity. Another, and presumably more serious problem, is that, especially during the 1950s and 1960s, companies employed widely different accounting

174

policies with respect to tangible assets. On the one hand one can find companies using highly conservative accounting policies, including accelerated depreciation of fixed assets to notional amounts and use of the base-stock method for inventories. At the other end of the spectrum one finds companies valuing some or all of their tangible assets at actual or approximate current cost. Despite these shortcomings, and mainly because of the lack of a feasible alternative, total assets will be used as the basic measure of size.

To take into account changes in size over time, one would ideally collect size data for each year during which a company is included in the sample. For practical reasons, size data were only collected at four set dates: 1950, 1960, 1970 and 1983, or the closest year for which data were available on censored companies[10]. This results in at least one and at most four size observations for each of the 140 companies in the sample. Sales data were collected for 1970 and 1980 as well, to provide support for the choice of total assets. For these two dates, total assets can be correlated with sales for most companies. Assets and sales are virtually equivalent in ranking companies according to size[11].

Overall relationship between disclosure and size

Table 5.4 shows a clear correlation between various size and disclosure measures. In the table, 'Size' is expressed in terms of (1) total assets and sales, (2) in terms of the commonly used logarithic transformation of assets and sales and (3) in terms of 'normalized sales'. The latter, indicated as average normalized size (ANS) is calculated in the same way as average normalized disclosure (AND; see section 5.4.2).

---

[10] Total assets have been used as presented in the balance sheet. The only systematic adjustment carried out consisted in adding back current liabilities when working capital was included on a net basis in total assets. Consolidated figures have been used when available. In a few instances this implied that data for years other than the set dates have been used.

[11] Correlation coefficients of assets with sales are 0.98 for 1970 (n = 60) and 0.99 for 1980 (n = 58).

175

Table 5.4
Correlation of various size and disclosure measures

Disclosure	n	Assets	Ln(Assets)	Sales	Ln(Sales)	ANS4583
AED4554	100	.40**	.44**			
AED5564	117	.38**	.42**			
AED6574	60	.25	.56**	.27	.57**	
AED7583	58	.23	.64**	.24	.67**	
AED4583	72					.53**
OFD	72					-.54**

Notes: ** p < .001
Subperiod correlations are based on all available companies; AED4583 and OFD correlations are based on all companies with seven or more observed first disclosures.
ANS4583 is the weighted average of the normalized size data over all appropriate subperiods.

As in other studies, using the logarithm of assets and sales results in stronger correlations than using the untransformed data. The absence of significant correlations between disclosure and untransformed size measures following 1965 represents the increasing skewness of the size distribution as the largest (multinational) companies grow more rapidly than the other companies. For logarithmic size measures, the relationship between disclosure and size measures is stronger for later periods. This may reflect an actual difference between the earlier and later periods regarding disclosure behaviour, or it may simply reflect the larger amount of 'noise' in the early size data because of disparate accounting practices[12]. For the years following 1975, size-measures based on sales and assets give similar results, which is not surprising given the high correlation between assets and sales.

The relationship between size and disclosure identified in table 5.4 can be visualized in terms of cumulative adoption curves. One would expect that the adoption curve representing smaller companies lies below and to the right of the curve representing larger companies, as in the stylized representation in figure 5.9. This ideal picture can be compared with figure 5.10 which shows the development of average total disclosure in the sample. In order to prepare figure 5.10, all companies were ordered into four size quartiles at each of the four set dates for which size data were collected.

Figure 5.10 adheres by and large to the pattern sketched in figure 5.9. The pattern is clear for the largest and smallest size groups. For the two middle size groups, the picture is slightly more complex: during the period 1945-1954, the curves coincide and for the 1955-1964 period, the order is reversed with the third largest size group disclosing on average better than the second size group. The significance of differences in disclosure between the second and third size group are hard to determine, if only because of the weaknesses of the size criterion used[13].

---

[12] Notably the contrast between the very conservative valuations practised by some companies and the valuations based on current cost used by other companies.

[13] Apart from issues of significance, order reversals as observed in figures 5.10 are not necessarily anomalous. In fact, general diffusion theory has recognized this phenomenon as the so-called 'Cancian dip' (Rogers, 1983). In many innovation diffusion situations, there is a positive relationship between socio-economic status and propensity to disclose. But for the middle ranges of 'socio-economic status' it frequently appears from empirical studies that the order of adoption is partially reversed.

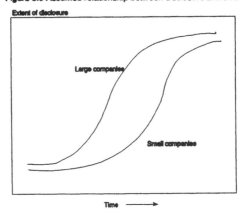

Figure 5.9 Assumed relationship between disclosure and size

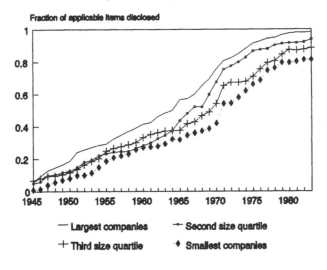

Figure 5.10 Disclosure and company size
(Total disclosure by size quartiles)

178

Size growth

An alternative relationship between size and disclosure is that *levels* of disclosure are related to size *growth*. From a contracting perspective, a growing company can be envisaged as engaged in a continuous expansion and reordering of the relationships between the various parties interested in the company. This process might be facilitated by the publication of high-quality general purpose financial statements. A general hypothesis might therefore be that growth, other things being equal, is associated with higher levels of disclosure.

Determining growth rates of size is hampered by a disclosure problem similar to that plaguing the determination of yearly size figures, as companies may change their accounting policies without disclosing this fact. Therefore, a company exhibiting a high rate of asset growth may simply be one that is eliminating its secret reserves. On the basis of published information, one can do little more than taking note of the existence of this problem.

It will be recalled that figure 5.8 contains a scatterplot of average disclosure scores against the direction of change in disclosure. Within this scatterplot, one can attempt to identify subgroups of companies defined in terms of size and size growth. One way to do this is to use size and size growth as dichotomous criterià by which companies can be divided in four groups:

- large, rapidly growing companies
- small, rapidly growing companies
- large, slowly growing (or declining) companies
- small, slowly growing (or declining) companies[14].

---

[14] The following definitions have been used. Large (small) firms are firms with ANS > 0 (ANS <0; for ANS: see note to table 5.4). Growth is determined by average yearly growth over the period for which data are available. Firms are classified as rapid-(slow-)growth firms if their average growth rates exceeds (falls short of) the average across all firms. In the preparation of graphs 5.11a-d, only firms for which data on 17 or more years are available have been included.

179

This classification of companies can be superimposed on the classification of companies in terms of average disclosure and disclosure change. The result is shown in the series of figures 5.11a-d, in which the relationship between average relative disclosure and trend of change in relative disclosure are plotted for each of the four size/size change groups defined here.

Although the data are not well suited to a formal analysis, it seems nevertheless appropriate to draw some conclusions on the relationship between size and disclosure. While it remains true that the companies with high relative disclosure scores are mostly large companies, it appears that maintaining or improving such a high relative position (upper right quadrant) is almost exclusively reserved to large, growing companies. Large companies with slow growth tend to be companies with higher than average disclosure, but for most of these companies this average represents the average of a declining trend. These companies start with relatively high disclosure, but are incapable of maintaining their advantage. Small companies with slow or negative growth are, with two conspicuous exceptions, all concentrated in the lower left quadrant, with a low and/or deteriorating relative disclosure position. Small but rapidly growing companies display a rather wide variety of experiences. Although many of them are located in the same position as small size/slow growth companies, others figure prominently in the upper left quadrant (worse than average but improving disclosure).

180

Fig 5.11a: small/low-growth companies

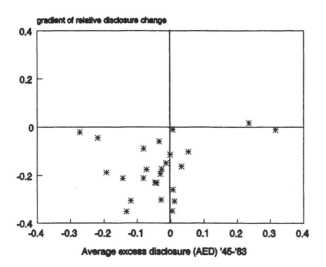

Fig 5.11b: small/high-growth companies

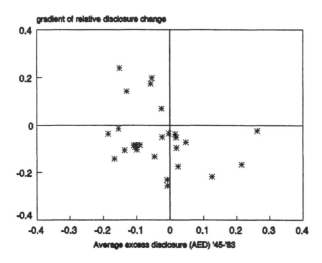

Fig 5.11c: large/high-growth companies

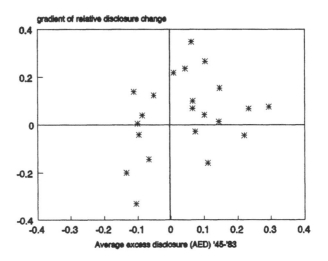

Fig 5.11d: large/low-growth companies

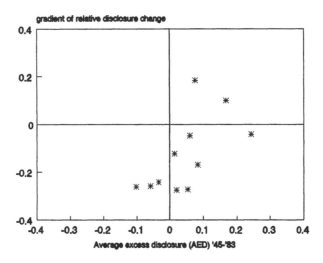

5.5.3 *Capital market activity*

The existence of a relationship between disclosure and the extent to which companies rely on the public capital market has frequently been mentioned or suggested in the literature. Examples of previous empirical work include Choi (1973), Firth (1980), Dahliwal (1979) and Meek, Roberts and Gray (1995).

On this issue, two types hypotheses can be formulated (*cf.* Frankel *et al.*, 1995), which will be investigated in this section:
- There is a *general* relationship between capital market activity and disclosure, in the sense that, over time, companies that rely more on the capital markets tend to disclose more.
- There is a *specific* relationship in the sense that increases in disclosure tend to coincide in time with new demands on the capital markets (*e.g.* Firth, 1980).

General relation between disclosure and capital market activity

In order to test the general hypothesis, companies have to be characterized as to their capital market activity over a longer period of time. This is done by means of two variables, share issues and use of bond financing.

Share issues The extent to which Dutch companies have raised capital by means of stock issues has varied considerably over time. In the immediate postwar years, notably in 1947, the number and volume of new issues was very large, so that (temporary) concerns were voiced about the ability of the capital market to continue to supply these large amounts of risk-bearing capital (Lentz and Ozinga, 1956). At the other end, Rietkerk (1986) has indicated that from the middle 1970s to the end of the period studied here, the net domestic supply of risk-bearing capital to Dutch companies virtually stopped. This shift away from share capital is said to have been induced by a number of factors including low real returns on equity holdings and unfavourable treatment of equity for tax purposes.

The decreasing reliance on share issues can be illustrated for the companies included in the present sample. For these companies, a complete listing of all their issues of common stock during the 1945-1983 period was compiled[15].

As indicated in figure 5.12, the percentage of sample companies issuing shares dropped from a peak of 15% in 1951 to 2-3% in the late 1970s. Combined with the falling number of listed companies over the same period (see figure 4.1), this meant a sharp fall in the total number of share issues.

As a result, the classification of companies as frequent or infrequent issuers depends on the period during which they were listed. Hence, for each company the expected or 'normative' number of share issues in any year is defined as the annual share issue percentage as displayed in figure 5.12. On this basis, a company listed in 1951 would be expected to have .15 issues that year, and a company listed throughout the period from 1945 to 1983 would be expected to have a total of 1.72 issues. Subtracting the expected number of issues from the actual number results in the number of excess issues (EXISS) of each company.

Use of bond financing As an alternative to issuing shares, companies can issue bonds. Owing to data availability, the characterization of companies in terms of their reliance on bond financing is rather less elaborate than that regarding share issues. A binary variable is used, indicating whether or not companies had bonds listed on the exchange at any moment during the relevant period.

Excess issues and bond financing are related to average normalized disclosure by means of multiple regression, with the results shown in table 5.5.

It appears that capital market activity is significantly related to (excess) disclosure, although the explanatory power of this factor, as indicated by R^2, is low. This might be caused by the division into subperiods, which may divide share issues from their disclosure effects: an issue towards the end of a subperiod may lead to

---

[15] Based on *Van Oss' Effectenboek*, and the *Effectengids* (various volumes 1945-1983), and on company financial statements.

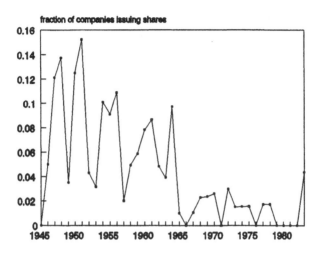

Figure 5.12 Share issues
(140 sample companies)

fraction of companies issuing shares

Table 5.5
Multiple Regression coefficients of Excess issues and bonds

	n	R^2	p (F)	Coefficients (probabilities)		
				EXISS*	BONDS	Constant
AND4554	100	.08	.02	.28	-.03	-.02
				(.01)	(.87)	(.85)
AND5564	117	.06	.01	.29	.08	-.01
				(.00)	(.68)	(.95)
AND6574	115	.06	.01	.30	.47	-.18
				(.16)	(.01)	(.09)
AND7583	66	.08	.02	.38	.58	-.40
				(.31)	(.02)	(.02)
AND4583	140	.10	.00	.18	.18	-.11
				(.00)	(.22)	(.56)

Exiss* :Excess issues during the appropriate subperiods

185

increased disclosure in the following years, which will, however, not be related to the previous issue.

One interesting, though not quite surprising aspect of the regression results is that in the course of the period significance shifts from share issues to bonds. In the two later sub-periods, from 1965 onwards, the fall in total share issues apparently diminishes the usefulness of share issues as a predictor of disclosure. For the entire period 1945-1983, though, share issues dominate use of bond financing as explanatory variable.

Relation of disclosure changes with specific share issues

A next step is to see whether increases in disclosure tend to concentrate around years in which shares are actually issued. If companies do review their financial reporting policies in connection with share issues, one would expect that they do so before the actual issue. Doing otherwise would leave the company with the same additional disclosure costs (if any), and without the benefit of facilitating the share issue by means of more extensive information. However, it is possible that more extensive disclosures will be made in the prospectus accompanying the offering, and will only later become part of normal reporting policy. Hence, in the following analysis, an increase in disclosure will be considered to coincide with a share issue in year t if the new disclosure appears in the financial statements covering year t-1 or t.

Given this definition, we can state the following hypothesis in the null-form: for each company, the proportion of its observed first disclosures that coincide with share issues is equal to the proportion of years containing or preceding a share issue relative to a company's life span within the sample. 'Observed first disclosure' is used as defined in section 5.2[16]. On this basis, the data shown in table 5.6 were compiled.

---

[16] However, for this particular purpose, disclosures made in first available financial statements over 1945-1948 were not counted as observed first disclosures.

Table 5.6
Concurrence of share issues and first disclosures

	number:	%
All observed financial years:	2984[17]	100
of which:		
years preceding or containing issues:	235	7.88
observed first disclosures:	792	100
of which:		
observed first disclosures		
coinciding with issues:	94	11.87

If first disclosures are uniformly distributed, the number of disclosures coinciding with issues follows a binomial distribution with p = 235/2984 and n = 792. Under this hypothesis, the probability of observing 94 or more coinciding first disclosures is negligible[18]. Hence, it can be concluded that a certain concentration of first disclosures around new issues did in fact take place. It should be kept in mind, though, that about half of the companies in the sample did not issue any shares at all in the observation period. Therefore, a large fraction of new disclosures can not be related at all to share issues. Nevertheless, the results permit the conclusion that for those companies that did issue shares, disclosure increases tended to concentrate around share issues[19].

---

[17] This is equal to the total number of financial statements sampled (3124) reduced by 140. For all companies, data considering the first year of listing were ignored since these years cannot contain observed first disclosures.

[18] The normal approximation results in a z-value of 4.17, p < .0002.

[19] For issuing companies only, 18.9% of observed first disclosures occurred during the 13.7% of financial years during or following which a share issue occurred. The probability of this occurrence under the null-

Multiple listings and multinational companies
Exposure to foreign capital markets can be an important influence on disclosure (Choi, 1973; Gray and Roberts, 1989). During most of the period, only four of the companies in the sample were listed on other exchanges. In a way, UNILEVER and KONINKLIJKE PETRO-LEUM had already been exposed to the British capital market before the war. In 1953 and 1954, PHILIPS, AKU and KONINKLIJKE PE-TROLEUM entered the New York capital market, followed by UNI-LEVER in 1961. Only in the second half of the 1970s did the prac-tice of listing shares (or certificates of shares) on other, continental european exchanges become more common. Among the sampled companies, HEINEKEN, KNP, OGEM, VAN OMMEREN, PAKHOED and VMF began to be traded on exchanges like Brussels, Paris, Frank-furt, Düsseldorf and Antwerp.

There are no indications that the listing on continental European exchanges did have any systematic effect on the disclosure of these last six companies. None of the companies, with the possible exception of KNP, shows any discernible increase in disclosure in the years surrounding their listing. On the contrary, the relative disclosure of OGEM and VAN OMMEREN continued to decline after their listing. VAN OMMEREN, being listed on four foreign exchanges, fell from the third highest to the fourth lowest decile in terms of total disclosure ranking.

Some of these companies were among the best disclosers in the sample (HEINEKEN and VMF being in the top decile for most of the time), but in all the record seems to be very mixed. The fact that these six companies had, on average, markedly higher disclosure level seems to be related primarily to their size.

Though there may be doubts about the impact of international listings among the next largest companies, it is clear that the four largest multinationals did figure prominently among the top disclosers (compare figure 5.5), a fact frequently ascribed to their foreign listings.

---

hypothesis is similarly small as for the entire sample.

188

This raises the question to what extent they can be identified with the 'innovators' in the Rogers' framework of innovation diffusion, that is, whether the multinationals were always the first to disclose new items of information. Table 5.7 lists the rankings of the four multinational companies on the five-point scale introduced in section 5.3.1. According to table 5.7, for most items one out of the four multinational companies was among the very first to disclose. It is, however, a rare occurrence to find more than one of the multinationals among the three to five (the number varies across items) 'innovators' with a score of '1'.

Table 5.7
Disclosure characterization of multinational companies by item

	UNILEVER	KONINKLIJKE PETROLEUM	PHILIPS	AKU/AKZO
Sales	1	2	2	2
Labour costs	3	2	2	4
# Employees	4	2	1	2
Consolidated	1	2	2	3
Tax costs	2	3	3	3
Tax liabilities	3	3	3	2
Current cost (Inc)	4	4	1	2
Current cost (Blnc)	5	5	1	2
Comp. figures	1	2	2	2
Funds Statement	1	1	3	2
Ind. segments	1	4	3	2
Geo. segments	1	3	3	3
Earnings p. share	2	1	2	2

Note: five-point rating as defined in section 5.3, with '1' referring to an early disclosure and '5' to a late disclosure.

UNILEVER appears to be the most consistent innovator, being among the first with important items as sales disclosure, consolidated financial statements, funds statement and segmental disclosure. AKU/AKZO on the other hand is never an 'innovator' although it figures prominently among the 'early disclosers'. The results for PHILIPS and KONINKLIJKE PETROLEUM are like those of AKU/AKZO with as most important examples the (not surprising) current cost disclosures of PHILIPS and the Earnings per share and Funds statement of KONINKLIJKE PETROLEUM with which it was clearly ahead of the rest. Especially with regard to these last two items, the influence of the foreign listings of KONINKLIJKE PETROLEUM appears most marked (the role of foreign influence on disclosure of individual items will be discussed more extensively in chapter 6).

In short, although PHILIPS, UNILEVER and KONINKLIJKE PETROLEUM are undeniably the most important 'innovators' in the sample, this conclusion can be qualified by the following two observations:

First, they appear to take turns in innovating, rather than being collectively at the forefront. In more than one instance, one of the three is among the 'innovators' while the other two follow with the 'early adopters', the 'early majority' or even later. Timing differences between the three can be material.

Second, and as an inevitable consequence of the previous observation, the three companies share the status of 'innovator' with a number of other companies.

Other companies that occasionally or repeatedly share this role are KROMHOUT (5 times), ARM (4 times), DOMANIALE MIJN, MÜLLER (twice) BEYNES, DORP, DRU, NDSM, HOEK, STOOMVAART NEDERLAND, STOOMVAART ZEELAND, LOHUIZEN, NKF, ROTTERDAMSCHE LLOYD, VAN OMMEREN and VERTO (once each). It is only to be expected that among the two-thirds of listed companies not included in the sample, there will be other companies with similar occasional early disclosures.

5.5.4 Disclosure and industry

A relationship between disclosure and industry can be explained in
two ways. First, it may be that disclosure is primarily related to
characteristics of individual companies (such as size, growth and
capital market activitities), and that industry effects are in fact the
reflection on the concentration of companies of particular types in
particular industries. Second, industry effects may be explained in
terms of the interaction of companies within an industry. On the
basis of the cost-benefit analysis of incremental disclosures explored
in chapter 2, it might be argued that, if some disclosures are accompanied by costs because of adverse action by competitors, such
competitive effects will be more severe in industries characterized by
more intense competition. From an innovation-diffusion perspective,
it might be argued that companies take their cue to adopt certain
innovations primarily from other companies with which they are
closely involved, *i.e.* from companies within the same industry.

When taken together, these arguments do not yield an unambiguous
overall hypothesis concerning the relationship between industry and
disclosure. The various effects may to a certain extent balance each
other: an internationally exposed industry may also be one that is
more competitive, so that the overall effect on disclosure is unpredictable.

Added to the difficulty of formulating unambiguous hypotheses is the
problem that 'industry' is hard to define. The CBS[20] standard
industry classification (SBI 1974) provides some guidance, but offers
little assistance in classifying companies with mixed activities.

These two difficulties combined make it difficult to proceed beyond
a general exploration of the relationship between industry and
disclosure. In order to make this attempt, companies have been
classified on the basis of annual report information following the
CBS-classification with a precision of at most two digits. These data
allow conclusions with regard to the two particular industry effects
discussed in the next subsections.

---

[20] CBS: Netherlands Central Bureau of Statistics.

191

Manufacturing versus trading companies

It appears that the disclosure pattern of manufacturing companies (CBI code 20 through 39) differs from that of trading (wholesale) companies (CBI code 61-64). This is illustrated by figure 5.13a-b, showing the scatterplots of average disclosure and change in relative disclosure introduced in section 5.3.3. Manufacturing companies appear to be evenly distributed through all quadrants. Trading companies are by and large limited to the lower-than-average disclosure positions in the left-hand part of the diagram, and tend to decline in terms of relative disclosure (lower-left quadrant). This result is comparable to that in Wagenhofer (1990:253). To explain this result it might be argued that barriers to entry, and hence the possible competitive losses due to disclosure, are generally lower in trading than in manufacturing.

'Strong' versus 'weak' manufacturing companies

The group of manufacturing companies can be divided according to 'industry strength'. Van Zanden and Griffiths (1989: 223-231) observe that major changes took place in the Dutch manufacturing sector during the postwar period, with 'strong' industries developing and 'weak' industries declining or even disappearing. It might be hypothesized that in 'strong' industries there would be a preponderance of companies with characteristics associated with good disclosure. Strong industries included the chemical, electrotechnical, metalworking and machine industries. Weak industries included textiles, clothing and food. When manufacturing companies in the sample are divided along these lines, the excess disclosures (see section 5.3) of each group can be compared. When this is done for the 1951-1973 period covered by the data in Van Zanden and Griffiths, it appears that the 'strong' industries do in fact manifest higher levels of disclosure, although the difference is not great[21].

---

[21] Strong (36 companies): AED5173 = .076 ; weak (20 companies): AED5173 = .003. Differences are significant (one-tailed) at the 5% level (t = 1.7147). The four multinationals were excluded from this analysis.

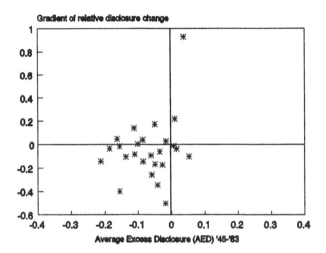

Fig. 5.13a Disclosure types by industry
Trading companies

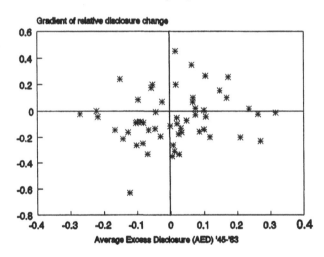

Fig. 5.13b Disclosure types by industry
Manufacturing companies

The weakness of the result is caused to a large extent by the textile industry. Although a 'weak' industry, the companies from that sector included in the sample distinguish themselves, on average, with quite high levels of disclosure. The 'weak' food industry, with the exception of HEINEKEN, adheres quite well to the pattern of a largely lower than average and declining disclosure.

In all, industry effects, if they exist, are not very strong. The data available for the present study do not allow very forceful conclusions (apart from the difficulty of arriving at a satisfactory industry classification, there is the problem that some industries are represented by only one or two companies), but it appears likely that if industry effects do exist, they are mainly company effects that happen to dominate particular industries.

5.5.5 Disclosure of newly listed versus delisting companies

The overall, or average level of disclosure in the sample of companies can change in two ways. On the one hand, there may be changes in the disclosures of listed companies. On the other hand, companies may be added or removed from the sample whose disclosure differs from that of the sample as a whole. If newly listed or delisting companies differ consistently from the average disclosure profile, either by disclosing less or by disclosing more, there may be a discernible effect on average disclosure. Reasons for expecting consistent differences include the following.

In the literature, it has often been asserted and confirmed by empirical studies that the extent of disclosure of unlisted companies is below that of listed companies (*e.g.* Cooke, 1989). As a rule, one would expect that at the time of listing, unlisted companies would have to revise their reporting policies and to extend their annual report disclosures. This is nothing more than a specific instance of the general association between capital market activity and extent of disclosure noted in section 5.5.3. For this reason, one would expect that the extent of disclosure of newly listed companies tends to be equal to the average level of disclosure in the year of their first listing. Alternatively, it is conceivable that newly listed companies disclose better than average. This might be caused by:

- 'Overshooting': since the 'average' extent to disclosure is hard to observe, companies may consider it prudent to disclose more rather than less in doubtful cases in order not to jeopardize the success of their public offering.
- Influence of role models: in deciding on an appropriate level of disclosure, the financial reports of the most prominent, or largest companies within the industry may receive relatively much weight.
- Industry effects: newly listed companies will tend to be active in growing rather than declining industries. Since the former tend to disclose slightly better than the latter (see section 5.5.4), this difference may be reflected in the disclosure practices of newly listed companies.

In all, for newly listed companies one would expect disclosure that is at least as good as average disclosure at the time of listing.
For delisting companies, the above argument can not simply be reversed, nor can it be expected that, in general, delisting companies tend to disclose less than the remaining listed companies. The reason for this is that companies may delist for two quite different reasons. One of these is financial distress leading to insolvency or even bankruptcy, the other being the opposite: financial health and good prospects, making a company an attractive candidate for acquisition or merger. One would not, as a rule, expect companies in distress to be among the very largest (since spectacular failures were comparatively rare during the period), nor to have been very active in the capital market in the period preceding their failure, nor to belong to thriving industries. But it is also possible that companies that are taken over belong in fact to the 'financial distress' group, and that their buy-out is a form of reorganization. For the group ending its listing by insolvency, lower than average disclosures are therefore expected. For the 'buy-out' group, no unambiguous prediction can be made.

195

In order to observe the actual relation between disclosure and changes in sample composition, companies are classified according to their mode of entry or exit from the sample. As in section 4.5, the main distinctions made are between mergers and acquisitions, and, within the group of acquisitions, between acquisitions by listed companies and acquisitions by unlisted companies and individuals (buy-outs). For each company, the average disclosure score (percentage of applicable items disclosed) was calculated for the first and the last year of its inclusion in the sample. The difference between these scores and the average score across all companies in these years ('excess disclosure') is averaged for each entry and exit group, with the result shown in table 5.8.

Table 5.8
Disclosure by mode of entry/exit compared with average disclosure

A. Additions to sample

type of change	n	average excess disclosure	t
new listing	54	.008	0.57
merger	16	.083	1.92*

B. Removals from sample

type of change	n	average excess disclosure	t
acquired by non-listed entity	28	-0.124	-4.01***
acquired by listed company	30	-0.019	-0.70
merger	23	0.026	0.66
insolvency or bankruptcy	13	-0.090	-3.00**

significance levels: *** p < .01, ** p < .05, * p < .10

196

The data in table 5.8 allow the following conclusions. Newly listed companies apparently model their disclosure on the average disclosure level in the year of entry. That is, they do not systematically seek to present more extensive disclosure than is common with companies that are already listed[22].

The reverse is not true for delisted companies. Companies that end their listing by severing all links with the stock exchange, either by insolvency or by takeover by an unlisted entity, have significantly lower levels of disclosure than the remaining listed companies. For the 'financial distress' group, this result is as expected. For the 'buy-out' group, this result may be interpreted as a dominance of negative reasons for take-over. It is also possible that their lower disclosures represent a size effect as it is likely that smaller companies predominate in this group.

There appears to be only a slight merger effect in the sense that merging companies do not differ significantly from average, whereas the resulting combination discloses slightly better than average. This may be the result of combining the best accounting policies of the combined companies.

5.5.6 Intercompany links

The influence on financial reporting fo individuals in top position in the organization has not received much attention in the disclosure literature (with the exception of Gibbins, Richardson and Water-house, 1990, 1992: chapter 5). Data availability limits investigation

---

[22] This conclusion is not without interest since imitative effects are not always accepted as satisfactory explanations of accounting practice:

> ...in many studies [of the positive accounting school], the explanatory power of the models is low (...) The alternative predictive model is that each firm uses the most common combination of accounting methods, a model with little explanatory appeal. The alternative model begs the question of what determines the majority accounting choice. Many accounting teachers would be uncomfortable with the explanation that managers choose their accounting procedures based on what most other firms are doing. (Watts and Zimmerman, 1990:10)

of these effects during the period studied here to two classes of people: members of the management board (*directie, (raad van) bestuur*) and members of the supervisory board (*raad van commissarissen*).

A rationale for investigating the influence of directors and supervisors can be derived from their legal function within the company. Throughout the period, preparing the financial statements has been the formal responsibility of the management board. Until 1970, the responsibility of the supervisory board was stated as 'supervising the drafting of the balance sheet and profit and loss account', before these were presented to the shareholders for approval, whereas subsequently (for large companies), the approbation of financial statements devolved on the supervisory board itself.

The joint responsibility for the contents of the financial statements was symbolized by the signing of the financial statements by all individual members of the management and supervisory boards[23]. The (legal) literature attests to the decisive role that directors and supervisors were expected to play in formulating the financial reporting policy of their company. This included the opinion that 'it is the task of the supervisory board to encourage the tendency towards a more open financial reporting' (Vecht, 1977: 167).

From the perspective of innovation diffusion, individuals can play an important role in transmitting knowledge of new disclosure options among companies. Instead of assuming that knowledge of contemporary disclosure practices is transmitted to all companies simultaneously and in a similar way (for instance, through mass media like the financial press), it may be assumed that each company is pro-

---

[23] Articles 42 and 52 of the pre-1970 Commercial Code; articles 42 and 52m of the post-1970 Commercial Code. Strictly speaking, the pre-1970 situation allowed for companies without supervisory boards and for supervisory board members without responsibility for the financial statements. In practice, it appears that nearly all listed companies had supervisory boards and that only a tiny minority of supervisors was not designated as so-called *balanscommissaris* (De Boer, 1957:24). See also the 1962 Hamburger committee report (*op.cit.*), p. 16.

vided with information through its own individual network of contacts. Moreover, even if individuals in top positions do not play an active role themselves in transmitting information on disclosure options and practices, the fact that a company recruits 'cosmopolitan' directors may represent an outward-looking stance within the organization as a whole.

Throughout the period there were numerous personal links among listed companies. Members of the management board of one company acted as supervisors with other companies, and many supervisors acted in that capacity for more than one company. Concern over cumulations of managerial or supervisory responsibilities in one person repeatedly surfaced in the postwar Dutch literature on company law and business administration.

It is conceivable that functioning in more than one company may have led to direct transmission of information on disclosure options. However, it is also possible to envisage the relationship between multiple directorships and disclosure in more general terms. Having directors or supervisors that serve with other companies as well may be an expression of a more fundamental quality of 'cosmopolitanness' that is frequently associated with innovativeness in the innovation-diffusion literature (Rogers, 1983:chapter 10). Appointing supervisors with broader experience may indicate a general willingness to stay involved with contemporary developments. 'Cosmopolitan' directors and supervisors need not necessarily be active in looking for improvements in financial reporting, but they may well be more willing to adopt changes in financial reporting suggested by others, such as the company's auditor.

Multiple board memberships as indication of 'cosmopolitanism'
A first way of looking at multiple board memberships is to see them simply as indications of interconnectedness with the world at large. The existence of links through multiple directorships to other companies, can serve from this point of view as an indication that a company is interested in drawing on the experience of other companies.

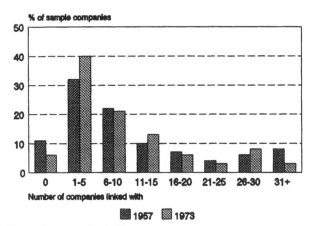

Figure 5.14 Multiple board membership
(Frequency distribution)

% of sample companies

Number of companies linked with

■ 1957 ▨ 1973

Note: 'Number of companies linked with'
refers to the number of listed companies
with which directors are shared

We can therefore define the variable LINKS as the number of other listed companies[24] with which a particular company shares (supervisory) directors. The values of LINKS have been calculated for sampled companies for 1957 and 1973[25]. For 1957, values of LINKS range from zero to 65. For 1973, there is a tendency towards smaller numbers of multiple directorships, which is a likely consequence of the falling number of listed companies. The maximum number of links falls to 41 (see figure 5.14). For both 1957 and 1973, correlations between LINKS and disclosure are quite high[26]. Before the conclusion is drawn that there is in fact a relationship between the two, it should be noted that LINKS is distinctly correlated with size.

---

[24] For this purpose data on all listed companies, not just those included in the sample, have been used.

[25] These years were chosen to represent the pre- and post-1970 period.

[26] The correlation coefficients between LINKS and AND are .39 for 1957 and .51 for 1973 (both significant at $p < .001$).

Multiple board memberships as communication channels

Rather than looking at the total number of links that a particular company, through its board members, has with the outside world, it is also possible to consider to which particular other companies a company is connected. This can be relevant, since a group of companies may have close links among each other, but few outside contacts, and be therefore, in effect, isolated.

If board members did play a role in communicating information on reporting practices, one would expect to find that board members link companies that are relatively homogeneous with regard to disclosure. In other words, the prediction of the disclosure of a particular company is improved if one knows the disclosure of the companies to which it is linked by multiple board memberships.

This is investigated for the years 1957 and 1973. For these years, a predicted disclosure can be computed for each company by calculating the average disclosure of all companies to which it is related by multiple board memberships. The same data for 1957 and 1973 linkages are used as in the previous section, with the added proviso that only companies with links by means of more than one director are included. In addition, to control for a possible size effect, companies in the upper size quartile were excluded as well. This leaves a total of 26 (17) companies for 1957 (1973), for which both actual and predicted disclosure are plotted in figure 5.15a-b. The dotted line in these graphs indicates the theoretically perfect relationship that would obtain if each company's disclosure were a perfect composite image of the disclosure of all companies that it was directly linked with.

As indicated by figure 5.15a, there is some correlation between actual and predicted disclosure for the 1955-1964 period, but also a clear overestimation of higher than average disclosure, and *vice versa*. For 1973, the picture is different and no clear relation between actual and predicted disclosure is apparent. When compared with the 1957 results, it can be observed that in 1973 there are hardly any companies with lower-than-average predicted disclosure. This implies that companies that are involved in multiple directorships are mostly related to good disclosers.

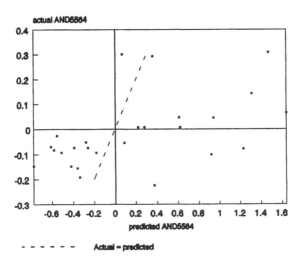

Fig. 5.15a 1957 Multiple directorships
as predictor of '55-'64 disclosure

Actual = predicted

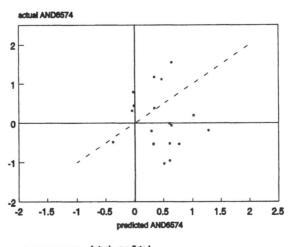

Fig. 5.15b 1973 Multiple directorships
as predictor of '65-'74 disclosure

Actual = predicted

Figure 5.15a can serve as a starting point in a further discussion of the disclosure practices of those smaller companies that were identified above as unexpectedly good disclosers (see also figure 5.5 and section 5.4.3). For some of these companies, the composition of their boards may help to explain their sometimes quite exceptional disclosure practices. Owing to the virtual absence of retrievable archival materials, discussing the influence of specific individuals on disclosure practices is limited to making informed guesses.

A closer inspection of the best disclosing companies in 1957 (19 companies out of 99 with a total disclosure score of 40% or more) reveals that many, though not all of them, had linkages that may have played a role in their disclosure behaviour.

Apart from the large multinational companies, a number of smaller companies appear as good disclosers, notably a number of companies in what may loosely be described as the metal-working industries: DRU, KROMHOUT, LOHUIZEN and in the second echelon THOMASSEN DRIJVER, GROFSMEDERIJ and BEGEMANN.

KROMHOUT, a shipbuilding company, had a relatively small board (two directors, three supervisors). The two directors had no outside positions, but each of the three supervisors did, bringing the company in contact with other high-disclosing boards. One of the supervisors was F.Q.H. den Hollander, former president of the national railways, a prominent member of the business establishment and a supervisory board member of KONINKLIJKE PETROLEUM. Another supervisor was P. Goedkoop Dzn, a member of the founding family who was also a supervisor with THOMASSEN DRIJVER, a manufacturer of metal packagings and also a company with quite good disclosure. At the THOMASSEN DRIJVER board (also fairly small, consisting of five supervisors) the KROMHOUT director would meet E.L. Schiff, a supervisor on the boards of PHILIPS and DRU, both high disclosers. DRU (heating equipment and other metal appliances) also had a small board of three supervisors, including P.W. Kamphuisen, a supervisory board member of AKU.

In a slightly different group were BEGEMANN, LOHUIZEN and GROFSMEDERIJ. Both BEGEMANN (machine building) and GROFSMEDERIJ (specialist forge) had on their board of supervisors A.H. Ingen

203

Housz, president of Hoogovens (not in the sample, but with a reputation for good disclosure[27]). Ingen Housz had been a member of the 1955 Rijkens committee on financial reporting, and would therefore have brought awareness of the report's recommendations to those company boards of which he was a member. BEGEMANN shared T.H. Ligthart as supervisor with LOHUIZEN (cast-iron productions), which shared another supervisor with Hoogovens.

At the risk of unduly complicating the picture, it can further be pointed out that the two groups outlined here were also interconnected. F.Q.H. den Hollander, of KROMHOUT and KONINKLIJKE PETROLEUM was also a supervisor with BEYNES, a rolling-stock manufacturer, and of VMF, a large machine-building firm. Both BEYNES and VMF shared supervisors with LOHUIZEN, while Ingen Housz was a supervisor on the board of VMF. Both BEYNES and VMF were quite good disclosers (ranking 27th and 36th out of 99).

The overall picture that emerges is that of a group of five or six smaller yet well-disclosing companies in the same industry. They had in common that their management and supervisory boards were quite small, and that a large fraction, usually a majority of their supervisors served with one or more of the large multinationals and/or with one or more of the other five. The fact that their boards were small appears to be of some importance. This factor sets them apart from other companies that were equally well connected, but where any board members with experience with well-disclosing companies were definitely outnumbered by others. This appears to apply in particular to the shipping sector. In that sector, networks in

---

[27] One factor underlying Hoogovens' disclosure may have been the European Community for Coal and Steel (EGKS). Among other things, the Community ran an extensive statistical programme, the results of which were generally presented as aggregates by country. Since Hoogovens was virtually the only Dutch steel mill, extensive information on the company could be extracted from EGKS-publications. Publication of these data in the company's annual report would therefore result in few additional proprietary costs (See Dankers and Verheul, 1993: 220).

terms of multiple directorships were even more tight than in the metallurgical sector, but the shipping sector did not distinguish itself by its disclosure.

The previous discussion does not exhaust the possible roles that personal links may have played in furthering increased disclosure. The list of the twenty best disclosing companies of 1957 contained a rather small and local Amsterdam company, ARM. ARM's financial statements of the early 1950s are quite remarkable, the company being among the very first to use photographs and full-colour printing. In addition to these outward embellishments, the information content of the ARM financial statements was rather high. An explanation offers itself in the person of its supervisory board member A.Th.E. Kastein, a well-known Amsterdam solicitor and member of the NIvA. His interest in financial reporting is shown by his attendance at the International Congress on Accounting (London, 1952; see Kastein, 1952). During the 1950s and 1960s he was the chairman of a NIvA study committee that served as the main focus of the NIvA's activities in the area of financial reporting. The hypothesis that the personal influence of Kastein played an important role in shaping ARM's reporting policies is reasonable[28].

As a final note, it should be observed that three of best disclosing companies in 1957 were not linked to any listed company at all. Evidently, being linked to other companies in this particular manner was at this point in time by no means a necessary condition to reach higher levels of disclosure.

5.5.7 *Auditors and early disclosure*
Although not strictly a characteristic of the disclosing company, 'audit firm' has frequently been employed in cross-sectional studies as a possible covariate of extent of disclosure. As indicated in

---

[28] According to J.W. Schoonderbeek, erstwhile secretary to the 'Kastein Committee', it is 'very plausible that Kastein has played a considerable role in reporting by ARM' (Letter from J.W. Schoonderbeek to the author, 1 February 1995).

section 5.5.1, the potential influence of audit firms on disclosure may also be envisaged in terms of the communication channel they provide among companies, or in terms of their possible roles as 'change agents'. The Dutch auditing profession has frequently been credited with playing an important role in the development of financial reporting. Alternatively, it has been alleged, with reference to the prewar and immediately postwar auditing profession that '[t]he auditors have followed practice faithfully, they didn't protest against insufficient publications and issued their certificates of correctness without qualifications', and 'it is certain that the Dutch auditor has contributed little or nothing to the improvement of published [financial statements]' (Burgert, 1953: 51, 56).

Even though an external audit was not legally required until the Act on Annual Financial Statements of 1970, most listed companies, though not all, were audited well before 1970. The data are therefore not suitable for conclusions on differences between audited and unaudited companies. Differences among audit firms might be observed, however. A null-hypothesis can be formulated that the number of early new disclosures by clients of a particular audit firm is proportional to that audit firm's market share. This involves the following steps:

1. Identify all observed switches from nondisclosure to disclosure (OFD; see footnote 5 to this chapter).

2. Identify all first disclosures falling into adopter categories 1-3 (pre-median disclosures) as defined in table 5.5 (total: 480 first disclosures).

3. Attribute first disclosures to the audit firm signing the financial statements in the year of first disclosure. A total of 94 different audit firms were involved with these first disclosures.

4. Calculate expected OFD for each audit firm as:

$$\sum_t (\ market\ share_{j,t} * total\ OFD_t\ )$$

In which *market share* is defined as the number of companies audited by firm *j* in year *t* divided by the total number of companies in the sample in year *t*.

Total observed first disclosure is calculated across all disclosure items, but only, as indicated above, for pre-median switches.

5. Expected and observed first disclosures by audit firm are compared by means of a Chi^2 test (grouping all audit firms with expected observations < 5 into one group). The results are not significant at the 10% level (see table 5.9).

The fact that there are hardly any differences among audit firms regarding timing of disclosure suggests that all firms have had, by and large, the same influence, regardless of how large that influence was. It is interesting to note, though, that the group of 'no auditor' does not differ in extent of disclosure from the other companies[29]. This fact, coupled with the absence of systematic guidance on financial reporting practice within the auditing profession before 1971, suggests the preliminary conclusion that the role of the auditing firms in furthering disclosure has in general not been large.

---

[29] See however Zeff *et al.* (1992:82-83) for the fact that, during the 1950s, companies might retain an auditor even though his opinion was not published in the financial statements.

Table 5.9
Audit firms and observed first disclosures

Firm	New disclosures by clients	
	Actual	Expected
Bianchi & Co	19	18.8
Wm K. de Brey	2	6.3
Burgmans	7	12.1
Dijker & Belt	4	5.4
Dijker, Bianchi & Co	18	12.6
Dijker, de Boer & Vink	8	5.9
Elles, Hamelberg & Co	5	6.8
Frese, Hogeweg, Meyer & Hörchner	13	11.4
Jonkers & De Jong	5	8.2
Van Kampen	7	8.1
Keuzenkamp & Co	10	9.9
Klynveld, Kraayenhof & Co	48	49.6
Th. & L. Limperg	7	5.2
Meyer & Hörchner	21	16.0
Moret, De Jong & Starke	11	8.4
Moret & Limperg	5	5.4
Moret & Starke	24	20.1
Nederlandse Accountants-Maatschap	20	15.9
Nietzman, Ten Hage & Kuijper	8	7.7
Paardekooper & Hoffman	6	8.4
Pelser, Hamelberg, van Til & Co	5	7.7
Price Waterhouse/		
Cooper Brothers[1]	11	5.8
De Tombe, Demenint & Co	4	6.1
Venker en Steenbergh	0	5.8
Wolff & Co	3	6.6
Wolfrat, Entrop en van Namen	8	5.1
All other (67) firms	133	123.8
No auditor	68	76.4
Total	480	480.0

Chi-square = 33.63801; $p > .10$

[1] Price Waterhouse/Cooper Brothers appear only once in the sample, as the joint auditors of Unilever.

5.6 Multivariate approach

Having discussed the relationship between overall disclosure and selected company characteristics, the final step is to investigate what remains of these individual effects when they are viewed in combination. The main tool for this investigation will be multiple regression of the various explanatory variables on average disclosure (measured by AND) for various subperiods.

Table 5.10 shows the correlation coefficients for some explanatory variables for the entire 1945-1983 period. There is reason for concern regarding the explanatory power of some variables when viewed in combination. Table 5.11 presents the results of a regression analysis of average total disclosure (AND) on four predictor variables: size, share issues, bond issues and whether or not the company is a trading company. Intercompany linkages have been omitted because of the high correlation with size, but also because data on these variables are not available for all companies or periods. The regression models for the various periods have been determined by stepwise forward regression.

Table 5.10
correlation coefficients of various independent variables

	ANS4583	TRADE	BONDS	EXISS4583	LINKS57
TRADE	-.15				
BONDS	.32**	-.11			
EXISS4583	.15	-.16	.19		
LINKS57	.74**	-.13	.20	.02	
LINKS73	.66**	-.19	.35*	.04	.60**

p* < .01; ** p < .001

Comparisons are pairwise with a minimum of 25 cases in each comparison. Variables as defined in previous sections.

Table 5.11

Multiple regression models of AND for various subperiods

	n	adj. R^2	coefficient estimates (p-values)				
			ANS*	TRADE	EXISS*	BONDS	Const.
Panel A: all companies							
AND4583	140	.34	.40 (.00)	-.42 (.01)	.13 (.00)	-	.07 (.24)
AND4554	100	.25	.37 (.00)	-	.26 (.00)	-	.02 (.74)
AND5564	116	.23	.34 (.00)	-.42 (.01)	.23 (.01)	-	.09 (.29)
AND6574	112	.40	.61 (.00)	-	-	-	.01 (.91)
AND7583	66	.41	.64 (.00)	-	-	-	-.13 (.18)
Panel B: all companies excluding multinationals							
AND4583	136	.25	.34 (.00)	-.42 (.01)	.14 (.00)	-	.05 (.39)
AND4554	96	.16	.28 (.00)	-	.26 (.00)	-.37 (.04)	.03 (.71)
AND5564	112	.09	-	-.43 (.03)	.25 (.00)	-	.032 (.73)
AND6574	108	.32	.63 (.00)	-	-	-	-.01 (.89)
AND7583	62	.39	.77 (.00)	-	-	-	-.08 (.43)

stepwise forward regression with entry criterion of $p < .05$
variables as defined in previous sections; ANS* and EXISS* refer to
the values for the appropriate period.

Panel A of table 5.11 shows the results for all companies. The fit of the models as indicated by R^2 is reasonably good when compared with typical cross-sectional disclosure studies[30]. It is evident that size as measured by ANS is the single most important variable in explaining differences in overall disclosure, although its importance varies across the various sub-periods. In the sub-periods up to 1965, TRADE and EXISS (excess issues relative to sample average) are admitted to the regression equation next to size, but after 1965 size alone plays a significant role. Moreover, after 1965, on the basis of size alone, R^2 attains the highest levels. The shifting relative importance of size compared to industry and share issues could reflect the difficulties in measuring size prior to the 1970 Act on Annual Financial Statements (WJO). The size measure, based on assets, may be distorted by the wider use of conservative valuation practices before 1965-1970. This explanation appears to be supported by the improving model fit after 1965. On the other hand, one might argue that the steep fall in the number of share issues after 1970 makes the corresponding variable less useful for the period after 1970. That the role of TRADE is similarly limited in time can perhaps be explained by the relationship between disclosure and exit mode indicated in section 5.5.4: almost one-half of the trading companies in the sample were delisted before 1970, most by liquidation or take-over. Especially this group should be characterized by less than average disclosure.

Since it is conceivable that the size effect as illustrated above depends on the influence of the very large multinational companies, panel B of table 5.11 shows the result of the same regression analysis, but with AKU/AKZO, PHILIPS, KONINKLIJKE PETROLEUM and UNILEVER omitted. As might be expected, the model fit declines, as does the role of the size variable. The effect is especially clear in

---

[30] For a multiple regression on a single-period disclosure index, Chow and Wong-Boren (1987) and Wagenhofer (1990c) find adjusted R^2 values of .15 and .279, respectively.

211

the 1955-1965 period, where the model fit is very low, and where size disappears altogether as a significant explanatory variable. For the sub-periods after 1965, however, the results with and without the multinational companies are by and large identical.

For the 1955-1964 period, with relatively low fits, an alternative model can applied with predicted (1957) disclosure (on the basis of the average disclosure of linked companies, see section 5.5.6) as additional independent variable. This variable is not significantly correlated with size and hence may provide additional explanatory power. Table 5.12 shows the results of the regression analysis with and without multinational companies. Introducing the linkage variable does improve the fit of the model to some extent, both with and without the multinational companies.

Table 5.12
Multiple regression including linkage variable

dependent variable: AND5564

	with multinationals	without multinationals
n	68	64
adj. R^2	.31	.17

coefficient estimates (p-values)

ANS5564	.39 (.00)	-
TRADE	-.62 (.02)	-.67 (.01)
EXISS5564	-	-
BONDS	-	-
PRED57	2.35 (.02)	2.13 (.03)
Constant	-.72 (.06)	-.61 (.09)

Notes to table 5.11 apply.

5.7 Conclusions

The outline of the development of disclosure throughout the postwar period is well established in the literature, and is clearly confirmed by this study. In addition, the materials presented in this chapter add some detail to this picture.

Both the Dutch and the international literature stress the importance of company size as a covariate of disclosure. According to the present study, size, almost regardless of definition, is the single most important covariate of disclosure. The more specific expectation that the four large multinational companies have been prominent among the companies with more extensive disclosures has been confirmed as well.

Apart from confirming this outline, the present study provides some details with which the general picture can be completed.

Size, though important, is not a guarantee of good disclosure, nor do large companies have a monopoly on introducing and improving disclosures. On the one hand, several very large companies, notably in the shipping sector, had average or even poor disclosure records. On the other hand, some middle-sized and small companies distinguished themselves with good to excellent disclosures. To some extent, these departures from the size-rule can be linked to changes in size. Size growth appears as a useful variable to explain why companies of similar size nevertheless display quite different disclosure histories. As a rule, declining company size is associated with a decline in relative disclosure position. This relationship between (relative) decline in size and disclosure is evident as well for companies delisted as a result of commercial misfortune. Companies ending their listing through failure or receivership disclose markedly less than average.

Departures from the rule that large companies disclose better appear to have been most widespread in the earlier part of the period. From the 1970s onwards, company size plays an increasingly important role in any description of disclosure development, almost to the point of driving other covariates into insignificance. This may partly be due to the difficulty of measuring size in the early part of the period, but, even allowing for this factor, there appear to be more size/disclosure order reversals in the 1940s and 1950s. This may perhaps be expanded into a more general statement that disclosure practices in the early part of the period were more of a random nature than in later years. This is highlighted by the occurrence of 'incidental disclosures', which occur quite frequently in the 1940s and 1950s, but not nearly as much in the later part of the period.

Another covariate that is helpful next to size is capital market activity. In the period until 1965, there is a tendency for increases in disclosure to occur in conjunction with share issues. After 1970, owing to the absence of share issues in significant numbers, this variable looses significance in distinguishing companies according to disclosure. It cannot be said that the overall level of disclosure has been raised by the practices of newly listed companies: on the whole, these companies model their disclosure on the average of the year in which they are first listed.

An industry effect has not been established by this study, apart from the general observations that trading companies tend to lag behind manufacturing companies. This, however, might as well be the result of a company-specific effect (declining economic position leading to less than average disclosure), that is disproportionally represented among trading companies. The absence of a specific industry effect may result from the limitations of the available data (too many industries represented by too few companies). It is, however, plausible that group effects on disclosure did not operate strictly along industry lines. Links between companies of different industries were illustrated in the discussion of the relation between disclosure and multiple board memberships. As with other co-variates, this variable is eclipsed by the effect of size from the 1970s onwards.

Chapter 6
Studies of individual disclosure items

6.1 Introduction

Whereas the previous chapter is primarily concerned with an investigation of the overall level of disclosure, and of differences in disclosure among companies, this chapter discusses the specific characteristics of individual disclosure items. The objective is to give an impression of the extent to which the adoption and diffusion processes of different items are comparable, or, to what extent they each display their own characteristics. The inductive approach followed in this chapter, which consists in effect of nine separate case studies, has the following structure.

First, the nine disclosure areas selected in chapter 4 are discussed in nine separate sections which form the main part of this chapter. These sections are arranged in a broadly chronological order. Although most of the disclosure elements studied here have been disclosed to some extent throughout the postwar period, most of them can be classified as belonging typically to subperiods as 'the 1950s' or the 'post-1970 period'.

Second, as far as feasible all items will be discussed with reference to a number of constant themes:

- The chronology of the appearance of the item in theory, professional literature and regulation;
- A broad outline of the reception of the item abroad, supported with quantitative data whenever available. The number of foreign countries discussed in this way varies from item to item owing to differences in data availability. In most cases, references are made to the United Kingdom and the United States. Empirical data for these countries are usually available from

Accounting Trends & Techniques and *Survey of Published Accounts*. Unless otherwise indicated, US and UK data are from these sources. Other countries (mainly Germany, and, more rarely, France) are discussed whenever information was available.

- The existence of possible 'change agents' or other forces influencing disclosure. Frequent references will be made to materials from chapter 3, relating to the institutional background of financial reporting in the Netherlands. Common points of reference include the Act on Annual Financial Statements (WJO) of 1970, the two Employers' reports on recommended annual reporting practices of 1955 and 1962, the Tripartite Study Group, the Enterprise Chamber, and the auditing profession.

Third, in the final section which follows the nine case-studies, these materials are integrated in a discussion of the similarities and differences between the items. Starting point of this discussion is Rogers' innovation-diffusion framework, specifically his listing of innovation characteristics that influence the rate of diffusion. The presentation within the main body of the chapter is guided by this end.

6.2 Sales

6.2.1 General

The movement towards disclosure of sales, or turnover, probably illustrates as well as any other change in disclosure the transition from earlier, more secretive, stages in the development of financial reporting to the present, relatively open practices. Sales are an elementary fact of business life, so that already in the early stages of thought on financial reporting it was obvious to all concerned that company managements possessed information regarding sales. On the other hand, disclosure of sales was relatively rare before the Second World War, because fear of competitors was widely perceived as a valid argument for not making this information public. Initially, legal provisions in most countries tended to accord considerable weight to the argument of competitive damage. Required sales disclosures were introduced only in the later stages of financial reporting regulation.

The country that took the lead in this development was the United States. Although total sales were 'long regarded as a profoundly important management secret' by US corporations (Ross, 1966:4), sales were already disclosed by around 60% of companies listed in New York before 1934 (Benston, 1969). By that time, the SEC started to require sales disclosure in the filed reports. The result was that sales were disclosed in published annual reports by 93% (98%) of US companies in 1950 (1960). In Europe, events proceeded more slowly, and the general nondisclosure of sales could be used to contrast the high esteem in which American managements held their investors with the paternalistic attitude towards stockholders common in Europe (Clapp, 1967:32-34).

Germany was the first country to adopt a position more similar to the US. Sales disclosure was made mandatory in 1960, but in the face of considerable opposition (Adler *et al.*, 1960). Some companies attempted to escape the consequences of disclosure by including distorting items in the disclosed sales figure. This led to certain remedial measures enacted in 1965 (Niehus, 1966).

Slightly earlier, it was observed that in the UK 'Sales (...) can legally be veiled from the owners' gaze; and there is little tendency for the voluntary concession of what is not demanded by law' (Baxter, 1956: 40). Ten years later, the disclosure of aggregate turnover was 'now gradually becoming more common', although the London Stock Exchange 'jibbed at including the disclosure of turnover among its new listing requirements' (Murray, 1965: 64). It took the Companies Act 1967 to achieve virtually full disclosure by the end of the 1960s.

The Dutch prewar literature tended to attach considerable weight to the competitive argument, and to excuse the nondisclosure of sales (*e.g.* Van Slooten, 1900: 258; Van Gruisen, 1937). In the postwar literature, the strength of the competitive argument against sales disclosure began to be played down. Spinosa Cattela (1948a) discussed the example of US reporting and argued that the amount of detail in the Dutch income statement had to be increased. He did foresee, though, that following the US example with regard to sales disclosure would 'in a small country like ours meet with much resistance'. Despite this and other advocacy of voluntary sales disclosure (*e.g.* Knol, 1948), there was rarely an outright demand for mandatory disclosure by all companies.

The development of opinion is illustrated by the differences between the two employers' reports of 1955 and 1962. The 1955 report merely mentioned that substitute disclosures had to be found when the disclosure of sales was judged to be detrimental to the company. The 1962 report stated: 'The objection, still current, that disclosure of sales figures would be detrimental in connection with competitors, can be considered valid in a limited number of cases only.'

An argument in favour of sales disclosure that gained in strength during this period was the fact that foreign competitors were increasingly compelled to disclose sales, apparently without suffering from detrimental effects (*e.g.* Sanders, 1963). Sales disclosure had become mandatory in Germany in 1960, and was proposed in the UK in the 1962 Jenkins report. In both countries, mandatory disclosure in the US was used as an argument in favour of domestic sales disclosure[1]. In this way, of course, the case for mandatory sales disclosure was strengthened by each nation adopting it.

In the end, sales disclosure was not strictly required by the 1970 Act on Annual Financial Statements. Companies were given the option of providing alternative disclosures, notably index figures showing changes in sales over time. The supporting documents to the law and the discussions in parliament made it clear, however, that sales disclosure would be appropriate except for small, undiversified

---

[1] See Farr (1955), le Coutre (1957) and Niehus (1958), for materials on Germany. In Britain, 'American witnesses who gave evidence before Jenkins were unanimous that disclosure of turnover (...) had caused no material harm' ('Turnover: What can be shown?', *Accountancy* (UK), vol. 74 no. 844, December 1963, p. 1121-1122).

enterprises. For most of the companies included in the present sample, therefore, there would have been a strong presumption that in their case sales disclosure became mandatory after 1970.

The opposition to mandatory sales disclosure in many countries leads to the hypothesis that this restistance was based on the existence of substantial proprietary costs of disclosure. Empirical investigation of this question has been limited to the effects of the 1934 (US) Securities and Exchange Act, with mixed results.
Benston (1969) doubted the necessity of the disclosure requirements of the Securities Acts. In Benston (1973) it was found that there was no measurable impact on securities prices of companies affected by the 1934 Act, that is, the 40 percent of companies that did not previously disclose their sales. Combined with the considerable voluntary disclosure before the Act, Benston concluded that the Act was not, in this regard, of great significance[2].

6.2.2 Comments on observed disclosure practices

Four different 'disclosure positions' were recognized with regard to sales (see Appendix A). Next to disclosure of the absolute amount of sales, either within or outside the income statement, two intermediate disclosures were distinguished: disclosure of a physical output measure and disclosure of an index number of sales.

Early disclosures

Figure 6.1 summarizes the development of sales disclosure over time. As can be seen, there were only slow increases in disclosure of the absolute amount of sales until the early 1960s, followed by a strong increase in the adoption rate during the 1965-1970 period.

---

[2] Benston's work has been the object of some methodological criticism, summarized in Chow (1984). Chow also attempted a more detailed study of consequences of the 1934 Act and concluded that there was, in fact, evidence of negative wealth effects for shareholders of previously nondisclosing companies.

Figure 6.1 Sales disclosure

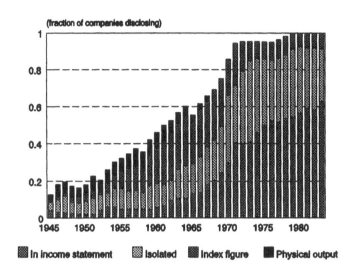

(fraction of companies disclosing)

■ In income statement   ▨ Isolated   ■ Index figure   ■ Physical output

During the 1940s and 1950s a group of companies was gradually formed that systematically disclosed sales, while another, larger group, disclosed sales irregularly or experimented with surrogates such as index numbers. If one leaves out, for the moment, the considerable number of companies that disclosed sales only incidentally, one is left with a quite small group of companies that disclosed or (started to disclose) their sales consistently during the 1945-1958 period. These companies form a rather disparate group, and the reasons for their early disclosure are not always obvious.

The sales disclosure by UNILEVER since 1945 is perhaps not surprising. The presence among sales disclosers of ARM and KROMHOUT, identified as progressive disclosers in the previous chapter, also seems natural. But why STOOMVAART ZEELAND was among the very first to publish an income statement headed by gross sales, or why WALVISVAART disclosed sales since 1945, is not clear. Both companies were to some extent government sponsored and hence shielded from domestic and foreign competition, which may have influenced their disclosure decisions.

In the early 1950s, AKU, KONINKLIJKE PETROLEUM and PHILIPS

started to disclose their sales, for reasons possibly connected with the New York listings they acquired at that time (see also section 5.5.3). Some companies (THOMASSEN DRIJVER, BLIKMAN SARTORIUS) made it explicit in their financial statements that they started to disclose on the recommendations of the Rijkens report (1955). ALBATROS remarked in its 1954 report, its first to contain a sales disclosure, that 'the demands of modern financial reporting entail a more detailed presentation of our balance sheet and income statement'. This statement may well have come from the company president, J.D. Waller, who was a member of the Rijkens committee.

Irregular disclosures and reversions to nondisclosure
A considerable number of companies disclosed their sales irregularly during the 1940s and 1960s. Some disclosed only once, for instance at the occasion of an anniversary, while others switched back and forth between disclosure and nondisclosure (*e.g.* ASW). Reversions to nondisclosure were mainly confined to companies that disclosed only an isolated sales figure, for instance in the directors' report. It was very rare, apart from situations of financial distress, for companies that had once integrated the sales figure in the income statement to stop disclosing sales. The only instances of this phenomenon were STOOMVAART ZEELAND and NBT, both discontinuing the practice of providing income statements headed by sales in the early 1950s almost as if suddenly becoming aware that their reports were, in this regard, out of line with the other companies. After 1960, reversions to nondisclosure occur only infrequently.

Influence of the 1970 Act
There can be little doubt that the 1970 Act had considerable influence on the disclosure of sales. In this respect, the Netherlands clearly contrasted with the United States were, prior to 1934, there had already been extensive voluntary disclosure by listed companies. Although the 1970 Act did not, strictly speaking, require the disclosure of sales, it was made clear along the way towards enactment that claiming potential competitive damage was going out of favour. The reduction in the importance attached to the competitive argument,

indicated above, was accompanied by a rise in sales disclosure throughout the 1960s, from about 20% in 1960 to 42% in 1968. The major change came in 1969-1971, however, when disclosure went up to 72%. After that, the percentage gradually increased to 90% in 1983. Evidently, many companies waited with their disclosure until it was certain that a law strongly inclined towards sales disclosure would be passed. In 1976, when most listed companies disclosed their sales, the Tripartite Study Group issued a Considered View that nondisclosure of sales was warranted only when management expected that 'substantial disadvantage to the enterprise' would ensue from this disclosure (IVb.2.11-12, December 1976).

Use of different disclosure formats
Given the perceived sensitivity of sales disclosure, many companies preferred to go through an interim stage before actually disclosing sales. About two-thirds of the companies that finally disclosed their absolute sales did so after an average of six years during which they disclosed either index figures of sales or physical measures of output. Evidently, physical measures of output are useful for companies with relatively homogeneous bulk production only (HEINE-KEN, DOMANIALE MIJN) or in the case of customized production of capital goods (NDSM). Hence, providing index figures was by far the most popular interim measure. Index figures were an innovation themselves. Before 1950, hardly any company used index figures to report sales, but they rapidly acquired popularity during the 1950s. During the 1960s, about 25% of companies disclosed index figures of sales, and it is therefore not surprising that their use was provided for in the 1970 Act. However, by 1970 index figures were already being superseded by disclosure of absolute sales. From 1970 to 1972, use of index figures dropped to about 10% of companies, a level at which it remained until 1980. After 1970, it was rare not to disclose at least an index of sales.
The 1970 Act did not prescribe that the income statement had to open with sales, or had to include a reconciliation of sales with profit. Traditionally, the income statement (or rather, profit- and loss account) opened with gross operating income from which items

222

like depreciation, interest and taxes were deducted to arrive at net income. This format was still allowed under the new Act.

More modern, or 'integrated' formats in which the income statement opened with sales were unknown in practice before the war, even though they had been recommended in 1938 with reference to American standards (Koppenberg, 1938)[3]. Integrated income statements began to be used sporadically in the early 1950s, mainly by the multinational companies (KONINKLIJKE PETROLEUM, PHILIPS, AKU) with a listing in New York[4]. UNILEVER also adopted the integrated income statement at the time of its New York listing, in 1961). The use of such statements began to expand in the late 1960s, even though they were not mentioned in the law being prepared at that time (see figure 6.1).

After 1970, however, the spread of the integrated income statement slowed, and a substantial fraction of companies continued with the traditional format. In this respect, the Tripartite Study Group provided no guidance. In the relevant sections of its considered views (I b.3.11, IV b.2) it adhered closely to the text of the law. It was not until the late 1970s and early 1980s that a number of large companies, including ALBERT HEYN, BYENKORF and BOSKALIS changed to an integrated income statement.

6.2.3 Summary

The disclosure of sales remained a sensitive issue during a considerable part of the period. Given the importance attached to sales disclosure in terms of its perceived benefits and costs, it is likely that

---

[3] Koppenberg's article referred to the widely circulated 1929 publication of the American Institute of Accountants, *Verification of Financial Statements*. This set of recommended auditing and accounting practices was endorsed by the Federal Reserve Board and 'attracted attention on both sides of the Atlantic' (Zeff, 1972:118).

[4] The transition in the annual reports of the multinational companies from T-shaped profit- and loss accounts to income statements opening with sales was ascribed by Brands (1953) to the requirements of the SEC.

most companies made conscious policy decisions regarding this disclosure. This is borne out by the way most companies chose to use interim disclosure formats in a way to balance carefully the demand for more disclosure against the perceived drawbacks of disclosure. Nevertheless, by 1970 the fear that sales disclosure would lead to heavy proprietary costs appears to have diminished. Although the law allowed companies to continue the use of interim formats such as index figures, the large majority of companies chose to disclose absolute sales figures. Sales disclosure can therefore be seen as an instance of a disclosure item that was part of the 'disclosure array' for a long time before a shift in perceptions of disclosure costs (brought about in particular by observation of foreign practice) led to increases in disclosure.

6.3 Comparative figures

6.3.1 General comments

Before the war, the practice of disclosing a column of previous year's figures in the balance sheet and profit and loss account was rare. Even though companies would provide little or no additional information by doing so, few provided this service to the readers of the financial statements. UNILEVER (since 1934), Heemaf NV (since 1937) and PHILIPS (since 1937/8) appear to be among the few companies who, before the War, published comparative figures[5].

During the immediate postwar years, the practice was continued on a limited scale. UNILEVER, one of the prewar disclosers, immediately showed comparative figures in its 1945 financial statements. The Anglo-Dutch company would have been aware of the fact that in the United Kingdom the provision of comparative figures had been recommended by the ICAEW in 1944, a recommendation included

---

[5] See also Munnik (1931: 30) and Koppenberg (1938).

Figure 6.2 Comparative figures

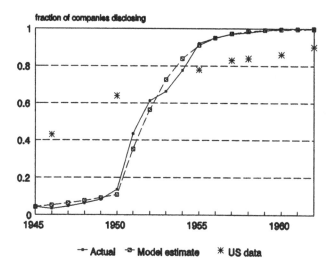

fraction of companies disclosing

-•- Actual   -□- Model estimate   * US data

as a requirement in the Companies Act 1948[6]. PHILIPS resumed the inclusion of comparative figures in 1946, in its first regular postwar annual report. Three years later, showing comparative figures was apparently still rare enough for the newspaper *Haagsche Post* to call attention to PHILIPS' 'commendable' comparative figures[7]. Other large companies like KONINKLIJKE PETROLEUM (1950) and AKU (1948) were preceded by a some smaller companies such as DORP (1946) and KROMHOUT (1947).

The change in the percentage of companies disclosing comparative figures is shown in figure 6.2. What is immediately clear is the sharp increase in disclosures following 1950. The change was so rapid that for a few years, disclosure levels were higher in the Netherlands than in the USA. In the latter country,

---

[6] *Recommendations of the Institute of Chartered Accountants in England and Wales*, No. 8, 'Form of balance sheet and profit and loss account', 1944; *Companies Act*, 1948, Schedule 8, 11(11) and 12(5).

[7] 'Philips verslag geeft Houvast', *Haagsche Post*, 8 July 1950, p. 14.

225

comparative figures were gaining ground more gradually (see figure 6.2)[8].

The most plausible explanation for the sudden expansion of disclosure of comparative figures is the fact that the Stock Exchange Association made one of its rare postwar attempts to influence financial reporting[9]. In a circular to members of the Stock Exchange dated October 1951, it was stated that:

It would be applauded by the Stock Exchange Association if the practice, already applied by a few companies, of including for the purpose of comparison the figures of the preceding year next to the figures of the current financial year, would henceforth be followed generally.[10]

The circular, which also included some other modest requests concering financial reporting, was supported in unambiguous terms by R. Besançon, a leading auditor who in 1954 would become NIvA-president:

We should hope that the leaders of our public companies show

---

[8] In 1940, *Accounting Research Bulletin* No. 6 (April 1940), asserted that 'The increasing use of comparative statements in the annual reports of companies is a step in the right direction' but, even though the SEC endorsed this and other CAP pronouncements, this did not amount to a formal requirement to include comparative figures in annual reports to stockholders. ARB No. 43 (1953) restated ARB No. 6 and asserted that it is 'ordinarily desirable' to publish comparative statements. According to Farr (1955) the disclosure of comparative figures was by no means common among German companies in the mid-1950s.

[9] See Van Berckel (1965), who credits the Stock Exchange Association for the fact that, by 1965, presenting comparative figures had become 'common practice'. See Zeff *et al.* (1992:chapter 3, *passim*) for the role of the Association in postwar financial reporting.

[10] Vereeniging voor den Effectenhandel (Bedrijfsgroep Effectenhandel), *Mededelingen van het Bestuur aan de Leden* no. 285, 15 October 1951, 'Publicatie van gegevens door naamloze vennootschappen'.

their appreciation of the moderation ever shown, in the face of many contrary demands, by the Stock Exchange Association, by complying loyally and with understanding, where this is still necessary, with these minimal publication requirements. And let me conclude by repeating that the auditor can perform a useful and grateful task by defeating the many unfounded objections against better publicity that so often show themselves to be still in existence. (Besançon, 1952:200)

6.3.2 A modelling approach

The impact of the Stock Exchange Association's circular can be illustrated by developing a simple model for the disclosure process depicted in figure 6.2. This figure shows, in addition to the actual disclosure data, the result of a simulation exercise which attempts to recreate the observed data by means of a model, derived from an innovation-diffusion context. It will be recalled from the discussion in chapter 4 that innovation-diffusion processes are generally characterized by 'S'-shaped diffusion curves. One of the more popular mathematical representations of this 'S'-shaped curve is the Bass (1969) model which interprets such curve shapes as the result of two forces influencing the diffusion of an innovation:

- An 'external influence' effect, such as the effect of mass media. This type of effect exerts an influence on all nonadopters that is constant over time.
- An 'internal influence' effect, which can be understood as the result of imitation or word-of-mouth communication. As the number of adopters increases over time, the strength of this influence increases as well.

The process depicted in figure 6.2 can be interpreted in these terms. Specifically, one might say that prior to 1951, the 'external influence' coefficient can be set equal to zero. That is, from 1945 to 1950, the growing disclosure of comparative figures can be assumed to rely entirely on the 'internal influence' diffusion effect produced

227

by mutual observation and imitation. Starting with 1951, an external factor indicating the presumed effect of the Stock Exchange circular comes into effect as well. It appears from figure 6.2 that a model along these lines is capable of matching the observed data quite closely[11]. It is therefore possible to conclude that the process by which comparative figures were introduced in Dutch financial statements took place *as if* before 1951, new disclosures occurred only because of an interaction and imitation effect, while from 1951 onwards new disclosures were mainly the result of a strong 'external influence' type of diffusion[12].

6.3.3 *Other potential influences on disclosure*

The rapid introduction of comparative figures in published annual reports following 1951 suggests that companies were not particularly concerned about this disclosure. This attitude, if it existed, contrasts with the continued and emphatic recommendations of comparative figures. While these recommendations may have been relevant to unlisted companies (which are not covered in this study), they can hardly have played a role in encouraging disclosure by listed companies.

In 1956, when more than 90% of the sampled companies were already disclosing comparative figures, the norms for the Henri Sijthoff award included the presentation of comparative figures as one of the three primary criteria to be applied, while citing the Stock

---

[11] Specifically, the model used is $N(t) = N(t-1) + a[1-N(t-1)] + bN(t)[1-N(t-1)]$, with $N(t)$: the percentage of disclosing companies in year t;
a: the external influence coefficient (0 for 1945-1950, .25 for 1951-1962);
b: the internal influence coefficient (.22 throughout).
Model coefficients are estimated according to the procedure described in Mahajan and Peterson (1985), $R^2 = .9936$.

[12] More or less equivalently, one might say that after 1951, new disclosures followed the pattern of a Markov-process in which each year about a quarter of nondisclosing companies started to disclose.

Exchange circular to stress the importance of this item[13]. Whereas this apparent oversight could be excused because of the rapid spread of comparative figures in the previous years, it is more difficult to understand why comparative figures had to be a matter for discussion when in 1968 the draft Act on Annual Accounts was introduced (see Zeff *et al.*, 1992: 177-78). These instances of relative unawareness of current actual practice are important to note. They illustrate the difficulties of observing and assessing the importance of new developments in disclosure at a time when systematic surveys of reporting practice were not available.

As distinct from individual auditors such as Besançon, quoted above, the Dutch auditors' organization can be ruled out as an alternative influence on disclosure, since the NIvA apparently played a reactive role in these developments. In 1952, the board asked the Advisory Committee on Professional Matters (CAB) to consider the 'phenomenon that, over the last few years more and more companies start to include for comparative purposes the figures for the preceding financial year, next to the figures relating to the current financial year.'[14] The NIvA did not take the lead in stimulating its members to encourage their clients to include comparative figures. Rather, at the time when the subject made its appearance in the NIvA literature, practice had already to a large extent accepted comparative figures. The discussions within the NIvA were confined to the auditor's duty to verify the comparative figures, and their coverage by the auditor's opinion (see also De Jong, 1956).

6.3.4 Summary

Compared to other disclosure items discussed in this chapter, the disclosure of comparative figures displays two interesting characteristics. First, this particular disclosure spread among companies with

---

[13] *Normen voor de beoordeling van Jaarverslagen* opgesteld voor de Henri Sijthoff Prijs (Amsterdam: Het Financieele Dagblad, 1956), p. 3.

[14] *De Accountant*, vol. 59 no. 3, November 1952, p. 219.

a rapidity that was not observed for any other item included in this study. It is true that a rapid diffusion of comparative figures is not in itself surprising, in the light of the presumably low or negligible proprietary costs associated with their disclosure. Yet, the actual observation of this rapid diffusion is useful since it occurred quite early in the postwar period, which suggests that even at that time financial reporting could be quite responsive to stimuli aimed at increased disclosure. Second, the comparative figures disclosure stands out because it can quite definitely be associated with a single important influence, the Stock Exchange memorandum of 1951.

6.4 Taxation

6.4.1 Introduction
The notion of deferred taxation was, at least as far as limited liability companies were concerned, a distinctly postwar development. Before the Second World War, Dutch companies were not subject to a tax on income or profit. Income was subject to taxation only to the extent that it was distributed as dividends. In the late 1930s, preparations for the introduction of an income tax were made. This tax became effective in the early 1940s[15]. Essentially, an income tax of this kind was retained until the present, although a number of important modifications occurred in 1947, 1950 and 1964.

An important aspect of the switch from a tax on dividends to an income tax was that, without further measures, retained earnings from before the new tax would escape taxation altogether. This was prevented by the transformation of part of retained earnings from previous periods into a 'tax-free' reserve on which the tax authorities retained a deferred claim[16]. Even if, in future, there would be no differences between taxable and reported income, this reserve confronted companies with the question of wether or not to recognize

---

[15] Besluit Winstbelasting 1940, Besluit op de Vennootschapsbelasting 1942.

[16] The so-called *Herleide overgangsreserve (H.O.R.)*

the deferred claim in their balance sheets. In 1947, additional scope for deferred taxation issues was created with the introduction of several other reserves that might be formed to reduce taxable income. In 1950, these were amalgamated with the earlier transition reserve into one type of temporarily tax-free reserve[17]. The cumulative effect of the various measures was that, by the early 1950s, the single remaining tax-free reserve 'had reached a considerable level in many companies' (Nierhoff, 1952:281). These reserves formed an important component of deferred tax claims. It was, however, a transitory source of tax deferrals since the regime of these reserves was not supposed to last indefinitely. At the same time, there came to be more general and more lasting sources of differences between taxable and reported income. One of the most important was the introduction, in 1950, of accelerated depreciation for tax purposes. It was gradually being recognized that there existed a broader problem of latent tax claims than that arising from the tax-free reserves[18].

Hence, in successive stages between 1940 and 1950, Dutch corporations were confronted with, and became more and more aware of, an increasingly complex issue of deferred taxation, an issue which they had not faced before. The newness of the phenomenon can be illustrated by a remark from Lafeber (1952: 351) that, to his knowledge, there was as yet no generally accepted name for the balance sheet item containing deferred taxes.

The same changes in the tax law that gave rise to the issue of deferred taxation also gave rise to an increased importance of tax costs as a disclosure. Whereas tax payments in the past had been tied to dividends, they were now tied to the assessment of profits by

---

[17] The so-called *Nieuwe Onbelaste Reserve (N.O.R.)*

[18] Roozen (1952:339) characterized it as a 'piepjong vraagstuk' (a 'fledgling issue'), and asserted that before, under the regime of a dividend tax, deferred taxation could not be considered to occur. Moreover, he extended the question of deferred taxation from the tax-free reserves to any difference that might occur between reported income (equity) and income for tax purposes.

the tax authorities. In an age of secret reserves and earnings management, readers of financial statements showed an understandable interest in disclosure of tax costs[19]. Evidently, this made some companies reluctant to provide extensive disclosures of both current and deferred tax charges and liabilities. Some apparently even turned the argument around by claiming that deferred tax liabilities did not need to be disclosed because they were balanced by secret reserves hidden elsewhere in the balance sheet (an argument rejected by Roozen, 1952:340).

By 1955, therefore, tax disclosure and disclosure of deferred liabilities were a recognized financial reporting issue for which no generally accepted solution was available (see also Soesbeek, 1955:256 and De Jong, 1964:42n).
It appears from the literature that the Rijkens report issued in that year did much to provide a standard for at least the disclosure aspect of the deferred tax issue. Burggraaff (1968) suggests that this report and its 1962 successor played an important role in elevating requests from the financial press for fuller disclosure of tax items to the level of a generally accepted reporting norm. The Rijkens report listed the topic of taxation among the three key reporting issues singled out for extensive treatment at the start of the report (the other two being secret reserves and current cost accounting, implying that accounting for taxes was on a level with these two important issues). It was recommended to disclose tax costs charged to this year's profits, even though it was conceded that for some companies nondisclosure might be justified because of potential competitive damage. Furthermore, tax costs were to be calculated over reported profits and should not necessarily equal taxes payable. Deferred tax obligations should be recognized, but not necessarily separately disclosed. If no

---

[19] As an example, the financial journalist Justus Meyer used disclosed tax data to arrive at a more realistic estimate of the 1949 income of Heemaf NV, a company that was evidently keen to report a very conservative measure of income ('Het Jaarverslag der Heemaf', *Haagsche Post*, 18 March 1950, p. 16).

deferred taxes were taken into account, this should be mentioned in the annual report. The 1962 Hamburger Committee report, although it largely reiterated the demands of its 1955 predecessor, was more specific regarding disclosures of tax liabilities. Whereas the Rijkens report had recommended including taxes payable in the 'Other payables' item, the Hamburger report called for separate disclosure. That deferred taxes were to be separately disclosed might be inferred, but it was not made explicit.

Although the right way to calculate tax deferrals remained a controversial issue until well into the 1980s, by the mid-1960s it was more or less agreed that the financial statements ought to provide information on both the tax charges in the income statement, and on tax liabilities included in the balance sheet[20]. This agreement in theory did not immediately translate into a completely homogeneous disclosure practice. Tempelaar (1966:272) notes that one of the three most common deficiencies in a sample of financial statements was the absence of information on taxes. But these deficiencies were soon to be eliminated by the enactment of the 1970 Act (WJO). The 1965 Verdam committee report proposed separate disclosure of current and deferred tax liabilities and tax charges in the income statement. The committee refrained, however, from pronouncing on the calculation of deferrals. Its recommendations were incorporated in the law.

---

[20] In 1962 a report on tax deferrals was published by a NIvA-subcommittee, installed in 1952 when the deferred tax issue was still young. Although the report prompted extensive discussion within the NIvA and in the literature, these discussions hardly touched on the disclosure aspect of (deferred) taxation. To the extent that disclosure was discussed, a reference was generally included to the Employers Organizations' reports. See Commissie van Advies inzake Beroepsaangelegenheden, 'De vraagstukken, welke samenhangen met de invloed van de latente belastingverhoudingen op de jaarrekening van de naamloze vennootschap', *De Accountant*, vol. 69 no. 1, September 1962, p. 40-51, and *De Accountant*, vol. 69 no. 8, April 1963, p. 524-543; also: 'Belastingen naar de winst in de jaarrekening', *De Accountant*, vol. 74 no. 2, June 1967, p. 35-46. The literature referred to includes de Jong (1964), Brok (1964), Burggraaff (1968) and Smulders (1968).

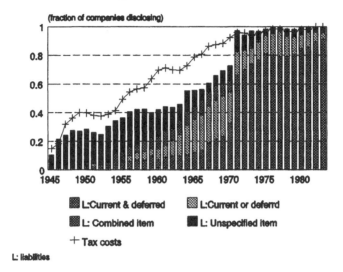

Figure 6.3 Tax disclosures

(fraction of companies disclosing)

■ L:Current & deferred	▦ L:Current or deferrd
▦ L: Combined item	■ L: Unspecified item
+ Tax costs	

L: liabilities

6.4.2 Comments on observed disclosure practices

Figure 6.3 shows the increase in disclosure of tax data by the sample companies. No comparative data for other countries are shown owing to a lack of published comparable time series.

The various disclosure positions distinguished in figure 6.3 include:

- The disclosure of the tax cost item charged to the profit- and loss account.
- Disclosures regarding the balance sheet tax liability.

With regard to the balance sheet item, various classes of disclosure are distinguished: the disclosure of an unspecified tax item, the disclosure of a single item with the indication that it consists both of current and deferred taxes, the disclosure of either current or deferred taxes and the disclosure of the two items separately (see also Appendix A).

234

Relationship between disclosures of tax cost and tax liabilities.

Given that tax costs and tax liabilities are closely related in terms of the journal entries required to enter them into a set of accounting records, it might be assumed that there would also be a fairly close relationship between the disclosures of the two items. A first indication of the strength of this relationship was provided in table 5.1, where it was found that the years of Observed First Disclosure of the two items were fairly strongly correlated[21]. Nevertheless, as figure 6.3 indicates, disclosure levels for tax costs were somewhat higher than those for tax liabilities through most of the pre-1970 period. This leads to the assumption that new disclosures of the two items often did not occur simultaneously, and that disclosure of tax costs usually preceded disclosure of tax liabilities. This is supported by the following observations:

- In the entire sample, there were 105 observed switches from nondisclosure to disclosure of tax costs and 95 switches in the same direction regarding tax liabilities. In 32 cases, the switches occurred simultaneously.
- An even lower fraction was observed for the reversions to nondisclosure: there were 9 simultaneous switches out of 53 tax costs reversions and 40 tax liability reversions[22].
- Roughly a third, therefore, of all disclosure switches occurred simultaneously for both items. The others occurred in a wide variety of circumstances, with the average time elapsing between the first disclosure of tax costs and the first disclosure of tax liabilities being slightly more than ten years. Occasionally, some 20 years elapsed between the first disclosure of tax costs and the

---

[21] $r = .4914$ ($p < .001$, $n = 69$). It will be recalled that a binary disclosure definition (see appendix A) was used to make this calculation.

[22] There were even some simultaneous switches in opposite directions: in two cases tax liabilities were disclosed in the year that disclosure of tax costs was discontinued, and two cases with switches in the opposite directions.

first disclosure of tax liabilities[23].

Main factors underlying changes in disclosure
It is likely that the factors governing tax disclosures were somewhat different from the factors underlying other disclosures. This is suggested not only by the somewhat irregular shape of the disclosure curve for tax cost disclosures, but also by the absence of a relationship between tax cost disclosure and size[24].
It is not easy to indicate the main influences on the disclosure process. On the one hand, the disclosures of tax costs and tax liabilities are sufficiently different to prevent easy generalisation. On the other hand, the number of potential explanations for the observed changes is quite large. Figure 6.3 shows a clear break in the series for tax liability disclosure in 1971. It is quite evident that for this disclosure item the 1970 Act had a major impact on the process of disclosure extension that had been going on since the early 1950s.
For tax cost disclosures, there was less scope for the Act to make an impact since by 1965 about 80% of companies were already disclosing this item.
Figure 6.3 suggests a more or less cyclical pattern in the extension of tax cost disclosure between 1945 and the middle 1960s, with periods of increases in disclosure alternating with periods of constant or even slightly decreasing disclosure. A similar pattern suggests itself for tax liabilities, before 1960. Figure 6.4 allows a closer look at these developments by showing observed changes from nondisclosure to disclosure by year.

---

[23] As in the cases of STOOMVAART NEDERLAND, DORP and GROF-SMEDERIJ.
[24] A cross-sectional analysis for 1960 shows that the tax cost disclosure percentages for companies of above (below) median size was 64% (66%), which is an insignificant difference. As an indication of the size effect with other disclosures it can be said that for sales disclosure the disclosure percentage for above (below) median size were 27% (11%), a difference significant at $p < .05$. For consolidated statements these figures were 50% (25%), significant at $p < .015$. Probabilities shown are based on the Fisher exact probability test.

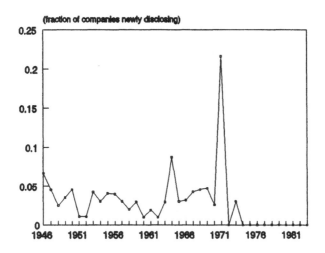

Figure 6.4a New tax disclosures
tax liabilities

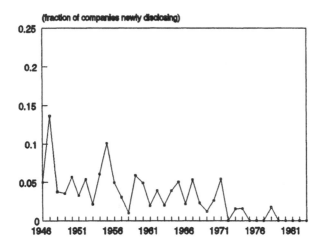

Figure 6.4b New tax disclosures
tax costs

237

Figure 6.4 shows that there were definite 'spikes' of new disclosures
of tax liabilities in the years 1964 and 1971. There appears to be
some indication of a slight fall in the rate of new disclosures in
1951-1952 and 1960-1962. For tax costs, the peak years with regard
to new disclosures appear to be 1947 and 1955.

It seems reasonable to relate the tax cost disclosures of 1955 (and
subsequent years) to the Rijkens report, especially in the light of the
importance attached to that report by contemporaries in promoting
thought on accounting for taxation.

It is tempting to relate the disclosures of 1947 and 1964 to the tax
law changes of those years on the ground that these changes in the
law focused attention on taxes and hence increased the probability of
new disclosures. The apparent tendency to disclose tax costs prior
to tax liabilities would explain why in 1947 the effect on disclosure
was primarily in terms of tax costs whereas in 1964 the main change
was in tax liability disclosure.

Reversions to non-disclosure

Both tax items show a rather high reversion rate. That is, the
number of observed switches to nondisclosure is high compared to
the number of observed switches to disclosure (see table 6.1, which
shows that for both items the number of reversions is about half the
number of new disclosures). This can, at least in part, be explained
by the fact that loss-making companies may have no tax obligation
and/or tax charges to report for a number of years. At least for
some companies, such as ADAM, ASSELBERG, ASW, GIESSEN, this
explanation appears to account for some of the fluctuation in disclosure: reported losses coincide with the disappearance of a tax item
from the financial statements. In this regard, it should be noted that
a company explaining in the notes to the financial statements that
there are no tax liabilities or tax charges to be reported because of
losses is considered to be disclosing its tax data.

Reversions are especially prominent during the years 1950-1952.
During those three years, 16 companies discontinued the disclosure
of tax costs (30% of all observed reversions for the entire 1945-1983
period). It seems that after the initial round of new disclosures

238

Table 6.1
Discontinued disclosure by item

Discontinuance ratio
(reversions to nondisclosure / observed new disclosures)

Geographical segments	56.4%
Tax costs	50.5%
Tax liabilities	42.1%
Number of employees	40.6%
Current cost / balance sheet	29.8%
Industry segments	28.6%
Current cost / income statement	27.8%
Sales	21.9%
Wage costs	13.3%
Earnings per share	7.4%
Consolidated statements	6.7%
Funds statement	1.7%
Comparative figures	1.1%

following 1947, a number of companies realized that the potential costs of disclosure (in terms of additional information on profit) might be too high, and therefore reverted to nondisclosure.

A number of these discontinued disclosures were achieved by combining taxes into an aggregate balance sheet and/or income statement item. This was a reporting device that gained considerable popularity during the earlier postwar period. The item would bear names like 'reserve for special purposes', 'reserve for miscellaneous purposes' or 'reserve for sundry interests'. In the notes to the financial statements a remark would be made to the effect that an unspecified provision for taxation was included in this reserve, which might either be fed by charges to the income statement or by allocations from retained earnings. The device remained quite popular until the disclosure requirements of the 1970 Act made it no longer acceptable.

An individual company

In some cases, insight may be gained into the difficulties that companies were faced with in providing tax disclosures, assuming they were willing to do so.

The 'Hoogovens' steel mills did not disclose any quantitative data on taxes until 1957. However, because of statements in the preceding years' annual reports, it is possible to obtain some insight into the circumstances surrounding the decision to start disclosing in 1957.

Starting with the 1954/55 annual report, the section of the directors' report discussing the balance sheet and income statement was significantly expanded. The more extensive discussions contained henceforth a paragraph on taxes. In the 1954/55 report, it was observed that 'regarding our tax situation, we are not yet capable of providing precise figures owing to our ongoing consultations with the tax authorities. (...) As soon as the tax assessments are established, we will disclose the tax liability separately in our annual report.'

The most likely explanation for this declared willingness to disclose tax data is the 1955 Rijkens report which appeared about six months before the Hoogovens annual report and which paid extensive attention to disclosure of taxes. It may be recalled (see section 5.5.6) that Hoogovens president A.H. Ingen Housz was a member of the Rijkens committee.

It took a while before the declared intention could be realized. Readers of the 1955 and 1956 annual reports were kept informed about the proceeding negotiations with the tax authorities (which centred on the acceptance by the tax authorities of the base stock method), but in both years it was stated that the company preferred not to give actual figures before the exact liability was known. Finally, in the 1957 annual report, it was stated that 'the moment has arrived to disclose our tax liabilities in the financial statements'. The company certainly did so, with a complete disclosure of current and deferred liabilities and a breakdown of tax costs in taxes payable and movements in deferred liabilities.

6.4.3 *Summary*

Tax disclosures were governed to a large extent by their own specific causes. This appears from the relatively small degree of association with other disclosures and the absence of the otherwise ubiquitous size effect. The factors operating on tax disclosure were primarily legal, connected with the progress of tax reform in the Netherlands. Changes in the tax structure gave rise to the issue of deferred taxation. The tax law revisions of 1947 and 1964 were accompanied by distinct improvements in disclosure. The 1970 Act also played a certain role in bringing about disclosure by the remaining nondisclosing companies.

As to non-legal influences, the data provide some support for the assertions in the contemporary literature that the employers' reports of 1955 and 1962 were an important factor in bringing about improvements in disclosure.

6.5 Employment-related disclosures

Regarding disclosure of employee-related data, two disclosure items were investigated: the disclosure of labour-related costs (primarily wages) and disclosure of the number of employees. Considerable differences in disclosure with regard to these two items can be observed, even though they show aspects of the same facet of the enterprise. By and large, companies appeared more willing to disclose the number of employees than their aggregate remuneration. This difference becomes apparent from figure 6.5, which shows the disclosure of both items over time. Whereas the number of companies disclosing employee numbers rises rather gradually, the number of companies disclosing wage costs remains low until the late 1960s, when a sudden increase occurs. The remainder of this section provides comments and backgrounds on these developments.

6.5.1 *Employee numbers*

Throughout the period, disclosure of employee numbers was not mandated by law. A disclosure requirement was introduced with the

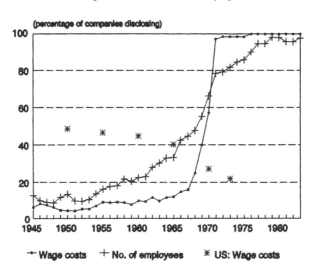

Figure 6.5 Disclosure of employee data

(percentage of companies disclosing)

-*- Wage costs   -+- No. of employees   * US: Wage costs

adaptation of Dutch law to the Fourth Directive in 1983. Nevertheless, from the middle 1950s onwards the number of companies disclosing employee numbers rose steadily to reach 90% or more in the mid-1970s. During the 1940s and 1950s, disclosure of employee numbers was to a large extent a matter of experimentation and incidental disclosure. As with sales disclosure, the number of new disclosures during the 1945-1954 period is almost balanced by the number of discontinued disclosures. Another illustration of the irregularity of disclosure is that during this ten-year period, a total of 27 companies started to disclose employee numbers. However, only 9 of these companies disclosed employee numbers for more than three consecutive years. Hence a complaint in the financial press that 'only few financial statements report on the number of employees.'[25]

From 1955 onwards, new disclosures began to outweigh discontinued

---

[25] 'Financiële publiciteit' in *Het Financieele Dagblad*, 6 January 1955, p. 1.

242

disclosures, although the latter remained substantial. An indication of a changing attitude is that the Norms for the Henri Sijthoff award (1956) suggested the disclosure of the number of employees in the directors' report.

Apparently, the 'jubilee factor' played a larger role with this item than with any other. It accounts to a considerable extent for the pattern of intermittent disclosure during the period up to 1955[26]. As noted by the financial journalist W.C. Posthumus Meyjes (1960), labour-intensity was frequently a subject shrouded in secrecy, except at anniversaries when the president might take pride in pointing out 'that he started out on his own and that now a thousand men earn a living in the company'. Examples of irregular disclosures include SMITS, which announced the recruitment of the 100th employee in its 1964 annual report; REEUWIJK (1964), which disclosed employee numbers at the occasion of its 50th anniversary; NIEAF, which in the 1949 annual report mentioned the current number of employees in the obituary of the company's founder; and SIMPLEX which on one occasion printed a group portrait of what it claimed was its entire staff. Anniversaries could also be the occasion for more structural changes in disclosure, as for BYENKORF which started disclosing employee numbers with its 1969/1970 annual report coinciding with the company's 100th anniversary.

The willingess of many companies to make incidental disclosures, and the gradual net increase of disclosure without a hint of legal compulsion suggest that any secrecy surrounding employment figures was based more on habit than on conviction. Companies were apparently not unwilling to provide the information when requested by shareholders or when they formed the impression that disclosure

---

[26] Another, incidental, factor was the Second World War: a number of companies made incidental disclosures of both casualties and total employee numbers in their retrospective narratives included in their first postwar annual reports.

was becoming majority practice[27]. What may have played a role is that it was rather hard to keep this particular type of information secret. As noted again by Posthumus Meyjes (*loc. cit.*), it was not too difficult to arrive at a reasonably correct estimate of the number of employees by 'chatting at the gate'.

Data on employee disclosures in other countries are rare. Chambers (1955:197) observed that employee numbers were 'commonly' disclosed in the United States, but that 'only a small proportion' of companies in England and Australia disclosed these data. If correct, this observation again underlines the superiority of US disclosures, and the fact that Dutch disclosures were not widely out of line with those in other parts of the English-speaking world.

6.5.2 Wage costs

From the postwar literature, it appears that disclosure of labour costs was seen as a fairly sensitive item. This becomes especially clear from the treatment of this topic in the various publications leading up to the 1970 Act on Annual Financial Statements.

As in other matters, the 1955 Rijkens report was perhaps the most outspoken advocate of disclosure: 'The disclosure of salaries, wages and social security contributions (...) can be deemed to be efficacious' (*is doelmatig te achten*) (p. 17)[28]. The 1962 Hamburger report adopted a more cautious tone: 'As appears from current

---

[27] In this light, it is intriguing that Munnik (1931:29) remarks that 'almost all' bank financial statements in a large survey of financial statements from the late 1920s 'gave particulars about the number of staff and changes therein'. However, according to Munnik, the banking sector distinguished itself by its good reporting practices.

[28] In the same report it was stated: '[In the directors' report] the most important developments regarding staffing and employee policy, wages and conditions of employment and the labour market can be reviewed.' (p. 19) and: 'Statistical summaries are appropriate for (...) number of employees, wages and salaries paid, social costs, additional provisions such as contributions to pension funds.' (p. 21).

practice, it is sometimes considered desirable to state separately [from total costs] the total of wages, salaries and social security costs in order to indicate the significance of the enterprise to the labour market. This can also be achieved by disclosing the number of employees in the annual report.' (p. 46)

This growing caution may well reflect the political nature of the debate on company law reform in which financial reporting began to be involved. The requirement to disclose wages and social security contributions was not included in the preparatory Verdam proposals for a law on company reporting. However, such a requirement was included in the 1968 draft law on the basis of an advice by the Social-Economic Council (SER)[29]. The auditors' organizations noted in their joint advice on the Verdam report[30] that the SER's suggestion for a separate disclosure of wage costs 'can not be founded on considerations of *bedrijfseconomie*'. They therefore guarded what amounted to a careful neutrality on the subject by stating that '[i]f separate disclosure of the item 'wages and social security contributions' is considered desirable for reasons other than [the requirement that the financial statements give insight as contained in] articles 2 and 3 of the law' care should be taken to arrive at a proper definitional treatment of the various items involved. A similar view was expressed by Groeneveld (1968:139) who remarked that the inclusion of a wage cost disclosure in the draft law was based on motives 'other than strictly financial information provision'[31].

---

[29] The SER is one of the most important advisory bodies to the Dutch government. It is routinely consulted on important economic legislation.

[30] Nederlands Instituut van Accountants, 'Nota van de besturen van het Nederlands Instituut van Accountants en van de Vereniging van Academisch Gevormde Accountants inzake het voorontwerp van de commissie Verdam van Wet op de jaarrekening van ondernemingen', *De Accountant*, vol. 72 no. 11, July/August 1966, p. 583-595.

[31] In Germany, disclosure of wage costs and, separately, social security contributions, was required from 1931 (or 1937) onwards. These disclosures were considered to be based on 'general economic and socio-political considerations' (Van Viegen, 1956: 277).

Figure 6.5 illustrates that wage cost disclosures were regarded as a somewhat sensitive issue during the 1960s. Throughout the 1950s and until 1967, the percentage of companies disclosing wage costs remained well below 20%. At the same time, it is clear that the unambiguous disclosure requirement inserted into the draft law in 1968 was effective. Between 1968 and 1971 (when the law became effective), the rate of disclosure sharply increased to just short of 100%. Some companies explicitly stated that their disclosures were motivated by the new law. UNILEVER (1968), DESSEAUX (1969/70) and BERGOSS (1970) disclosed wage costs before it became strictly necessary and motivated this change as an anticipation of the new legal requirements.

Developments in the United States provide an interesting comparison with the Dutch data. In the US, employment cost disclosures were not, during this period, mandatory under GAAP. Around 1950, there was a considerable extent of voluntary disclosure. However, as indicated by figure 6.5, disclosure of employment costs in the USA declined continuously from 1950 onwards[32]. In both the Netherlands and the USA, therefore, there was no evidence of a lasting willingness to disclose wage costs voluntarily. In the Netherlands, however, full disclosure was achieved by the imposition of regulation whereas in the United States the absence of regulation meant a gradual decline in disclosure.

Post 1970-occurences further support that wage cost disclosures were primarily influenced by the 1970 Act. Around 1970, there was apparently some uncertainty on what constituted the legal minimum of disclosure. Once this became clear, there is a distinct tendency to fall back on the legal disclosure minimum.

Labour costs can be broken down into components as wages and salaries, pension contributions and social security payments.

---

[32] It was remarked at the end of the 1960s that 'An increasing number of companies (...) are omitting any presentation of the amount of employment costs from their annual reports' (*Accounting Trends and Techniques*, 1969:167).

Whether the law required a breakdown was not immediately obvious from either the law itself or the accompanying Explanatory Memorandum. Some commentators (Vecht, 1968:313) appeared to favour a separate disclosure. But post-enactment commentators (IJsselmuiden, 1972:196, Sanders, Burgert and Groeneveld, 1975:287) assumed that the disclosure could be made as one single item.

What the data show is that, over the entire 1945-1983 period, there are only 14 companies who, for varying lengths of time, broke down their labour costs into various components (such as pension costs). This low percentage in itself suggests an unwillingness on the part of companies to provide the disclosure, a suggestion that is reinforced by the observation that only five of these 14 companies continued the more detailed disclosure to the end of the observation period. The other nine sooner of later fell back to a lower level of disclosure. Before 1970, this lower level was in all cases (four instances) no disclosure of labour costs at all. After 1970, the five companies who reduced their disclosure all fell back on the legal minimum of disclosing a total 'labour cost' item.

Given that legal requirements played an important role in introducing wage cost disclosures, it is interesting to investigate in some detail the disclosures of this item before 1965, when no legal requirements were either in force or in preparation. From 1945 to 1968, two important characteristics of the Dutch economy were a tight labour market and a so-called 'guided wage policy'[33]. The latter aimed, through a fairly elaborate mechanism of central negotiation and government controls, to restrain wage increases with a view to protecting the competitiveness of Dutch industry. The former ensured that wages were frequently under upward pressure and that the policy was difficult to implement. As a result, wages rose with leaps and bounds and years of relative stability alternated with years of double-digit wage increases. Figure 6.6 matches for each year in

---

[33] See Windmuller, de Galan and Van Zweeden (1983, chapter V and p. 215 for details on wage movements).

247

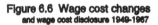
**Figure 6.6 Wage cost changes
and wage cost disclosure 1949-1967**

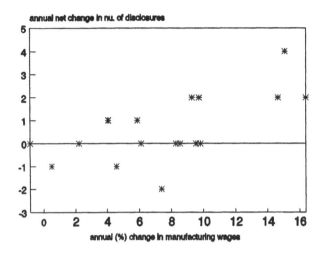

the period 1949-1967 the increase in wages with the change in the number of companies disclosing wage costs in that year's annual report.   Data on wage increases are those for the year-on-year percentage increases in nominal manufacturing wages[34].   It appears that the fitful developments in wages left their mark in companies' annual reports: in years with a higher than average growth in wages, the number of companies disclosing wage costs tends to increase, whereas this number remains constant or falls (on a net basis) in years with lower than average wage increases[35].

This phenomenon might be explained by assuming that any item that is brought to the attention of a company's management because it is affected by a serious disturbance has an increased likelihood of disclosure.   It is also possible that more purposeful disclosures occurred and that some company managements might want to draw

---

[34] Nominal weekly wages in manufacturing as reported in International Labour Organization (ILO), *Year book of labour statistics* 1950-1975.

[35] $r = .605$, which is significant at the .01 level.

attention to the negative consequences of rapid wage increases by means of disclosure of the total wage bill. The data at hand do not support a choice between these two explanations.

6.5.3 Summary

The data suggest that wage cost disclosure was more controversial than disclosure of the number of employees. In fact, it appears that without regulatory support, wage cost disclosure would not have become very widespread. US data tend to support this conclusion. Those companies that did disclose wage costs before 1965 appear to have done so at least in part in response to labour market developments. The 1970 Act, which did have its intended effect on wage cost disclosure, also appears to have had a side effect on the disclosure of the number of employees: even though there was no reference to disclosure of employee numbers, there was an increase of disclosure in the years around 1970.

6.6 Consolidated financial statements

6.6.1 Introduction

Consolidated financial reporting is, like the funds statement, a distinctly recognizable reporting innovation that has attracted much attention in the literature. A number of previous studies is therefore available, both with regard to the Netherlands and other countries, on the development over time of this type of reporting[36].

---

[36] The most important historical studies on the spreading of consolidated reporting include: Bores (1934, general), Kitchen (1972, UK), McKinnon (1984, Japan), Whittred (1986, Australia), Bircher (1988, UK) Edwards (1991, UK), Blommaert (1995, Netherlands). Studies attempting to analyze consolidated reporting on the basis of specific theoretical models include Whittred (1987) and Blommaert (1995), who use a derived demand approach, and Parker (1977), who uses an innovation-diffusion perspective.

In the mid-1920s, the consolidated balance sheet could be regarded in Europe as 'something new, distinctly American in origin' (Hatfield, 1927:279). Knowledge of the device spread fairly rapidly beyond the United States, however. As indicated by Kitchen (1972), consolidated reporting was well-known in Great Britain before the Second World War, even though this was not reflected by a commensurate extent of published consolidated statements. This changed when the 1948 Companies Act required the publication of consolidated financial statements.

In Germany, consolidation was a well-known topic in the literature before the Second World War. Whether or not companies should be required to publish consolidated financial statements was an important issue in the debate on company law reform in the 1930s (Fuchs and Gerloff, 1954:15). The result was limited to a clause introduced in 1931 which gave the government the right to regulate the publication of group accounts by decree. This clause was not acted upon, nor were companies keen to start publishing consolidated accounts voluntarily. The first voluntary publications occurred in the early 1950s[37]. At the same time, moreover, consolidation received an unexpected encouragement. As one of the many consequences of the War, consolidated accounts were imposed on German financial reporting practices. The Allied occupation authorities charged with reorganizing German industry and dismantling the large conglomerates inserted a clause in the model articles of incorporation for successor companies in the coal and steel industries, that required these companies to publish consolidated financial statements. In this way, an element of US reporting practice was transplanted directly to Germany (Wietzke, 1962:12). This requirement was in force for a short period only, but it did have a lasting effect. A small number of the affected companies continued to publish consolidated statements on a voluntary basis[38]. A requirement to publish consoli-

---

[37] Fuchs and Gerloff (1954:138); cf. Weiß (1949).
[38] Adler, Düring, Schmaltz (1972:III,3); cf. Fettel (1958).

dated financial statements was imposed for the first time on all companies (AGs) by the 1965 Company Law.

In the Netherlands, it could be claimed in 1926 that there existed hardly any discussion of consolidation in the literature, and that many Dutch auditors did not appreciate the importance of the consolidated balance sheet (Ten Haven, 1926). The auditing textbook *Leerboek der Accountancy* (Nijst, 1929) devoted a chapter to publications by holding companies in which various alternatives, including consolidated statements, were discussed. This text emphasized the need to protect the publishing companies, and competitive damage was advanced as a plausible reason for not publishing consolidated statements. In keeping with this cautious attitude, Blommaert (1995) found only 11 listed Dutch companies that published consolidated financial statements before the Second World War[39].

From ten Haven's (1926) assertions, but also from the basis of retrospective assessments by Groeneveld (1962) and Goudeket (1961), it appears that consolidation was at first accepted as a tool for internal use rather than as an element of external financial reporting. Loos (1940) repeated ten Haven's call for Dutch auditors to promote an accounting tool that had proven its usefulness in the US, but which appeared only 'sporadically' in the Netherlands.

It was only during the decade following the War that consolidated financial statements began to be regarded as an important element of up-to-date external financial reporting. According to Hofman (1950:387), there were two reasons why consolidated external reporting, which after all had been known in the US for about half a century, attracted attention in the Netherlands in the late 1940s.

First, a large number of Dutch companies had extensive interests in the Dutch East Indies which, in 1950, became independent as Indonesia. Before the war, assets and liabilities held in the East Indies

---

[39] See also Polak (1933:30-31) for a summary review of contemporary Dutch practices.

could be integrated in the financial statements without difficulty owing to the free convertibility of colonial currency. With independence, however, currency convertibility was no longer guaranteed. Assets and liabilities in Indonesia had to be treated as if they belonged to foreign subsidiaries over which the parent company no longer had full control. Therefore, many companies and their auditors were for the first time confronted with issues of consolidation of foreign subsidiaries.

Second, the Companies Act 1948 required publication of consolidated financial statements by English holding companies. This did attract some attention in the Dutch literature, and it was pointed out that Dutch accounting and Dutch auditors ought not, in this respect, to fall behind other nations (Spinosa Cattela, 1947; *cf.* Spinosa Cattela 1948b:chapter 15).

Moreover, the British requirements had direct implications for the two Anglo-Dutch multinationals, UNILEVER and KONINKLIJKE PETROLEUM. The first consolidation of UNILEVER in 1945[40] and the announcement by KONINKLIJKE PETROLEUM in 1950 that it would soon follow suit were considered as landmark events by Hofman (*op.cit.*).

When opinions could be aired without imposing strict obligations, consolidated reporting for external purposes began to be recommended, as in the 1955 Rijkens report and the 1956 Henri Sijthoff norms. The Stock Exchange Association, however, did not go as far as to require consolidated financial statements (something which the London Stock Exchange had done in 1939). In 1951, the Association declared that it had considered this option, but that the consequences of this step could not be assessed to their full extent. It contented itself 'for the time being' with urging listed companies to provide a list of subsidiaries, 'if possible accompanied by extensive

---

[40] Blommaert (1995) cites the year 1928 as the start of UNILEVER's consolidation. This was, however, a one-off event on the occasion of the merger between the Dutch and the British company. During the 1930s, the company did not publish consolidated statements.

information'[41].

As explained more fully in Blommaert (1995), the 1970 Act did not contain a strict legal requirement to provide consolidated financial statements. Consolidation was presented as an option next to combined or separate subsidiary financial statements. Of course, for all companies with more than a very small number of subsidiaries, presenting consolidated financial statements would be the only practical way to comply with the legal requirements.

6.6.2 Comments on observed disclosure practices

Figure 6.7 summarizes the introduction of consolidated financial reporting in the Netherlands. In presenting the percentage of companies that include consolidated financial statements, it is possible either to take a percentage of all companies, or to take into account that for companies without subsidiaries publication of consolidated financial statements is not relevant.

In figure 6.7, the data on 'gross' and 'net' disclosure percentages refer to this distinction. As indicated in Appendix A, this distinction is often of a judgmental nature. Indications of the spread of consolidation in other countries are included for comparison. Complete series were generally not available for these countries[42].

Blommaert (1995) contains a major study of the development of consolidated financial reporting by Dutch listed companies during the 20th century. Rather than presenting an extensive analysis of the sample data, this section will concentrate on comparing and supple-

---

[41] Vereniging voor den Effectenhandel, 'Publicatie van gegevens door naamloze vennootschappen', *Mededelingen van het bestuur aan de leden*, No. 285, 15 October 1951.

[42] The UK figure is based on *Survey of Published Accounts*. Unfortunately, no UK data before 1967 are available, except those in Bircher (1988) for the largest 40 British companies. The Companies Act (1967) ended the period during which consolidated statements might be provided on a voluntary basis. The US data are derived from *Accounting Trends & Techniques*. Data before 1959 were not available. The Australian data are taken from Whittred (1986), the Canadian data from Murphy (1988).

Figure 6.7 Consolidated reporting
(Publication of consolidated statements)

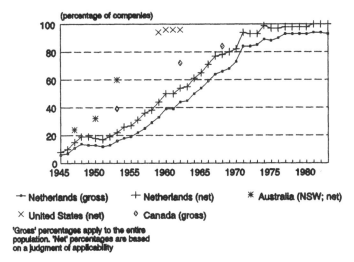

— Netherlands (gross)   + Netherlands (net)   * Australia (NSW; net)

× United States (net)   ◊ Canada (gross)

'Gross' percentages apply to the entire
population. 'Net' percentages are based
on a judgment of applicability

menting some of Blommaert's results with data from the present
study.

Blommaert's data on first consolidations correspond well with those
used in this study[43]. The Blommaert study did not contain data that
allowed a precise estimation of the overall rate of adoption of consolidated financial statements.

Compared with other disclosures documented in this chapter, the
diffusion of consolidated financial statements is characterized by a
fairly smooth and almost constant increase in disclosure for the
twenty years between 1950 and 1969. Blommaert noted that in the
period around 1960 and in the years leading up to the 1970 Act there
were important changes in the rate of new consolidations. This

---

[43] For some companies, the years of first consolidation recorded in the
two studies differed. Repeated scrutiny of the financial statements showed
that such deviations were mainly due to different choices of whether consolidation of a subset of subsidiaries only results in a proper consolidated
financial statement. Hence, this study uses first consolidation data that
depart, in a small number of cases, from those in the Blommaert study.

254

pattern is confirmed by the present study as well, although the number of new consolidations around 1960 in this study does not depart much from the trend. The smooth pattern is related to the rarity of reversions to nondisclosure. Only one instance of reversion was observed. There is no indication of the sort of experimentation that was observed with some other items.

Although the foreign data shown in figure 6.7 are somewhat fragmentary, the suggestion is clearly that the Netherlands did to some extent lag behind the English-speaking countries in the adoption of consolidated financial statements. It should be remembered that the results may not always be strictly comparable. Differences may arise especially in determining the 'applicability' of consolidation. Furthermore, the difference with Canada, where consolidation did not become mandatory until a relatively late date, is not very great. Nor can it be assumed that German companies displayed a greater willingness to consolidate voluntarily (see above). As to France, consolidation was still in its infancy during the early 1960s[44].

Consolidation and the incidence of subsidiaries
One basic explanation for the spread of the consolidated financial statement would be the growing use of subsidiary companies. Mergers and takeovers occurred throughout the postwar period, but especially during the 1960s. In the early 1960s, mergers became sufficiently widespread to bring about a growing awareness of the 'merger phenomenon' (see Van Sloten, 1963, for various references). By the end of the decade, the volume of mergers and acquisition had swollen to a veritable merger wave (see figure 4.1). Figure 6.8 compares the increasing number of consolidating companies with the number of companies showing investments in one or more other companies in their parent company balance sheet. The

---

[44] 'in neither France nor Germany is a holding company obliged to publish accounts for the group. (...) [s]ome French companies are already beginning to do so on a voluntary basis' (Most, 1964:10).

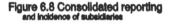

Figure 6.8 Consolidated reporting
and incidence of subsidiaries

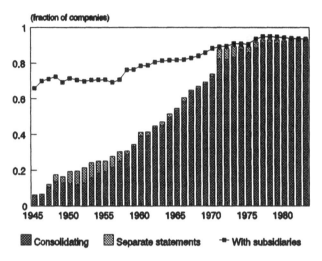

(fraction of companies)

■ Consolidating   ▨ Separate statements   --■-- With subsidiaries

financial statements of many companies did not provide the information necessary to distinguish between controlling and minority shareholdings[45]. The percentage of companies with subsidiaries (shown in figure 6.8) is therefore an overstatement of the number of companies for which consolidation was appropriate.

Until the late 1950s, the percentage of companies without subsidiaries, and for which consolidation was therefore certainly inappropriate, remained stable around 30%. By 1960, this percentage starts to fall, corresponding indeed with the increase in consolidation noticed by Blommaert. About 25 sample companies acquired investments during the period studied. In 40% of these cases, this coincided

---

[45] Article 42 of the Commercial Code did require the separate disclosure of investments *(deelnemingen)* in other companies. According to Van der Heijden (1929:355), 'investments' were not defined in terms of control but in terms of the relationship between the operations of the investing and investee companies. This provision makes it unlikely that investments were hidden in other balance sheet items, but it does not guarantee that all investments shown were controlled by the investing company.

with a first consolidation. For the other 60%, first consolidation happened on average 7 to 8 years after the acquisition of the first investment. Changes in investments in other companies were apparently an important, but not a decisive factor in the spread of consolidated reporting, as a large proportion of companies started to consolidate rather later than they might have done.

Interim formats

A possible interim format between no and full consolidation is the inclusion of separate financial statements of major subsidiaries in the parent annual report. This approach to disclosure was not widely used. Figure 6.8 shows two periods when an appreciable percentage of companies published separate financial statements: from the late 1940s to the late 1950s, and in the early 1970s.

During the late 1940s, reporting of separate financial statements was limited almost exclusively to trading and mining companies with a clear distinction between overseas operations and the metropolitan parent company. HV ROTTERDAM, FRANSCH SOUDAN, TWENTSCHE HANDEL, HVA, REISS, LINDETEVES, ALGEMENE EXPLORATIE, DORP, MAINZ fall into this group. These companies typically published separate financial statements for the domestic and overseas operations, the latter usually in local currency. Companies with investments in the Dutch East Indies/Indonesia were regarded as problematic because of uncertainties regarding currency convertibility. A number of auditors preferred non-consolidation and separate reporting in local currency in this case (Hofman, 1950:422-23). This problem (and hence the need for separate financial statements) was ended by the nationalization of Dutch investments in Indonesia in 1957. Around 1970, a number of companies disclosed separate financial statements apparently in response to the demands of the 1970 Act. OOSTZEE, GROFSMEDERIJ and REEUWIJK published separate statements for a few years before changing to consolidation.

6.6.3 Summary

The introduction of consolidated reporting was achieved roughly between 1950 and 1970 in a process of constant disclosure expansion. Although the 1970 Act did have a role to play in persuading the last nondisclosers, the diffusion of consolidated reporting was far advanced by the later 1960s. The background of this phenomenon was a process of increasing merger and acquisition activity starting in the middle 1950s and peaking in 1969.

6.7 The Funds Statement

6.7.1 Introduction

In the US, the idea of explaining changes in balance sheet items like cash or working capital in terms of changes in other balance sheet items can be traced back to the 19th century. Embryonic funds statements are reported to have been in use by various companies throughout the second half of the 19th century, while the funds statement made its entry into the textbooks in the first decades of the 20th century. But acceptance as a tool for financial analysis did not imply acceptance as an element of public financial reporting. Only four out of 60 surveyed US companies published a funds statement before 1925 (Rosen and DeCoster, 1969). A survey by Kempner (1957) revealed that in the middle 1950s about one-half of US audit firms regularly included a funds statement in their long-form audit report to clients. The accounting staff of many large clients already prepared funds statements for internal use themselves. Again, the inclusion of funds statements in reports to stockholders lagged behind: for the same period, Käfer and Zimmerman (1967) cite a number of studies reporting that funds statements were included in (depending on the sample of reports surveyed) not more than 35% of published financial statements.

It was not until 1961 that an AICPA research study (*Accounting Research Study No. 2*) on the subject appeared. This was followed in 1963 by APB Opinion No. 3, which contained the opinion that companies should in general include a funds statement in their

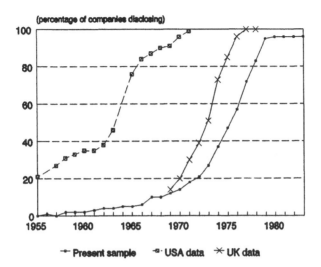

Figure 6.9 Adoption of funds statements

(percentage of companies disclosing)

— Present sample   -⊡- USA data   ✳ UK data

published financial statements.

The adoption of funds statements by US companies as reported in *Accounting Trends & Techniques* is charted in figure 6.9. This shows that the real breakthrough of the funds statement occurred in the US as late as the middle 1960s. In the 1962 volume of *Accounting Trends & Techniques,* this phenomenon received the following comment:

> As may be noted (...), the trend here is strongly in favor of the statements of sources and applications of funds (...). The "funds statement" is no innovation in the field of accounting, but it is becoming more prominent, and is now to a greater extent taking its place among the statements covered by the auditor's report. (p. 17)

According to Rosen and DeCoster (1969:133), credit for this development must not be given to the APB, whose recommendations in Opinion No. 3 were 'vague', but rather to the New York Stock Exchange and the Federation of Financial Analysts 'who strongly advocated its use'. APB Opinion 19, which required the publication of a funds statement from 1971 onwards, merely confirmed previous developments. According to data published in Murphy (1988:277), the adoption of the funds statement in Canada went virtually parallel with that in the United States.

Previous studies, notably by Dijksma (1984, 1987) point out that the the funds statement has but a short history in the Netherlands. However, the main difference between the two countries lies in the early adoption history, which in the US goes back well before the War, whereas the first published funds statements in the Netherlands date from the late 1950s. When data from the present study and US data are compared, as in figure 6.9, it appears that as far as adoption on a substantial scale is concerned, the Netherlands was about ten to fifteen years behind the US.

Compared to the UK, the Netherlands certainly was not far behind. In 1961, the funds statement could be presented in Britain as a new device from the United States, that was hardly if at all used in British annual reports[46]. According to remarks in Murray (1965: 69-70), Käfer and Zimmerman (1967:109) and Hendriksen (1969-:24), it seems unlikely that more than a handful of British companies included funds statements in their financial statements during the first half of the 1960s. Figure 6.9 shows that around 1970, practices in the Netherlands and the United Kingdom were approximately similar. After 1970, the funds statement spread more rapidly in the UK than in the Netherlands, at first on a voluntary basis, and from 1975 onwards under the influence of SSAP 10.

In Germany, the funds statement had traditionally occupied an important place in the literature on company finance and planning. As documented in Käfer and Zimmerman (1967), the notion of the *Bewegungsbilanz* went back to prewar finance textbooks. It is also

---

[46] See 'Points from published accounts: the source and application of funds', in: *Accountancy* (UK), vol. 72 no. 813, May 1961, p. 298. The article was illustrated by a funds statement from a Newfoundland company since, apparently, no British examples were at hand.

true that the relevance of developments in the US for German reporting were perceived rather quickly by at least some German authors. Holzer and Schönfeld (1962:564) raised the question 'whether [the introduction of the proposals of *Accounting Research Study No. 2*] would not influence the published annual reports of European companies'. An expanding use of funds statements in annual reports was in fact observed during the middle 1960s, indicating that German practice was (by a rough calculation), perhaps three years ahead of the Netherlands[47].

The available data on France do not allow a strict comparison but suggest that French companies were about equally swift, or lagged somewhat behind, the Netherlands in actual disclosure practice[48].

6.7.2 Origin and diffusion of Dutch fund statement disclosures

The funds statement did not make its appearance in the Dutch literature until the late 1950s[49], when the funds statement also

---

[47] Flohr (1964) reported that at that time '20 to 25 mainly large companies' in Germany published a funds statement. According to Käfer and Zimmerman (1967:115n) 'Only a few years ago one would only occasionally find such statements in German annual reports (...) This is different today: An examination of the annual reports of eighteen of the largest German corporations showed that in 1962 (...) eleven, and in 1963 (...) thirteen included fully developed capital flow statements (about two-thirds in the form of a funds statement)'. According to the data in table 6.2, it appears reasonable to estimate the total number of funds statements published in the Netherlands in 1967 at about 15. Allowing for at least twice as many listed companies in Germany would make this comparable with the 1963/1964 data for Germany.

[48] Boussard and Colasse (1992) state that 'in the late 1950s and early 1960s (...) a few French banks and some French companies started to use funds statements'. In 1968, an 'influential' model statement was published by the institute of auditors (OECCA). By 1981, '60 % of registered companies' disclosed a funds statement.

[49] However, Dijksma (1987) has documented various instances of funds statement technology being used in financial analysis and education in the Netherlands before the Second World War.

261

began to be used in annual reports. The 1955 Rijkens report did not call for a funds statement. It was recommended that 'especially the liquidity position be elucidated' in the directors' report (p. 19). A slightly more extensive note could be found in the 1962 successor report: 'To enhance the insight in the manner in which the company is being financed, it is suggested for consideration to pay attention [in the directors' report] to the sources and application of funds during the current and some previous financial years' (p. 49). The difference in wording between the two reports neatly coincides with the appearance of the first funds statements in Dutch annual reports as documented in table 6.2. Since the first adoptions all occurred well within the period with which this study is primarily concerned, and because these were adoptions by large, relatively well-documented companies, it is possible to reconstruct the circumstances of these first disclosures in more detail than for other items discussed in this chapter. The first adoptions will be discussed on a company by company basis.

Unilever

UNILEVER's 1956 funds statement appears to be first of its kind in the Netherlands. Although it is possible that proto funds-statements did appear sporadically in the early part of the century, as they did in the US, it is probably correct to identify part of UNILEVER's 1956 annual report as the first postwar example of a formal analysis of changes in liquidity (Dijksma, 1987:27). This 1956 statement, presented in the body of the text of the directors' report rather than as a separate table, explained changes in liquid assets as the combined result of retained earnings with depreciation added back, net investment in fixed assets and working capital, and 'other' transactions.

But even though a good case can be made to regard it as the first funds statement, this particular passage did have clear antecedents in the annual reports of previous years. It is likely that those involved in the gradual evolution of UNILEVER's annual reports would have considered the epithet 'first funds statement in the Netherlands', which suggests a distinctly recognizable innovation, as inappropriate.

Table 6.2
First disclosures of funds statements 1956-1970[50]

Year of first disclosure	Company
1956	UNILEVER
1958	KONINKLIJKE PETROLEUM
1960	Hoogovens[51]
1961	VLISSINGENS KATOEN
1962	OGEM
1963	KLM
1964	AKU
1966	TEXTIEL UNIE
1967	INDOHEEM
	MÜLLER
	KEY
1968	NKF
1969	BYENKORF
	ACF

Since 1951, the UNILEVER annual report included a section of graphical representations to illustrate developments over time. One of these, shown from 1951 to 1953 and again in 1955, displayed in two parallel stacked bars on the one hand the investment in fixed assets and working capital, and on the other hand the sources of

---

[50] On the basis of Scholten (1962:221-2), it appears plausible that this listing is complete for the years until 1961, that is, for the first four disclosing companies. Zwagerman (1970) reports that 11 listed companies disclosed a funds statement in 1967, which would indicate that the listing in table 6.2 is a comprehensive presentation of funds statement disclosure by listed companies until 1967. This is not particularly likely, given that the table is basically the result of a sample of 30% of listed companies.

[51] In fact, Hoogovens 1960 disclosure was part of a long incidental discussion of the financial position in the directors' report. It was not until 1964 that the company started to publish funds statements on a regular basis.

263

finance consisting of retained income, current cost depreciation and issues of securities. Readers were invited to observe the large extent to which the company relied on retained earnings to finance its expansion, and to observe (in an accompanying diagram), the large share of earnings absorbed by taxation. In this way, the company used its annual report to reiterate a message that was a main theme in its public policy statements throughout the early 1950s, that financing through retained earnings was essential, and that high taxes were a potential threat to economic development[52].

In 1956, the notion of sources and application of funds that was implicitly in these graphical representations was combined with other elements of the directors report. This had, in a separate section on 'Finance', already for a number of years included as part of the narrative items like the change in liquid assets and the amounts raised by issues of securities. In 1956, all these elements were combined, still in the text of the narrative, into a tabular format which linked them all together in an arithmetically closed addition. This, then, was the first funds statement.

The direct motivation for this change was probably the extraordinary level of liquidity attained by the company in 1956 as a result of the Suez crisis, a factor mentioned in this context in the directors' report. The company may have felt the need to explain the large increase in net liquid assets by a more elaborate statement. This may also explain why the 'funds statement' did not reappear in the 1957 annual report, when net liquid assets had fallen again to more normal levels. However, in 1958, the process repeated itself. The company was again compelled to explain a huge increase in liquidity as a result of various incidental circumstances (sales of subsidiaries, currency movements) and it resorted again to the inclusion of a 'funds statement' in the directors report. By this time, it may have

---

[52] See for UNILEVER's emphasis on internally financed growth: Wilson/Baudet (1968:135-6). See also the 1948 and 1949 addresses by UNILEVER chairman P. Rijkens to the general meeting of shareholders and the 1956 lecture 'Het bedrijfsleven en de belastingen' (All published as brochures by the company).

been decided that this type of information was useful on a permanent basis as well, and it remained an element of the financial statements that eventually evolved into the modern cash flow statement.

The conclusion should therefore be that UNILEVER, rather than introducing the funds statement as a conspicuous innovation in 1956, merely arrived through gradual evolution at a convenient format to convey messages particular to its situation in the 1950s. It was only subsequently that these statements came to be seen as a useful permanent fixture of the annual report.

Koninklijke Petroleum

The first funds statement published by KONINKLIJKE PETROLEUM in 1958 did have a somewhat similar origin. It too appeared originally as a statement to bring a particular message across, rather than as a general-purpose increase in disclosure. In the 1958 annual report, the company included a separate table labelled 'Sources and applications of funds' which was, in effect, an approximated cash-flow statement. It was included in a section of the directors' report headed 'Influence of taxation on growth' and the accompanying text pointed out that a very large part of the huge revenues of the group were paid out to various governments in the form of taxation, and that of the remaining income a large fraction had to be retained to finance heavy capital expenditures. The company apparently realized, as did UNILEVER in the same year, that this type of table might also be useful as a regular disclosure. This transition to a general purpose funds statement is neatly illustrated in the 1959 annual report. This included again a similar table, this time in a separate section of the directors' report headed 'Sources and application of funds'. In the accompanying text it was stated that '[t]his table has been prepared to place the very large amounts received by the Group companies from sales to customers all over the world in a proper perspective, that is, in relation to the equally large expenditures that must be made out of these revenues. This year, there are no specific comments to make on these figures, although we might point out that the total amount paid in some form of taxation or another to the government, has increased again' (1959 report, p. 17).

265

Hoogovens

Around 1960, the Dutch steel company Hoogovens arrived at an important juncture in its development as it approached the capacity limits of its core rolling mill installed in 1952. Further growth would entail a new round of core capacity expansion involving large investments. Moreover, it was decided that further growth should no longer merely consist of increasing output of the basic sheet steel, but that there should be a strategic shift towards a wider product range including profile steel and non-steel metals such as aluminum (see also Dankers and Verheul, 1993:chapter 2). In the 1959 and 1960 annual reports, these strategic shifts were discussed. In the 1960 annual report, this discussion focused on the way the large financing requirements of the coming expansion would be met. To elucidate this discussion, a 7-year summary of sources and application of funds was included as part of the narrative. As with the first UNILEVER and KONINKLIJKE PETROLEUM funds statements, this first Hoogovens funds statement was an incidental disclosure, included to illustrate a rather specific point. In the 1961 annual report, no analysis of sources and application of funds was included. Instead, the directors' report focused on another specific problem of expansion and included, for this year only, detailed analyses of movements in its workforce. In the 1962 annual report, there was a short note on the realization of the expansion plans unveiled in the 1960 annual report. This included, as part of the narrative and without separate title, a short analysis that could formally be classified as a funds statement: it balanced the figures for investment in fixed assets and working capital with retained earnings, depreciation, increases in liabilities and decreases in liquid assets. This was not repeated in the 1963 annual report. It was only in 1964 that the company started to include, on a regular basis, separate tables in the directors' report entitled 'movements in liquidity', and which were, in effect, proper funds statements.

The next generation

In the early 1960s there is a shift in funds statement disclosure. The funds statement was by now not necessarily a statement to be used to explain extraordinary situations, but had become, as indicated by the practice of KONINKLIJKE PETROLEUM, a standard element that might usefully be included in all financial statements on a regular basis. It had become a distinctly recognizable and 'adoptable' innovation.

The gradual emergence of the funds statement as a distinct phenomenon is reflected in the Dutch literature. Because of its relatively late appearance, a more complete reconstruction of the 'discovery' of the funds statement in the literature can be given here than is possible for other items. The emergence of the funds statement is closely linked to prof. B. Pruijt of the Rotterdam School of Economics. Pruijt was involved in a number of instances where the funds statement emerged in the period 1958-1962, and he can therefore, to a certain extent, be credited with the status of 'change agent' with regard to this particular innovation.

Pruijt appears to have discovered the funds statement for himself in the late 1950s. In a 1956 article, Pruyt discussed the impossibility of complying with the recommendation in the Rijkens to give insight into liquidity by means of a balance sheet, however well ordered. The alternative of a funds statement was not mentioned. In a 1961 article[53], Pruyt presented the funds statement as a new and promising phenomenon, one that had not spontaneously evolved in Dutch practice. As sources, he referred to publications on national income accounting by general economists, and to US textbooks on financial statement analysis.

During this period, Pruijt also supervised the PhD-thesis of Th.M. Scholten (published as Scholten, 1962) which contained an extensive discussion of the first funds statements in Dutch annual reports. Finally, Pruijt was an active member of the Hamburger committee which prepared the 1962 Employers' recommendations on financial reporting. These various activities presumably reinforced each other, and support the assumption that Pruijt played a pivotal role in spreading knowledge of the funds statement in the Netherlands.

---

[53] Recognized by Dijksma (1987) as the first Dutch publication on the use of the funds statement in external financial reporting.

It can therefore hardly be coincidental that the next company to publish a funds statement, in 1961, was VLISSINGENS KATOEN, a middle-sized company with which Pruijt served as a member of the Supervisory Board. In the 1961 financial statements, a separate table of sources and applications of funds was introduced, together with a summary in graphical form. These data were explicitly presented as general purpose information to be provided on a regular basis next to the customary balance sheet and income statement. That it was Pruijt's influence that played a role in this adoption, is supported by the conclusion of Scholten that VLISSINGENS KATOEN's funds statement was similar to the one indicated by Pruijt in his 1961 article (Scholten, 1962:227)[54].

In the following years, there were more instances of companies adopting 'general-purpose' funds statements. OGEM was the first to follow in 1962. For this company, there is no readily available explanation in terms of 'change agents'. Starting with its 1962 annual report, the company thoroughly refurbished the layout and contents of its hitherto fairly traditional financial statements. On this occasion, it may have looked around for 'state of the art' reporting practices and have found them, for instance, in the recommendations of the Hamburger report published a year earlier. A funds statement was included without comment as a separate table at the back of the report, among other statistical summaries.

Next in line were KLM (1963) and AKU (1964). In the case of KLM, a vestige of the previous 'special purpose' funds statement can be discerned. The company started to disclose funds statements during a period of considerable financial difficulties. In 1962, the

---

[54] It is, however, likely that Pruijt's interest in funds statements was temporary. He never published any other article on the subject, and he did not avail himself of the first opportunity of publishing a funds statement himself. In the middle 1960s, he was made president of Steenkolen Handelsvereeniging NV. This large private company started to publish its financial statements in 1968 on a voluntary basis. Although these statements were remarkable enough for their generous disclosure (see Brands, 1969), they did not contain a funds statement until 1972.

government had to step in with additional funding and a standby credit facility to prevent liquidity shortages. The initial funds statements were included to illustrate that, despite grave problems, the company's liquidity position was still sufficient and that there was no need to call upon the government credit facility. The funds statement was retained as a permanent feature of the report in later years. It is also quite possible that the sudden upsurge in the use of funds statements in the USA played a role in the disclosures by KLM and AKU, since both companies were listed in New York. As illustrated in figure 6.9, the adoptions of these two companies coincided with the final breakthrough of the funds statement in the USA.

PHILIPS, the only other company listed in New York at the time, did not publish a funds statement until 1972. A reason for this may have been a conviction within the company that a traditional funds statement linked to a current cost balance sheet and income statement would not provide much insight because of the large influence of 'elements of bookkeeping' on such a statement. This view was put forward by P.C. Breek, a board member of Philips, in 1974 (Breek, 1974).

Later adoptions

By the mid-1960s, a number of factors could influence the decision of individual companies to adopt funds statements. Apart from developments in the USA, which were made known to the Dutch in review articles like Diephuis (1966), there were the recommendations in the domestic literature. There was also a small number of well-known companies publishing funds statements on a regular basis. But although this could provide sufficient justification for any company considering publishing a funds statement, it apparently provided little active encouragement. The percentage of companies publishing a funds statement did not reach 20% until well into the 1970s. Around 1972/3, however, diffusion of the funds statement began to take off. By 1979, about 90% of the listed companies published a funds statement.

Developments from 1972 to 1979 should perhaps be characterized as an 'internal influence' diffusion process, because there are few

269

discernible outside influences that might be used to explain the increase in funds statement usage after 1972:

- The 1970 Act on Annual Financial Statements did not mention the funds statement. In itself, this was not too surprising since the law aimed primarily at codification of existing practice and was limited in scope to the traditional financial statements: balance sheet and income statement. It would, however, not have been surprising to find references to the funds statement in the extensive literature produced in the course of the enactment process[55].
- The Tripartite Study group set up to produce guidance on financial reporting following the 1970 Act did not publish a statement on the funds statement until 1979, when adoption was virtually complete. Even then, its guidance was very general and widely criticized (*e.g.* Rietkerk, 1981).
- In its first (1977) pronouncement, the Enterprise Chamber (OK) ruled that funds statements, when published on a voluntary basis together with the financial statements, were part of the financial statements as defined by the law. This pronouncement may have increased attention for the funds statement, but it did not contain any formal encouragements to publish them.
- A similar increase in attention without formal encouragement was provided by the publication of IASC's ED 7 in 1976.

One possible source of external influence may be identified, however. The norms of the Henri Sijthoff award for the best annual report were changed in 1968 and 1974. At the time of the 1968 change, the funds statement was not mentioned. In 1974, though, the funds statement was included among the basic requirements

---

[55] In this literature, an important theme was the extent to which the balance sheet could meet the proposed legal requirement that it give 'insight into the liquidity of the enterprise'. Even though it was widely assumed that the balance sheet could not do this, there was no discussion of a possible role for the funds statement in this regard.

defining eligibility for the award. Apart from any influence of the Sijthoff award, it seems likely that the funds statement began to be adopted in the course of the 1970s for want of opposition rather than because of active encouragement. It was perceived as a low-cost innovation that was increasingly common, but real enthusiasm for the funds statement was still rare by the late 1970s. A 1979 survey (reported in Klaassen and Schreuder, 1981) showed that the funds statement ranked rather low in importance according to financial statement readers. Vecht (1977) did not think that the typical funds statement published in the mid-1970s provided any useful information in addition to the balance sheets on which it was typically based.

6.7.3 Summary

The first funds statements evolved during the late 1950s. As was demonstrated for UNILEVER, the precursors of the funds statement were verbal discussions of particular financing problems in the directors' report. The supporting figures in these discussions gradually took on the format of funds statements. When they had reached this stage of a distinctive format and label, other companies started to include funds statement as a regular element of their annual report. From the middle 1960s onwards, funds statement adoption proceeded smoothly, resulting in a regular 'internal influence' diffusion pattern, apparently largely unaffected by any outside influences.

6.8 Disclosure of current cost data

6.8.1 Introduction

Current cost accounting[56] has been advocated in theory in the Netherlands since the 1920s and was quite well-known as an alternative

---

[56] The distinctly Limpergian construct of *vervangingswaarde* is best translated as 'current value accounting'. In this section, 'current cost accounting' is used as a more general term to denote all attempts to incorporate specific price changes in the financial statements.

for historical cost accounting by the end of the 1930s (see Cam-fferman, 1994b). Prewar usage of current cost accounting in pub-lished annual reports was rare, however, and largely confined to partial applications. In the early 1950s more pronounced forms of current cost accounting began to be adopted by a number of compa-nies. The most conspicuous of these was PHILIPS, which used a full-fledged system of current cost accounting starting with its 1951 financial statements (see Groeneveld, 1953; Brink, 1992). On the basis of this example, current cost accounting was recommended in the 1955 and 1962 employers' reports. At least among auditors, current cost accounting was considered by many to be the clearest indicator of the high quality of accounting thought and practice in the Netherlands.

It was not until the middle 1960s, however, that empirical data became available on the actual extent of current cost accounting practice in the Netherlands. In surveys reported in Tempelaar (1966) and Foppe (1965), 10 to 20% of listed companies (depending on the definitions used) applied some form of current cost account-ing. During the 1970s, more systematic data were gathered, but the conclusion was that there was only slow progress in the movement towards more widespread adoption of current cost accounting[57].

Despite the slow development of practice, theoretical attention for current cost accounting increased during the 1970s (see Groeneveld, 1979; for a review). One of the more important stimulants for further reflection was the topicality of inflation accounting in the English-speaking world during that period. Current cost accounting also played an important role in the deliberations of the Tripartite Study Group and in the preparations for the adaptation of Dutch law to the Fourth Directive (Zeff et al., 1992, chapters 5 and 6).

---

[57] See the NIvRA biennial survey, *Onderzoek Jaarverslagen*, and *Vijftig jaarverslagen — Gewogen en te licht bevonden*, Economisch Instituut der Rijksuniversiteit Utrecht (Leiden: Stenfert Kroese, 1975).

6.8.2 Comments on observed disclosure practices

Figure 6.10 shows the development of current cost applications over time, broken down into categories indicating various degrees of disclosure. In the literature, many elaborate classifications of current cost applications have been suggested to describe the various degrees of comprehensiveness with which current cost accounting may be applied (see, for instance, Slot and Vijn, 1979, ch. 16). In this section, the discussion will be limited to three types or gradations of current cost accounting:

- Partial supplementary data: indications in the notes to the financial statements of current costs of selected assets or the effect of current cost accounting on selected income statement items.
- Partial financial statement applications: the main, or supplementary financial statements, are in part based on current cost accounting.
- Full financial statement applications: current cost accounting is used for all applicable items in the (main or supplementary) balance sheet and income statement.

Figure 6.10 shows that there was only limited use of current cost data in the financial statements themselves until the 1970s. Before that time, companies mainly limited themselves to partial supplementary data. Full financial statement applications of current cost accounting remained rather rare.

At the peak, in 1983, 8 out of 46 companies showed full current cost financial statements. Together with partial financial statement applications, almost half the companies eventually included some current cost data in their financial statements. By the 1970s, of course, in many countries accounting for inflation had become the subject of intensive discussion, and by that time current cost accounting could no longer be assumed to be a purely Dutch phenomenon.

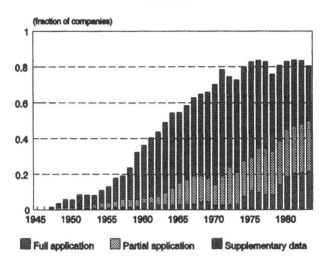

Figure 6.10a Current cost data
balance sheet

(fraction of companies)

■ Full application   ▨ Partial application   ■ Supplementary data

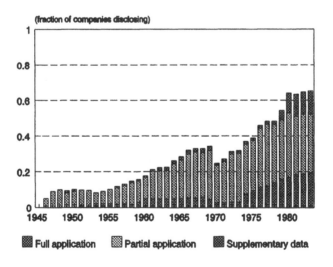

Figure 6.10b Current cost data
income statement

(fraction of companies disclosing)

■ Full application   ▨ Partial application   ■ Supplementary data

274

Interim formats

Most companies that applied some form of current cost accounting did not do so straight away. Rather, the preferred course during the 1950s and 1960s was to meet calls for current cost accounting by disclosing in the notes an indication of the current cost of major fixed assets. For this particular purpose, the notion of 'insured value' ('verzekerde waarde') enjoyed a spell of considerable popularity, which can be explained by the fact that it was directly available without additional costs. The two employers' reports did recommend supplemental disclosure of the current costs of assets, but they did not mention that insured value might be used as an approximation of current cost. In fact, this approximation was frowned upon by the more rigorous theorists (see Vecht, 1981: 93; Slot and Vijn, 1979:81). It was suggested mainly by those outside the audit profession, such as the Wiardi-Beckman report of 1959 (p. 122), the financial journalist Posthumus Meyjes (1960:262) and the Society for Investor Protection[58].

In 1973, the Tripartite Study Group expressed its view (in an exposure draft) that 'the disclosure of insured value, which occurs frequently in practice, is (...) of limited value and can, in certain circumstances, be misleading' (IIa1).

The importance of 'insured value' as a preparatory stage for current cost accounting is shown by the fact that, of the 31 companies that switched to some form of current cost accounting in both balance sheet and income statement, 19 did so after a number of years during which they just disclosed 'insured value'. Those that adopted current cost without this interim stage were either very large companies (such as NSU, UNILEVER, KONINKLIJKE PETROLEUM) for which there was probably not a large cost advantage in gathering data on this particular approximation of current costs, or pioneers (PHILIPS, AKU, NIJVERDAL) that adopted current cost when 'insured value' was not yet a common disclosure.

---

[58] Vereniging Effectenbescherming, letter 14 July 1965 to SER relative to Verdam committee report.

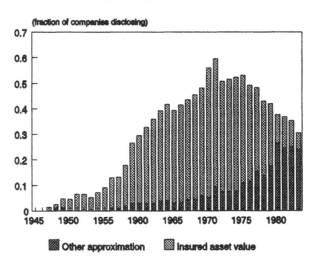

Figure 6.11 Current cost data
types of supplementary data

(fraction of companies disclosing)

■ Other approximation   ▨ Insured asset value

The development over time of supplementary balance sheet data is shown in figure 6.11. As can been seen, the provision of this sort of information reached its peak in 1971. After that, most of the decline can be attributed to companies moving on to more advanced stages of current cost disclosure. It does not seem unreasonable to attribute at least part of the transition to other approximations of current cost observed from 1975 onwards to the Tripartite Study Group's discouragement of insured value. Whereas in other instances discussed in this chapter there appeared to be no ground to assume a large role for the TO in furthering disclosure among listed companies, in this case where it tried to discourage a disclosure, it appears to have been quite successful.

Current cost data within the financial statements
The extent of current cost usage in the financial statements themselves (that is, partial or full applications in main or supplementary balance sheet and income statement) is shown in figure 6.12. From this figure, it is evident to what extent current cost accounting was in fact a 1970s phenomenon: it was not until 1965 that the adoption rate

276

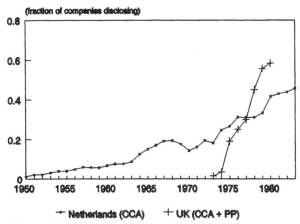

Figure 6.12 Inflation Accounting
In the Netherlands and the UK

(fraction of companies disclosing)

— Netherlands (CCA)   + UK (CCA + PP)

Figures refer to partial or full
applications of CCA (PP) in either main
or supplementary statements

reached 10%. By 1983, though, almost half (21 companies) of the surveyed companies used current cost data for at least part of the items in both the balance sheet and income statement (or supplementary statements). The fact that, by the early 1980s, current cost accounting was for most companies a rather recent phenomenon can also be stated in another way. By 1983, two-thirds of the companies with at least partial financial statement applications of current cost had started to do so in or after 1971. Only three companies (PHILIPS, HEINEKEN and NIJVERDAL) could trace their current cost accounting back to the 1950s while four others had started during the 1960s[59].

Comparison with UK disclosure
During the 1970s, various forms of accounting for inflation were introduced in UK accounting standards. Between 1971 and 1980, an

---

[59] AKU had started in 1953, but AKZO discontinued the practice between 1969 and 1974.

277

almost annual series of study reports, exposure drafts and final accounting standards were published which turned accounting for inflation into a major accounting issue[60]. The resulting changes in accounting practice are shown in figure 6.12 as well. Comparisons between the Dutch and the UK series should be made with some caution since the data may not, owing to the definitions used, be strictly comparable. Moreover, the UK data contain a (small) component of Purchasing-Power disclosures which are not included in the Dutch data. Nevertheless, it can be concluded that, as a minority practice, current cost accounting developed in the Netherlands well before it developed in the UK. However, regulatory pressure in the UK led to a sharp increase in disclosure in that country between 1974 and 1979. By the later 1970s, the UK led the way in accounting for inflation, at least in terms of the crude measure of the number ofcompanies that did at least disclose some information on this topic.

Current cost disclosures and inflation
Figure 6.12 shows an acceleration in reporting current cost figures following 1964, and a decrease in the percentage of disclosing companies around 1970. Closer observation of the data shows that the fall in the number of disclosing companies around 1970 is due to (a) the fact that a disproportionate number of companies being delisted in the late 1960s merger wave were current cost users and (b) to an almost complete temporary standstill in new current cost disclosures around 1970.
In general terms, it is not too difficult to relate the increase in current cost disclosures to the rate of inflation. As indicated in figure 6.13, current cost disclosures began to take off when the rather stable price level of the 1950s and 1960s gave way to sustained inflation. The very large price increases after 1974 coincide

---

[60] An ASC discussion paper was published in 1971. This formed the basis for ED 7 (1973) and SSAP 7 (1974). In September 1975, the Sandilands report was published. This led, in turn, to ED 18 (1976), the socalled Hyde Guidelines (1977), ED 24 (1979) and, finally, SSAP 16 (1980).

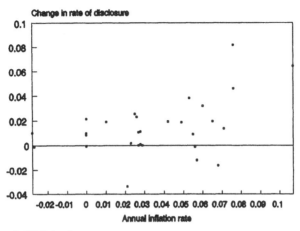

Figure 6.13 New current cost disclosures
and rate of inflation 1963-1983

Change in rate of disclosure

Inflation rate: CBS index of
manufacturing input prices

neatly with rather marked increases in current cost adoptions.
Drawing detailed conclusions about the relation of current cost
adoptions with inflation is plagued by the difficulty of defining
inflation. The data used in figure 6.13 are based on the producers'
price index. Using a headline inflation rate can result in rather
marked differences within individual years, although the overall
trend remains unchanged.

In addition to attributing the drop in current cost disclosures around
1970 to a temporary falling or levelling inflation rate, it is also
possible to point towards inherent difficulties with current cost
accounting that began to be evident around that time. Awareness of
the theoretical deficiencies of the traditional current cost approach
began to spread in the later 1960s (see Camfferman and Zeff, 1994).
An indication of a changing attitude to current cost accounting is
found in Blom (1967) who provides a critical review of the difficulties and dangers of applying current cost accounting in practice.
Blom concludes:

I think — and I have found support in conversations with many

279

directors and supervisory directors and with some auditors — that the objections against current cost financial statements are being felt ever more strongly. I therefore expect that we will go back to the traditional and internationally customary 'historical financial' balance sheets and income statements (p. 68).

Blom also points out that a number of companies that had adopted current cost accounting in the past because their competitors had done it or because their shareholders had asked for it, now regretted that decision. These companies often did not go back openly to historical costs. But because they omitted further revaluations of their assets, their financial statements would in a number of years revert automatically to a historical cost basis.

Blom's assertions are to some extent borne out by the facts of this survey, notably the drop in the number of new current cost adoptions in the late 1960s points in this direction. To what extent companies did relinquish current cost accounting without formal reinstatement of assets at historical cost was not systematically surveyed. Blom's prediction as to the continuing decline of current cost accounting was overtaken by the onset, in the 1970s, of an inflation more severe than before, and by a spell of international attention to current cost accounting that temporarily mitigated any possible concerns regarding international conformity of Dutch reporting practice.

Comments in annual reports

Company financial statements do shed some light on the perceptions of current cost disclosures by companies. Compared to other changes in disclosure, which usually were not commented upon, the incorporation of some form of current cost data in the financial statements was more often the subject of comments. In some cases (DRU, 1963; KORENSCHOOF, 1960), requests by shareholders were cited as reasons for additional disclosures. BYENKORF (1979/80) mentioned a more general growth in demand for insight in current costs. HEINEKEN (1957) strove for 'more clarity' in financial statement presentation, while SMITS (1964) used current cost data to 'give our balance sheet a more modern form'. In an unconcerned disregard of the preceding fifty years of theory development, REE-SINK (1979) started to value inventory at current cost 'in conformity with new insights'. INTERNATIO-MÜLLER included supplementary data in 1983 'also with a view to the Fourth Directive'.

Reasons for not or no longer supplying current cost data were also occasionally given. From 1977 to 1983, VAN OMMEREN apologized for not giving information on a current cost basis owing to 'the ongoing discussion in academic and business circles' and because 'sharp price fluctuations' made the application of current cost accounting difficult for this particular company.

Finally, VIHAMIJ BUTTINGER stopped after three years in 1973 because supplying current cost data was 'not really practicable'.

A case of extensive footnote explanation of additional disclosures can be found in the financial statements of KONINKLIJKE PETROLEUM (see also Grob, 1995). For this company, the reasons for addition or deletion of supplementary schedules were the developments in standard-setting in the English-speaking world. Its first inclusion of supplementary data on the basis of general price level accounting coincided with SSAP 7 (1974); current cost data were added when required by SSAP 16 (1979) and scrapped together with that statement. In other comments during the later 1970s, the company extensively explained its lack of confidence in the various accounting standards with which it had to comply[61]. For this particular company, at any rate, inclusion of current cost data was hardly a matter of voluntary disclosure at all.

The same appears to be true of UNILEVER, which professed to have used current cost data since the early 1950s for internal purposes (De Jong, 1980:18), but which only started the disclosure of supplemental financial statement data as late as 1976. On this occasion, as in 1980, when the supplementary data were much expanded, the company averred to have followed British standards (the Hyde Guidelines and SSAP 16, respectively). The Dutch pronouncements

---

[61] See also 'Shell vecht ED 24 (current cost) aan', *De Accountant*, vol. 86 no. 5, January 1980, p. 266.

of 1979 were mentioned to indicate that the company considered compliance with the British standards as equivalent with compliance with their Dutch counterparts.

Current cost disclosures and audit firms
Current cost accounting found its origins and its most enthusiastic promotors within the Dutch auditing profession. But within that profession, there were serious doubts and dissenting views as well. This can be illustrated by the following quotes from a published series of interviews with leading Dutch auditors from the postwar period (Schoonderbeek and De Hen, 1995):

> When I stopped practicing, I no longer had any client who did not prepare its financial statements on the basis of current values. (p. 3)

> Everybody tried in practice to be a propagandist for the application of current value by clients. Sometimes this succeeded in an internal trial. On the rarest of occasions it succeeded in the published annual report. (p. 50)

> I think that, insofar as in the Netherlands current value accounting is used, this has for the great majority of cases been encouraged by auditors (...). I used to recommend current value accounting, whenever this was useful. This advice was generally followed, albeit not always in the published annual report. (p. 60-61)

> With all large clients we pleaded the cause of current value accounting, and with success. (p. 66)

> I never recommended [current value accounting] to anyone. I discussed it sometimes with clients, but I never was a current value apostle. (p. 90)

Given these and other assertions[62], it appears useful to investigate the relationship between audit firms and current cost disclosures. One can examine this relationship by comparing
- the market shares of audit firms estimated on the basis of sample market shares, with
- the number of current cost disclosers among the clients of a particular firm relative to the total number disclosing companies in a particular year.

The significance of these comparisons is difficult to judge, though, because of (1) the relatively small number of disclosures through most of the period, (2) because of the small market shares of all except the largest firms, and (3) because of the continuous changes in the populations of audit firms and companies.

A rough indication of significance may be obtained by considering for each audit firm the number of current cost disclosers[63] among its clients in a particular year as the outcome of a binomial distribution[64]. On that basis, 10 out of 91 firms are identified as having, for one or more years, relatively many current cost disclosers among their clients. None of these cases appeared after 1973, suggesting that if a relationship of sorts existed, it did so only before that date. Six of these cases can be discounted as chance incidents during

---

[62] See, for instance, Klaassen (1975: 76), who reports on interviews with company managements on their motives for adopting current cost accounting. Six out of 29 companies mentioned that 'the attitude of the auditor had been of major importance' in the decision to adopt current cost accounting.

[63] In this case, and in the remainder of this section, current cost disclosure is narrowly defined as partial *or* full adoption in balance sheet *and* income statement.

[64] With the probability of success (p) equal to the total disclosure rate across all companies for that year, and n equal to the number of clients of the specific firm. A second simplification is to approximate the binomial with the normal distribution, which strictly speaking is unwarranted. The combined effect of these approximations is to overestimate the significance of relations between audit firms and current cost disclosures.

transition periods since they refer to short periods in the middle 1960s and early 1970s, when, as indicated above, there were considerable changes in the total number of disclosures. In all, the numbers appear to be insignificant in the sense that (with one possible exception, see below) there were no audit firms in the sample that displayed a clear and lasting tendency to have relatively many current cost disclosers among its clients.

These results are underlined by a more precise test of a less general hypothesis: whether current cost disclosures are associated with large audit firms. For the selected years 1963 and 1980, the relationship between audit firm size (measured by sample market share) and current cost disclosures was investigated. It was found that for both years, although current cost disclosures by clients of large firms were in excess of what might be expected on the basis of the firms' sample market share, these differences were not significant[65].

The fact that current cost disclosures among clients were more or less proportional to market share meant that during the 1950s, when the number of audit firms was large, quite a number of audit firms had current-cost using clients. The six companies using some form of current cost accounting in balance sheet and income statement during the 1950s retained five different audit firms. Among these,

---

[65] Audit firm size and current cost disclosures 1963 (1980)

	large firms	small firms
clients using current costs	6 (20)	3 (1)
clients not using current costs	45 (24)	41 (8)

Chi^2 values (with continuity correction) are insignificant at the 10% level.
'large' audit firms are defined as firms with greater than average market share.
'clients using current costs' have fully *or* partially adopted current cost accounting in *both* balance sheet and income statement.

Klynveld, Kraayenhof & Co. was prominent with two celebrated current cost users (PHILIPS and AKU) among its clients. But smaller firms also had their share of clients using current cost accounting. A very small audit firm like the one-man firm of M. Janssen[66] assisted in the adoption of a rather elaborate form of current cost accounting by DRU which coincided with the far better known adoption by PHILIPS in 1951.

The point that current cost disclosures tended to occur in harmony with audit firm market share is illustrated in figure 6.14. The two panels compare the data for the audit firms Klynveld, Kraayenhof & Co and Moret & Limperg, both combined with their respective predecessor firms. For the group of firms forming Moret & Limperg, the actual number of current cost disclosures follows quite closely the pattern suggested by the firm's market share. For the Klynveld firms, there is some indication that during the 1950s and early 1960s there was an excess of current cost using clients, but this had disappeared by 1970. In the years 1974-1976, Klynveld clients joined in the second wave of current cost adoptions. The firm, or rather, its clients, were a few years ahead of the remainder of the sample in choosing current cost accounting practices.

In all, it can be concluded that it is unlikely that there were large differences among Dutch audit firms regarding persistency or success in persuading their clients to provide current cost accounting information. Although it can therefore be tentatively concluded that all firms were equally active in this regard, no conclusions can be drawn regarding the level of their activity. On this issue, one still has to rely on assertions in the literature, as quoted in this section, that a large number of auditor regularly advocated current cost accounting.

---

[66] This firm would, through various mergers, later become a part of Dijker & Doornbos, and hence of Coopers & Lybrand.

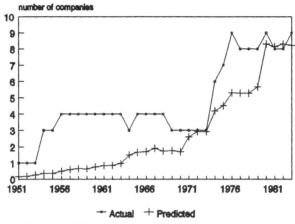

Figure 6.14 CCA adopters by audit firm
KKC constituent firms

KKC: Klynveld, Kraayenhof & Co
Prediction on the basis of market share

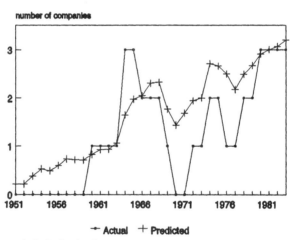

Figure 6.14b CCA adopters by audit firm
Moret & Limperg constituent firms

Predictions on the basis of market share

6.8.3 *Summary*

In the development of current cost disclosures, two stages can be distinguished. The first stage lasted until the late 1960s. During this period, the absence of significant attention for current cost accounting abroad meant that developments were governed by domestic circumstances only. Fairly widespread attitudes in favour of current cost led some pioneering companies to adopt rather elaborate systems of providing current cost information during the 1950s and 1960s. A more typical reaction was for companies to disclose some readily available supplementary data, most often the insured value of fixed assets.

During the 1970s, a second stage began. In this stage, high inflation and international attention for inflation accounting were accompanied in the Netherlands by a quickening of the pace of new current cost disclosures. In both stages, there is no evidence that particular Dutch audit firms can be associated with current cost adoptions by client companies.

6.9 Earnings per share

Compared with the United States, the ratio of earnings per share gained popularity but slowly in the Netherlands. According to a casual survey by Barr (1972), earnings per share started to be disclosed in US annual reports during the 1920s, with the practice gradually increasing in the 1930s. In the late 1940s and early 1950s, earnings per share had already been well-established in the United States as a tool of financial analysis for a considerable time (Myer, 1952:51,244). There are few indications that earnings per share was used at all in the Netherlands before or shortly after the war.

Earnings per share became a familiar notion in the Netherlands following the listing of the shares of KONINKLIJKE PETROLEUM in New York in 1954. This listing focused attention in the Netherlands on the importance attached in the United States to price-earnings ratios and hence to earnings per share:

287

The Dutch investor, not aware of the notion of the price:earnings-ratio (...) has had the opportunity in recent months to become acquainted with this concept. This phrase can frequently be encountered in the financial press these days, especially in observations on the shares of Royal Dutch Petroleum. These shares have become very popular with the American public since they were listed on the New York Stock Exchange. This popularity is based primarily, so it is said, on the very low P:E-ratio of the shares of Royal Dutch Petroleum relative to American oil shares. (Gans, 1954:918)

In 1955, J.M. Vecht commented on the relative unfamiliarity of Dutch investors with the notion of earnings per share and he provided a possible explanation for this phenomenon when he discussed the influx of American investment into the Amsterdam Stock Exchange during 1954:

One had to recognize the fact, peculiar [to those accustomed to] the Dutch circumstances, that the American investor calculates with the so-called 'price-earnings ratio', that is, with the ratio of the share price to *earned* (and therefore not *distributed*) income. This ratio, which represents the 'earning capacity' of the company, is decisive for the American investor even though he will, of course, take other factors into account. (...) The Dutch investor calculates mainly with returns, that is, with the relationship between share price and *distributed* income, probably because the impossibility of calculating earnings per share on the basis of financial reporting as practised by the majority of companies. (Vecht, 1955:67).

As is indicated below by the discussion of developments in the UK, another reason for the fact that earnings per share were relatively unknown in the Netherlands may have been the existence of a tax on dividends rather than profits before the war. Since the amount of taxes depended on the dividend policy, studying trends in after-tax earnings on a per share basis, or comparing price- earnings ratios,

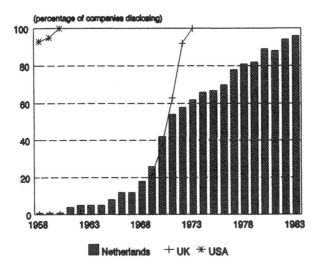

Figure 6.15 Earnings per share

(percentage of companies disclosing)

■ Netherlands   + UK   ✳ USA

was not very useful.

Finally, it has been observed that 'ratios were alien to Limperg's way of looking at things' (Gans, 1979: 120). In the same place, it is observed that Limperg shared the contemporary focus on dividend yield rather than on share price. Given Limperg's influence on auditor education, this may provide a further reason for a relative disinterest in the earnings per share figure in the Netherlands.

During the late 1950s, the first disclosures by sample companies were observed. The first to disclose was indeed KONINKLIJKE PETROLEUM, the company allegedly responsible for the sudden increase in attention to earnings per share in the Netherlands. It was followed in 1960 by OGEM (also among the first to disclose a funds statement, around the same time, see paragraph 6.7). Other large companies as PHILIPS (1961), UNILEVER (1962) and AKU (1965) followed suit. Earnings per share disclosure developed along an almost classical S-curve (figure 6.15).

During the 1960s, earnings per share apparently gained a growing foothold in the investment community. In 1962, earnings per share were included in a new serial publication on key data of listed securities[67]. But its popularity continued to be hindered, on the one hand, by established stock exchange practices and, on the other hand, by the alleged deficiencies of financial reporting. In the middle 1960s, at least a substantial minority of investors continued to think primarily of share prices and dividends in terms of percentages of face value. There was, in fact, a degree of controversy over the method to be used in share price quotations at the Stock Exchange. Proponents of listing in terms of guilders (rather than percentages of face value) conceded that it would be helpful to relate the absolute share price to some other amount, such as earnings per share: 'But this is quite difficult because earnings are calculated in various ways. The chaotic situation in financial reporting by companies in this country precludes uniformity of calculation.' (Verwayen, 1963:224; see also Haccoû, 1963).

It is difficult to trace how the importance attached to earnings per share increased during these years because of a lack of published material on the subject of financial statement analysis. Existing indications suggest that this increase was rather slow. In 1973, earnings per share was still presented as a novelty of which the use was spreading gradually as a result of the US example (De Reus, 1973). It was claimed that a 1974 textbook on financial statement analysis was about the first such book in the Netherlands (Slot and Vecht, 1974:v). By that time, however, earnings per share had taken its place among the standard financial statement ratios, although it was not until 1977 that the association of investment analysts recommended a standard procedure for calculating earnings per share (Boissevain and Van Doorn, 1977).

---

[67] *Kerngetallen* van ter beurze van Amsterdam genoteerde Nederlandse effecten (Amsterdam: Amsterdamsche Bank, March 1962-). Entries included earnings per share, cash flow per share and price-earnings ratios. The editors of the series had decided to include the earnings per share data on the basis of a study of US financial reporting and financial analysis. The assistance of W. Sprey (ABN-Amro bank) and H. Haarbosch in preparing this footnote is gratefully acknowledged.

The disclosure of earnings per share data in annual reports spread rather slowly. The otherwise extensive recommendations of the 1955 Rijkens report did not include a reference to earnings per share although it did suggest inclusion of a few related ratios (such as income and dividends as a percentage of share capital). The 1962 Hamburger report went no further than a general recommendations to include 'ratios' in the report of directors. One might expect that the financial community would be rather more early in demanding earnings per share figures, but the 1956 statement of norms for the Henri Sijthoff award (sponsored by the leading financial newspaper) did not mention any ratios, let alone earnings per share. It is therefore not surprising to find that, until 1965/1967, the number of companies publishing earnings per share data remained low.

Around 1970, though, one can observe a sudden surge in publications. The reason for this change is not evident. A relationship with the WJO suggests itself because for companies of all size groups, there are strong increases in disclosure in 1970 and/or 1971. There is, however, no hint in the law itself or in its preparatory documents about the publication of financial ratios. Yet, it is conceivable that the drafting of the law induced a number of companies to review their financial reporting policies as a whole, and not just those aspects covered by the law. Comments in company financial statements on the inclusion of earnings per share are extremely rare. In one instance (NIERSTRASZ, 1971) it was remarked that '[i]t has come to our attention that shareholders value the inclusion in the financial statements of some ratios on Nierstrasz stock'. This suggests that at least for some companies that started to publish earnings per share around 1970, the primary motive was simply that the disclosure was 'in the air'.

In the United Kingdom, earnings per share was also a relatively late arrival. Whereas in the Netherlands, initial attention to earnings per share had developed because of the listing of KONINKLIJKE PETRO-LEUM in New York, in the United Kingdom the catalyst was the Corporation Tax introduced by the Finance Act of 1965:

The concept of earnings per share is still relatively new in this country. Until 1965 investors and investment analysts tended to work in terms of dividend yield and cover. The Finance Act 1965 (...) meant that there were two distinct breaks in the basis of computation of yields and covers between 1965 and 1967. There was thus a quite natural tendency to look at what other countries were doing, and most investment journals and investment analysts began to talk in terms of P/E ratios. (...) [T]his interest in P/E ratios brought a corresponding interest in earnings per share. There had been little or no discussion of earnings per share in this country for the simple reason that (if earnings are taken to be the amount available for ordinary shareholders after tax) the different rates of tax paid on distributed and non-distributed profits meant that earnings (and hence the earnings per share) varied with the level of dividend.[68]

In addition, Holmer (1971) mentions the prevalence of no-par shares in the US to explain the general US practice of stating dividends on a per share basis, with earnings per share as a natural extension. In the UK, where no-par shares did not exist, dividends were generally discussed as percentages of par value.

In the UK, the topic of earnings per share was rapidly covered by the newly developing accounting standards. In March 1971, an exposure draft was issued which was converted into SSAP 3 in February 1972. The resulting disclosures, compared with those in the Netherlands, are shown in figure 6.15. Unfortunately, the UK data source does not go further back than 1969/1970[69], so that the development of disclosure on a voluntary basis can only be compared for about two years. Nevertheless, it is clear that around 1970, the extent of disclosure reached in the Netherlands and in the UK, in both countries without any form of regulation, was more or

---

[68] 'ED4 and the new Corporation Tax', *Accountancy* (UK), vol, 82 no. 935, July 1971, p. 364.

[69] *Survey of Published Accounts*, published since 1968/1969. Earnings per share have been included since the 1969/1970 issue.

less equal. Both countries[70] were equally behind the United States, where disclosure of earnings per share had become universal in the late 1950s. After 1971, disclosure in the UK rapidly outpaced that in the Netherlands, owing to the influence of SSAP 3[71].

In the Netherlands, accounting standards did not play a comparable role. If the Considered Views of the Tripartite study group did play a role at all in furthering disclosure among listed companies, they could have done so for the smaller companies only. Guidance on earnings per share was published for the first time in december 1976[72], at a time when almost three-quarters of the listed companies did already disclose this item. The study group did not recommend the publication of earnings per share data, but merely observed with some understatement (see figure 6.15) that '[i]t does happen that an earnings per share figure can be found in the financial statements of companies. The financial press tends to pay much attention to this figure and its development.' The Study Group advised that if a company displayed an earnings per share figure without any notes, readers should be able to rely on the figure being calculated according to a recommended procedure. Although the wording of this statement was not very strong, it may have provided the required impetus to raise the disclosure level to (nearly) 100% in 1983. New disclosures had levelled of since 1972/3, but picked up again in 1977/8.

---

[70] A comparison with Germany might also be helpful, but empirical data appear to be lacking. In Germany, earnings per share had apparently been known for some time, but in terms of financial statement disclosure, earnings per share were apparently not very widespread by 1969 (see 'Gutachten des amerikanischen Instituts zur Berechnung des Gewinns pro Aktie', *Die Wirtschaftsprüfung*, vol. 22 no. 24, 15 December 1969, p. 709-10).

[71] A survey by Gray (1978a) shows that (large) UK companies disclosed earnings per share at that time to a significantly greater extent than companies in other Western European countries. The difference is attributed to the influence of UK accounting standards.

[72] *Beschouwingen naar aanleiding van de wet op de jaarrekening van ondernemingen*, issue nr. 5, December 1976.

Summary

Disclosure of earnings per share was closely linked with changes in the environment in which Dutch companies operated. Before the War, meaningful earnings per share calculations were hindered by the tax system. Even when the tax system was changed, earnings per share calculations (and the associated measure of the price-earnings ratio) gained ground only slowly in stock exchange practices. The latter development was clearly influenced by a growing awareness of US practices. When earnings per share did begin to play a role in financial analysis, companies reacted swiftly to provide these figures as a new annual report disclosure.

6.10 Segment reporting

6.10.1 Theoretical views on segment disclosure

In the United States, '[f]ew issues (...) have been as enduring or as controversial as that of segment reporting.'[73] This is true for other countries as well. These controversies have resulted in a voluminous literature on segmental reporting, dealing with the theoretical, practical and regulatory aspects of segment reporting. This section briefly discusses some of the theoretical aspects of the disclosure of segment data[74]. Section 6.10.2 discusses the development of segment reporting as a reporting 'issue' in the Netherlands and abroad. Section 6.10.3 comments on the survey data of the present study.

At a theoretical level, the relevance of segment reporting can be discussed in terms of the informational value of increasingly detailed information. Ronen and Livnat (1981) point out that segmental reporting allows writing more refined contracts and this change in market structure will be either neutral or positive in value to society

---

[73] Advisory Committee on Corporate Disclosure to the Securities and Exchange Commission, quoted in Horwitz and Kolodny (1980).

[74] No attempt is made to produce an extensive review. For further references see, for instance, Swaminathan (1991).

as a whole. In very general terms, they prove in the context of an analytical model that *if* management's objective is to maximize wealth or utility of investors, disclosing segment information is superior to not disclosing. Of course, this conclusion does not provide a firm basis for a prediction regarding the actual extent of voluntary disclosure of segment data.

Voluntary segment reporting by individual companies might be explained by its effect on cost of capital. Generally speaking, segment reporting may reduce information asymmetry. This point is explored by Greenstein and Sami (1994), who show that companies disclosing segment data for the first time following the new SEC requirement of 1970 (see below), experienced a relatively greater reduction in their bid-ask spreads. This is seen as evidence of the lower transaction costs resulting from reduced information asymmetry. A relationship between segmental information and share prices has been established in a number of studies (*e.g.* Ronen and Livnat, 1981; Prodhan and Harris, 1989). Horwitz and Kolodny (1980:418) summarize a number of studies exploring the relationship between segment reporting and forecast ability, and conclude that 'segment sales data can be utilized to improve earnings forecasts and to make better investment decisions, but that the availability of segment profit numbers provides no marginal benefit.' These studies do not explain why some firms choose not to disclose segment information, given that these disclosures appear to have a positive effect on share prices and share price volatility (Gray and Radebaugh, 1984). Part of this explanation may be provided by the notion of proprietary costs of disclosure. Reluctance to disclose segment information may be the result of a perception of large costs (notably competitive damage) resulting from such disclosures. Gray and Roberts (1989) surveyed a number of British multinationals, in order to establish a ranking of the perceived net costs of disclosure of a broad range of disclosure items. The results indicated that profits segmented by line of business on the basis of a narrow segment definition ranked as the most 'costly' disclosure out of the various items in the study. It was also found that using coarser segment definitions would result in significantly lower perceived net costs for all types of segment disclosures.

Thus, a model can be constructed explaining why there may be equilibria of partial disclosure of segment information. To translate such models into accurate predications of practice is complicated by the possible forms of segment reporting. Horwitz and Kolodny (1980:419) indicate that many of the conclusions regarding the effects of segment disclosure on share price or incurred costs are dependent on the amount of detail and on the way of calculating segment figures. That is, segment data may be so contaminated by inappropriate choice of segments and cost and revenue allocations that the resulting figures do not amount to meaningful disclosures. Defects like these may impede straightforward predictions regarding the voluntary provision of segment information.

In sum, segment reporting has been shown to be significantly related to a complex set of factors including rather distinct company perceptions of costs and benefits of disclosure, beliefs and decisions of share market participants and hence share price behaviour. In other words, it has been demonstrated that some forms of segment reporting are associated, in the minds of company managements and in terms of share price behaviour, with the economics of the disclosing company. Although in theory this true for many other disclosures, segment reporting is one of the few items where extensive research has provided proof of the existence of these links. Both the amount of research directed at this disclosure item and the research findings support the assumption that economic consequences are more pronounced with segment reporting than with many other disclosures.

6.10.2 Segment reporting as a financial reporting issue

As early as 1951, before segment reporting was an issue in any country, the US SEC required registrants to disclose 'the relative importance' of major products and product groups. Rapid growth in mergers and especially in diversified acquisitions during the 1950's and 1960's gave rise to demands for substantially more detailed information by line of business (Barr, 1967). However, this demand was not immediately met by changes in practice. Segmentation of

296

sales was characterized by Horngren (1958:85) as a 'tendency (...) already evident in a few scattered annual reports'.

In 1965, the US Senate's Subcommittee on Anti-Trust and Monopoly prodded the SEC into reconsidering the sufficiency of its 1951 requirement[75]. When the SEC publicly declared its interest in the issue, this gave rise to a flurry of activity by the APB, the Financial Executives Institute and various other interested parties. The APB issued Statement No. 2, *Disclosure of Supplemental Information by Diversified Companies* in 1967. In this document, the Board revealed its preference for voluntary extensions of disclosure rather than for mandatory guidelines. The SEC, however, chose not to rely on voluntary disclosures. Relying on the recently published Wheat Report, it successively required comprehensive line of business reporting (*i.e.* segmentation of both revenues and profits) in registration statements (1969), Form 10-K filings (1970) and corporate annual reports to stockholders (1974). Whether or not the SEC was correct in opting rather quickly for mandatory disclosure rather than awaiting the results of a system of voluntary disclosures as advocated by the APB remained the subject of extensive debate throughout the 1970's (see Horwitz and Kolodny, 1980). This remained true even when the FASB in effect endorsed the comprehensive disclosure of both revenues and profits for both industry and geographical segments in SFAS 14 (1976). In all, attention for segment reporting in the United States developed rapidly in second half of the 1960's. By the middle 1970's, the current regulatory framework was by and large in place.

In the United Kingdom, a requirement to provide segmented data on revenue and income for lines of business was included in the Companies Act 1967 (S. 17) and effective from the middle of 1968 onwards. At the time, this was regarded as going 'much beyond the

---

[75] Information on the chronology of events in the US has been derived from Barr (1969), Skousen (1970), Zeff (1972) and Horwitz and Kolodny (1980).

current disclosure requirements in the United States' (Hendriksen, 1969:27). An escape clause was provided, however, since judgment regarding segment materiality was left to management, and because management might abstain from publication altogether on the grounds of possible competitive damage. These regulations remained largely unaltered until SSAP 25 (1990).

In the Netherlands, disclosure of segment data developed into a reporting issue somewhat later than in the US. In the Netherlands, segmental reporting received much attention from the middle 1970's to the early 1980's, whereas, as indicated above, segment reporting figured prominently in the US literature of the later 1960's. Statements on segmental reporting in the Dutch literature before 1970 are rare. The 1955 Rijkens report did suggest in general terms that the information in the directors' report be 'focused on' *(toegespitst op)* main lines of business, but this recommendation did not reoccur in the 1962 successor report. Against this background, it is not surprising that the 1970 Act on Annual Financial Statements did not contain a requirement to segment either sales or income. The law did contain a requirement that the figures of the income statement 'are analyzed and explained in the notes according to standards acceptable in the [relevant] industry'. This requirement might, at first sight, be constructed as a segmentation requirement. But according to Sanders, Burgert and Groeneveld (1975:283), this interpretation was not correct. In their opinion, the law protected the diversified companies by not requiring a breakdown of sales, and the smaller companies by allowing the publication of index figures for sales. The 1970 Act therefore left segmental reporting entirely in the realm of voluntary disclosures.

Some attention to segmental reporting appears to have developed in the late 1960's, in the wake of developments in the United States[76].

---

[76] Around that time, it was observed by a leading Dutch auditor that an income statement showing income by line of business 'is, at least in terms of published financial statements, in our country the rarest of exceptions. Neither are such statements usual in the United States, although voices can

298

At the end of the 1960's, a wave of mergers and acquisitions significantly altered the corporate landscape in the Netherlands (see figure 4.1), but there is no indication that this resulted immediately in a call for more segmental information. Yet, by 1972, awareness of the issue had spread sufficiently to bring the topic before a NIvRA study meeting where the desirability and feasibility of segment reporting was discussed by accountants employed in industry (reported in Wilschut, 1973). According to the introductory material supplied for the discussion, the question was phrased primarily with reference to recent developments in the United States and the United Kingdom. Similarly, Frederiks (1973) discussed segment reporting on the basis of developments in the English-speaking world. During 1972/3, the issue was placed on the agenda on the NIvRA's committee on financial reporting, the CAJ, which served as a preparatory committee for the Tripartite Study Group[77].

Around the middle 1970's, segment reporting had definitely become a current issue. References to segment reporting began to emerge with increasing frequency in wider circles:

- In February 1974, a revised version of the draft Fourth Directive was published. Citing the British example, the new draft included a requirement to segment both sales and operating income according to areas of activity and geographical areas (article 41 paragraph 6). The NIvRA reacted negatively to this change and proposed to eliminate the geographical segmentation and to allow a broader definition of activity segments[78].

---

recently be heard in that country calling for a presentation of results by line of activity.' (Burggraaff, 1968:169)

[77] Nederlands Instituut van Registeraccountants, *Jaarverslag 1972/73*, p. 87.

[78] Nederlands Instituut van Registeraccountants, Commissie Ondernemingsrecht, '(Gewijzigd) voorstel voor vierde EEG-Richtlijn', *De Accountant*, vol. 81 no. 5, January 1975, p. 313-323, in particular p. 319.

- In October 1974, new norms for the Henri Sijthoff prize were announced. These included, for the first time, the 'recommendation' to segment income and sales according to line of business.

- IASC's ED 3 on consolidated financial statements, issued in December 1974, did contain a requirement to specify main balance sheet headings geographically. In its comments, a NIvRA committee suggested in effect an expansion of the requirement by stating that a geographical breakdown of 'invested capital and/or turnover' might be more appropriate[79]. That a geographical breakdown was rejected in the comments on the Fourth Directive was presumably due to the fact that different committees were involved in drafting the two responses.

- In an address to NIvRA members in April 1975, Labour Union representative W. Kok identified segmented reporting as an inevitable appurtenance of the increasing democratisation of the enterprise (Kok, 1975). This speech evidently drew on previous work within the labour unions (see Nabbe (1974)) and was elaborated in a July 1976 brochure on the information demands of employees issued by one of the main Federations of Labour Unions[80].

- In a series of meetings of auditors employed in industry, late in 1974, the topic was studied on the basis of the FASB's drafts for SFAS 14 (Kas, 1975).

---

[79] Nederlands Instituut van Registeraccountants, College voor Beroeps-vraagstukken, 'De geconsolideerde jaarrekening en de methode van de vermogenswaarde voor deelnemingen', *De Accountant*, vol. 81 no. 11, August 1975, p. 700-702.

[80] *Open boek: Een nota over de behoefte van werknemers aan informatie over hun onderneming* (Amsterdam: Federatie Nederlandse Vakbeweging, 1976), p. 6, 10.

- Finally, in April 1975, segment reporting was introduced into the Act on Annual Accounts (WJO) of 1970. A member of the lower house of parliament used the occasion of an otherwise largely technical reorganization of legal matter to introduce successfully an amendment calling in general terms for segment information according to lines of business[81].

The new requirement did much to keep attention to the issue of segment reporting alive, but provided certainly no definitive settlement. The requirement was formulated rather generally, and required interpretation to establish its exact extent. Already in October 1975, a NIvRA commentator observed after extensive quotes from the parliamentary record that 'for the time being, no concrete figures on the breakdown of operating income according to different classes of goods and services can be expected'[82]. Similar views were aired by Boukema (1976) and Beckman (1977).

A more decisive indication of the extent of the required disclosure was provided by the Enterprise Chamber. In a verdict pronounced in 1980, it was ruled that 'the parliamentary history [of the segmentation requirement introduced in 1975] does not give a clear answer to the question in what way the required insight must be provided. There are differences of opinion in the literature. In practice, no fixed pattern of behaviour has developed of how to implement the requirement.'[83]

This ruling confirmed the interpretation that a verbal indication of the contribution of the various lines of business to operating income was sufficient to comply with the disclosure requirement (Beckman,

---

[81] For details, see Zeff *et al.* (1992:232-234)

[82] 'Voorstellen tot wijziging WJO aangenomen', *De Accountant*, vol. 82 no. 2, October 1975, p. 60-62.

[83] OK 3 April 1980 (HAL). In earlier cases, the court had ruled in a similar way that segmental information was not required (OK 20 January 1977 (DE) and OK 26 January 1978 (Eggerdink)). These pronouncements, however, dealt with financial statements over 1974 and 1975 when the new segmental disclosure requirement did not yet apply.

1981:520)[84]. While numerical segmental disclosures therefore remained in effect non-mandatory, further developments ensured that the issue continued to receive attention.

In February 1977, the Tripartite Study Group (TO) issued a statement on segmental reporting[85]. Although the study group had by then been rather severely criticized for not taking firm positions, it did take a rather forward stance on segment reporting (Zeff *et al.*, 1992:240). Segmenting sales according to major product groups was simply prescribed, a numerical breakdown of operating income according to product groups was 'emphatically' recommended, while geographical segmentation of sales, gross margin and number of employees was recommended without adverbial qualification.

In the latter half of the 1970's, a number of international developments also directed attention towards segment reporting. The OECD Code of Conduct for Multinational Companies (1976, 1979), the UN International Standard of Accounting and Reporting for Transnational Corporations (1977) and IASC's E 15 (March 1980) all dealt with segment reporting.

A similar impetus came from the European Community. As indicated above, drafts of the Fourth Directive on Company Law required comprehensive segmental information from February 1974 onwards. It was this change that gave support to the introduction of the requirement to segment operating income into Dutch law in 1975. However, the adopted version of the Directive published in July 1978 restricted the segmentation requirement to sales, which had to be segmented according to both lines of business and geo-

---

[84] The assertion of Horwitz and Kolodny (1980: 420) that '[a]t the present time, no foreign law or stock exchange rule mandates public disclosure of profits attributable to industry or geographic segments', was therefore strictly speaking correct as far as the Netherlands was concerned. It seems unlikely, though, that the authors were aware of the careful interpretation required to arrive at this conclusion.

[85] Draft *Beschouwing* IV b.2. 'Detaillering van omzet en bedrijfsresultaat'. Included in Issue no. 5, dated December 1976 but published February 1977.

graphical areas. As a result, the Act to adapt Dutch law to the Fourth Directive dropped the reference to segmentation of operating income included in the law in 1975. Although a number of Dutch observers professed their disappointment (*e.g.* Helderman, 1981:280; see also Zeff *et al.*, 1992:306-307), this 'step backwards' (IJssel-muiden, 1981:92) was also reflected in the position of the successor to the Tripartite Study Group, the Council on Annual Reporting, which in 1984 subtly toned down its recommendation to disclose segmented operating income in the wake of the change in the law (Zeff *et al.*, 1992: 327-328).

Summing up, segmental reporting was introduced as an issue in Dutch financial reporting around 1970 through awareness of developments in the United States. Soon, however, the issue acquired a local momentum because of the link with the contemporary tendency towards increased corporate accountability and *vermaatschappelijking*, and because of the uncertainty introduced through the changes in position in the successive drafts of the Fourth Directive. Towards 1983, however, the situation was clarified both by court pronouncements and by the draft Act to adapt Dutch law to the Fourth Directive. Segmentation of sales was to become unavoidable. Segmentation of operating income, though still favoured in sections of the literature and in the largely advisory statements of the IASC and the Dutch Council on Annual Reporting (RJ), was not to become mandatory.

6.10.3 Empirical results
The development of disclosure for line of business and geographical segmentation is charted in figure 6.16. Comparable US and UK data on line of business segmentation are added. Comparative data on geographical segmentation are not shown since US and UK data were either available on an irregular basis or were classified in a way to impede comparability with the Dutch data. In interpreting the figure, it should be remembered that it shows the percentage of companies making any sort of numerical segmental disclosure, that

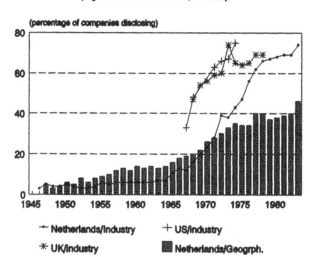

Figure 6.16 Segmental disclosures
(segmentation of revenues and/or income)

(percentage of companies disclosing)

- Netherlands/Industry   + US/Industry
* UK/Industry   ▨ Netherlands/Geogrph.

is, either of income or of sales, or of both. Needless to say, these companies form a rather heterogeneous group. For instance, companies merely breaking down sales into export and domestic sales are treated as equal with companies providing both sales and profit by as many as five or more geographical areas. As far as numerical disclosures are concerned, figure 6.16 therefore presents the most favourable interpretation of the extent of segmental disclosure. In order to increase comparability with the UK and US data, no correction was made for applicability. A check on the representativeness of the present sample by means of the results of previous cross-sectional studies provides satisfactory results[86].

---

[86] The sample data for 1976 and 1977 are comparable to those reported in Beckman and Van Rijn (1979), the data for 1983 compare moderately well with those in Van der Gaag (1986). In general, disclosure rates in the present sample are slightly but not significantly higher than those in the Beckman and Van Rijn sample. Apart from chance effects, these difference might also be explained by the fact that the Beckman and Van Rijn sample included some non-listed companies. The Van der Gaag study included all

Disclosure levels

For both types of segmentation, the percentages of disclosing companies remained low throughout the 1960's. It was not until 1969 that disclosures of both types were made by one-fifth of the sampled companies. Around 1970, the percentage of companies disclosing line of business information starts to grow at an accelerated pace, while geographical disclosures continue to increase at a more steady rate of one to two percentage points per annum.

Regarding line of business disclosures, it can be observed that, from about 1967 to 1975, developments in the Netherlands followed behind the United Kingdom and the United States by about five years. Given that disclosure in both the US and the UK was influenced if not downright directed by regulation, whereas in the Netherlands it was not, and given that segment disclosures are generally considered as rather sensitive, the fact that disclosure practices in the Netherlands lagged only a few years behind those in the UK and in the US is quite remarkable[87].

Nevertheless, regulation did start to make a difference after 1975. From that year onwards, segment reporting was made mandatory for US published annual reports, while strict materiality criteria applied. The result was that segment reporting became universal for US companies. In the UK and the Netherlands, no materiality criteria

---

non-financial listed companies. The 1983 percentage of geographical disclosures is identical to the present sample. Van der Gaag reports a 62% disclosure of line of business data, while rate in the present sample is 74%.

[87] On the basis of these data, Gray's (1978b) conclusion that the higher incidence of segment reporting among UK as opposed to continental multinationals in 1972/3 was due to a higher degree of efficiency of the UK equity market appears questionable. It seems more likely that the single most important influence on UK disclosure had been the 1967 Companies Act. In the Netherlands, a comparable legal provision introduced in 1975 brought disclosure swiftly to UK levels, but even before that date disclosure had risen significantly above the UK pre-legislation level of the late 1960's. This conclusion is further reinforced by Gray and Radebaugh (1984) who attribute the higher level of disclosure in the US compared to the UK to differences in regulation.

were in force, with the result that more companies might plausibly claim to be in a single class of business only. As indicated in figure 6.16, disclosure percentages in the UK and the Netherlands converged after 1975, suggesting that materiality judgments were made with approximately the same effect. Strictly speaking, though, the Dutch law did not require explicitly that numerical segmental information be provided. The disclosure percentage found for Dutch companies represents therefore a larger component of voluntary behaviour than that of their British counterparts.

Segmentation and consolidation
Segmentation, especially segmentation along industry lines, is a way to partially undo the effects of consolidation. In this light, it is not surprising to find that in the sample, segmentation by line of business generally follows the adoption of consolidated reporting. In only four out of 140 companies some form of segmental information according to line of business was provided prior to the inclusion of consolidated financial statements[88]. In all other cases, segmentation coincided with or followed consolidation, or did not occur at all.
As shown in table 5.1, there is a certain correlation between consolidation and segment reporting. That is, companies that consolidate early are likely to be early disclosers of segment reporting as well, although the average interval elapsing between first consolidation and disclosure of segment information by line of business was 10.4 years[89]. This average hides considerable variation, ranging from simultaneous disclosure to a maximum time lag of 38 years.

Industry versus geographical segmentation
For the earlier part of the period, geographical segmentation was slightly more widespread than segmentation by line of business, although the difference is not likely to be much in excess of the

---

[88] In none of the four cases did the timing difference exceed four years.

[89] This average is calculated for the 31 companies for which observed first disclosure (OFD) data are available for both consolidation and industry segments.

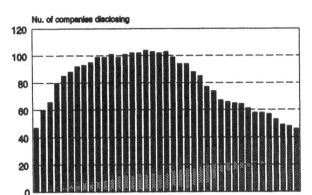

Figure 6.17 Segmental disclosures
Geographical and industry segments

range of sampling error. It is interesting to note that after 1970, disclosure of line of business information started to outgrow geographical segmentation, resulting in a significant gap by 1983. This appears to contrast with the findings of Gray and Roberts (1989) who report that company managements generally perceive geographical segmentation as less costly, and hence more amenable to voluntary disclosure, than line of business information. A closer look at the relationship between geographical and line of business reporting seems therefore warranted.

Figure 6.17 displays the absolute numbers of companies broken down into the various combinations of line of business and geographical segmentation. This chart demonstrates in the first place that large numbers of companies in the sample never arrived at the stage of considering any form of segment reporting at all: the merger wave of the late 1960's occurred before segment reporting was practised by more than a small minority. Furthermore, it can be seen that, with the conspicuous exception of UNILEVER (about which more below), the combination of both line of business and geographical segmentation did not appear until 1962. Not before the

307

early 1970's did more than a handful of companies disclose both types of segmental information. By then, however, companies disclosing geographical information only formed a disappearing minority. From about 1976 onwards, geographical information was an 'additional' disclosure, provided by companies that also provided line of business disclosures.

Discontinued disclosure

As shown in table 6.1 (above), the 'discontinuance ratio' for geographical information is the highest across the sample of disclosure items. One-yearly, or incidental disclosures account for a considerable share of this high rate of 'discontinuance'. One-off disclosures might occur for a number of reasons. The jubilee factor did play a role, but less obviously than with employee disclosures. In one instance of incidental disclosure, (VLISSINGEN KATOEN, 1947) a geographical distribution of sales was given in the report of directors to support an argument against the government's exchange rate and balance of payments policies.

Looked at in closer detail, discontinuance of geographical segment disclosure appears to be constant throughout the 1945-1983 period. It might be described as a process of attrition in which every year on average ten percent of the companies disclosing geographical information stops providing that type of disclosure. For individual companies, the reason for discontinued disclosure may, of course, simply be the discontinuance of a line of business or of activities in a geographical area. For the population as a whole, though, it is unlikely that by the early 1980's less than half of the companies had any foreign activities or export sales (as would be the case if figure 6.16 described a situation of full disclosure). In fact, Van der Gaag (1986) reports an increase in the percentage of companies disclosing geographical information from 45% to 66% between 1983 and 1984. Since this increase may be related to impending legislation, there had apparently been some room for a voluntary expansion of geographical segment reporting.

This again appears to contradict the findings of Gray and Roberts (1989) mentioned earlier. It may well be, though, that this differ-

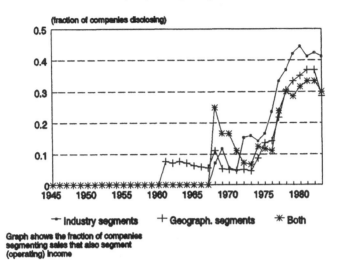

Figure 6.18 Income segmentation
by companies segmenting sales

(fraction of companies disclosing)

— Industry segments + Geograph. segments * Both

Graph shows the fraction of companies
segmenting sales that also segment
(operating) income

ence is caused by the fact that the Gray and Roberts study was limited to multinationals. In the present study, this subgroup shows no signs of reversion regarding geographical information. A tendency for geographical information to decline during the 1970's and 1980's was found in the Rennie and Emmanuel (1992) study, which, like the present one, was based on a wider sample of UK companies.

Segmentation of operating income

As evidenced by the literature discussed above, segmentation of income has been more controversial than segmentation of sales. On the one hand, companies have been reluctant to provide breakdowns of operating income out of fear for competitive disadvantages. On the other hand, it has been claimed that such disclosures of (operating) income as have been provided have been of limited use owing to the occasionally arbitrary allocations of costs and revenues involved. The companies in the sample showed a marked reluctance to disclose details on (operating) income. Figure 6.18 shows companies disclosing details of income as a percentage of companies breaking down sales (There are only a few instances of companies that show details

309

of income without showing a breakdown of sales). Before 1975, only a handful of companies provided details on income. After 1975, and apparently as a result of the change in the law, there is a marked increase in the provision of segmented income data. Interestingly enough, this applies to geographical segmentation as well, even though this was not mentioned in the law. Hence, the willingness to provide details on income does not vary substantially between line of business and geographical segmentation. Nor are companies that segment sales according to both criteria more willing to provide details on income than companies that segment sales according to only one criterion.

Influence of the law
There was a definite increase in disclosure of line of business information during the period 1966-1974, that is, before segmentation was explicitly mentioned in the law (see figure 6.16). It is possible that the 1970 Act on Annual Financial Statements prompted an overall revision of financial reporting practices, including areas not covered by the law. A similar development was noted for the funds statement. The text of the 1970 Act regarding the income statement was rather general, and could give rise to the conclusion that some sort of segmentation was appropriate (see above).
The 1976 modification of the law, even though it did not impose a strict requirement to provide numerical segment information, did have an effect on segmentation of operating income[90]. As indicated by figure 6.18, this effect applied to line of business and geographical segmentation even though the latter was not covered by the law.
A number of companies discontinued the practice of disclosing segmented operating income in the latter 1970's, apparently after realizing that such was not, after all, strictly required by law.

---

[90] In the case of PHILIPS, a statement by one of its directors (Breek, 1974) shows that the company was not enthusiastic about segmenting operating income. Nevertheless, the following year the company showed operating income by line of business. In this case, the law appears to have exerted a direct influence.

BERGOSS seems to offer an instance of such behaviour. More importantly, though, is that figure 6.18 shows that the number of such reversions in the later 1970's was limited.

Finally, there is no evidence that the 1976 amendment influenced the disclosure of segmented sales in a significant way. This latter observation is important when an attempt is made to disentangle the effects of the law from the effects of the relevant Considered View issued by the Tripartite Study Group in 1977. As was indicated above, this publication prescribed the segmentation of sales in rather strict terms, while the segmentation of operating income was recommended. If this publication did influence disclosure, it seems likely that there should have been an impact on segmented sales disclosure as well as a change in segmented operating income. Since only the latter was observed, there is no reason to attribute a strong influence to the study group.

Company characteristics and segmental disclosures

There can be no doubt that UNILEVER led the way in segmental reporting in the Netherlands. Already by 1947, it distinguished itself by extensive geographical and line of business breakdowns of sales which were highly acclaimed by the financial press (see Zeff *et al*, 1992:75-77). The extent of its lead on other companies can be appreciated by noting that between 1947 and 1962, it was the only company to provide both types of breakdown. Another indication of its lead was that a PHILIPS chairman considered it necessary, halfway down this period, to justify why his company would *not* publish geographical and line of business breakdowns (Otten, 1954:9). UNILEVER was not the first to provide a segmentation of income[91], but it was the first to provide 'comprehensive' segmentation (in 1968). In all these developments, it was not just ahead of its Dutch counterparts, but also of most American and British companies.

---

[91] Within the sample, that distinction goes to VAN OMMEREN, which, in an otherwise rather traditional profit and loss account, showed the balances of the trading accounts of its various activities since 1947.

Previous studies have found that large, multiple listed companies are prone to be early and/or more extensive disclosers of segment information (Salamon and Dhaliwal, 1980; Rennie and Emmanuel, 1992; Bradbury, 1992a). This is supported by the present sample. The multiple-listed companies HEINEKEN, KNP, VAN OMMEREN, PAKHOED and VMF (see section 5.4.3.) are, together with the larger multinationals, conspicuous among those disclosing some form of segmental information before 1970. However, this observation can be qualified in a number of ways:

First, the meaning of 'segmental disclosure' is not constant throughout the period. Since the late 1960's, segmental disclosures are usually thought of as separate schedules in the notes to the financial statements. In the late 1940's and early 1950's, however, companies might disclose segmental information in the context of the traditional profit- and loss account. Usually, such a profit and loss account would show the combined balance of all trading accounts (*exploitatierekeningen*) as one credit item, which would be offset with depreciation, taxes and sundry expenses. Some companies, however, would show the balances of the trading accounts separately, providing, in effect, a segmentation of gross income. In this way, it might be argued that the early segmental disclosure of VAN OMMEREN (since 1947) was little more than the result of the strong link between the ledger accounts and the published financial statements which had characterized financial reporting in its early stages.

ARM, already identified in chapter 5 as a rather exceptional discloser, did provide exceptional disclosures even though its financial statements were cast in a traditional form. Since 1945, it published not just its profit and loss account, as required by law, but also its trading account. In the latter statement, it showed on the credit side its revenues divided into four groups, and on the debit side the totals for various expense categories. It is implausible that this high level of detail was not the result of a deliberate reporting policy.

Table 6.3
Segmentation by size group

	Geographical		Line of Business	
Year:	1960	1980	1960	1980
Number of companies:	14	20	6	36
Size group:				
1 (largest)	29%	65%	67%	44%
2	14%	25%	-	39%
3	43%	10%	17%	11%
4 (smallest)	14%	-	17%	6%
	----	----	----	----
	100%	100%	100%	100%

Notes:
'Size groups' as defined in section 5.5.2
'Segmentation' refers to segmentation of sales and/or income.

Second, a number of the larger companies began to disclose segmented information either before they acquired foreign listings or
before foreign exchanges began to demand segmented information.
Therefore, their subsequent listing status may simply be another size
covariate, just as their segmental disclosures.

Third, there are a number of exceptions in the form of other companies without foreign listings who turned out among the early
disclosers as well. This is true mainly for geographical segmentation, however. As far as line of business information is concerned,
the only unexpected disclosures are those by ARM, mentioned
above, and BATENBURG, which showed the balances of the various
trading accounts from 1955 to 1961. Otherwise, early line of
business reporting was dominated by the large companies.

A considerably larger number of smaller companies provided at least
minimal geographical breakdowns during the 1950's (often exports
as a percentage of total sales), such as DRU, KROMHOUT, BEGE-
MANN, VULCAANSOORD and ENOT. In this respect, they preceded

313

the large multinationals who, with the exception of UNILEVER, did not provide geographical breakdowns until the middle or late 1960's. These multinationals made good their late start by the quality of their subsequent disclosures, however: they were all among the six companies in the sample providing 'comprehensive' disclosures at any one time (UNILEVER (since 1968), AKZO (since 1974), KONINKLIJKE PETROLEUM (since 1975), PHILIPS (since 1977), INTERNATIO-MÜLLER (1977-1982) and PAKHOED (since 1978)). The perceived applicability of geographical segment disclosures appears to have diminished over time. Table 6.3 summarizes segment disclosures by size group for 1960 and 1980.

Although the 1960 data refer to rather small numbers of observations, the conclusion still seems warranted that the middle-sized and small companies (size groups 3 and 4) provided a substantial share of the geographical disclosures in 1960. By 1980, though, geographical disclosures had become the preserve of the large and very large companies. Given the very small number of 1960 disclosures, it is difficult to draw strong conclusions with regard to line of business reporting.

Fourth, a number of companies, though not providing numerical information, did provide rather extensive verbal information on industry and geographical segments of their business (*e.g.* MULLER, since 1945).

6.10.4 Summary

There are definite changes over time in the pattern of segment data disclosure. Obviously, companies had to disclose sales before segmentation of sales could be considered. Hence, disclosure levels before the late 1960's are quite low. During this period, the companies that did provide some form of segmentation were slightly more likely to provide a simple form of geographical segmentation rather than any kind of line of business reporting.

Around 1970, a clear change in reporting practices occurred, which can be traced to developments in the United States a few years earlier. The time lag in disclosure practices between the Netherlands on the one hand and the United States and the United Kingdom on the other is not particularly large, especially not when the different impact of regulation is considered.

In was not only the extent of disclosure which changed around 1970. During the 1950's and 1960's, segmental reporting was rather evenly distributed among companies of various size. During the 1970's, segment reporting (especially in its more elaborate forms) became largely the preserve of the larger companies.

The 1976 amendment appears to have had an influence on disclosure of segmented operating income. Segmentation of operating income increased after 1976, in a roughly equal measure for segmentation of both geographical and line of business criteria.

6.11 Discussion and conclusions

This section combines the results of the previous nine studies of individual disclosure items. This inductive process of drawing comparisons can be structured by drawing on the concepts of innovation-diffusion studies. First, an innovation-diffusion approach allows a formal comparison of the various processes of disclosure change in terms of the speed or rate of diffusion. This comparison is the subject of section 6.11.1. Second, innovation-diffusion studies have developed a number of relevant characteristics or dimensions of innovations which help to understand differences in the rate of diffusion. Section 6.11.2. contains a comparison of the disclosure items by means of these characteristics or dimensions. Third, apart from an adopter-characteristics and an innovation-characteristics perspective, an 'infrastructure' perspective on innovation-diffusion can play an important role. In this context, the innovation 'infrastructure' consists largely of a number of external influences on disclosure, such as the role of the law. These external influences are discussed on a comparative basis on section 6.11.3.

6.11.1 Overall diffusion patterns

As has been illustrated by the various diagrams throughout this chapter, the process of disclosure extension of almost all items studied here was characterized by the type of 'S'-shaped curves usually associated with processes of innovation diffusion. The impression conveyed by these graphical representations can be formalized by fitting an appropriate, S-shaped curve to the data. This also makes it possible to arrive at a numerical indication of differences in rate of diffusion among disclosure items.

In the diffusion literature, a number of mathematical models have been proposed to describe various types of S-shaped functions (see, for instance, Mahajan and Peterson, 1985). As indicated above (section 6.3), an elementary yet frequently used model is the internal-influence model proposed by Bass (1969). In this model, the number of new adoptions in each period is determined by the numbers of adopters and non-adopters in the previous period. In other words, the number of new adopters in a particular period is explained in terms of the effects of imitation induced by mutual communication and/or observation among potential adopters.

Applied to the changes in disclosure, the model can be formulated as:

$$N(t) = N(t-1) + b * N(t-1) * [1-N(t-1)]$$

in which $N(t)$ is the number of disclosing companies at time t. The coefficient b, or the 'coefficient of internal influence' represents the strength of the assumed 'imitation effect', with high values for the coefficient b indicating a rapid diffusion of the disclosure in question[92].

An internal influence model may be expected to work well for annual report disclosure:

---

[92] It will be recalled that in section 6.3 an extended or 'mixed-influence' model was used in which an 'external influence' was recognized next to the 'internal influence' factor.

The internal influence model is most appropriate when an innovation is complex and socially visible, not adopting it places members at a 'disadvantage', the social system is relatively small and homogeneous, and there is a need for experiential and or legitimizing information prior to adoption. (Mahajan and Peterson, 1985:18-19)

Financial statement disclosure by listed companies meets these conditions, albeit to varying degrees for different items. At least as an approximation, this type of model appears to be useful to describe changes in disclosure during this period.
The (discrete) internal-influence model described above can be approximated by a (continuous) exponential function. The results of fitting such a function to the data are presented in table 6.4[93].
For most disclosure items, the model fits the data quite well. High values of (adjusted) R^2 are the rule in diffusion studies, though. Hamlin, Jacobson and Miller (1973) posit on the basis of a wide survey of diffusion studies that fitting S-shaped models typically results in an R^2 of .98 or higher. With the present data, however, it can easily be illustrated that such good fits do not necessarily indicate that an appropriate model has been selected. The flexibility provided by two parameters to be estimated is apparently sufficient to produce a good fit even for the labour cost item, for which an internal influence model is clearly incorrect. In a previous section, it was argued that the single most important influence on the rapid increase in disclosure of this item was the introduction of a legal requirement in 1970. For this item (and in the case of funds statements), a good fit was obtained by means of an extremely low

---

[93] The curve used here explains N(t), the fraction of disclosing companies at time t, in the following way:

$$N(t) = 1 / (1 + (1-N(0))/N(0) * e^{\char`\^} (b * t))$$

in which b is the coefficient of internal influence and N(0) is fraction of disclosing companies in the year of first observation.

Table 6.4
Estimates of internal-influence model parameters

Disclosure item[1]	coefficient of internal influence (b)[2]	initial disclosure N(0)	adj. R^2
Geographical segments	.08	.042	.965
Current cost	.10	.016	.973
Tax liabilities	.13	.123	.917
Tax costs	.14	.206	.979
Consolidation	.16	.051	.995
Industry segments	.18	.003	.982
Sales	.19	.012	.963
Employee number	.19	.018	.972
Earnings per share	.29	.001	.988
Funds statement	.44	1.87E-9	.991
Comparative figures	.71	.008	.994
Labour costs	.85	1.09E-9	.972

Notes:
1. A binary disclosure definition was used as defined in Appendix A, with current cost disclosure defined as partial or full application in both balance sheet and income statement.
2. Results are based on nonlinear regression.

estimate of the initial disclosure percentage. Similarly, the fit for comparative figures reported in table 6.4 is good (and the b-coefficient suggests a high degree of imitation), while the more detailed analysis of section 6.3 has shown that there is reason to believe that at least part of the disclosure process for this item should be explained in terms of external influence.

Even with these qualifications, the data in table 6.4 help to make a point that might also have been apparent from inspection of the various figures in this chapter. Although the basic shape of the diffusion curves is similar across most items, the rapidity of diffusion can differ considerably. These differences are further considered in section 6.11.2.

6.11.2 Innovation characteristics

Rogers' (1983) list of innovation characteristics that influence the adoption process can be used to structure the interpretation of the data presented in this chapter. According to this approach, the rate of adoption of an innovation is associated with certain qualities of the innovation itself. These qualities include:

- *Advantage:* the advantages of the innovation, as perceived by the adopters, relative to what it supersedes.
- *Compatibility:* the degree to which the innovation is in harmony with existing values, past experiences and needs of the adopters.
- *Complexity:* the degree to which the innovation is difficult to understand and use.
- *Trialability:* the degree to which an innovation can be tried on a limited basis.
- *Observability:* the degree to which the results of an adopted innovation are easily observed by other potential adopters.

Since Tritschler (1970), the applicability of these criteria to accounting innovations has been asserted by various authors (*e.g.* Parker, 1977). This section therefore considers whether the differences in rates of adoption documented in the previous section can be interpreted in terms of differences among disclosure items in terms of these five characteristics.

A summary of the results is shown in table 6.5. Inevitably, this table is more of the nature of a descriptive summary of the data, than a conclusive proof that these criteria are in fact applicable or yield the expected conclusions. All that table 6.5 attempts to do is to make clear that this framework can assist in arriving at a plausible interpretation of the observed developments in disclosure. For this purpose, table 6.5 ranks the disclosure items according to general indicators of the rapidity and extent of adoption: the final rate of voluntary disclosure and the number of years elapsing between initial and final disclosures.

319

Table 6.5
Summary presentation of innovation characteristics and key adoption data

	% final vol. discl. (year)	10-90% (years)	Advantage	Complexity	Trialability	Observability
Geo segments	46% (1983)	≥ 27	-	-/+	+	-
Tax liabilities	73% (1970)	≥ 26	-	-	+	-
Sales	91% (1983)	32	-	+	-	-/+
Current Cost	46% (1983)	≥ 20	-/+	-	-	-
Consolidation	93% (1983)	30	-/+	-	-	+
Tax costs	92% (1970)	≥ 25	-	-	+	-
Industry segments	74% (1983)	≥ 19	-	-/+	+	-
Labour costs	57% (1970)	8	-	+	-	-
Employee number	98% (1983)	≥ 20	+	+	+	-
Earnings per share	96% (1983)	16	+	+	-	+
Funds statement	96% (1983)	11	+	+	-	+
Comparative figs	100% (1960)	5	+	+	-	+

Ordering of disclosure items

The ordering of disclosure items in table 6.5 according to the rapidity and extent of diffusion provides an indicative rather than exact ranking of the ease with which an item was adopted. Two measures have been used, while a simple average ranking determined the order in table 6.5.

The first measure is the final percentage of voluntary disclosure. This is the percentage of disclosing companies observed immediately before disclosure of that item became mandatory[94], or the percentage observed in 1983.

The second measure of the difficulty or ease with which an item was adopted is the length of time between the year in which 10% of the companies disclosed that item and the year in which disclosure reached 90%. The limitation of the study to the period between 1945 and 1983 means that for a number of items no data are available on when disclosure reached the 10% or 90% mark. The table shows these items by means of $\geq$ signs, but for purposes of ranking these signs were ignored[95].

Advantage

The criterion of 'advantage' is difficult to apply in a straightforward manner to financial statement disclosures. Theoretically, of course, disclosures represent a balance of costs and benefits. In practice, however, it is difficult to rate disclosure items objectively in terms of the net benefits they are seen to provide. For some items, especially sales and segmented data, previous empirical studies have demonstrated relationships between disclosure and share price develop-

---

[94] This may result in overstatement of the final degree of voluntary disclosure since some companies may anticipate the imposition of a disclosure requirement. The resulting disclosures cannot strictly be regarded as 'voluntary'.

[95] It will be observed that the ordering in table 6.5 corresponds largely with the ranking in table 6.4. The differences can be attributed to the fact that for the calculations in table 6.4 no distinction was made between mandatory and voluntary disclosure.

321

ments, suggesting that disclosures are valued by investors. For other items, however, like disclosure of tax data, it can only be shown by reference to the professional literature that there has been an explicit demand for their disclosure. Given this difficulty in assessing benefits, the benefits of all disclosures are assumed to be more or less equal for the purpose of arriving at the summary presentation in table 6.5. In other words, 'advantage' has been interpreted as absence of major perceived proprietary costs. This criterion has been operationalized by reference to the Dutch literature discussed in the previous sections. On this basis, sales, segmentation, labour costs and the two tax items have been classified as being associated with significant costs ('-') whereas the other items were not ('+'). Consolidation and current cost accounting, though not generally perceived as sensitive during this period, might be accompanied by substantial implementation costs and are hence rated '-/+'.

Complexity
Complexity refers to the difficulty of understanding and using an innovation. Compared with many technological innovations, innovations in annual report disclosure can generally not be considered as inordinately difficult to understand. Most items are therefore considered to be not complex ('+'). The exceptions are current cost accounting, consolidation and tax disclosures, all of which require more extensive calculations or fairly advanced technical accounting knowledge. Segment disclosures are scored '-/+' to indicate that full-fledged segment reporting is quite complex, but that simple forms of sales segmentation are not.

Trialability
Trialability refers to possibility of trying an innovation on a limited scale. In the context of financial statement disclosure, this can be interpreted in two ways.
One possibility is to see trialability as the possibility of disclosing an item incidentally, without a commitment to disclose the item again in subsequent years. Theoretically (see chapter 2), such incidental disclosures are feasible only with regard to data of which it is known

or plausible that they are only incidentally available to the company. Otherwise, discontinued disclosure should be prevented by an 'adverse selection' mechanism. From this perspective, only the tax disclosures are 'trialable' since it is not always known with certainty that a nondisclosing company is in fact faced with a tax liability. It will be recalled from table 6.1 that the tax items have, in fact, very high rates of reversion to nondisclosure.

Another interpretation of trialability considers the extent to which limited forms of implementation are possible. For segmental reporting, consolidation, current cost accounting and sales disclosure, the use of interim disclosure formats may have facilitated the movement towards full disclosure. For instance, it appears plausible that the custom of using index figures of sales made the gap between no disclosure and full disclosure easier to bridge. The data do not always allow a precise distinction, however. For segment disclosure, for instance, it can be argued that trialibility is enhanced by the possibility of choosing a coarse segment definition first, which can subsequently be refined.

In general, the observations from table 6.1 have been used to assign scores with regard to trialability. That is, the observation of high rates of reversion to nondisclosure has been interpreted as an indication of trialability[96].

Observability

Strictly speaking, all financial reporting innovations are equally observable since they are all included in published annual reports. Nevertheless, a judgmental scoring of observability has been attempted based on the experiences gained during the data collection for this study. Disclosures within the directors' report are less easily found by a quick perusal of an annual report, whereas items like the funds statement and consolidated reporting occur generally on

---

[96] The only departure from table 6.1 concerns the current cost item, which in table 6.5 is interpreted more narrowly, in terms of 'balance sheet and income statement applications'.

separate pages and are easily spotted. Earnings per share and sales, although generally not shown on the face of the financial statements, since the late 1950's often appeared on a page of 'key figures' and are therefore considered 'observable'.

Compatibility
No attempt has been made to score compatibility. At a technical level, almost all these disclosures are incremental, and can easily be added without disturbing the remainder of the annual report. Possible exceptions are the current cost and tax items which may entail some reorganization of other financial statement items. On the whole, differences in compatibility would seem to be negligible. This is also true at a more general level, where compatibility is often interpreted as 'being compatible with overall value systems or outlooks'. On this level, compatibility may differ among companies but even in this case one would probably find that companies with extensive disclosures will find an additional disclosure rather more compatible than more secretive firms.

The preceding discussion of the scorings in table 6.5 makes it clear that these scores are to a considerable extent open to discussion. Nevertheless, the resulting pattern appears to be helpful in interpreting differences in disclosure among items. It does at least provide a workable framework to distinguish between the more extreme differences in diffusion patterns among items. A plausible case can be made that the items in the lower (upper) end of table 6.5 are indeed different in important respects and hence show quite different disclosure development patterns. An important implication for this line of research appears to be that a search for more objective or accurate indicators of such factors as 'trialability' and 'complexity' may well yield good results.

Figure 6.19 Total changes in disclosure
by year, all companies

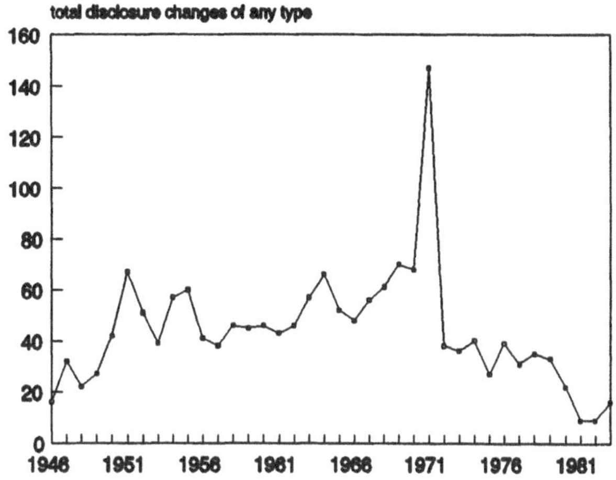

total disclosure changes of any type

6.11.3 *External influences on disclosure*

Throughout this chapter, a number of external influences on disclosure have been discussed. This section recapitulates the findings regarding the most important of these various influences.

The law

There can be little doubt that the 1970 Act on Annual Financial Statements was an important influence on disclosure. This is illustrated by figure 6.19 which shows the total number of changes in disclosure (of any kind) observed for each year. The exceptional nature of the year 1971, the first financial year to which the new law applied, is evident. There is some indication of a rise in disclosure in the few years preceding the law, but the extent of this anticipatory effect pales in comparison with the direct effect observed when the

325

law came into force[97].

What is interesting from a voluntary disclosure perspective, of course, is the fact that for many if not all items the years preceding 1970 also showed considerable disclosure activity. By a rough calculation, each of the sample companies made a change in its disclosure of the items studied here every other year. When one also considers the disclosures not covered in this study, the picture emerges of a fairly steady rate of change in disclosure throughout the 1950's and 1960's. Across all the items studied here, this process of voluntary disclosure extension resulted in rather high disclosure percentages prior to the imposition of legislation. As indicated in table 6.5, all items were disclosed voluntarily by at least about half of the companies before disclosure became strictly mandatory. Even though for some items (*e.g.* wage costs) the anticipation of legal requirements causes some overstatement of the effects of voluntary behaviour, the overall conclusion is justified that substantial advances in disclosure were achieved before 1965.

The main impact of the law was therefore that it made certain disclosures mandatory that were already to a large extent disclosed voluntarily. The most conspicuous example is the provision of consolidated data. Moreover, it has been noted in this chapter that there were noticeable increases in disclosure even in areas were the law provided little or no guidance. These effects were observed in particular in the cases of employee number disclosure and earnings per share disclosure. These items were not covered by the law, but disclosure increased nevertheless in 1970 and 1971.

A similar effect was observed with the 1976 amendment. Although geographical segmentation was not covered, there was a marked increase in geographical segmentation of operating income in the years following this law.

---

[97] This tends to confirm contemporary impressions. Louwers (1972a, 1972b) observed that many companies would have to give considerably more information as a result of the 1970 Act. Frijns (1979) thought in retrospect that the law called for more detailed reporting than customary until then.

Other domestic influences

The 1955 and 1962 reports are generally credited with a major influence on Dutch financial reporting in the postwar period. For some disclosure items, notably the disclosure of tax data, it was found that there was evidence of a relation between increased disclosure and the contents of these reports. But even when no such evidence was found, it could generally be concluded that, in conformity with contemporary opinion, the recommendations of the two reports were definitely ahead of practice. Even though their recommendations were often softened by escape clauses, the general impression of the two reports, when compared with contemporary practice, is quite progressive. Figure 6.19 does in fact show that there were considerable movements in disclosure in the two financial years ending after the publication of the two reports[98]. The case for attributing these movements to the two employers' reports becomes stronger when the data on comparative figures are excluded from total number of disclosure changes by year. This flattens the peak shown in figure 6.19 for 1950-1952, and makes it clear that 1954-1955 and 1963-1964 are exceptions to an otherwise fairly stable level of annual disclosure change between 1950 and 1966.

This chapter provides also some material for assessing the role played by the Tripartite Study Group (TO) after 1970. References to the study group in company financial statements are very rare, but that in itself is no reason to assume that the Considered Views of the study group did not influence financial reporting. After all, the number of references to the 1955 and 1962 employers' reports was also rather small. It is more important to notice that this chapter has shown that, in contrast to the two employers' reports, statements by the study group on disclosure issues were published in general at times when many or most companies already disclosed the items in

---

[98] The 1955 report was published in April, which at that time would have meant that most companies would not yet have published their 1954 annual report. The 1962 report was published in October, which meant that the 1963 annual reports were the first it might influence.

question. As far as the disclosures considered in this chapter are concerned, the most favourable interpretation of the work of the study group is that it may have influenced the disclosures by the 'late majority' or 'laggard' companies. The study group may have played this role in the case of sales disclosure, segment reporting, the funds statement and earnings per share disclosure. Moreover, it should be kept in mind that this chapter deals only with listed companies, whereas the Considered Views of the study group were intended to apply to non-listed companies as well. Nevertheless, the contrast in terms of progressiveness of recommendations between the study group and the two employers' committees (to which the study group was in a sense the successor), is striking.

Foreign influence
It has been shown in this chapter that for most items, disclosure levels in the Netherlands were consistently lower than in the United States. With respect to that country, there existed therefore a differential that could serve as a stimulus for imitation. With respect to other countries, the existence and extent of any disclosures differentials is less clear, owing to the fragmentary nature of the available data. However, the conclusion appears to be justified that during the late 1960's, disclosure levels in the Netherlands were roughly comparable to those in the United Kingdom[99]. Especially with regard to items like earnings per share disclosure and the fund statement, differences between the two countries are slight indeed. Following 1970, a high degree of standard setting activity in the UK

---

[99] This does contradict the findings of Barrett (1977) who found that UK disclosure levels in the period 1963-1972 where throughout comparable to those in the US, whereas the Netherlands was found to be on a level with Japan, Sweden and Germany. Barret's study deals only with small samples of very large companies, and the results may therefore not be comparable with the present study. However, the impact of increasing regulation in the United Kingdom is ignored by Barrett even though this would seem to account for a considerable share of disclosure expansion in the UK over this period.

resulted, at least for some disclosures, in a gap between UK and Dutch disclosure levels. As a result, UK financial reporting could serve once again as an example for Dutch financial reporting.

Cross-border listings played a role in transmitting the influence of these two potential role models. The possible role of international business in this regard has been discussed for the United Kingdom (as a recipient country) by Cook (1989), and has also frequently been suggested with regard to the Dutch multinationals. This possibility has to some extent already been explored in section 5.5.3. In that section it was concluded that, although the large multinationals were usually at the forefront of disclosure, there frequently were smaller, domestic companies with disclosures to match those of the large multinationals.

In this chapter, three cases were reported in which a foreign listing was an immediate cause of reporting change in the Netherlands:

-   The listing of KONINKLIJKE PETROLEUM in New York was found to have played a distinct role in the introduction of the earnings per share disclosure in the Netherlands.
-   The New York listings of PHILIPS, KONINKLIJKE PETROLEUM and AKU coincided with the adoption, by these companies, of modern integrated income statements which hitherto had been unknown in Dutch practice[100].
-   The fact that UNILEVER and KONINKLIJKE PETROLEUM were 'listed'[101] in London helped to bring the reform of the Companies Act 1948 under the attention of the Dutch, notably with respect to the requirement to provide consolidated financial statements.

An international listing probably played a role in the funds statement

---

[100] The income statements of ARM and STOOMVAART ZEELAND, although integrated in the late 1940's, represent the final development of the traditional T-shaped profit and loss account rather than the modern income statement.

[101] By means of their British sister-companies.

disclosure of KONINKLIJKE PETROLEUM, which was among the first to disclose. However, UNILEVER developed a funds statement long before it went to New York and before KONINKLIJKE PETROLEUM. PHILIPS definitely came in the rear with regard to the funds statement, indicating that its foreign listings initially played no role in this respect. For current cost accounting a reverse effect could be observed. UNILEVER and KONINKLIJKE PETROLEUM finally started to disclose current cost data when they were required to do so by foreign accounting standards in the 1970's, even though many Dutch companies had preceded them at home.

Apart from the effect of multiple listings, the US and UK example were effective because of the awareness of foreign practices in the Netherlands. This was most clearly seen from the data on segment reporting. A few years after that had become an issue in the United States, in the late 1960's, the subject began to be discussed quite intensively in the Netherlands as well with frequent references to the US situation. This was accompanied by an increase in disclosure which also lagged some five years behind that in the United States.

A certain parallelism between developments in the Netherlands and those in the United States and/or the United Kingdom was found for all disclosures that developed fully after 1970 (segmentation, current cost data, the funds statement and earnings per share). In these cases, the time-lag with respect to the United States could be in the order of magnitude of ten to 15 years, whereas the time-lag relative to the United Kingdom was typically much shorter.

In the case of earlier disclosures for which the US example might have been relevant (sales, consolidation) developments in the Netherlands lagged behind to such an extent that a link is hard to discern. This would support the conclusion that the direct influence of the US example had definitely grown stronger around 1970. This conclusion would be in harmony with the opening of the Dutch auditing towards foreign accounting and auditing practices that occurred during the 1960's (see also section 3.4.3).

Chapter 7
Summary and discussion

7.1 Introduction

This study started with the question of how financial reporting in the Netherlands developed during the four decades following the Second World War, given that, during that period, financial reporting throughout the Western World was undergoing an important transformation. In conformity with the perceptions of this period expressed in the Dutch and international literature, this question was stated with particular reference to the development of annual reporting disclosure on a voluntary basis.

An important aspect of change in financial reporting internationally during this period was the large increase in the amount and detail of information disclosed in annual reports. In many countries, including, in 1970, the Netherlands, new legislation was introduced aimed at increasing mandatory disclosure. The distinguishing feature of the Netherlands was that disclosure had remained unregulated for longer than in many other countries, but that, nevertheless, the quality and extent of disclosure in the Netherlands reputedly had improved not significantly less than in leading but more regulated countries like the United Kingdom.

In short, financial reporting in the Netherlands during this period allegedly could be seen as an unusually extensive and successful experiment in voluntary financial reporting reform. The purpose of this study was to arrive at a better understanding and appreciation of this episode in the development of Dutch financial reporting. This study was based mainly on two sets of primary source materials: the contemporary Dutch professional literature, and a sample of published annual reports of listed companies. This chapter summarizes the results of this study, by discussing the main characteristics of the process of annual reporting change in the Netherlands.

In chapter 1, three levels were distinguished at which the development of disclosure in the Netherlands could be studied: the level of individual disclosure items, the level of the disclosing company, and the national level. In this chapter, the results of this study will be summarized with reference to these three levels in the sections 7.2 through 7.4. Section 7.5 discusses the limitations of this study and possibilities for further research.

7.2 Individual disclosure items

7.2.1 General features

In chapter 2, a general framework was provided for the interpretation of disclosure phenomena. This framework relies heavily on the economic rationality of disclosure decisions in order to summarize some of the 'universal' aspects of disclosure that apply in any financial reporting situation in a modern market economy. It was found that, on this basis, a case can be made *a priori* for the existence of forces pushing for the non-mandatory disclosure of all information relevant for investment decisions and for the ordering of corporate governance. This tendency to disclose is tempered by a number of complicating factors, notably the issue of information structure knowledge and the existence of disclosure costs.

It was also found that a translation of these economic interpretations of disclosure from a signalling or agency perspective to the context of routine financial statement disclosure required some additional steps that are not frequently taken in the analytical literature. In chapter 4, an innovation diffusion framework was suggested as a possible approach to fill this lacuna.

In chapter 6, the actual disclosures made by sample companies in the 1945-1983 period with regard to nine different disclosure areas were studied in some detail. At a most elementary level, it was found that there was, in fact, a rather substantial extent of voluntary disclosure in the annual reports studied. Throughout the period, companies continuously expanded their disclosure with the result that many items were already being disclosed by about half or a majority of companies before disclosure was made mandatory by changes in the law in 1970 or 1983.

Especially with regard to the period before 1970, there seems to be no room for excessively pessimistic assessments. While it is obvious that the extent of disclosure was still far removed from current levels, there was definite progress. Mueller's (1972) impression of the 'sad state' of European financial reporting in the late 1950s, cited in chapter 1, should at least for the Netherlands be qualified by the remark that there was no stagnation but rather constant improvement in the direction of the US example posited by Mueller.

As might be expected from any detailed study, the process of voluntary disclosure extensions was found to be highly complex, and to vary considerably in its particulars across disclosure items. Yet, it was also found that the main outlines of disclosure development in the Netherlands were quite clearly discernible, and that these outlines were amenable to interpretation within the broad frame of reference of 'universal' disclosure characteristics outlined above. It seems reasonable to interpret the process of disclosure expansion largely in terms of actively managed disclosure. This conclusion is based primarily on the following observations.

- Differences in rapidity and extent of voluntary disclosure among items can be related to features of the information such as perceived costs, the certainty with which outside parties can assume that information is available within the company and the complexity of the disclosure.
- Already early in the period, companies were quite responsive to stimuli for disclosure extension.
- Quite careful use was made of interim formats of disclosure, which indicates an active interest in balancing costs and benefits of disclosure. Use of 'low cost' solutions to demands for more disclosure (*e.g.* disclosure of insured value as an approximation of current cost of assets, disclosure of index figures rather than absolute amounts of sales) was frequently observed.

Hence, to understand the process of voluntary disclosure expansion in the postwar Netherlands, it is not necessary to assume that the working of 'ordinary' factors influencing disclosure was largely suspended. In particular, there appears to be no need to assume an unusually large concentration of managerial goodwill in the Netherlands during this period. While, as noted above, it would be incorrect to view the 1950s and 1960s as an era of stagnation, it would be equally incorrect to assume a 'golden age' in which voluntary improvements in reporting were brought about for no other reason than a detached desire to further the cause of good financial reporting. Changes in the law were required to persuade sometimes substantial numbers of remaining nondisclosing companies, or to impose some uniformity on disclosure practices.

The general conclusion that the process of disclosure expansion was, in very general terms, characterized by a considerable degree of apparent rational disclosure management can be refined or modified on the basis of more detailed results of this study. The more important observations include the following.

7.2.2 Sources of new disclosures

New disclosures can be introduced into the array of relevant potential disclosures in a variety of ways. Sources of new disclosures found in this study include changes in taxation laws (resulting in disclosures of deferred tax items), changes in Stock Exchange practice and the language of financial analysis (the introduction of price/earnings ratios and earnings per share in the course of the 1950s) and the movement towards enterprise democratization in the 1950s and 1960s (resulting in demands for wage cost disclosures).

Foreign reporting practices, especially in the United States, also played an important role as sources of new disclosures. Awareness of foreign practices could turn existing theoretical knowledge of potential disclosures into effective demand for the disclosure of these items. This was observed in the case of sales disclosure and the introduction of consolidated information. Both items were recognized as theoretically conceivable but, for the time being, impracticable disclosures long before the US and/or UK examples made them part of the regular disclosure array.

Foreign practices could also be an immediate source of new disclosures. In this way, the segment reporting issue was transplanted from the United States to the Netherlands in a relatively short period around 1970.

7.2.3 Changes over time

A question that must be considered in this context is whether the nature of the disclosure process changed in the course of the postwar period. It is unmistakable that 1970 marks a watershed in the development of financial reporting. As was pointed out in chapter 3, this is not merely because of the 1970 Act, but also because of a number of other developments occurring more or less simultaneously: the mergers and acquisition wave of the late 1960s which altered the corporate landscape, the corresponding merger wave in the audit profession, the advent of accounting standard setting at home and abroad, and finally, the advent of the Fourth Directive. It would have been surprising if these developments had not left their mark on the process of disclosure change. Yet to point out the difference of pre- and post-1970 disclosure on the basis of the detailed studies of disclosure items in chapter 6 is not a straightforward task, because it involves the comparison of disclosure behaviour with respect to quite different items (*e.g.* earnings per share versus tax cost disclosure).

Two indications that might point in the direction of change are:

- The more widespread occurrence of 'incidental' disclosures and reversions to nondisclosure before 1970. This might indicate a growing rationalization or self-consciousness of the disclosure process in the course of the period, which would in turn leave less room for experiment.

- Time lags between the 'invention' of an item and its acceptance in the regular disclosure array appear to diminish towards the end of the period. This becomes clear when the transmission from theory to practice is compared of consolidated reporting (spanning the 1920-1950 period) and of segment reporting (from the late 1960s to the early 1970s). A possible explanation for this tendency towards more rapid dissemination of new disclosures might be a growing awareness of disclosure practices of other companies, or more intense mutual observation. However, on the basis of developments sketched in chapter 3, it is also plausible to attribute some influence to a growing awareness of developments abroad.

It cannot, however, confidently be concluded that all changes in disclosure were effected more rapidly in the 1970s than, say, in the 1950s. It is true that the disclosure of earnings per share and the funds statement (both occurring in the 1970s) were models of rapid and smooth diffusion processes. But on the other hand, so was the spread of comparative figures in the early 1950s. And the examples of current cost and segmental disclosures suggest that after 1970 there might still be considerable reluctance to disclose new items.

7.3 Companies

The second level of analysis is that of the disclosing company. The particular question asked here is to what extent companies differed in their participation in the process of disclosure expansion, and what company characteristics were associated with these differences. This question was addressed in particular in chapter 5.

The relationship between company characteristics and disclosure has received extensive attention in the existing literature on empirical disclosure research. A review of this literature was provided in chapter 4. From this review, it appeared that previous studies had largely been confined to cross-sectional studies.
From the longitudinal data on Dutch companies, it appeared that companies were not necessarily consistent in their disclosure over time. That is, early disclosure of one item by a particular company

was not always associated by early disclosure of other items. Even though a general tendency towards to consistent disclosure could be established, a number of companies went through quite distinct phases in terms of apparent willingness to increase disclosure. An approach was developed to capture the entire disclosure performance of a company over a longer period of time in a single number.

On the basis of these measurements, it was found that there were clear differences among companies with regard to the participation in the overall process of disclosure expansion. Not all companies shared in the disclosure improvement reported in the preceding section.

These differences among companies could to some extent be related to company characteristics that were found to be relevant in earlier empirical work. In some instances, the longitudinal nature of this study allowed some refinements or extensions of previous results.

7.3.1 Company characteristics

Previous studies of voluntary disclosure have consistently found that size was the most important covariate of extent of disclosure. This was clearly confirmed by the present study, even though size was measured by the rather crude accounting data that were available. A refinement of the general association between size and disclosure was introduced by the finding that changes in (relative) size were associated with changes in (relative) disclosure. In particular, large but slow-growing companies did on the whole disclose better than average, but were gradually falling behind in the extent of their disclosure.

Differences in capital market activity appeared to be a second important characteristic, although the importance of this factor declined with the overall tendency, manifest from 1970 onward, to rely less on issues of risk-bearing capital. Differences over time in overall capital market activity may obviously play a role in explaining differences across empirical studies with regard to the significance of this covariate.

A particular combination of size and capital market activity was displayed by the small group of four multinational enterprises with listings on foreign exchanges (AKU / AKZO, KONINKLIJKE PETRO-LEUM (Shell), PHILIPS and UNILEVER. As might be expected, these companies tended to be among the best disclosing companies. However, it was found that these companies were not necessarily the first to disclose new items. A typical pattern was for one or two of the four to be among the very first disclosing companies while the others would follow later, sometimes after considerable numbers of smaller companies had preceded them. In terms of disclosure innovation during the postwar period, it would presumably be fair to give more credit to UNILEVER than it usually receives.

Differences in disclosure among industries could only be established in general terms. Trading companies tended to disclose less than manufacturing companies, and within the group of manufacturing companies there was a slight association between industry 'strength' and extent of disclosure.

As an alternative to an industry grouping, this study attempted a grouping on the basis of intercompany link through multiple director-ships. It was found that, especially for the earlier part of the period, such links do provide insight in disclosure behaviour even though further work needs to be done to refine these measures.

7.3.2 Generational effect

Another way of looking at the relationship between company charac-teristics and disclosure is to consider the changes in the Dutch corporate landscape during this period. By the end of the period, the population of listed companies had changed in important respects because of strong size growth, new listings, financial distress and a veritable mergers and acquisitions wave during the 1965-1975 period. It can be argued that corporate demographics were an important mechanism of disclosure change during this period. It was found that new listings typically conformed to 'average' disclosure practices in the year of their listing, whereas delisting companies tended to disclose less than average. A clear generational effect is discernible in the disappearance of large numbers of older com-

338

panies, typically listed from well 1940 and active in traditional sectors as shipping and international trade. These companies tended to be less innovative in their financial reporting, and their delisting contributed to the overall impression of disclosure improvement. The company perspective, therefore, reinforces the tentative conclusion of change in the disclosure process indicated in section 7.2.

7.4 The national level

In the preceding sections, it was indicated that the process of disclosure extension in the Netherlands could be interpreted to a large extent in 'universal' terms of disclosure management, dissemination of knowledge, group behaviour and economic considerations. Any differences between the Netherlands and other countries must be seen, therefore, largely as differences in degree rather than kind.

The question whether financial reporting in the Netherlands did show unusually early or high levels of voluntary disclosure was addressed in chapter 6. Unfortunately, limited data availability prevented the systematic comparison across disclosure items of the Netherlands with countries other than the United Kingdom and the United States.

Compared with the United States, disclosure in the Netherlands typically lagged behind. However, as indicated above, the gap appeared to be narrowing in the course of the period, from roughly 40 years in the case of sales disclosure, to about fifteen years in the case of the funds statement and less than ten years with regard to segment disclosures.

No great differences in voluntary disclosure were apparent with regard to the United Kingdom. Clear examples of more or less simultaneous development are provided by the data on the funds statement and earnings per share disclosure. In the course of the 1970s, disclosure in the UK began to grow more rapidly than in the Netherlands, but this difference can probably largely be attributed to the more rigorous accounting standards introduced in the UK.

The fragmented data available for other European countries do not indicate that these were significantly ahead of the Netherlands in terms of voluntary disclosure.

The conclusion that, in many respects, financial reporting in the Netherlands developed parallel to that in the United Kingdom is important for two reasons.

First, the United Kingdom has generally been regarded as being ahead of other European countries in terms of the development of financial reporting. In the Netherlands itself, British reporting was before the war perceived as the most relevant example to follow.

Second, as documented in chapter 3, even though the Netherlands mirrored the British approach to reporting regulation until the Second World War, the 1948 (UK) Companies Act was not followed by comparable Dutch legislation until 1970. Therefore, from the late 1940s to the late 1960s, Dutch financial reporting was in fact able to match or approximate British standards of reporting, even though the regulatory regime was lighter in the Netherlands.

A somewhat similar pattern is observable in the 1970s, with particular reference to segment reporting. Despite the absence of a requirement similar to that in force in the United Kingdom since 1967, segmentation by line of business was clearly spreading in the Netherlands during the first half of the 1970s.

As discussed in chapter 3, the fact that Dutch financial reporting was developing largely in line with international developments but without the support of regulation was recognized in the Netherlands during the 1950s and 1960s. The fact that disclosure continued to lag behind that in the United States was, for some observers, a reason to call for increased regulation. To others, however, the fact that financial reporting was improving on a voluntary basis was a sign of the effectiveness of a peculiarly Dutch approach to financial reporting. In chapter 3, the development of this notion of a 'Dutch system' of financial reporting and reporting regulation was investigated. It was found that its main trait was a belief in the beneficial working of the free interaction between company managements who where willing to comply with reasonable demands for disclosure, and a competent auditing profession that could interpret these continuously changing demands. The sample of financial reports in this study justifies the contemporary belief that this voluntary system was in fact resulting in a continuous expansion of disclosure on a voluntary basis. In this sense, the existence and working of a 'Dutch system' can be considered to have their basis in facts.

However, the adoption of a wider perspective allowed by the time elapsed since the end of the 1945-1983 period results in some qualifying remarks concerning the uniqueness of this 'Dutch system'. In chapter 3, it was found that the period of relatively light regulation in the Netherlands could be seen as a temporary interval. Taking the period from the middle 19th century to the later 20th century as a whole, it can be observed that company law, in sofar as it impinged on annual report disclosure, was developing under the influence of basically similar forces throughout Western Europe. In most countries, mandatory publication of financial statements was introduced into the law during the 1870-1930 period, in order to replace earlier systems of preventive government supervision of limited liability companies. Later during the 20th century, reporting laws were changed in countries like the United Kingdom, Germany and the Netherlands to reflect social concerns over the role of large enterprises in a democratizing society. Still later, the harmonization of company law in the context of European union became another common cause of change. The Netherlands participated in all these developments, but timing differences attributable largely to factors operating in the legal sphere (and not primarily germane to financial reporting) resulted in a period of relatively unregulated financial reporting from *circa* 1930 to 1970.

During the interval of light regulation, some forces influencing financial reporting practice that were active elsewhere as well were given a relatively free rein, and could therefore play a more conspicuous role than elsewhere. One of the most important of these forces was the role of the organized Dutch employers. This study has found that many of their 1955 and 1962 recommendations were in fact considerably ahead of contemporary practice. Even though immediate changes in practices could only be discerned in a small number of cases (notably tax disclosures), the claim that their recommendations did indeed play a unique and effective role in the changing of Dutch financial reporting seems not unreasonable.

A summary assessment of Dutch financial report disclosure in the postwar period would therefore be that it was different from that in other countries, but in a more limited sense than in the area of income determination and valuation. Whereas in the latter two areas fundamental differences did and still do exist (for instance in the influence of taxation on financial reporting), differences in attitude towards disclosure regulation were of a more transitory nature. The Netherlands temporarily set itself apart from neighbouring countries because of timing differences in the long-term development of company law, which was moving in the same general direction as that in other European countries. This resulted in 'window of opportunity' for voluntary financial reporting. This opportunity was not wasted. A process of voluntary improvements in disclosure was brought about, that was, however, governed by common, that is, not typically Dutch, factors.

7.5 Limitations and suggestions for further research

The limitations of this study flow to a large extent from its exploratory character. As indicated in chapter 1, an amount of detail or precision in the investigation of particular aspects of disclosure was sacrificed in order to obtain a wide view of the development of disclosure in the Netherlands. This implies that further research is possible along a number of lines that could only briefly be touched, or dealt with in a less than exhaustive manner in this study. The most important limitations, and hence, areas for further research are related to:

- The focus on listed companies. An important reason for this limitation, which can probably not easily be undone, is the limited availability of annual report data for unlisted companies. This limitation is important when possible influences on disclos-

342

ure are discussed that may work differently for unlisted companies. In the present study, this may apply in particular to the role of the auditor and the influence of the guidance on annual reporting produced by the Council on Annual Reporting (RJ) and its predecessor. An extension of this study to the area of unlisted companies might be desirable, but would probably have to be preceded by a separate research effort directed at opening up and documenting the existing collections of annual reports of these companies held at various locations in the Netherlands.

- The selection of disclosure items. Essentially, the items studied here are all examples of items that were introduced with at least moderate success in the course of the 1945-1983 period. That is, no items were included that were already being disclosed on a large scale at the beginning of the period, that only began to be disclosed at the end of the period or that enjoyed only a brief spell of popularity before disappearing from published annual reports. This may have introduced a certain 'innovation bias' into the study. Discontinued disclosures have received some attention in this study, but might well be an object of further study.

- Measurement and analysis. In general, this study has relied on rather simple measurements and techniques. The extent to which information was given on the various disclosure items was measured by binary scales or by three- or four-point ordinal scales. Aggregation of these data to measures of aggregate disclosure also followed simple procedures. Finally, explanatory variables, such as size, capital market activity or industry were also measured by unsophisticated procedures. Further research might well make considerable progress in measurement issues of this kind. In particular, more refined ways may be sought to make operational the notion of 'innovation characteristics' imported from diffusion theory. In this study, these characteristics were assessed in a very general way on the basis of the historical materials described in chapter 6. More sophisticated assessments of costs and benefits of disclosure, complexity and trialability might well result in a better understanding of the unmistakable differences in the disclosure process among items. A particular 'innovation characteristic' that ought to be further explored is the degree of 'fineness' of disclosures: since it is possible to disclose particular items at varying levels of detail, the relationship between the 'quality' of disclosure and the willingness to disclose can be further explored.

Despite a small number of multivariate analyses, this study consists in general of univariate analyses. One type of interaction effect that is neglected in this way is the interaction among disclosure elements. A simple example of interaction found in this study is that disclosure of segment information does not precede the disclosure of consolidated data. More subtle interactions include the observed effect that changes in the law with respect to one disclosure item may coincide with non-mandatory disclosure extensions in related areas. In the same way, interaction between numerical and verbal, or between annual report disclosure and other disclosure channels, can be investigated.

Finally, a particular concern would be the resolution of problems involved in applying standard analytical techniques, such as survival analysis, to company data that are seriously disturbed by mergers and acquisitions.

The preceding limitations and research suggestions relate to the empirical study of annual report data. Other areas where future research may be fruitful include:

-   The process by which knowledge of new disclosures is spread among the potential disclosers. The effects of education, the financial press and the role of the auditor in this respect can be further investigated. This would presumably require a different type of approach in which in-company case studies, surveys or 'oral history' approaches might be used.

-   The international background. This study has relied heavily on materials from English-speaking countries, with regard to both the historical background sketched in chapter 3 and the published data on the extent of disclosure in other countries used for comparative purposes in chapter 6. While even the comparison between the Netherlands and the United Kingdom in terms of the development of attitudes towards reporting and reporting regulation might bear further inquiry, this is certainly true with respect to other continental European countries. The production of comparable time series on the development of reporting practices in the main European countries seems to offer an hitherto unexplored area of research in accounting history.

Appendix A
List of disclosure items

This appendix contains particulars on the disclosure data gathered from company financial statements. A general discussion of the process by which these items have been selected can be found in chapter 4.

Definitions
The disclosures described in this appendix are referred to in the main body of this book by three different expressions:
The basic element in this study is the *disclosure item*. A total of 13 disclosure items have been distinguished. The data collected for each company in this study consist of a string of 13 scores for each year during which the company was included in the sample.
Some of these disclosure items are fairly closely related. For this reason, the 13 items can be grouped into nine *disclosure areas*. These nine areas correspond to the nine sections of chapter 6. They are listed here in the same broadly chronological order in which they are discussed in chapter 6.
The annual scores for each of the 13 items were either binary (disclosure or nondisclosure), or based on a larger number of possible scores. For instance, for the disclosure item 'sales', four different modes of disclosure (apart from nondisclosure) were distinguished. In this way, a total of 30 different *disclosure positions* were distinguished for these items.

Scoring
Specific issues in scoring are indicated in 'remarks' following the description of each item. An important general issue is the difference between consolidated versus parent-company data. In general, a company has been credited with a disclosure when *either* consolidated or parent-company data on a particular item (*e.g.* sales) were disclosed.

Binary scoring
In some cases (notably in chapter 5), it was found useful to reduce the scores on all items to a binary scoring. Where this has been done, the definitions of binary disclosures listed below have been used, unless otherwise indicated.

Disclosure:

Area	Item	Name & disclosure positions

1

    1   **Sales**
- 0. no disclosure
- 1. disclosure of quantities/physical units sold
- 2. indexed values or growth rates of revenues
- 3. absolute sales figure, not reconciled to operating income in income statement
- 4. absolute sales figure, reconciled to operating income in income statement.

Binary score: 0-2 nondisclosure; 3-4 disclosure

Remarks:
- . Position 1, 'quantities sold' is applicable only in case of relatively undiversified bulk production or in case of a relatively small number of construction-type projects that can be enumerated.
- . Disclosure of change on previous year (rather than multi-period data) is scored '2'.
- . A score of '3' in most cases refers to a sales disclosure in the directors' report or the note to the financial statements. Only in rare cases was the sales figure provided on the face of the income statement without a reconcilliation of sales to net income.

2

    2   **Comparative figures**
- 0. no disclosure
- 1. disclosure

Remark:
Disclosure is assumed to occur when both balance sheet and income statement contain comparative figures for major groupings (in a few instances, companies started to provide comparative figures for one of the two main statements. This practice was never continued for more than two years).

3   *Taxation*

    3   **Tax costs**
- 0. disclosure
- 1. no disclosure

348

Remark:

In case of losses and carry forward of losses, tax costs may be zero. In such cases, a note on the effect of losses explaining the absence of a tax item is considerd as disclosure of tax costs.

4   **Tax liabilities**

0. no disclosure of tax item
1. disclosure of tax item of unspecified composition
2. disclosure of one tax item with notes indicating mixed (current/deferred) composition
3. separate disclosure of either deferred or current liabilities
4. separate disclosure of both current and deferred liabilities.

Binary scores: 0 no disclosure, 1-4 disclosure.

Remark:

Deferred liabilities are assumed to be disclosed even if only the temporary tax-free reserves based on the tax-regime of the 1940s and 1950s are disclosed (see also section 6.4.1).

4   *Employment data*

5   **Labour cost data**

0. no disclosure
1. disclosure of total costs
2. labour costs subdivided into categories as pension costs or social security contributions.

Binary score: 0 nondisclosure; 1-2 disclosure

Remark:

Disclosure of labour costs as a percentage of total costs when total costs are given at another location in the financial statements is considered as disclosure.

6   **Number of employees**

0. no disclosure
1. disclosure

Remark:

Employee data for part of the enterprise only count as disclosure if it can be assumed that the employees referred to are not the staff of a mere holding company and therefore amount to a more than negligeable fraction of total staff. This issue arises mainly when the number of Dutch staff is disclosed, but not the number of staff overseas.

349

7   **Consolidated financial statements**
0. no disclosure
1. disclosure of separate financial statements of major subsidiaries
2. disclosure of either consolidated balance sheet or consolidated income statement
3. disclosure of both balance sheet and income statement.
9. not applicable

Binary score: 0-1, 9 no disclosure, 2-3 disclosure

Remark:
Consolidation is considered to be not applicable when there is no
indication of 'Investments' in the parent balance sheet. When
'Investments' are included in the parent balance sheet, consolidation is considered to be in order unless the investments are
explicitly presented as minority holdings.

8   **Funds statement**
0. no disclosure
1. disclosure

Remark:
Includes any analysis in tabular format that relates income statement data to cash-flow figures or changes in working capital.

Current cost data

9   **Income statement**
0. no disclosure of current cost data
1. indication of current cost equivalents of selected cost items
in notes
2. selected cost items in income statement on current cost
basis
3. income statement (main or supplementary) fully on current
cost basis.

10   **Balance sheet**
0. no disclosure of current cost data
1. indication of current costs of selected assets in notes
2. selected assets in balance sheet valued at current cost
3. balance sheet (main or supplementary) fully on current cost
basis.

Binary scores: 0 no disclosure, 1-3 disclosure

Remarks:
. Disclosure of insured value (*verzekerde waarde*) is considered as 'indication of current costs of selected assets in notes'.
. Accelerated depreciation or additional credits to 'replacement provisions' are not considered as current cost figures without an indication that the amount of these charges has been determined with some reference to current costs.
. Use of the base-stock method does not count as current cost basis for costs of goods sold.
. One-off revaluations of assets result in a 'no disclosure' score for years following the revaluation unless the revaluation is yearly referred to.

8

11 **Earnings per share**
0. no disclosure
1. disclosure

Remark:
. Disclosure is assumed to occur when a per share figure is given for an actually outstanding type of share (Eg: per ordinary share of *f* 25,-) rather than for a round number of share capital (Eg: per *f* 1000,- of share capital).

9 *Segment data*

12 **Industry (line of business) segments**
0. no disclosure
1. segmentation of sales only
2. segmentation of (operating) income only
3. segmentation of sales and (operating) income
9. not applicable

13 **Geographical segments**
0. no disclosure
1. segmentation of sales only
2. segmentation of (operating) income only
3. segmentation of sales and (operating) income
9. not applicable

Binary scores: 0, 9 no disclosure; 1-3 disclosure

Remarks:
. Even if absolute sales are not disclosed, a percentagewise

breakdown of sales nevertheless counts as disclosure of segmented sales.

Geographical disclosure is considered to be applicable as soon as 'exports' are referred to in the financial statements. Hence, a break-down between 'domestic' and 'export' is considered sufficient to count as 'segmentation'.

Appendix B
Company sample

This appendix lists the companies of which the financial statements were studied. For each company, the following data are presented. In SMALL CAPITALS the label used to refer to the company in the text. Labels like these are used rather than the more cumbersome and sometimes changing full names. The next two columns present information on the financial years for which financial statements were surveyed, the full names of the companies (including major name changes) and information on predecessor (Pr) or successor (Sc) companies included in the sample.

Company label	Years surveyed	Full name and affiliations
ACF	1967-1983	ACF Amsterdam Chemie Farmacie NV. Pr: BANDOENG KININE
ADAM	1945-1970	NV Delftsche Leerlooierij en Drijfriemenfabriek v/h Alex Adam (since 1962: Koninklijke Fabrieken Adam NV)
AIR	1958-1983	Automobiel Industrie Rotterdam NV
AKU	1944/45-1968	Algemene Kunstzijde Unie NV. Sc:AKZO
AKZO	1969-1983	Akzo NV. Pr: AKU
ALBATROS	1945/46-1958/59	Albatros Superfosfaatfabrieken NV
ALBERT HEYN	1948-1983	Albert Heyn NV (since 1973: Ahold NV)
ALBERTS	1945-1959	NV Houthandel v/h G. Alberts Lzn & Co
ALGEMENE	1940/46-1967	NV Algemeene Exploratie Maatschappij
AMSTEL HOTEL	1948-1968	NV Amstel Hotel Maatschappij
APELDOORN ZEPPELIN		
	1950/51-1965	Apeldoornse Nettenfabriek Von Zeppelin & Co NV
ARM	1945-1983	NV Amsterdamsche Rijtuigmaatschappij
ASSELBERG	1954-1979	Asselberg's IJzerindustrie en Handelmaatschappij NV (Since 1976: Asselbergs Holland NV)
ASW	1945-1975	A.S.W. Apparatenfabriek NV
AUDET	1973-1983	NV Associatie van Uitgevers van Dagbladen en Tijdschriften

353

AVIS	1945-1965	NV Verffabrieken Avis
BALLAST-NEDAM	1968-1983	Ballast-Nedam Groep NV. Pr: NAM
BANDOENG KININE		
	1958-1965	Bandoengsche Kininefabriek Holland NV. Sc: ACF
BATENBURG	1955-1983	NV Electrotechnisch Installatiebedrijf en Handelsbureau v/h P. Batenburg (Since 1982: Batenburg Beheer NV)
BEERS	1961-1983	Beers' Zonen NV
BEGEMANN	1954-1983	NV Koninklijke Nederlandsche Machine-fabriek v/h E.H. Begemann
BENSDORP	1960-1971	Bensdorp Internationaal NV
BERGOSS	1964-1980	Koninklijke Tapijtfabrieken Bergoss NV
BEYNES	1945-1957	Koninklijke Fabrieken van Rijtuigen en Spoor-wagens J.J. Beynes NV
BLAAUWHOED	1945-1966	NV Blaauwhoedenveem-Vriesseveem (since 1954: Blaauwhoed NV) Sc:PAKHOED
BLIKMAN SARTORIUS		
	1949/50-1956/57	Blikman & Sartorius NV
BOSKALIS	1970-1983	(Since 1977: Koninklijke) Boskalis West-minster (Since 1980) Group NV
BUTTINGER	1959-1969	Buttinger NV
BYENKORF	1956-1983	NV Magazijn "de Bijenkorf" (since 1965: Bijenkorf Beheer NV; since 1971 KBB NV)
CARP	1944-1969	NV J.A. Carp's Garenfabrieken
CETECO	1945-1983	Curaçaosche Handel-Maatschappij NV (Since 1970: NV Handel- en Industrie-maatschappij "Ceteco")
DESSEAUX	1959/60-1983/84	Taptijfabriek H. Desseaux NV
DOMANIALE MIJN	1944/45-1964/65	Domaniale Mijn-Maatschappij NV
DORP	1946-1983	NV v/h G.C.T. van Dorp & Co
DRU	1948-1969	Koninklijke Fabrieken Diepenbrock & Reigers NV
DUIKER	1961-1981	Duiker Apparatenfabriek NV
ECONOSTO	1970-1983	Econosto NV
ELECTROLASCH	1954-1966	NV Nederlandsche Electrolasch Maatschap-pij. Sc: HCG
ENOT	1954-1972	NV Nederlandsche Optische Industrie E.N.O.T.
ERIKS	1978-1983	Eriks NV
FEARNLEY	1975-1979	Fearnley NV. Pr: OOSTZEE
FURNESS	1944/45-1983	Furness' Scheepvaart- en Agentuur Maat-schappij NV (Since 1968: Furness NV)
FRANSCH SOUDAN		
	1947/48-1957/58	NV Société Commerciale du Soudan Fran-çais (Fransch Soudan Handel Maatschappij)
GAMMA	1972-1983	Gamma Holding NV. Pr: TEXOPRINT

GERZON	1940/41-1947/48	Gebroeders Gerzon's Modemagazijnen NV
GIESSEN	1957-1983	C. van der Giessen & Zonen's Scheepswerven NV (Since 1962: Van der Giessen - de Noord NV)
GROENHOEDENVEEM		
	1945-1954	NV Groenhoedenveem
GROFSMEDERIJ	1944/45-1976	NV Koninklijke Nederlandsche Grofsmederij
HOLDOH	1956-1983	NV Drentsch-Overijsselsche Houthandel (Since 1979: NV Holdoh, since 1982: NV Holdoh-Houtunie)
HANDELSCOMPAGNIE		
	1950-1966	Handelscompagnie NV
HAVENWERKEN	1946-1967	(Koninklijke) Nederlandsche Maatschappij voor Havenwerken NV
HBG	1968-1983	Hollandsche Beton Groep NV. Pr: HBG, HCG
HBM	1945-1967	Hollandsche Beton Maatschappij NV. Sc: HBG
HCG	1966-1967	Hollandse Constructie Groep NV. Pr: ELECTROLASCH, HCW Sc: HBG
HCW	1944/45-1965	NV Hollandsche Constructiewerkplaatsen. Sc: HCG
VAN DER HEEM	1949-1963	Van der Heem NV. Sc: INDOHEEM
HEINEKEN	1944/45-1983	Heineken's Bierbrouwerij Maatschappij NV
HOEK	1945-1983	NV W.A. Hoek's Machine- en Zuurstoffabriek
HOLLAND HANDEL		
	1946-1960	NV Handelsvereeniging "Holland"
HOLLAND MEEL	1945-1956	Stoom-Meelfabriek "Holland" NV
HOLLANDIA	1949-1961	Koninklijke Hollandia Fabrieken van Melkproducten en Voedingsmiddelen NV
HOLL. MELKSUIKER		
	1948-1969	NV Hollandsche Melksuikerfabriek
HOOIMEIJER	1951-1971	A. Hooimeijer & Zonen NV
HOUTVAART	1945-1973	NV Houtvaart
HVA	1941/47-1982	NV Handelsvereeniging "Amsterdam" (since 1959: Verenigde H.V.A.-Maatschappijen NV)
HV ROTTERDAM	1940/47-1969	NV Internationale Crediet- en Handelsvereeniging "Rotterdam" Sc:INTERNATIO -MÜLLER
IJSFABRIEKEN	1940/46-1956	NV Unie van IJsfabrieken
INDOHEEM	1964-1968	Indoheem NV (since 1968: Indola NV) Pr: VAN DER HEEM
INTERNATIO-MÜLLER		
	1970-1983	Internatio-Müller NV. Pr: HV ROTTERDAM, MÜLLER

JAVA-CHINA PAKET

	1940/46-1969	Koninklijke Java-China-Paketvaartlijnen NV. Sc: NSU
JONGENEEL	1945-1970	NV Houthandel v/h P.M. & J. Jongeneel (since 1970: Jongeneel NV)
KAISER	1950-1956	Nederlandsche Kaiser-Frazer Fabrieken NV
KEY	1945-1982	NV Houthandel v/h G. Key. Sc: PONT
KLENE	1945-1983	NV Fabriek van Chocolade en Suikerwerken J.C. Klene & Co (since 1950: Klene's Suikerwerkfabrieken NV)
KNP	1945-1983	Koninklijke Nederlandsche Papierfabriek NV (since 1973: Koninklijke Nederlandse Papierfabrieken NV)

KONINKLIJKE PETROLEUM

	1945-1983	NV Koninklijke Nederlandsche Petroleum Maatschappij
KORENSCHOOF	1944/45-1969/70	"De Korenschoof" NV
KOUDIJS	1944-1971/72	NV Koudijs' Voederfabrieken B.K.
KROMHOUT	1944/45-1964	Kromhout Motoren Fabriek D. Goedkoop Jr NV
LINDETEVES	1940/47-1974	Lindeteves NV (since 1958: Lindeteves-Jacoberg NV)
LOHUIZEN	1945-1963	NV "Industrie" v/h van Lohuizen en Co.
MAINTZ	1946/47-1969	NV Handelsvennootschap v/h Maintz & Co
MARIJNEN	1945-1971	NV Technisch Bureau Marijnen
MATUBEL	1965-1972	Matubel NV
MÜLLER	1940/45-1969	Wm. H. Müller & Co NV. Sc:INTERNATIO-MÜLLER
NAM	1945-1967	NV Nederlandsche Aanneming Maatschappij. Sc: BALLAST-NEDAM
NBM	1971-1983	NV Verenigde NBM-Bedrijven
NBT	1940/53-1964	NV Nederlandsche Bioscoop Trust (since 1953: NV Nederlandsche Bioscoop Theaters). Sc: MATUBEL
NDSM	1945-1967	Nederlandsche Dok en Scheepsbouw Maatschappij Vof (Annual report jointly issued by the listing vehicles NV Nederlandsche Scheepsbouw Maatschappij and Nederlandsche Dok Maat-schappij NV)
NKF	1945-1969	NV Nederlandsche Kabelfabrieken
NETAM	1949-1976	NV Nederlandsche Tank- Apparaten- en Machinefabriek "Netam"
NIEAF	1948-1975	NV Nederlandsche Instrumenten- en Electrische Apparatenfabriek "NIEAF"
NIERSTRASZ	1947-1983	NV v/h Nierstrasz (since 1969: Nierstrasz NV)
NSU	1969-1983	NV Nederlandsche Scheepvaart Unie (Since 1977: Koninklijke Nedlloyd Groep

NV) Listed since 1915 as a pure holding company but only since 1969 as a company with operational activities. Pr: JAVA CHINA PAKET, ROTTERDAMSCHE LLOYD, STOOMVAART NEDERLAND

NIJVERDAL	1954-1983	Koninklijke Stoomweverij te Nijverdal NV (since 1957: Koninklijke Textielfabrieken Nijverdal-ten Cate NV)
OGEM	1948-1980	NV Overzeese Gas- en Electriciteitsmaatschappij (until 1949 Nederlandsch-Indische Gas-Maatschappij)
VAN OMMEREN	1947-1983	Phs van Ommeren NV
OOSZTEE	1940/46-1974	NV Stoomvaartmaatschappij "Oostzee". Sc: FEARNLEY
OVING	1964-1977	Oving NV (since 1970: Oving-Diepeveen NV; since 1972: Oving-Diepeveen-Struycken NV)
PAKHOED	1967-1983	Pakhoed Holding NV. Pr: BLAAUWHOED
PAPIER GELDERLAND		
	1957-1971	NV Papierfabriek "Gelderland" (since 1963: Gelderland-Tielens Papierfabrieken NV)
PARKHOTEL	1952-1970	NV Parkhotel en -Restaurant
PHILIPS	1944/45-1983	NV Philips' Gloeilampenfabrieken
PONT	1948-1983	NV Houthandel v/h William Pont (since 1969: Koninklijke Houthandel William Pont NV)
REEUWIJK	1945-1980	NV Maatschappij voor woninginrichting P. van Reeuwijk
REINEVELD	1945-1971	Machinefabriek Reineveld NV
REISS	1948-1978	NV Handelsvereeniging v/h Reiss & Co
ROTTERDAMSCHE LLOYD		
	1940/46-1969	Koninklijke Rotterdamsche Lloyd NV (since 1968: NV Koninklijke Rotterdamsche Lloyd-Wm Ruys & Zonen) Sc: NSU
ROMMENHÖLLER	1945-1983	NV Maatschappij tot Exploitatie der C.G. Rommenhöller'sche Koolzuur- en Zuurstofwerken (since 1973: Maatschappij Rommenhöller NV)
REESINK	1958/59-1983	H.J. Reesink & Co NV (since 1973: Reesink NV)
SCHOKBETON	1946-1980	NV Schokbeton
SCHUITEMA	1959-1983	NV Gebr. D. Schuitema (since 1977: Schuitema NV)
SIMPLEX	1947/48-1963/64	NV Simplex Machine- en Rijwielfabrieken
SMITS KLEDING	1956-1967	Kledingindustrie H. Smits & Co NV
STEVIN	1968-1977	Stevin Groep NV (until 1971: Van Hattum

en Blankevoort Beheer NV). Sc: VOLKER
STEVIN

STOOMVAART NEDERLAND
                1940/46-1969   Stoomvaart Maatschappij "Nederland" NV
STOOMVAART ZEELAND
                1945-1983   Stoomvaart Maatschappij "Zeeland" Koninklijke Nederlandsche Paketvaart NV

STORK	1945-1953	Koninklijke Machinefabriek Gebr. Stork & Co NV. Sc: VMF
SWAAY	1961-1967	Maatschappij voor Industriële Ondernemingen Gebr. van Swaay NV. Sc: HV ROTTERDAM
TELS	1947-1962	L.E. Tels & Co's Handelmaatschappij NV
TEXOPRINT	1964-1971	Texoprint NV (since 1969: Hatéma-Texoprint NV) Pr: VLISSINGENS KATOEN Sc: GAMMA
TEXTIEL UNIE	1966-1971	Koninklijke Nederlandse Textiel-Unie NV

THOMASSEN DRIJVER
                1948-1969   Blikemballagefabriek Thomassen en Drijver NV (since 1965: Thomassen & Drijver-Verblifa NV)

TWENTSCHE KABEL
'   1953-1983   NV Twentsche Kabelfabriek (since 1980: NV Twentsche Kabel Holding)

TWENTSCHE HANDEL
                1949-1968   NV Twentsche Overzee Handel Maatschappij

UNILEVER	1945-1983	Unilever NV (until 1951: Lever Brothers & Unilever NV)
VAROSSIEAU	1961-1968	Varossieau & Cie NV Lakfabrieken
VERSCHURE	1945-1964	Verschure & Co's Scheepswerf en Machinefabriek NV
VERTO	1945-1983	NV Vereenigde Touwfabrieken (since 1972: NV Verto)

VIHAMIJ BUTTINGER
                1970-1981   Vihamij-Buttinger NV
VLISSINGENS KATOEN
                1945/46-1963   NV P.F. van Vlissingen & Co's Katoenfabrieken. Sc: TEXOPRINT

VMF	1954-1983	Verenigde Machinefabrieken NV Stork-Werkspoor. Pr: STORK
VOLKER STEVIN	1978-1983	Volker Stevin NV. Pr: STEVIN
VRIES TEXTIEL	1948-1965	B.I. de Vries & Co Textiel NV
VULCAANSOORD	1950-1975/76	NV Vulcaansoord
WALVISVAART	1946/47-1965/66	Nederlandse Maatschappij voor de Walvisvaart NV
WERNINK	1951-1979	NV Wernink's Beton Maatschappij NV (since 1960: Wernink's Beton- en Aan-

		neming Maatschappij NV; since 1970: Vandervliet Wernink NV)
WIJK & HERINGA	1949-1983	Van Wijk & Heringa NV (until 1959: Leidsche Textielfabriek Gebrs. van Wijk & Co NV)
ZEEVAART	1940/45-1976	NV Maatschappij Zeevaart
ZUID HOLLAND BIER	1945-1960	NV Zuid-Hollandsche Bierbrouwerij NV

References

The following pages contain the references to all publications cited by means of the 'author (year)' system in the text. References to newspaper articles, company financial reports, unsigned notes in professional journals, committee reports, sources of statistical data, legal materials and professional regulations (mainly accounting standards) are included in footnotes to the text.

Adler, H., K. Schmaltz, K.-H. Forster and R. Goerdeler, 'Der Ausweis der Umsatzerlöse in der neuen Gewinn- und Verlustrechnung', *Die Wirtschaftsprüfung*, vol. 13 no. 23, 1 December 1960, p. 628-638.

Adler, H., Düring and K. Schmaltz, *Rechnungslegung und Prüfung der Aktiengesellschaft*, 4th edition, vol. 3 (Stuttgart: C.E. Poeschel Verlag, 1972).

Akerlof, George A., 'The market for "lemons": quality uncertainty and the market mechanism', *Quarterly Journal of Economics*, vol. 84 no. 3, August 1970, p. 488-500.

Amerongen, F. van, 'Dutch Accounts', *Accountancy* (UK), vol. 74 no. 838, June 1963, p. 497-500.

Bao, Ben-Hsien, and Da-Hsien Bao, 'Lifo adoption: A technology diffusion analysis', *Accounting, Organizations and Society*, vol. 14 no. 4, 1989, p. 303-319.

Barr, Andrew, 'Corporate financial reporting: The developing debate on "Line of business" disclosure - Establishing criteria for line of business disclosure', *Management Accounting* (NAA), vol. 49, section 1, December 1967, p. 18-22.

Barr, Andrew, 'Financial reporting by conglomerates', address before the 23rd Annual Conference of Accountants, University of Tulsa, April 23, 1969, in: *Written Contributions of Selected Accounting Practitioners*, Vol. 3: Andrew Barr (Department of Accountancy, University of Illinois at Urbana-Champaign, 1980), p. 564-577.

Barr, Andrew, 'Accounting yesterday, today and tomorrow', *The International Journal of Accounting*, vol. 8 no. 1, Fall 1972, p. 1-15.

Barrett, M. Edgar, 'Financial reporting practices: Disclosure and comprehensiveness in an international setting', *Journal of Accounting Research*, vol. 14 no. 1, Spring 1976, p. 10-26.

Barrett, M. Edgar, 'The extent of disclosure in annual reports of large companies in seven countries', *The International Journal of Accounting*, vol. 12 no. 2, Spring 1977, p. 1-25.

Barth, Mary E., and Christine M. Murphy, 'Required financial statement disclosures: Purposes, subject, number, and trends', *Accounting Horizons*, vol. 8 no. 4, December 1994, p. 1-22.

Bass, F.M., 'A new product growth model for consumer durables', *Management Science*, vol. 15 no. 5, January 1969, p. 215-227.

Baxter, William T., 'The inadequacy of financial accounts', in [booklet of the] *Summer school at St. Andrews University*, 21st to 26th September, 1956 (Edinburgh: The Institute of Chartered Accountants of Scotland, 1956), p. 38-54.

Baxter, William T., 'The future of company financial reporting', in: Thomas A. Lee (editor), *Developments in Financial Reporting* (Oxford: Philip Allan Publishers Ltd, 1981), p. 270-292.

Bazley, M., P. Brown and H.Y. Izan, 'An analysis of lease disclosures by Australian companies', *Abacus*, vol. 21 no. 1, March 1985, p. 44-63.

Beckman, H., 'Winstsplitsing per produktgroep in de jaarrekening', *TVVS*, vol. 20 no. 9, September 1977, p. 245-253.

Beckman, H., 'Het arrest van de ondernemingskamer inzake de jaarrekening 1977 van de HAL/Ultramarco', *Maandblad voor Accountancy en Bedrijfshuishoudkunde*, vol. 55 no. 9, October 1981, p. 517-520.

Beckman, H., and J.M.A. van Rijn, 'Financiële informatie per produktgroep en de praktijk van de jaarverslaggeving', *TVVS*, vol. 22 no. 6, June 1979, p. 193-200.

Beekhuizen, Theo, and Paul Frishkoff, 'A comparison of the new Dutch accounting act with generally accepted American accounting principles', *The International Journal of Accounting*, vol. 10 no. 2, Spring 1975, p. 13-22.

Beerenborg, J. 'Openbaarheid en unificatie van balansen', *Accountancy*, vol. 5 no. 58, December 1907, p. 151-155.

Belkaoui, Ahmed Riahi, *Accounting Theory*, 3rd edition (London: Academic Press, 1992).

Benjamin, James J., and Keith G. Stanga, 'Differences in disclosure needs of major users of financial statements', *Accounting and Business Research*, vol. 7 no. 27, Summer 1977, p. 187-192.

Benston, George J., 'The value of the SEC's accounting disclosure requirements', *The Accounting Review*, vol. 44 no. 3, July 1969, p. 515-32.

Benston, George J., 'Required disclosure and the stock market: An evaluation of the Securities Exchange Act of 1934', *American Economic Review*, vol. 63 no. 1, March 1973, p. 132-155.

Benston, George J., 'Public (U.S.) compared to private (U.K.) regulation of corporate financial disclosure', *The Accounting Review*, vol. 51 no. 3, July 1976(a), p. 483-498.

Benston, George J., *Corporate Financial Disclosure in the U.K. and the U.S.A.* (Lexington: Saxton House, 1976(b)).

Benston, George J., 'Disclosure under the Securities Acts and the proposed federal securities code', *Journal of Accountancy*, October 1980, p. 34-45.

Berckel, J.J.L. van, 'Verslaggeving en publiciteit in Nederland', *TVVS*, vol. 8 no. 7, November 1965, p. 173-178.

Berendsen, J.G., *Maatschappij, onderneming en accountant* (Amsterdam: VU Uitgeverij, 1990).

Berle, Adolf A., and Gardiner C. Means, *The Modern Corporation and Private Property* (New York: Macmillan, 1932).

Besançon, R., 'Kanttekeningen bij de "Mededelingen" van het bestuur der Vereeniging voor den Effectenhandel betreffende "Publicatie van gegevens door naamloze vennootschappen"', *Maandblad voor Accountancy en Bedrijfshuishoudkunde*, vol. 26 no. 5, May 1952, p. 198-200.

Bevis, Herman B., *Corporate Financial Reporting in a Competitive Economy* (New York: Macmillan, 1965).

Bindenga, A.J., 'De oordeelsfunctie van de public accountant in perspectief', in:

W.J. van der Hooft and F.D. Zandstra (editors), *Accoord,* Afscheidsbundel prof.drs A.A. de Jong (Rotterdam: Erasmus Universiteit, 1976), p. 211-226.

Bindenga, A.J., 'De accountant en zijn verantwoordelijkheid', in: C. Boneco, M.P.B. Bonnet, R.L. ter Hoeven and J. Maat (editors), *fMA kroniek 1993,* (Rotterdam: Vakgroep Kosten- en Winstbepalingsvraagstukken, Faculteit der Economische Wetenschappen, 1993), p. 7-20.

Bindenga, A.J., 'Het vakgebied externe verslaggeving in ruime zin', in: M.N. Hoogendoorn, J. Klaassen and F. Krens (editors), *Externe verslaggeving in theorie en praktijk,* vol. 1 (Den Haag: Delwel Uitgeverij, 1995), p. 7-15.

Bircher, Paul, 'The adoption of consolidated accounting in Britain', *Accounting and Business Research,* vol. 19 no. 73, Winter 1988, p. 3-13.

Bloembergen, E., 'De structuur van de onderneming', *TVVS,* vol. 4 no. 10, February 1961, p. 223-231.

Blom, F.W.C., 'Bezwaren en gevaren van vervangingswaardebalansen', *TVVS,* vol. 10 no. 3, March 1967, p. 63-68.

Blommaert, J.M.J., *Consolideren & informeren,* Een onderzoek naar de informatieve waarde van de geconsolideerde jaarrekening (Houten: Educatieve Partners Nederland, 1995).

Boer, H. de, *De commissarisfunctie in Nederlandse, ter beurze genoteerde, industriële naamloze vennootschappen, bezien van organisatorisch standpunt* (Amsterdam: J.H. de Bussy, 1957).

Boissevain, R.L., and R.J.W.B. van Doorn, 'Correctie van cijfers per aandeel (aanbeveling voor een uniforme methodiek)', *Maandblad voor Accountancy en Bedrijfshuishoudkunde,* vol. 51 no. 3, March 1977, p. 120-137.

Bores, Wilhelm, 'Geschichtliche Entwicklung der konsolidierten Bilanz (Konzernbilanz), *Zeitschrift für Handelswissenschaftliche Forschung,* vol. 28 no. 3, March 1934, p. 113-136; no. 4, April 1934, p. 209-222; no. 6, June 1934, p. 327-336.

Boukema, C.A., 'Juridische voorschriften inzake verslaggeving in Europees perspectief', in: J.W. van Belkum (editor) *De wet op de jaarrekening in perspectief* (Tilburg: Universitaire Pers Tilburg, 1975), p. 75-83.

Boukema, C.A., 'Nieuw rechtspersonenrecht', *Maandblad voor Accountancy en Bedrijfshuishoudkunde,* vol. 50 no. 7, July/August 1976, p. 382-387.

Boussard, Daniel, and Bernard Colasse, 'Funds-flow statement and cash-flow accounting in France: evolution and significance', *The European Accounting Review,* vol. 1 no. 2, December 1992, p. 229-254.

Bradbury, Michael E., 'Voluntary disclosure of financial segment data: New Zealand evidence', *Accounting and Finance* (AAANZ), May 1992(a), p. 15-26.

Bradbury, Michael E., 'Voluntary seminannual earnings disclosures, earnings volatility, unexpected earnings and firm size', *Journal of Accounting Research,* vol. 30 no, 1, Spring 1992(b), p. 137-145.

Brands, J., 'De nieuwe verslagstaten der levensverzekering-maatschappijen', *Maandblad voor Accountancy en Bedrijfshuishoudkunde,* vol. 26 no. 6, June 1952, p. 232-234.

Brands, J., 'Het jaarverslag van de naamloze vennootschap', *De Naamlooze Vennootschap,* vol. 30 no. 11/12, February/March 1953, p. 209-215.

Brands, J., 'Beroepsuitoefening in internationaal verband', *Maandblad voor Accountancy en Bedrijfshuishoudkunde,* vol. 28 no. 9, October 1954, p. 411.

Brands, J., 'Het jaarverslag van de open naamloze vennootschap', in *De Naamlooze*

Vennootschap, vol. 33 no. 2, May 1955, p. 21-25.

Brands, J., 'Openheid bij de naamloze vennootschap: het jaarverslag 1968 van de Steenkolen-Handelsvereeniging N.V. te Utrecht', *Economisch-Statistische Berichten*, 27 August 1969, p. 822-825.

Breek, P.C., *Nieuwe ontwikkelingen in de jaarverslaggeving*, Address delivered at the awarding of the Henri Sijthoff Prize, 11 December 1974 (Amsterdam: Het Financieele Dagblad, 1974).

Brezet, J.C., 'Nieuwe tendenties in de gepubliceerde jaarrekening?', in *Economisch-Statistische Berichten*, 7 October 1953, p. 796-798.

Brink, H.L., 'A history of Philips' accounting policies on the basis of its annual reports', *The European Accounting Review*, vol. 1 no. 2, December 1992, p. 255-275.

Brok, A.L., 'Latenties terzake van de vennootschapsbelasting', *Maandblad voor Accountancy en Bedrijfshuishoudkunde*, vol. 38 no. 6, June 1964, p. 224-246.

Brouwer, E.A., 'De grote belegger en de verslaggeving door N.V.'s', *De Naamlooze Vennootschap*, vol. 40 no. 8/9, November/December 1962, p. 127-128.

Brown, Lawrence A., *Innovation Diffusion*, A new perspective (London/New York: Methuen, 1981).

Burchell, Stuart, Colin Clubb and Anthony G. Hopwood, 'Accounting in its social context: Towards a history of value added in the United Kingdom', *Accounting, Organizations and Society*, vol. 10 no. 4, 1985, p. 381-413.

Burgert, R. 'Publicaties van naamloze vennootschappen', in: L.H. Belle, J. Brands, D.H. Brummelman, A.C.J. Jonkers and J.A.F.M. Lindner (editors), *Opstellen ter gelegenheid van een kwart eeuw V.A.G.A.* (Rotterdam, Vereniging van Academisch Geschoolde Accountants, [1953]).

Burgert, R., 'Spiegel der accountancy in U.S.A: 1954 Annual Meeting Papers', *Maandblad voor Accountancy en Bedrijfshuishoudkunde*, vol. 29 no. 8, September 1955, p. 361-365; vol. 29 no. 9, October 1955, p. 412-417; vol. 30 no. 5, May 1956, p. 220-231.

Burgert, R., 'De accountant en de Ondernemingskamer', *De Accountant*, vol. 86 no. 1, September 1979, p. 12-15.

Burgert, R., 'Tien jaar wet en rechtspraak omtrent de jaarrekening van ondernemingen', *Maandblad voor Accountancy en Bedrijfshuishoudkunde*, vol. 56 no. 4, April 1982, p. 158-176.

Burgert, R., M.A. van Hoepen and H.F.J. Joosten, *De jaarrekening nieuwe stijl*, volume 1, Inleiding + wetteksten en EEG-richtlijnen, 9th ed. (Alphen aan den Rijn: Samsom H.D.J. Tjeenk Willink, 1995).

Burggraaff, J.A., 'De presentatie van de belasting naar de winst in de resultatenrekening', *Maandblad voor Accountancy en Bedrijfshuishoudkunde*, vol. 42 no. 3, March 1968, p. 168-175.

Burton, John C., 'Discussion of voluntary corporate disclosure: The case of interim reporting', *Journal of Accounting Research*, Supplement to vol. 19, 1981, p. 78-84.

Bushman, Robert M., 'Public disclosure and the structure of private information markets', *Journal of Accounting Research*, vol. 29 no. 2, Autumn 1991, p. 261-276.

Buzby, Stephen L., 'Selected items of information and their disclosure in annual reports', *The Accounting Review*, vol. 49 no. 2, April 1974, p. 423-435.

Buzby, Stephen L., 'Company size, listed versus unlisted stocks, and the extent of financial disclosure', *Journal of Accounting Research*, vol. 13 no. 1, Spring 1975, p. 16-37.

Camfferman, Kees, 'Goed koopmansgebruik en maatschappelijk aanvaardbare normen', in: C.M.T. Boneco, R.L. ter Hoeven, R.F. Speklé and R. van der Wal (editors), *fMA-kroniek 1994* (Rotterdam: Vakgroep Kosten- en Winstbepalingsvraagstukken, Faculteit der Economische Wetenschappen, 1994(a)), p. 183-196.

Camfferman, Kees, 'Schmidt, Limperg and the dissemination of current cost accounting in the Netherlands', *The International Journal of Accounting*, vol. 29 no. 4, Winter 1994(b), p. 251-264.

Camfferman, Kees, and Stephen A. Zeff, 'The contributions of Theodore Limperg Jr (1879-1961) to Dutch accounting and auditing', in: J.R. Edwards (editor), *Twentieth-Century Accounting Thinkers* (London: Routledge, 1994).

Cerf, A.R., *Corporate Reporting and Investment Decisions* (Berkely: The University of California Press, 1961).

Chambers, R.J., *The Function and Design of Company Annual Reports* (London: Sweet and Maxwell, 1955).

Chandra, Gyan, 'A study of the consensus on disclosure among public accountants and security analysts', *The Accounting Review*, vol. 49 no. 4, October 1974, p. 733-742.

Chandra, Gyan, and Melvin N. Greenball, 'Management reluctance to disclose: An empirical study', *Abacus*, vol. 13 no. 2, December 1977, p. 141-154.

Choi, Frederick S., 'Financial disclosure and entry to the European capital market', *Journal of Accounting Research*, vol. 11 no. 2, Autumn 1973(a), p. 159-175.

Choi, Frederick S., 'Financial disclosure in relation to a firm's capital costs', *Accounting and Business Research*, vol. 3 no. 12, Autumn 1973(b), p. 282-292.

Choi, Frederick S., and Gerhard G. Mueller, *International Accounting*, 2nd edition (Englewood Cliffs, NJ: Prentice-Hall, 1992).

Chow, Chee W., 'Financial disclosure regulation and indirect economic consequences: An analysis of the sales disclosure requirement of the 1934 Securities and Exchange Act', *Journal of Business Finance and Accounting*, vol. 11 no. 4, Winter 1984, p. 469-483.

Chow, Chee W., and Adrian Wong-Boren, 'Voluntary financial disclosure by Mexican corporations', *The Accounting Review*, vol. 62 no. 3, July 1987, p. 533-541.

Clapp, Charles L., 'National variations in accounting principles and practices', *The International Journal of Accounting*, vol. 3 no. 1, Fall 1967, p. 29-42.

Coelingh, J.P., 'De jaarverslaggeving uit het gezichtspunt van een ondernemer', *De Naamlooze Vennootschap*, vol. 43 no. 1/2, April/May 1965, p. 5-6.

Coenenberg, Adolf, Peter Möller and Franz Schmidt, 'Empirical research in financial accounting in Germany, Austria and Switzerland: A review', in: Anthony G. Hopwood and Hein Schreuder (editors), *European Contributions to Accounting Research*, The achievements of the last decade (Amsterdam: Free University Press, 1984), p. 61-82.

Comiskey, E.E., and R.E.V. Groves, 'The adoption and diffusion of an accounting innovation', *Accounting and Business Research*, vol. 2 no. 5, Winter 1972, p. 67-75.

Cook, A. 'International business: A channel for change in United Kingdom accounting', in: A.G. Hopwood (editor), *International Pressures for Accounting Change* (Hemel Hempstead: Prentice Hall International, 1989), p. 33-42.

Cooke, T.E., 'Disclosure in the corporate annual reports of Swedish companies', *Accounting and Business Research*, vol. 19 no. 74, Spring 1989, p. 113-121.

Cooke, T.E., 'An assessment of voluntary disclosure in the annual reports of Japanese corporations', *The International Journal of Accounting*, vol. 26 no. 3, 1991, p. 174-189.

Cooke, T.E., 'The impact of size, stock market listing and industry type on disclosure in the annual reports of Japanese listed corporations', *Accounting and Business Research*, vol. 22 no. 87, Summer 1992, p. 229-237.

Copeland, Ronald M., and John K. Shank, 'LIFO and the diffusion of innovation', *Journal of Accounting Research*, supplement to vol. 9, 1971, p. 196-230.

Coret, H.J.A., 'Enige meningen omtrent uitbreiding van de attestfunctie', *De Accountant*, vol. 83 no. 6, February 1977, p. 294-299.

Cosman, C.A., 'Welke beginselen moet eene wettelijke regeling der Naamlooze Vennootschappen huldigen ten aanzien van het kapitaal van de vennootschap?', *Handelingen der Nederlandsche Juristen-Vereeniging*, vol. 3, 1872, no. 1, p. 69-117 with discussion in no. 2, p. 69-129.

Courtis, John K., 'The reliability of perception-based annual report disclosure studies', *Accounting and Business Research*, vol. 23 no. 98, Winter 1992, p. 31-43.

Coutre, W. le, 'Das Bruttoprinzip', *Zeitschrift für Betriebswirtschaft*, vol. 27 no. 3, March 1957, p. 141-147.

Cowen, Scott S., Linda B. Ferreri and Lee D. Parker, 'The impact of corporate characteristics on social responsibility disclosure: A typology and frequency-based analysis', *Accounting, Organizations and Society*, vol. 12 no. 2, 1987, p. 111-122.

Craswell, A.T., and S.L. Taylor, 'Discretionary disclosure of reserves by oil and gas companies: An economic analysis', *Journal of Business Finance and Accounting*, vol. 19 no. 2, January 1992, p. 295-308.

Da Costa, Richard C., Jacques C. Bourgeois and William M. Lawson, 'A classification of international financial accounting practices', *The International Journal of Accounting*, vol. 13 no. 2, Spring 1978, p. 73-85.

Dankers, J.J., and J. Verheul, *Hoogovens 1945-1993*, Van staalbedrijf tot twee-metalenconcern (Den Haag: SDU Uitgeverij, 1993).

Darrough, Masako N., and Neal M. Stoughton, 'Financial disclosure policy in an entry game', *Journal of Accounting and Economics*, vol. 12, 1990, p. 219-243.

Darrough, Masako N., 'Disclosure policy and competition: Cournot vs. Bertrand', *The Accounting Review*, vol. 68 no. 3, July 1993, p. 534-561.

De Paula, F.R.M., *Developments in Accounting* (London: Pitman & Sons, 1948).

De Paula, F.R.M., *The Principles of Auditing*, 12th edition by F. Clive de Paula (London: Pitman & Sons, 1957).

Degenkamp, J.Th., 'Actueel jaarrekeningenrecht', in: W. Verhoog *et al.*, *Actueel jaarrekeningenrecht*, Nivra geschrift 30 (Deventer: Kluwer, 1983).

Déking Dura, J., *Handhaving der rechten van obligatiehouders* (Amsterdam: van Munster & Zoon, 1886).

Dhaliwal, Dan S., 'Improving the quality of corporate disclosure', *Accounting and*

Business Research, vol. 10 no. 40, Autumn 1980, p. 385-391.

Dhaliwal, Dan S., Barry H. Spicer and Don Vickrey, 'The quality of disclosure and the cost of capital', *Journal of Business Finance and Accounting*, vol. 6 no. 2, Summer 1979, p. 245-280.

Diamond, Douglas W., 'Optimal release of information by firms', *The Journal of Finance*, vol. 40 no. 4, September 1985, p. 1071-1094.

Diephuis, G., 'De jaarrekening (met bijbehorende informatie)', *Maandblad voor Accountancy en Bedrijfshuishoudkunde*, vol. 40 no. 11, December 1966, p. 475-485.

Dijksma, J. 'De staat van herkomst en besteding der middelen in Nederlandse jaarverslagen', *Maandblad voor Accountancy en Bedrijfshuishoudkunde*, vol. 49 no. 8, September 1975, p. 369-379.

Dijksma, J., 'De staat van herkomst en de besteding der middelen in Nederland: een overzicht', in J. Bulte, K.J. Steeneker and R. van der Wal (editors), *Gehandhaafd*, Opstellen aangeboden aan drs J.C. Brezet (Rotterdam: Erasmus Universiteit, 1984), p. 161-188.

Dijksma, J., *Staat van Herkomst en Besteding van Middelen* (Groningen: Wolters Noordhoff, 1987).

Dijksma, J., and C. van Halem, 'Kwaliteit van de in Nederlandse jaarverslagen besloten informatie: een empirisch onderzoek', *Maandblad voor Accountancy en Bedrijfshuishoudkunde*, vol. 51 no. 4, April 1977, p. 189-202.

Dontoh, Alex, 'Voluntary Disclosure', *Journal of Accounting, Auditing & Finance*, vol. 4 no. 4 (new series), Fall 1989, p. 480-511.

Doorne, F.F. van, 'Uniformiteit in jaarrekening, boekhouding en kostprijsbepaling', *Maandblad voor Accountancy en Bedrijfshuishoudkunde*, appendix to vol. 12 no. 11, December 1935, p. 33-58.

Dye, Ronald A., 'Disclosure of nonproprietary information', *Journal of Accounting Research*, vol. 23 no. 1, Spring 1985, p. 123-145.

Dye, Ronald A., 'Proprietary and nonproprietary disclosures', *Journal of Business*, vol. 59 no. 1, April 1986, p. 331-366.

Dye, Ronald A., and Sri S. Sridhar, 'Industry-wide disclosure dynamics', *Journal of Accounting Research*, vol. 33 no. 1, Spring 1995, p. 157-174.

Edwards, J.R., 'The accounting profession and disclosure in published reports, 1925-1935', *Accounting and Business Research*, vol. 6 no. 24, Autumn 1976, p. 289-303.

Edwards, J.R., *A History of Financial Accounting* (London/New York: Routledge, 1989).

Edwards, J.R., 'The process of accounting innovation: the publication of consolidated accounts in Britain in 1910', *The Accounting Historians Journal*, vol. 18 no. 2, December 1991, p. 113-132.

Elliott, Robert K., and Peter D. Jacobson, 'Costs and benefits of business information disclosure', *Accounting Horizons*, vol. 8 no. 4, December 1994, p. 80-96.

Emmanuel, Clive, and Neil Garrod, *Segment Reporting*, International issues and evidence (Hemel Hempstead: Prentice Hall in Association with the Institute of Chartered Accountants in Engeland and Wales, 1992)

Emmerik, E.Th. van, 'Quo vadis ?', *De Accountant*, vol. 84 no. 3, November 1977, p. 170-174.

Farr, Gerhard, 'Eigenheiten der amerikanischen Bilanzierung und Rechenschaftslegung', *Zeitschrift für Betriebswirtschaft,* vol. 25 no. 11, November 1955, p. 642-649.

Feltham, G.A., and J.Z. Xie, 'Voluntary financial disclosure in an entry game with continua of types', *Contemporary Accounting Research,* vol. 9 no. 1, Fall 1992, p. 46-80.

Fettel, Johannes, 'Konzernbilanzen', in: H. Seischab and K. Schwantag (editors), Nicklisch' *Handwörterbuch der Betriebswirtschaft,* 3rd edition, vol. II (Stuttgart: C.E. Poeschel Verlag, 1958), p. 3331-3333.

Firth, Michael A., 'A study of the consensus of the perceived importance of disclosure of individual items in corporate annual reports', *The International Journal of Accounting,* vol. 14 no. 1, Fall 1978, p. 57-70.

Firth, Michael A., 'The impact of size, stock market quotation, and auditors on voluntary disclosure in corporate annual reports', *Accounting and Business Research,* vol. 9 no. 36, Autumn 1979, p. 273-280.

Firth, Michael A., 'Raising finance and firms' corporate reporting policies', *Abacus,* vol. 16 no. 2, December 1980, p. 100-115.

Fishman, Michael J., and Kathleen M. Hagerty, 'Disclosure decisions by firms and the competition for price efficiency', *Journal of Finance,* vol. 44 no. 3, July 1989, p. 633-646.

Flohr, Günter, 'Bewegungsbilanzen in Geschäftsberichten deutscher Aktiengesellschaften', *Die Wirtschaftsprüfung,* vol. 17 no. 12, 15 June 1964, p. 313-322.

Foppe, H.H.M., 'De verzorging van de vorm bij de opstelling van de jaarrekening', *Maandblad voor Accountancy en Bedrijfshuishoudkunde,* vol. 25 no. 1, January 1951, p. 27-32.

Foppe, H.H.M., 'Het getrouwe beeld in de gepubliceerde jaarrekening', *Economisch-Statistische Berichten,* 27 October 1965, p. 991-993.

Forker, John J., 'Corporate governance and disclosure quality', *Accounting and Business Research,* vol. 22 no. 86, Spring 1992, p. 111-124.

Frankel, Richard, Maureen McNichols and G. Peter Wilson, 'Discretionary disclosure and external financing', *The Accounting Review,* vol. 70 no. 1, January 1995, p. 135-150.

Frederiks, P.G.G., 'Publikaties door gediversificeerde ondernemingen', *Maandblad voor Accountancy en Bedrijfshuishoudkunde,* vol. 47 no. 9, October 1973, p. 418-424.

Frederiks, P.G.G., 'The regulations for publication of annual accounts according to the Financial Statements Act in the Netherlands, compared with those in force in the USA and those under the draft of a fourth directive of the EEC', *Journal UEC,* vol. 9 no. 3, July 1974, p. 158-165.

Frijns, J.W., 'Het Tripartiete Overleg: Zienswijze van een werkgeversvertegenwoordiger', *De Accountant,* vol. 85 no. 10, June 1979, p. 657-660.

Frost, Carol A., and Grace Pownall, 'Accounting disclosure practices in the United States and the United Kingdom', *Journal of Accounting Research,* vol. 32 no. 1, Spring 1994, p. 75-102.

Fuchs, Hermann, and Otto Gerloff, *Die konsolidierte Bilanz* (Köln: Verlag Dr Otto Schmidt, 1954).

Gaag, J.J. van der, 'Segmentatie', in: J. Dijksma (editor), *Jaar in - jaar uit,* Verslag van een empirisch onderzoek van jaarrapporten over de jaren 1983-1984 (Groningen: Wolters-Noordhoff, 1986), p. 169-195.

Gal-Or, Esther, 'Information sharing in oligopoly', *Econometrica,* vol. 53 no. 2, March 1985, p. 329-343.

Gal-Or, Esther, 'Information transmission - Cournot and Bertrand equilibria', *Review of Economic Studies,* vol. 53, 1986, p. 85-92.

Gans, M.P., 'Misverstanden omtrent het begrip price:earnings-ratio', *Economisch-Statistische Berichten,* vol. 39 no. 1954, 17 November 1954, p. 918-919.

Gans, M.P., 'De financieringstheorie van Limperg', in: J.W. Schoonderbeek and G.G.M. Bak (editors), *Reflecties op Limperg* (Deventer: Kluwer, 1979), p. 117-129.

Geertman, J.A., 'Neuere Bestrebungen zur Vereinheitlichung der Jahresabschlüsse in Holland', *Die Wirtschaftsprüfung,* vol. 8 no. 16, August 1955, p. 365-368.

Gibbins, Michael, Alan J. Richardson and John Waterhouse, 'The management of corporate financial disclosure: Opportunism, ritualism, policies and processes', *Journal of Accounting Research,* vol. 28 no. 1, Spring 1990, p. 121-143.

Gibbins, Michael, Alan J. Richardson and John Waterhouse, *The Management of Financial Disclosure: Theory and Perspectives,* Research Monograph No. 20 (Vancouver: The Canadian Certified General Accountants' Research Foundation, 1992).

Goudeket, A., 'Consolidatie', *Maandblad voor Accountancy en Bedrijfshuishoudkunde,* vol. 35 no. 4, April 1961, p. 82-88.

Gray, S.J., 'Statistical information and extensions in European financial disclosure', *The International Journal of Accounting,* vol. 13 no. 2, Spring 1978(a), p. 27-40.

Gray, S.J., 'Segment reporting and the EEC multinationals', *Journal of Accounting Research,* vol. 16 no. 2, Autumn 1978(b), p. 242-253.

Gray, S.J., and L.H. Radebaugh, 'International segment disclosures by U.S. and U.K. multinational enterprises: A descriptive study', *Journal of Accounting Research,* vol. 22 no. 1, Spring 1984, p. 351-360.

Gray, Sidney J., and C.B. Roberts, 'Voluntary information disclosures and the British multinationals: Corporate perceptions of costs and benefits', in: A.G. Hopwood (editor), *International Pressures for Accounting Change* (Hemel Hempstead: Prentice Hall International, 1989), p. 116-139.

Gray, Sidney J., Gary K. Meek and Clare B. Roberts, 'Market versus regulatory pressure on disclosure decisions by US and UK multinationals', Paper presented at the 14th Annual Congress of the European Accounting Association, Maastricht, 1991.

Gray, Sidney J., Gary K. Meek and Clare B. Roberts, 'International capital market pressures and voluntary annual report disclosures by U.S. and U.K. Multinationals', *Journal of International Financial Management and Accounting,* vol. 6 no. 1, 1995, p. 43-68.

Greenstein, Marilyn Magee, and Heibatollah Sami, 'The impact of the SEC's segment disclosure requirement on bid-ask spreads', *The Accounting Review,* vol. 69 no. 1, January 1994, p. 179-199.

Grinten, W.C.L. van der, 'Is het wenselijk voor de zogenaamde besloten naamloze vennootschap in de civielrechtelijke wetgeving bijzondere voorzieningen te treffen, al dan niet met invoering van een afzonderlijke rechtsvorm ?', *Handelingen der Nederlandse Juristenvereniging,* vol. 83 I-1, 1953, p. 43-100.

Grob, J.V., 'De Jaarrekening van Koninklijke Olie: Het jaarverslaggevingsbeleid van de "Koninklijke" tussen 1954 en 1994', unpublished masters thesis, Vrije

Universiteit Amsterdam, 1995.

Groeneveld, G.L., 'Nieuwe tendenties in de gepubliceerde jaarrekening', prae-advies Accountantsdag 3 October 1953, *De Accountant*, vol. 60 no. 1, September 1953, p. 3-35.

Groeneveld, G.L., 'De geconsolideerde jaarrekening', *TVVS*, vol. 4 no. 10, February 1962, p. 233-239.

Groeneveld, G.L., 'Het ontwerp van wet op de jaarrekening van ondernemingen', *TVVS*, vol. 11 no. 6, June 1968, p. 133-144.

Groeneveld, G.L., (Limperg/Groeneveld) *Leer van de accountantscontrole* (Deventer: Kluwer, 1976).

Groeneveld, G.L., (Limperg/Groeneveld) *Waarde, winst en jaarrekening* (Deventer: Kluwer, 1979).

Grossman, Sanford J., 'The informational role of warranties and private disclosure about product quality', *Journal of Law and Economics*, vol. 24 no. 3, December 1981, p. 461-483.

Gruisen, J.O. van, 'De gepubliceerde jaarrekening der industriëele naamlooze vennootschap', *De Naamlooze Vennootschap*, vol. 16 no. 6, September 1937, p. 161-165.

Haccoû, J.F., 'Verslaggeving, verantwoording en voorlichting door de besturen van N.V.'s', *TVVS*, vol. 5 no. 6, October 1962, p. 117-122.

Haccoû, J.F., 'Notering van aandelen', *TVVS*, vol. 5 no. 9, January 1963, p. 193-198.

Hageman, Ch., 'Het proces Lord Kylsant', *Maandblad voor Accountancy en Bedrijfseconomie*, vol. 9 no. 4, April 1932, p. 55-59.

Hakansson, N.H., 'On the politics of accounting disclosure and measurement: An analysis of economic incentives', *Journal of Accounting Research*, vol. 19, Supplement 1981, p. 1-35.

Hakansson, N.H., J.G. Kunkel and J.A. Ohlson, 'Sufficient and necessary conditions for information to have social value in pure exchange', *Journal of Finance*, vol. 37 no. 5, December 1982, p. 1169-1182.

Hall, F.A. van, *Verdediging van de onafhankelijkheid des handels bij het oprigten van Naamlooze Maatschappijen*, (Amsterdam: de erven H. Gartman, 1834).

Hamlin, Robert L., R. Brooke Jacobson and Jerry L.L. Miller, *A Mathematical Theory of Social Change* (New York, NY: John Wiley, 1973).

Hartog, G., 'Accountantsverklaring en verantwoordelijkheid', *De Accountant*, vol. 39 no. 13, December 1933, p. 458-496.

Hasselt, B.Th.W. van, *De literatuur over het wetsontwerp op de naamlooze vennootschappen, critisch samengevat* (Leiden: A. Vilders, 1919).

Hatfield, Henry Rand, 'What is the matter with accounting?', *The Journal of Accountancy*, vol. 44 no. 4, October 1927, p. 267-279.

Haven, H. ten, 'Jaarrekening van holding cy's en concern centrales', *Maandblad voor Accountancy en Bedrijfshuishoudkunde*, vol. 3 no. 5, May 1926, p. 67-70; no. 6, June 1926, 85-87.

Hawkins, David F., *Corporate Financial Disclosure, 1900-1933*, A study of management inertia within a rapidly changing environment (New York, NY: Garland, 1986).

Heijden, E.J.J. van der, *Handboek voor de Naamloze Vennootschap naar Nederlands Recht*, 1st edition (Zwolle: Tjeenk Willink, 1929); 6th edition, with W.C.L. van der Grinten (Zwolle: Tjeenk Willink, 1955).

Heijden, E.J.J. van der, 'Het wetsontwerp Nelissen-Heemskerk - I', *De Naamlooze Vennootschap,* vol. 4 no. 2, May 1925(a), p. 33-36.

Heijden, E.J.J. van der, 'Het wetsontwerp 1925 op de Naamlooze Vennootschap', *Maandblad voor Accountancy en Bedrijfshuishoudkunde,* Appendix to vol. 2 no. 10, November 1925(b).

Helderman, J.G.P.M., 'Gesegmenteerde informatie in de jaarrekening', *De Accountant,* vol. 87 no. 5, January 1981, p. 278-281.

Hen, P.E. de, J.G. Berendsen and J.W. Schoonderbeek, *Hoofdstukken uit de geschiedenis van het Nederlandse accountantsberoep na 1935* (Amsterdam/Assen: NIVRA/van Gorcum, 1995).

Hendriksen, Eldon S., 'Disclosure - Insights into requirements in the United Kingdom', *The International Journal of Accounting,* vol. 4 no. 2, Spring 1969, p. 21-32.

Hobgood, George, 'Voluntary disclosure in 1968 annual reports', *Financial Executive,* vol. 37 no. 8, August 1969, p. 64-69.

Hofman, E.A., 'Enige beschouwingen over geconsolideerde jaarrekeningen (Verslag studievergadering, November 1950)', *De Accountant,* vol. 57 no. 7, March 1951, p. 383-428.

Holmes, Geoffrey, 'Earnings per share: A measure of sustainable growth', *Accounting and Business Research,* vol. 1 no. 2, Spring 1971, p. 118-144.

Holzer, H. Peter, and Hanns-Martin Schönfeld, 'Die Bewegungsbilanz als Bestandteil des veröffentlichten Jahresabschlüsses in den USA', *Die Wirtschaftsprüfung,* vol. 15 no. 21, 1 November 1962, p. 558-564.

Honig, G.N., 'Waarom publiceerde Honig N.V. haar jaarverslag?', *De Nederlandse Industrie,* 1963, p. 639-640.

Horngren, Charles T., 'Disclosure: 1957', *The Accounting Review,* vol. 32 no. 4, October 1957, p. 598-604.

Horngren, Charles T., 'Disclosure: What next?', *The Accounting Review,* vol. 33 no. 1, January 1958, p. 84-92.

Horwitz, Bertrand, and Richard Kolodny, 'Segment reporting: hindsight after ten years', *Journal of Accounting, Auditing and Finance,* vol. 4 no. 3, Fall 1980, p. 20-35.

Hossain, Mahmud, Lin Mei Tan and Mike Adams, 'Voluntary disclosure in an emerging capital market: Some empirical evidence from companies listed on the Kuala Lumpur Stock Exchange', *International Journal of Accounting,* vol. 29 no. 4, 1994, p. 334-351.

Hossain, M., M.H.B. Perera and A.R. Rahman, 'Voluntary disclosure in the annual reports of New Zealand companies', *Journal of International Financial Management and Accounting,* vol. 6 no. 1, 1995, p. 69-87.

Hossain, Mahmud, and Mike Adams, 'Voluntary financial disclosure by Australian listed companies', *Australian Accounting Review,* vol. 5 no. 2, November 1995, p. 45-55.

Huussen-De Groot, F.M., *Rechtspersonen in de 19e eeuw,* Een studie van privaatrechtelijke rechtspersonen in de 19e-eeuwse wetgeving van Frankrijk, Nederland en Duitsland (Leiden: Universitaire Pers, 1976).

IJsselmuiden, Th.S., *Wet op de jaarrekening* (Deventer: Kluwer, 1972).

IJsselmuiden, Th.S., *De jaarrekening en het jaarverslag* (Deventer: Kluwer, 1981).

Indjejikian, Raffi J., 'The impact of costly information interpretation on firm disclosure decisions', *Journal of Accounting Research*, vol. 29 no. 2, Autumn 1991, p. 277-301.

Jacobs, Leonard, 'Ervaringen uit de praktijk van de nieuwe wet op de N.V. met betrekking tot het jaarverslag', *Accountancy*, vol. 30 no. 330, July/August 1932, p. 106-107.

Janssens, C.H.A.J., 'Eénvormige balanspublicaties', *Accountancy*, vol. 25 no. 276, August/September 1927, p. 126.

Jensen, M.C., and W.H. Meckling, 'Theory of the Firm: Managerial Behavior, Agency Costs and Ownership Structure', *Journal of Financial Economics*, vol. 3, October 1976, p. 305-360.

Jong, J. de, 'Vergelijkende cijfers in het jaarverslag', *Maandblad voor Accountancy en Bedrijfshuishoudkunde*, vol. 30 no. 4, april 1956, p. 167-170.

Jong, J. de, 'Latenties terzake van de vennootschapsbelasting', *Maandblad voor Accountancy en Bedrijfshuishoudkunde*, vol. 38 no. 1, January 1964, p. 42-54.

Jong, J. de, 'Problemen bij de invoering van actuele waarden in de jaarrekening van Unilever', in: W. Verhoog *et al.* (editors), *Toepassing van actuele waarden in de jaarrekening - deel 2*, NIVRA Geschriften 20 (Amsterdam/Deventer: NIVRA/Kluwer, [1980]), p. 16-26.

Jovanovic, Boyan, 'Truthful disclosure of information', *The Bell Journal of Economics*, vol. 13 no. 1, Spring 1982, p. 36-44.

Jung, Woon-Oh, and Young H. Kwon, 'Disclosure when the market is unsure of information endowment of managers', *Journal of Accounting Research*, vol. 26 no. 1, Spring 1988, p. 146-153.

Käfer, Karl, and Vernon K. Zimmerman, 'Notes on the evolution of the statement of sources and application of funds', *The International Journal of Accounting*, vol. 2 no. 2, Spring 1967, p. 89-121.

Kahl, Alfred, and Ahmed Belkaoui, 'Bank annual report disclosure adequacy internationally', *Accounting and Business Research*, vol. 11 no. 43, Summer 1981, p. 189-196.

Karelse, F.M.A., '"Accounting principles" in de branding', *Maandblad voor Accountancy en Bedrijfshuishoudkunde*, vol. 39 no. 4, April 1965, p. 131-141.

Kas, J., 'Informatieverstrekking door gediversificeerde ondernemingen', *De Accountant*, vol. 81 no. 10, June/July 1975, p. 643-645.

Kastein, A.Th.E., 'Het Sixth International Congress on Accounting 1952', *Maandblad voor Accountancy en Bedrijfshuishoudkunde*, vol. 26 no. 10, November 1952, p. 423-428.

Kempner, Jack J., 'Funds statement practices of certified public accounting firms', *The Accounting Review*, vol. 32 no. 1, January 1957, p. 71-82.

Keuzenkamp, T., Thema 3 'Prüfung des Jahresabschlusses', Nationalbericht 10, Niederlande, in: *Kongreß-Archiv des V. Internationalen Prüfungs- und Treuhand-Kongress* (Berlin: 1938), Band B, p. 169-198.

King, Ronald R., and David E. Wallin, 'Voluntary disclosures when seller's level of information is unknown', *Journal of Accounting Research*, vol. 29 no. 1, Spring 1991(a), p. 96-108.

King, Ronald R., and David E. Wallin, 'Market-induced information disclosures: An experimental markets investigation', *Contemporary Accounting Research*, vol. 8 no. 1, Fall 1991(b), p. 170-197.

Kitchen, J., 'The accounts of British holding company groups: development and attitudes to disclosure in the early years', *Accounting and Business Research*, vol. 2 no. 2, Spring 1972, p. 114-136.

Klaassen, Jan, *De Vervangingswaarde,* Theorie en toepassing in de jaarrekening (Alphen aan den Rijn: Samsom, 1975).

Klaassen, Jan, 'An accounting court: The impact of the Enterprise Chamber on financial reporting in the Netherlands', *The Accounting Review,* vol. 55 no 2, April 1980, p. 327-340.

Klaassen, J., 'Het institutionele kader van de jaarverslaggeving in Nederland', in: J.P.C.M. van den Hoeven, A. de Bos and C.D. Knoops (editors), *fMA-kroniek 1991* (Groningen: Wolters-Noordhoff, 1991), p. 69-75.

Klaassen, J., and G.G.M. Bak, *Externe verslaggeving,* 3rd edition (Leiden/Antwerpen: Stenfert Kroese Uitgevers, 1993).

Klaassen, Jan, and Hein Schreuder, 'Corporate report readership and usage in the Netherlands', *Maandblad voor Accountancy en Bedrijfshuishoudkunde,* vol. 55 no. 2/3, February/March 1981, p. 101-117.

Klaassen, Jan, and Hein Schreuder, 'Accounting research in the Netherlands', in: Anthony G. Hopwood and Hein Schreuder (editors), *European Contributions to Accounting Research,* The achievements of the last decade (Amsterdam: Free University Press, 1984), p. 113-131.

Kleerekoper, I., 'Een beoordeling van het rapport van de Commissie Jaarverslaggeving d.d. juli 1962 vanuit het gezichtspunt van de openbare accountant', *De Naamlooze Vennootschap,* vol. 40 no. 8/9, November/December 1962, p. 137-141.

Knap, Ger. H., 'De publiciteit van de N.V.', *De Naamlooze Vennootschap,* vol. 9 no. 11, February 1931, p. 334-335.

Knol, H.D.M., *Civielrechtelijke aansprakelijkheid van directie en commissarissen van naamlooze vennootschappen volgens Nederlandsch recht* (Zwolle: Tjeenk Willink, 1936).

Knol, H.D.M., 'Jaarverslagen', *Maandblad voor Bedrijfsadministratie,* vol. 52 no. 618, September 1948, p. 97-99.

Knol, H.D.M., 'Een rapport inzake de jaarrekening en het jaarverslag', *Maandblad voor Bedrijfsadministratie,* vol. 59 no. 699, June 1955, p. 97-99.

Koert, J.A., *Winstverdeeling bij Nederlandsche naamlooze vennootschappen* (Wageningen: H. Veenman & Zonen, 1934).

Kok, W., 'De maatschappelijke behoefte aan ondernemingsinformatie', *De Accountant,* vol. 81 no. 7, March 1975, p. 422-424.

Koppenberg Jr, W.C., 'Uniformiteit van de jaarrekening', *Maandblad voor Accountancy en Bedrijfshuishoudkunde,* vol. 12 no 9, October 1935, p. 129-132.

Kraayenhof, J. 'The profession in the Netherlands, sixty years of growth and development', *The Accountant,* vol. 133 no. 4215, October 1st, 1955, p. 382-390.

Kraayenhof, J., 'Rede van de heer J. Kraayenhof', *De Accountant,* vol. 74 no 1, May 1967, p. 16-19.

Kreps, David M., and Robert Wilson, 'Sequential equilibria', *Econometrica,* vol. 50 no. 4, July 1982, p. 863-894.

Kruisbrink, K., 'Over de inhoud van het Amerikaanse begrip "Generally Accepted Accounting Principles"', *Maandblad voor Accountancy en Bedrijfshuishoudkunde,* vol. 39 no. 4, April 1965, p. 142-144.

Kruize, F.H., 'Recente opvattingen omtrent de jaarverslaggeving van de n.v.',

Maandblad voor Handelswetenschappen, vol. 33 no 8, 1961, p. 117-118.

Lafeber, A.F., 'Latente belastingschulden', *Maandblad voor Accountancy en Bedrijfs-huishoudkunde*, vol. 26 no. 8, September 1952, p. 349-352.

Lampe, Jac., 'Eenige beschouwingen naar aanleiding van het wetsontwerp-1925 op de naamlooze vennootschap' *Maandblad voor Accountancy en Bedrijfshuishoud-kunde*, Appendix to vol. 2 no. 10, November 1925.

Lanen, William N., and Robert E. Verrecchia, 'Operating decisions and the disclosure of management accounting information', *Journal of Accounting Research*, vol. 25, Supplement 1987, p. 165-189.

Lang, Mark, and Russel Lundholm, 'Cross-sectional determinants of analyst ratings of corporate disclosure', *Journal of Accounting Research*, vol. 31 no. 2, Autumn 1993, p. 246-271.

Laterveer, E.L.Th., 'De accountant - een wereldhervormer?', in: R. Burgert, A.A. de Jong, A.C.M. van Keep and J.G. de Weger (editors), *Tot de Orde geroepen*, Opstellenbundel ter gelegenheid van het 40-jarig bestaan van de Vereniging van Academisch Gevormde Accountants (Deventer: A.E. Kluwer, 1967), p. 181-187.

Leftwich, Richard W., Ross L. Watts and Jerold L. Zimmerman, 'Voluntary corporate disclosure: The case of interim reporting', *Journal of Accounting Research*, vol. 19, Supplement 1981, p. 50-77.

Lentz, T., and A. Ozinga, 'Een onderzoek naar de emissie-bedrijvigheid van industriële, commerciële en transportondernemingen in Nederland na de Tweede Wereldoorlog', *Maandblad voor Accountancy en Bedrijfshuishoudkunde*, vol. 30 no. 4, april 1956, p. 146-166.

Loos, J., 'De geconsolideerde jaarrekening', *Maandblad voor Accountancy en Bedrijfshuishoudkunde*, vol. 17 no. 8, September 1940, p. 142-148; vol. 17 no. 9, October 1940, p. 161-166; vol. 17 no. 10, November 1940, p. 188-193.

Louwers, P.C., *Sincerity in Financial Reporting*, A Paper presented at the 20th Summer School of The Institute of Chartered Accountants of Scotland, at St Andrews University, September 17, 1972(a).

Louwers, P.C., 'Verslag van de Accountantsdag 1971 van het Nederlands Instituut van Registeraccountants', *De Accountant*, vol. 78 no. 6, February 1972(b), p. 257-263.

Mahajan, Vijay, and Robert A. Peterson, *Models for Innovation Diffusion*, Quantita-tive applications in the social sciences No. 48 (Beverly Hills/London/New Delhi: Sage Publications, 1985).

Maijoor, Steven, *The Economics of Accounting Regulation*, Effects of Dutch accoun-ting regulation for public accountants and firms (Maastricht: Datawyse, 1991).

Marston, Claire L., and Philip J. Shrives, 'The use of disclosure indices in accoun-ting research: A review article', *The British Accounting Review*, vol. 23 no. 3, September 1991, p. 195-210.

McKinnon, J.L., 'Application of Anglo-American principles of consolidation to corporate financial disclosure in Japan', *Abacus*, vol. 20 no. 1, June 1984, p. 16-33.

McKinnon, S.M., 'A Cost-Benefit Study of Disclosure Requirements for Multinati-onal Corporations', in *Journal of Business Finance & Accounting*, vol. 11 no. 4, Winter 1984, p. 451-468.

McNally, Graeme M., Lee Hock Eng and C. Roy Hasseldine, 'Corporate financial reporting in New Zealand: An analysis of user preferences, corporate characteristics and disclosure practices for discretionary information', *Accounting and Business Research*, vol. 13 no. 49, Winter 1982, p. 11-20.

McNichols, Maureen, and Brett Trueman, 'Public disclosure, private information collection, and short-term trading', *Journal of Accounting and Economics*, vol. 17 no. 1/2, 1994, p. 69-94.

Meek, G.K., Clare B. Roberts and Sindney J. Gray, 'Factors influencing voluntary annual report disclosures by U.S., U.K. and continental European multinational corporations', *Journal of International Business Studies*, vol. 26 no. 3, 3rd Quarter 1995, p. 555-572.

Meek, G.K., and S.J. Gray, 'Globalization of stock markets and foreign listing requirements: voluntary disclosures by continental European companies listed on the London Stock Exchange', *Journal of International Business Studies*, vol. 20 no 3, Summer 1989, p. 315-338.

Mees, M., 'Welke beginselen moet eene wettelijke regeling der Naamlooze Vennootschappen huldigen ten aanzien van het kapitaal der vennootschap?', *Handelingen der Nederlandsche Juristen-Vereeniging*, vol. 3, 1872, no. 1, p. 61-68 with discussion in no. 2, p. 69-129.

Meijer, W.N., and K. van Tilburg, 'Najaarsconferentie 1978', *De Accountant*, vol. 85 no. 6, February 1979, p. 398-401.

Meyerson, R., 'Incentive compatibility and the bargaining problem', *Econometrica*, vol. 47 no. 1, January 1979, p. 61-73.

Milgrom, Paul R., 'Good news and bad news: representation theorems and applications', *The Bell Journal of Economics*, vol. 12 no. 2, autumn 1981, p. 380-391.

Milgrom, Paul R., and John Roberts, 'Relying on the information of interested parties', *The Rand Journal of Economics*, vol. 17 no. 1, Spring 1986, p. 18-32.

Moore, Michael L., and Stephen Buzby, 'The quality of corporate financial disclosure: A comment', *The Accounting Review*, vol. 47 no. 3, July 1972, p. 581-584.

Morris, Richard D., 'Signalling, agency theory and accounting policy choice', *Accounting and Business Research*, vol. 18 no. 69, Winter 1987, p. 47-56.

Most, Kenneth S., 'How bad are European accounts ?', *Accountancy* (UK), vol. 75 no. 845, January 1964, p. 9-15.

Mueller, Gerhard G., 'An international view of accounting and disclosure', *The International Journal of Accounting*, vol. 8 no. 1, Fall 1972, p. 117-134.

Munnik, H., 'De publieke verantwoording der naamlo?ze vennootschap in het jaarverslag', *Maandblad voor Accountancy en Bedrijfshuishoudkunde*, Appendix to vol. 8 no. 11, December 1931, p. 26-42.

Murphy, George J., *The Evolution of Selected Annual Corporate Financial Reporting Practices in Canada 1900-1970* (New York, NY: Garland, 1988).

Murray, A.F., 'What investors want from company accounts', in: [booklet of the] *13th Summer School at the University of St. Andrews*, 18th to 22nd June 1965 (Edinburgh: The Institute of Chartered Accountants of Scotland), p. 43-81.

Myer, John N., *Financial Statement Analysis*, Principles and technique, 2nd ed. (New York: Prentice-Hall, 1952).

Nabbe, J.P.M., 'De informatiebehoefte van werknemers en hun representanten', *Maandblad voor Accountancy en Bedrijfshuishoudkunde*, vol. 48 no. 7, July/August 1974, p. 293-305.

Napier, Christopher, and Christopher Noke, 'Accounting and the law: an historical overview of an uneasy relationship', in: Michael Bromwich and Anthony Hopwood (editors), *Accounting and the Law* (Hemel Hempstead: Prentice Hall International, 1992) p. 30-54

Napier, Christopher, 'The history of financial reporting in the United Kingdom', in: Peter Walton (editor), *European Financial Reporting - A History* (London: Academic Press, 1995), p. 259-283.

Nathans, J., 'Grondslagen voor de verslaggeving', in: *Facetten van het accountants-beroep*, Een bundel opstellen van registeraccountants ('s-Gravenhage: W.P. van Stockum & Zoon, 1969), p. 76-82.

Newbould, G.D., and K.W. Wilson, 'Alternative measures of company size, A note for researchers', *Journal of Business Finance and Accounting*, vol. 4 no. 1, Spring 1977, p. 131-132.

Newman, Paul, and Richard Sansing, 'Disclosure policies with multiple users', *Journal of Accounting Research*, vol. 31 no. 1, Spring 1993, p. 92-112.

Niehus, Rudolph J., 'Die Gewinn- und Verlustrechnung in der Praxis amerikanischer Abschlußprüfung und Berichterstattung', *Die Wirtschaftsprüfung*, vol. 11 no. 18, 15 September 1958, p. 485-491.

Niehus, Rudolph J., 'Stock corporation law reform in Germany and the public accountant', *The International Journal of Accounting*, vol. 1 no. 2, Spring 1966, p. 25-41.

Nierhoff, A., 'Latente belastingschulden en haar betekenis voor de balans', *Maandblad voor Accountancy en Bedrijfshuishoudkunde*, vol. 26 no. 7, July 1952, p. 279-284.

Nijst, J.J.M.H., *Leerboek der accountancy*, deel IIIb, *De accountants-controle in de practijk*, eerste gedeelte ('s-Gravenhage: NV Uitgeversmaatschappij v/h G. Delwel, 1929).

Nobes, Christopher W., 'A judgmental international classification of financial reporting practices', *Journal of Business Finance and Accounting*, vol. 10 no. 1, Spring 1983, p 1-19.

Nobes, Christopher W., and Robert H. Parker, *Comparative International Accounting*, 4th edition (Hemel Hempstead: Prentice Hall International, 1995).

Otten, P.F.S., *Het beleid van Philips ten aanzien van de voorlichting aan aandeelhouders* (Eindhoven: Philips' Gloeilampenfabrieken, 1954).

Parker, Robert H., 'Explaining national differences in consolidated accounts', *Accounting and Business Research*, vol. 7 no. 27, Summer 1977, p. 203-207.

Parker, Robert H., 'The study of accounting history', in: Michael Bromwich and Anthony Hopwood (editors), *Essays in British Accounting Research* (London: Pitman, 1981), p. 279-293.

Parker, Robert H., and Christopher W. Nobes, *An International View of True and Fair Accounting* (London/New York: Routledge, 1994).

Philips, F.J., 'Het probleem van verslaggeving, verantwoording en voorlichting door de besturen van naamloze vennootschappen bezien vanuit het gezichtspunt van de grote publieke N.V.', in *De Naamlooze Vennootschap*, vol. 40 no. 8/9, November/December 1961, p. 117-120.

Polak, L., 'De verslaglegging door holdingcompanies en enkele opmerkingen omtrent de accountantscontrole bij deze lichamen', *Maandblad voor Accountancy en Bedrijfshuishoudkunde*, Appendix to vol. 10 no. 11, December 1933, p. 25-

56.

Posthumus Meyjes, W.C., 'Verslaggeving door naamloze vennootschappen', *TVVS*, vol. 2 no. 11, 1960, p. 257-268.

Postlewaite, A., 'Asymmetric information', in: John Eatwell, Murray Milgate and Peter Newman (editors), *Allocation, Information and Markets*, The New Palgrave (London: Macmillan, 1989), p. 35-38.

Prodhan, Bimal K., and Malcolm C. Harris, 'Systematic risk and the discretionary disclosure of geographical segments: An empirical investigation of US multinationals', *Journal of Business Finance and Accounting*, vol. 16 no. 4, Autumn 1989, p. 467-492.

Pruyt, B., 'Het jaarverslag en de liquiditeit', *De Naamlooze Vennootschap*, vol. 34 no. 1, April 1956, p. 1-5.

Pruyt, B., 'Herkomst en besteding der middelen van een onderneming', *De Naamlooze Vennootschap*, vol. 39 no. 1, April 1961, p. 1-5.

Pruyt, B., 'Financiële verslaggeving van een europese naamloze vennootschap', *De Naamlooze Vennootschap*, vol. 49 no. 1/2, April/May 1971, p. 40-41.

Putten, A. van, 'An entrepreneur's view of voluntary cooperation in formulating supplementary rules regarding external financial reporting', in: J.W. Schoonderbeek, A. van Putten and J. Bloemarts, *The Tripartite Accounting Standards Committee*, Pilot (Netherlands) 10 (Amsterdam: Nederlands Instituut van Registeraccountants, 1980), p. 10-13.

Raffournier, Bernard, 'The determinants of voluntary financial disclosure by Dutch companies', Paper presented at the 17th Annual Congress of the European Accounting Association, Venice, April 1994.

Rennie, E.D., and C.R. Emmanuel, 'Segmental disclosure practice: Thirteen years on', *Accounting and Business Research*, vol. 22 no. 86, Spring 1992, p. 151-159.

Reiman, J.D., and J.J.M.H. Nijst, *De accountant als controleur*, Handleiding bij het controleeren van administratiën (Zwolle: W.E.J. Tjeenk Willink, 1906).

Rietkerk, G., 'Cash flow verantwoording; een kritische analyse van het voorontwerp van een beschouwing inzake de staat van herkomst en besteding van middelen van het tripartiete overleg', *Maandblad voor Accountancy en Bedrijfshuishoudkunde*, vol. 55 no. 7/8, July/August 1981, p. 373-383.

Rietkerk, G., 'De verstopte markt voor risicodragend vermogen', *Economisch Statistische Berichten*, vol. 71 no. 3589, 15 January 1986, p. 65-69.

Rietschoten, A. van, 'Critiek op de sinds 1931 geldende bepalingen in het Duitsche vennootschapsrecht', *Maandblad voor Accountancy en Bedrijfshuishoudkunde*, vol. 11 no. 4, April 1934, p. 87.

Reus, C. de, 'APB Opinions No. 14: "Convertibles" en No. 15 "Winst per aandeel"', *Maandblad voor Accountancy en Bedrijfshuishoudkunde*, vol. 47 no. 1, January 1973, p. 27-33.

Roberts, Robin, 'Determinants of corporate social responsibility disclosure: An application of stakeholder theory', *Accounting, Organizations and Society*, vol. 17 no. 6, 1992, p. 595-612.

Rogers, Everett M., *Diffusion of Innovations*, 3rd edition (New York, NY: The Free Press/MacMillan, 1983).

Ronen, Joshua, and Joshua Livnat, 'Incentives for segment reporting', *Journal of Accounting Research*, vol. 19 no. 2, Autumn 1981, p. 459-481.

Ronen, Joshua, and Varda (Lewinstein) Yaari, 'The disclosure policy of the firm in an efficient market', *Review of Quantitative Finance and Accounting,* vol. 3 no. 3, September 1993, p. 311-24.

Roozen, L.J.M., 'Het vraagstuk van de latente belastingschuld', *Maandblad voor Accountancy en Bedrijfshuishoudkunde,* vol. 26 no. 8, September 1952, p. 339-343.

Rosen, L.S., and Don T. DeCoster, '"Funds" statements, A historical perspective', *The Accounting Review,* vol. 44 no. 1, January 1969, p. 124-136.

Ross, Stephen A., 'Disclosure regulation in financial markets: Implications of modern finance theory and signalling theory', in: F.R. Edwards (editor), *Issues in Financial Regulation* (New York: McGraw-Hill, 1979), p. 177-202.

Salamon, Gerald L., and Dan S. Dhaliwal, 'Company size and financial disclosure requirements with evidence from the segmental reporting issue', *Journal of Business Finance and Accounting,* vol. 7 no. 4, Winter 1980, p. 555-568.

Sanders, P., 'Verantwoording van het bestuur in de publieke naamloze vennootschap', in: *Rechtskundige Opstellen,* aangeboden aan Prof. Mr R.P. Cleveringa (Zwolle: N.V. Uitgevers-Maatschappij W.E. Tjeenk Willink, [1952]), p. 329-362.

Sanders, P., 'De jaarrekening der naamloze vennootschap en de verantwoording van het bestuur', in *De Naamlooze Vennootschap,* vol. 40 no. 11/12, February/March 1963, p. 194-198

Sanders, P., 'De vierde Richtlijn en onze Wet op de Jaarrekening', *TVVS,* vol. 15 no. 1, 1972, p. 1-15.

Sanders, P., G.L. Groeneveld and R.Burgert, *De Jaarrekening Nieuwe Stijl,* Commentaar op de wet op de jaarrekening (Alphen aan den Rijn: Samsom Uitgeverij, 1975).

Schiff, Allen, 'Annual reports in the United States: A historical perspective', *Accounting and Business Research,* vol. 8 no. 32, Autumn 1978, p. 279-284.

Schmalenbach, E., *Dynamische Bilanz,* 6th edition (Leipzig: G.A. Gloeckner Verlagsbuchhandlung, 1933).

Schoenfeld, Hans-Martinn, 'New German regulations for the publication of financial statements', *The International Journal of Accounting,* vol. 5 no. 2, Spring 1970, p. 69-88.

Schoepp, F., *De naamlooze vennootschap en haar aandeelhouders* ('s-Gravenhage: H.P. Leopold's Uitgevers-Maatschappij N.V., 1939).

Scholten, Th. M., *De liquiditeit van de onderneming* (Leiden: Stenfert Kroese, 1962).

Schoonderbeek, J.W., 'Ontwikkelingen in de regels voor de jaarrekening', in: W.C.L. van der Grinten and J.M.M. Maeijer (editors), *De Jaarrekening en de Vierde EEG-Richtlijn* (Deventer: Kluwer, 1981), p. 3-9.

Schoonderbeek, J.W., and P.E. de Hen, *Getuigen van de geschiedenis van het Nederlandse accountantsberoep,* 20 interviews (Assen/Amsterdam: van Gorcum/NIVRA, 1995).

Schroeff, H.J. van der, 'Het rapport van de commissie-Verdam en de rapporten van de werkgeversverbonden inzake de verslaggeving van ondernemingen', *Maandblad voor Accountancy en Bedrijfshuishoudkunde,* vol. 39 no. 6, June 1965, p. 225-231.

Schröer, Thomas, 'Company law and accounting in nineteenth-century Europe: Germany', *The European Accounting Review,* vol. 2 no. 2, September 1993, p. 335-345.

Scott, George M., 'Private enterprise accounting in developing nations', *The International Journal of Accounting*, vol. 4 no. 1, Fall 1968, p. 51-65.

Singhvi, Surendra S., 'Characteristics and implications of inadequate disclosure: A case study of India', *The International Journal of Accounting*, vol. 3 no. 2, Spring 1968, p. 29-43.

Singhvi, Surendra S., and Harsha B. Desai, 'An empirical analysis of the quality of corporate financial disclosure', *The Accounting Review*, vol. 46 no. 1, January 1971, p. 129-138.

Skinner, Douglas J., 'Why firms voluntarily disclose bad news', *Journal of Accounting Research*, vol. 32 no. 1, Spring 1994, p. 38-60.

Skousen, K. Fred, 'Chronicle of events surrounding the segment reporting issue', *Journal of Accounting Research*, vol. 8 no. 2, Autumn 1970, p. 293-299.

Slooten, G. van, *Verplichte openbaarmaking van balans en winst- en verliesrekening van naamlooze vennootschappen* (Den Haag: J. Hoekstra & Co., 1900).

Slooten, G. van, 'Wettelijke Regeling van de publicatie der jaarstukken van Naamlooze Vennootschappen', *Accountancy*, vol. 10 no. 111, October 1912, p. 109-110; vol. 10 no. 113, December 1912, p. 148-151; vol. 11 no. 114, January 1913, p. 4-7; vol. 11 no. 115, February 1913, p. 19-20.

Slot, R., 'Jaarverslag en rentabiliteit', *De Naamlooze Vennootschap*, vol. 33 no. 6, September 1955, p. 81-93.

Slot, R., 'Het beste jaarverslag', *Maandblad voor Handelswetenschappen en Handelspraktijk*, vol. 30 no. 12, October 1958, p. 169-171.

Slot, R., and J.M. Vecht, with J.G. Geverink and J.G.L. Verdurmen, *Zicht op cijfers*, Een inleiding tot de analyse van jaarrekeningen (Amsterdam/Brussels: Agon Elsevier: 1974).

Slot, R., and R.M. Vijn, *De ontwikkeling van het winstbegrip*, Van nominalisme naar "inflation accounting", 2nd edition (Leiden: Stenfert Kroese, 1979).

Sloten, P.J. van, 'Enige aspecten van het fusieprobleem', *Maandblad voor Accountancy en Bedrijfshuishoudkunde*, vol. 37 no. 5/6, May/June 1963, p. 178-183.

Smulders, G.B.A.M., 'Uniformiteit van jaarrekeningen', *Maandblad voor Accountancy en Bedrijfshuishoudkunde*, vol. 39 no. 4, April 1965, p. 126-130.

Smulders, G.B.A.M., 'De verantwoording van de vennootschapsbelasting in de jaarrekening', *Maandblad voor Accountancy en Bedrijfshuishoudkunde*, vol. 42 no. 7, July 1968, p. 354-359.

Soesbeek, K. 'Het jaarverslag', *Maandblad voor Accountancy en Bedrijfshuishoudkunde*, vol. 29 no. 6, juni 1955, p. 255-257.

Solomons, David, *Making accounting policy*, The quest for credibility in financial reporting (New York, Oxford University Press, 1986).

Sorter, George H., Selwyn W. Becker, T. Ross Archibald and William H. Beaver, 'Accounting and financial measures as indicators of corporate personality, Some empirical findings', in: Robert K. Jaedicke, Yuji Ijiri and Oswald Nielsen (editors), *Research in Accounting Measurement* (Evanston: American Accounting Association, 1966).

Spinosa Cattela, J.E., 'Is meerdere publicatie door onze N.V.'s gewenscht?', *De Naamlooze Vennootschap*, vol. 9 no. 10, January 1931, p. 291-293.

Spinosa Cattela, J.E., 'De openbaarmaking van jaarrekeningen bij holding-companies', *Maandblad voor Accountancy en Bedrijfshuishoudkunde*, vol. 21 no. 7, July 1947, p. 224-227.

Spinosa Cattela, J.E., 'Publicatie van jaarstukken in Amerika en Nederland', *Maandblad voor Accountancy en Bedrijfshuishoudkunde*, vol. 22 no. 1, January 1948 (a), p.15-18.

Spinosa Cattela, J.E., *Inleiding tot de leer van de accountantscontrôle* (Leiden: H.E. Stenfert Kroese's Uitgevers Maatschappij N.V., 1948 (b)).

Steenmijer, J.A., *Ontwikkelingen in de jaarverslaggeving door ondernemingen* (Groningen: Rijksuniversiteit Groningen, 1976).

Steiger, J.H. 'Tests for comparing elements of a correlation matrix', *Psychological Bulletin*, vol. 87 no. 2, March 1980, p. 245-251.

Sternheim, A., 'Wetgevers-wee', *De Kroniek van Dr.A. Sternheim*, vol. 6 no. 176, 1 April 1929, p. 322-323.

Sternheim, A., 'Iets over den vorm der accountantsverklaring', *De Bedrijfseconoom*, vol. 11 no. 6, December 1933, p. 65-67.

Stewart, Ian C., 'The ethics of disclosure in company financial reporting in the United Kingdom 1925-1970', *The Accounting Historians Journal*, vol. 18 no. 1, June 1991, p. 35-54.

Tempelaar, A.F., 'Accountancy in Groot Brittanië', in: A. Mey and A.F. Tempelaar (editors), *Beknopte Encyclopedie der Accoutantscontrôle* (Utrecht: De Haan, 1952) p. 110-111.

Tempelaar, A.F., 'De jaarverslaggeving van naamloze vennootschappen, beschouwingen naar aanleiding van hoofdstuk IV van het rapport "Herziening van het Ondernemingsrecht" van de commissie Verdam', *De Accountant*, vol. 72 no. 1, September 1965, p. 26-51.

Tempelaar, A.F. 'De jaarverslaggeving van naamloze vennootschappen', *De Accountant*, vol. 72 no. 5, January 1966, p. 271-292.

Tempelaar, A.F., 'Rede van de voorzitter van het N.I.v.R.A., de heer A.F. Tempelaar', *De Accountant*, vol. 74 no. 1, May 1967, p. 10-16.

Tempelaar, A.F., 'Ontwerp van wet op de jaarrekening van ondernemingen', *De Accountant*, vol. 75 no. 3, July 1968, p. 665-666.

Teoh, Siew Hong, and Chuan Yang Hwang, 'Nondisclosure and adverse disclosure as signals of firm value', *Review of Financial Studies*, vol. 4 no. 2, 1991, p. 283-313.

Tinker, A.M., and M.D. Neimark, 'The role of annual reports in gender and class contradictions at General Motors: 1917-1976', *Accounting, Organizations and Society*, vol. 12 no. 1, 1987, p. 71-88.

Tonkin, D.J., *World Survey of Published Accounts* (London: Lafferty Publications, 1984).

Traas, L., 'De jaarrekening als bedrijfseconomisch kompas?', in: A. de Bos, J.P.C.M. van den Hoeven and C.D. Knoops (editors), *fMA-kroniek 1991* (Groningen: Wolters-Noordhoff, 1991), p. 41-58.

Tricht, Gerard Johan Walraven van, *Iets over het toezicht bij de oprichting van naamlooze vennootschappen* (Leiden: P. Somerwil, 1880).

Tritschler, Charles E., 'A sociological perspective on accounting innovation', *The International Journal of Accounting*, vol. 5 no. 2, Spring 1970, p. 39-67.

Trueman, Brett, 'Why do managers voluntarily release earnings forecasts ?', *Journal of Accounting and Economics*, vol. 8, 1986, p. 53-71.

Tyra, Anita I., 'Financial disclosure patterns in four European countries', *The International Journal of Accounting*, vol. 5 no. 2, Spring 1970, p. 89-101.

379

Valkhoff, J., *Een Eeuw Rechtsontwikkeling*, De vermaatschappelijking van het Nederlandse privaatrecht sinds de codificatie (1838-1938) (Amsterdam: N.V. de Arbeiderspers, 1938).

Valkhoff, J., 'Naar vernieuwing van het Engels vennootschapsrecht', *Maandblad voor Accountancy en Bedrijfshuishoudkunde*, vol. 20 no. 4, April 1946, p. 94-107.

Vecht, J.M., 'De verslaggeving van de naamloze vennootschap', *Maandblad voor Bedrijfsadministratie en -Organisatie*, vol. 58 no. 685, April 1954, p. 57-60.

Vecht, J.M., 'De effectenbeurs in 1954', *Maandblad voor Bedrijfsadministratie en - Organisatie*, vol. 59 no. 697, April 1955, p. 67-70.

Vecht, J.M., 'Naar een vennootschapskamer?', *Maandblad voor Accountancy en Bedrijfshuishoudkunde*, vol. 34 no. 2, February 1960, p. 42-49.

Vecht, J.M., 'Jaarverslaggeving: Een nieuw rapport', *Maandblad voor Accountancy en Bedrijfshuishoudkunde*, vol. 37 no. 3, March 1963, p. 117-121.

Vecht, J.M. 'De wettelijke regeling van de jaarrekening', *Maandblad voor Bedrijfsadministratie en -Organisatie*, vol. 72 no. 857, August 1968, p. 309-314.

Vecht, J.M., *Onderneming en jaarverslag*, 5th edition (Alphen aan den Rijn: Samsom, 1977).

Vermeer, B., 'Het jaarverslag', *Maandblad voor Bedrijfsadministratie en -Organisatie*, vol. 59 no. 702, September 1955, p. 158-161.

Verrecchia, Robert E., 'The use of mathematical models in financial accounting', in *Journal of Accounting Research*, vol. 20, supplement 1982, p. 1-42.

Verrecchia, Robert E., 'Discretionary disclosure', *Journal of Accounting and Economics*, vol. 5, 1983, p. 179-194.

Verrecchia, Robert E., 'Endogenous proprietary costs through firm interdependence', *Journal of Accounting and Economics*, vol. 12, 1990(a), p. 245-250.

Verrecchia, Robert E., 'Information quality and discretionary disclosure', *Journal of Accounting and Economics*, vol. 12, 1990(b), p. 365-380.

Verwayen, J.E., 'Het aandelennoteringssysteem in Nederland', *TVVS*, vol. 5 no. 10, February 1963, p. 223-228.

Viegen, B. van, 'De jaarrekening van "Aktiengesellschaften" en de controle daarvan door "Wirtschaftsprüfer"', *Maandblad voor Accountancy en Bedrijfshuishoudkunde*, vol. 30 no. 6, June 1956, p. 256-286; vol. 30 no. 7, July 1956, p. 317-346.

Visser, L.E., *De naamlooze vennootschap* Volgens de wet van 2 juli 1928, stb. no. 216 ('s-Gravenhage: Boekhandel vh. Gebr. Belinfante N.V., 1929).

Volmer, J.G.Ch., (V***), 'Balansen en hare publicatie', *De Accountant*, vol. 3 no. 1, August 1897, p. 1-2.

Volmer, J.G.Ch., *De winstrekening en de vermogensbalans* (Den Haag: Delwel, 1914).

Volmer, J.G.Ch., 'Openbaarheid en financieele aansprakelijkheid', *De Naamlooze Vennootschap*, vol. 4 no. 2, May 1925, p. 36-38.

Volmer, J.G.Ch., 'Een fabrieksbalans (Verslag Nederlandsche Gist- en Spiritusfabrieken over 1925)', *De Naamlooze Vennootschap*, vol. 5 no. 3, June 1926, p. 65-67.

Volmer, J.G.Ch., 'Het wetsontwerp op de naamlooze vennootschappen', *De Naamlooze Vennootschap*, vol. 6 no. 2, May 1927, p. 33-36.

Volmer, J.G.Ch., 'Welke eischen moeten aan de te publiceren stukken gesteld worden', *De Naamlooze Vennootschap*, vol. 7 no. 12, March 1929, p. 375-377.

Vries, Johan de, *Een eeuw vol effecten*, Historische schets van de Vereniging voor de Effectenhandel en de Amsterdamse Effectenbeurs 1876-1976 (Amsterdam: Vereniging voor de Effectenhandel, 1976).

Vries, Johan de, *Lion Markus en de comptabiliteit in Nederland omstreeks 1900*, Mededelingen der Koninklijke Nederlandse Akademie van Wetenschappen, afd. Letterkunde, nieuwe reeks, deel 46, no. 4 (Amsterdam: B.V. Noord-Hollandsche Uitgevers Maatschappij, 1983).

Vries, Johan de, *Geschiedenis der Accountancy in Nederland*, Aanvang en ontplooiing, 1895-1935 (Assen/Maastricht: Van Gorcum, 1985).

Wagenhofer, Alfred, 'Voluntary disclosure with a strategic opponent', *Journal of Accounting and Economics*, vol. 12, 1990(a), p. 341-363.

Wagenhofer, Alfred, 'The demand for disclosure and actual disclosure by firms', Paper presented at the 13th Annual Congress of the European Accounting Association, Budapest, 1990(b)

Wagenhofer, Alfred, *Informationspolitik im Jahresabscluß*, Freilwillige Informationen und strategische Analyse (Leipzig: Physica-Verlag: 1990(c)).

Wallace, R.S. Olusegun, 'Corporate financial reporting in Nigeria', *Accounting and Business Research*, vol. 18 no. 72, Autumn 1988, p. 352-362.

Wallace, R.S. Olusegun, Kamal Naser and Araceli Mora, 'The relationship between the comprehensiveness of corporate annual reports and firm characteristics in Spain', *Accounting and Business Research*, vol. 25 no. 97, Winter 1994, p. 41-53.

Walton, Peter, 'The export of British accounting legislation to Commonwealth countries', *Accounting and Business Research*, vol. 16 no. 64, Autumn 1986, p. 353-357.

Walton, Peter, *European Financial Reporting*, A history (London: Academic Press, 1995).

Watts, Ross L., and Jerold Zimmerman, 'Towards a positive theory of the determination of accounting standards', *The Accounting Review*, vol. 53 no. 1, January 1978, p. 112-134.

Watts, Ross L., and Jerold Zimmerman, 'Positive accounting theory: A ten year perspective', *The Accounting Review*, vol. 65 no. 1, January 1990, p. 131-156.

Weisglas, M., *Public relations*, Een terreinverkenning (Amsterdam: Elsevier, 1955).

Weiß, Alfred, 'Die Rechnungslegungsvorschriften des Companies Act 1948', *Die Wirtschaftsprüfung*, vol. 2 no. 2, February 1949, p. 60-78; vol. 2 no. 3, March 1949, 118-125.

Wel, Frans van der, 'Internationalisatie van de Nederlandse jaarverslaggeving', *Maandblad voor Accountancy en Bedrijfseconomie*, vol. 66 no. 12, December 1992, p. 584-591.

Whittred, G., 'The evolution of consolidated financial reporting in Australia', *Abacus*, vol. 22 no. 2, September 1986, p. 103-120.

Whittred, G., 'The derived demand for consolidated financial reporting', *Journal of Accounting and Economics*, vol. 9, 1987, p. 259-286.

Wietzke, Günter, *Der konsolidierte Jahresabschluß und seine besonderen Probleme in der deutschen und anglo-amerikanischen Bilanzierungspraxis* (Berlin: Duncker & Humblot, 1962).

Wilschut, K.P.G., 'Enige vraagstukken met betrekking tot de jaarrekening', *De Accountant*, vol. 79 no. 11, July/August 1973, p. 538-547.

Wilson, Ch., *Unilever in de tweede Industriële Revolutie 1945-1965*, Dutch edition by H. Baudet (Den Haag: Martinus Nijhoff, 1968)

Windmuller, J.P., C. de Galan and A.F. van Zweeden, *Arbeidsverhoudingen in Nederland* (Utrecht/Antwerpen: Het Spectrum, 1983).

Wong, Jilnaught, 'Economic incentives for the voluntary disclosure of current cost financial statements', *Journal of Accounting and Economics,* vol. 10, 1988, p. 151-167.

Zanden, J.L. van, and R.T. Griffiths, *Economische geschiedenis van Nederland in de 20e eeuw* (Utrecht: Het Spectrum, 1989).

Zeff, Stephen A., *Forging Accounting Principles in Five Countries,* A history and an analysis of trends (Champaign, Ill: Stipes Publishing Co., 1972).

Zeff, Stephen A., Frans van der Wel and Kees Camfferman, *Company Financial Reporting,* A historical and comparative study of the Dutch regulatory process (Amsterdam: North-Holland, 1992).

Zeylemaker Jzn, Jb., *Verleden, heden en toekomst van de naamloze vennootschap,* (Zwolle: N.V. Uitgevers-Maatschappij W.E.J. Tjeenk Willink, [1946]).

Zwagerman, C., 'Informatie omtrent de herkomst en de besteding der middelen in het jaarverslag', *Maandblad voor Accountancy en Bedrijfshuishoudkunde,* vol. 44 no. 2, February 1970, p. 76-85.